Traumatic Pasts in Asia

Traumatic Pasts in Asia

*History, Psychiatry, and Trauma
from the 1930s to the Present*

Edited by Mark S. Micale and Hans Pols

berghahn
NEW YORK • OXFORD
www.berghahnbooks.com

First published in 2021 by
Berghahn Books
www.berghahnbooks.com

© 2021, 2024 Mark Micale and Hans Pols
First paperback edition published in 2024

All rights reserved. Except for the quotation of short passages for the purposes of criticism and review, no part of this book may be reproduced in any form or by any means, electronic or mechanical, including photocopying, recording, or any information storage and retrieval system now known or to be invented, without written permission of the publisher.

Library of Congress Cataloging-in-Publication Data

Names: Micale, Mark S., 1957- editor. | Pols, Hans, editor.
Title: Traumatic pasts in Asia : history, psychiatry, and trauma from the 1930s to the present / edited by Mark S. Micale and Hans Pols.
Description: New York : Berghahn, 2021. | Includes bibliographical references and index.
Identifiers: LCCN 2021026221 (print) | LCCN 2021026222 (ebook) | ISBN 9781800731837 (hardback) | ISBN 9781800731844 (ebook)
Subjects: LCSH: Psychic trauma--Asia--History--Case studies. | Cultural psychiatry--Asia--Case studies. | Asia--History--Psychological aspects--Case studies. | Asia--Historiography--Case studies.
Classification: LCC DS32.5 .T73 2022 (print) | LCC DS32.5 (ebook) | DDC 616.85/210095--dc23
LC record available at https://lccn.loc.gov/2021026221
LC ebook record available at https://lccn.loc.gov/2021026222

British Library Cataloguing in Publication Data
A catalogue record for this book is available from the British Library

ISBN 978-1-80073-183-7 hardback
ISBN 978-1-80539-150-0 paperback
ISBN 978-1-80539-564-5 epub
ISBN 978-1-80073-184-4 web pdf

https://doi.org/10.3167/9781800731837

Contents

List of Illustrations	vii
Preface and Acknowledgments	x

Introduction. History, Trauma, and Asia   1
Hans Pols and Mark S. Micale

Chapter 1. Tropical Stupor? An Investigation into Patients Affected by Earthquakes and Tropical Weather in Colonial Taiwan   35
Harry Yi-Jui Wu

Chapter 2. Male Hysteria in Modern Japan: Trauma, Masculinity, and Military Psychiatry during the Asia-Pacific War   58
Eri Nakamura

Chapter 3. Atomic Trauma: Japanese Psychiatry in Hiroshima and Nagasaki   78
Ran Zwigenberg

Chapter 4. "Yankee-Style Trauma": The Korean War and the Americanization of Psychiatry in the Republic of Korea   96
Jennifer Yum-Park

Chapter 5. "No PTSD in Vietnam": Psychological Trauma, Psychic Shock, and the Biology of War Suffering in the Context of the American War   128
Narquis Barak

Chapter 6. Psychological Trauma and Suffering in Long Distance Friendships Involving Political Prisoners in Indonesia   164
Vannessa Hearman

Chapter 7. Haunting and Recovery in Post-Khmer Rouge Cambodia   186
Caroline Bennett

Chapter 8. A Field of Happiness: Space, Trauma, and Existential
Precarity among China's Sent-Down Youth   205
Hua Wu

Chapter 9. Performing Songs as Healing the Trauma of the 1965
Anti-Communist Killings in Indonesia   226
Dyah Pitaloka and Mohan J. Dutta

Chapter 10. Healing Our Sacrifice: Trauma and Translation in the
Burmese Democracy Movement   245
Seinenu M. Thein-Lemelson

Chapter 11. Beyond PTSD: The Politics of Visibility in a Kashmiri
Clinic   268
Saiba Varma

Chapter 12. War Memorials: Materializing Traumatic Pasts and
Constructing Memories of the Asia-Pacific War   289
Maki Kimura

Afterword. Traumatic Pasts, Haunting Futures   315
Byron J. Good

Index   337

Illustrations

Figures

Figure 1.1.	Patients receiving emergency care. Courtesy Institute of Taiwan Studies, Academia Sinica. Yang Zhaojia photos: LJK_08_01_0150008.	45
Figure 1.2.	Patients waiting at Taichung Hospital. Courtesy Institute of Taiwan Studies, Academia Sinica. Yang Zhaojia photos: LJK_08_01_0160009.	47
Figure 4.1.	Cover page of "Nomenclature and Method of Recording Psychiatric Conditions" issued by the United States Joint Armed Forces. An original copy was found in Yu's personal archive. © Jennifer Yum-Park.	116
Figure 4.2.	Yi Pong-gi, co-author of *Eunuchoidism: A Clinical Case Study*, is pictured with Matthew Parrish MD, a US Army psychiatrist who was Yi's mentor at the 121 Evacuation Hospital in 1954. Parrish was chief psychiatric consultant to the Surgeon General of the Army during his time in Korea. Image courtesy of Yi Pong-gi.	119
Figure 5.1.	Reburial Ceremony in Tho Van, 1998. © Narquis Barak.	150
Figure 5.2.	Tuy reading from his battlefield journal, Tho Van 1998. © Narquis Barak.	154
Figure 5.3.	Tai and his daughter, Tho Van 1998. © Narquis Barak.	155

Figure 6.1.	Patricia Cleveland-Peck's collection of Pudji Aswati's letters and a copy of the article she wrote to raise funds for former political prisoners in the Quaker newsletter, *The Friend*. © Vannessa Hearman.	166
Figure 6.2.	Four former political prisoners meeting Patricia Cleveland-Peck in Malang in 1989. Pudji is seated next to Cleveland-Peck. Image courtesy of Dennis Cleveland-Peck.	173
Figure 8.1.	Farmer's Hut at the Happiness Field Cadre School. Image taken on August 21, 2017. © Hua Wu.	210
Figure 8.2.	Sent-Down Youth's Dorm at the Happiness Field Cadre School. Image taken on August 21, 2017. © Hua Wu.	219
Figure 8.3.	Visiting Old Town Center at the Happiness Field Cadre School. Image taken on August 21, 2017. © Hua Wu.	220
Figure 9.1.	Dialita Concert *Songs of Survivors*. Taman Ismail Marzuki, Jakarta, 13 December 2017. © Dyah Pitaloka.	228
Figure 10.1.	Naingkyin community and their supporters perform the traditional *aleipyu* ceremony during an anniversary memorialization of the 8888 pro-democracy demonstrations and massacres. © Seinenu M. Thein-Lemelson.	247
Figure 10.2.	Photos and names of fallen martyrs from the democracy movement were put on display at a political *pwe* (festival) organized by the naingkyin community. © Seinenu Thein-Lemelson.	255
Figure 12.1.	*The Statue of a Girl of Peace* in Wiesent, Germany, replica of the memorial in front of the Japanese Embassy in Seoul, Korea. © Maki Kimura.	291
Figure 12.2.	The Memorial Cenotaph for the Victims of the Atomic Bomb with a stone inscription in the Hiroshima Peace Memorial Park framing the Peace Flame and the A-Bomb Dome. © Maki Kimura.	301
Figure 12.3.	The Peace Memorial Hall for the Atomic Bomb Victims in Nagasaki. © Maki Kimura.	301

Figure 12.4.	Steps leading to the memorial for Korean victims in the Okinawa Peace Memorial Park with the Peace Memorial Hall behind. © Maki Kimura.	303
Figure 12.5.	Monument walls of the Cornerstone of Peace in the Okinawa Peace Memorial Park. © Maki Kimura.	304
Figure 12.6.	A memorial for the *Himeyuri* Students at Arakawa Shore, Okinawa. © Maki Kimura.	305

Tables

Table 1.1.	Number of patients presenting symptoms.	45
Table 2.1.	The number of newspaper articles using hysteria / *zōsōbyō*. Source of data: online article database of *Yomiuri Shimbun* (https://database.yomiuri.co.jp/rekishikan/) and *Asahi Shimbun* (https://database.asahi.com/index.shtml). Both accessed on 21 Dec. 2020/.	69
Table 2.2.	The number of hysterical patients at Kōnodai Military Hospital by diagnosis and military rank.	70
Table 2.3.	The number of patients with neurasthenia at Kōnodai Military Hospital by military rank.	72

Preface and Acknowledgments

Traumatic Pasts in Asia: History, Psychiatry, and Trauma from the 1930s to the Present is the first comparative, trans-Asian examination of the history of psychological trauma in any language. The idea for the book originated at a conference on "Psychiatry, Trauma, and History in a Global Age: The View from Australasia" organized by Elizabeth Roberts-Pedersen at the University of Newcastle, Australia, on 19 May 2017. At that conference, the two editors shared independently made observations with one another: from our respective vantage points on different sides of the Pacific and in different hemispheres, we had both taken notice of a cluster of young scholars with works in progress that sought for the first time to apply critical trauma theory to research in Asian history. This new work, which potentially formed a nascent subfield of study, was, however, uncoordinated professionally and dispersed geographically. We thank Libby Roberts-Pedersen for providing the occasion for this meeting of the minds as well as for organizing the first international and interdisciplinary symposium ever on global trauma history.

The next step was to meet these scholars, learn in greater detail about the work they had underway, and have them interact with one another. To this end, we sponsored two day-long workshops—one at the University of California, Los Angles, and the other at the University of Sydney. The UCLA workshop overlapped with the annual meeting of the American Association for the History of Medicine in May 2018. The Sydney gathering took place in July 2018 and coincided with the annual meeting of the Australian Society of Asian Studies. We thank the Sydney Southeast Asia Centre for providing support for both workshops and the assistance of the School of History and Philosophy of Science at the University of Sydney in organizing the second event. We are grateful for their indispensable support.

We wish to thank everyone who attended the workshops for making them such successful and memorable occasions, including several people who ended up not contributing to the book but who donated important ideas and insights to the emerging project. These includes Claire Edington from the University of California, San Diego; Rosalind Hearder from Melbourne; Adam Lowenstein of the University of Pittsburgh, and John Boulton from the University of Newcastle. We were also honored to have in attendance at the Los Angeles workshop Paul Lerner, co-editor of the original *Traumatic Pasts* volume published some twenty years earlier.

At the workshops, we were struck by how interesting and original (and interconnected) the presentations were. From a diversity of disciplines and a wide range of national backgrounds, the presenters time and again brought to light new sources, settings, approaches, populations, and findings in writing the history of trauma. We came away from both workshops convinced of the desirability, feasibility, and timeliness of bringing this new scholarship together into a major collected volume. From the discussions at the workshops, another basic conviction guiding the project became apparent: an anthology like this one should extend beyond the regional compartmentalizations that characterize academic Asian Studies—"East," "South," "Southeast," and so on—and aspire to be as broadly and comparatively Asian as possible. This approach, it is now clear, has brought out countless patterns and linkages that would not otherwise have emerged.

For their sponsorship of the book, and their role in helping to shape it intellectually, we thank Berghahn Books and in particular Chris Chappell and Vivian Berghahn. Very unfortunately, an increasing number of university presses today, both in the United States and the United Kingdom, only rarely accept edited volumes of essays—regardless of the importance of the subject under study or the eminence of the book's contributors. The cited motives for this new policy are changes in technologies of reading and declining sales figures. As all scholars know, the best of such essay collections not only advance specialized knowledge; they can also become basic, paradigmatic contributions to a given field of inquiry. Considering the new publishing environment, we are especially thankful that *Traumatic Pasts in Asia* found safe and welcoming harbor with Berghahn Books.

At Berghahn, we acknowledge the helpful assessments of three anonymous reviewers. We especially thank Jason Crouthamel for his excellent commentary on the entire manuscript in draft form. Mykelin Higham, Sulaiman Ahmad, their colleagues and their staff ably shepherded the manuscript through production, a task that required grappling with citations in eight different languages.

Most of all, we would like to express our deep gratitude to the volume's twelve contributors for their willingness to publish their work in the book, to make multiple revisions, and for their patience in the face of various delays. Doubtless when they committed to the project, they had no idea the editors would be so demanding. Individually and collectively, their essays convinced us of what at the outset of the undertaking was only an intuition: the "second wave" of historical trauma studies is likely to be shaped powerfully by the study of Asia, and this new body of scholarship must incorporate, but also move decisively beyond, World War I/Holocaust/Vietnam War studies at the center of the first corpus of commentary on trauma history.

We want to give an additional shout out to contributors who labored under especially challenging circumstances: Jennifer Yum-Park wrote her chapter on Korean military psychiatry with a newborn in the household; Harry Yi-Jui Wu managed to produce his essay while teaching in Hong Kong against the backdrop of daily political turmoil; and Narquis Barak distilled her voluminous research materials into a remarkable retelling of the PTSD story from the perspective of the North Vietnamese civilian victims while working full-time in the health care industry. For their home city hospitality, Mark Micale would like to thank Maki Kimura in London, Caroline Bennett in Wellington, and Seinenu Thein-Lemelson and Robert Lemelson in Los Angeles. For providing a thoughtful epilogue to the book, we thank Byron Good, whose work has long represented the scholarly gold standard in the medical anthropology of Asia. We thank Sahar Tavakoli for compiling the index. Hans Pols wishes to thank Stephanie Oak, Warwick Anderson, Byron Good, and Mary-Jo DelVecchio Good for their continuous encouragement. We also want to salute the somewhat parallel historiographical enterprise of Peter Leese (Copenhagen), Jason Crouthamel (Grand Rapids, Michigan), Julia Barbara Köhne (Berlin), and Ville Kivimäki (Tampere, Finland). In several edited volumes, both published and forthcoming, this trans-Atlantic team is enlarging the chronology and geography of historical trauma studies, highlighting new sites of world-historical suffering, and setting high scholarly and intellectual standards for the field.

Finally, a note on the times: Although the two workshops underpinning *Traumatic Pasts in Asia* took place earlier, the bulk of the book's constituent chapters were finalized and the manuscript was assembled in 2020. When we began the project, the editors and authors thought of trauma as an experience inherent in a succession of past catastrophes (wars, genocides, dictatorships, natural disasters) beginning in the second quarter of the twentieth century. But throughout 2020 "traumatic" events again and again became the stuff of the daily news, including a once-in-a-century disease pandemic, global market recessions, mass unemployment, Armageddon-like forest fires in Australia and California, and, in the United States, widespread racial unrest and a highly destabilizing presidential election. Perhaps the fact that the book is now successfully published in the face of these adversities is a contemporary instance of human resilience in trying times.

Mark Micale (Los Angles)
Hans Pols (Sydney)

About Djoko Pekik and his painting Go to Hell Crocodile!

Indonesian painter Djoko Pekik (b. 1937) was arrested in November 1965, shortly after General Suharto seized power in Indonesia, because of his association with LEKRA, an artist's organization with links to the Indonesian Communist Party. He was detained until 1972. In his works, he criticizes Suharto's dictatorial regime as well as colonialism, capitalism, corruption, exploitation, and human rights abuses in Indonesia and elsewhere.

"Go to Hell Crocodile!" (2014) is a very large (2 by 6 m; 6 by 18 ft) painting about the controversial Grasberg mine in West Papua (the large vortex in the centre of the painting), which used to be owned by the international conglomerate P. T. Freeport. The Grasberg mine is one of the largest gold and copper mining operations in the world, employing nearly 20,000 laborers. Human rights abuses at the giant site are notorious, the immense profits from the operation disappear in bank accounts outside the country, and the environmental decimation is vast. The title of the painting was inspired by a famous slogan of Sukarno, who preceded Suharto as Indonesia's president, when addressing the United States protesting its political meddling and the activities of profit-seeking American companies in Indonesia: "Go to Hell with your Aid!" In Indonesia, the figure of the crocodile is generally associated with corruption.

In the lower center of the image, two men hold sharpened bamboo spears directed at the giant fire-breathing crocodile. During the war of Indonesian independence against Dutch colonial forces (1945–1949), young people often used sharpened spears carved from local bamboo trees as weapons. The tallest of the two figures, with a white beard and ponytail, bears an uncanny physical resemblance to the artist.

We wish to express our sincere thanks to artist Djoko Pekik for his permission to reproduce his painting *Go to Hell Crocodile!* for the cover of this book. We also thank his son Gogor Bangsa, and Ninik Supartini and Baskara T. Wardaya for their assistance.

Introduction

HISTORY, TRAUMA, AND ASIA

Hans Pols and Mark S. Micale

In the early morning of 21 April 1935, the people of Taiwan experienced the deadliest earthquake in the island's recorded history. During World War II, hundreds of thousands of girls and women were forced into sexual slavery by the Japanese Imperial Army. In August 1945, a heretofore unknown and unimaginable weapon of mass destruction was detonated over the Japanese cities of Hiroshima and Nagasaki, instantly vaporizing a quarter million inhabitants, most of them civilians. In 1947, former British India underwent partition, splitting into two independent dominion states—a majority-Hindu India and majority-Muslim Pakistan—a process leading to the violent deaths of hundreds of thousands of people and the displacement of millions. On the Korean peninsula, between 1950 and 1953, and then again in Vietnam, during the 1960s until 1976, savage civil wars pitted pro-Communists in the north against anti-Communists in the south, along with their supporting superpowers, China, the Soviet Union, and the United States. In Indonesia, in 1965–66, between 500,000 and a million citizens—mostly Communists and their alleged sympathizers—were purged by right-wing militias supported by the armed forces of Suharto's authoritarian regime. Mao Tse Tung's Cultural Revolution began at the same time and went on for ten years. In a drive to resist liberalization and return China to pure Communism, Red Guard paramilitary groups roamed across the country, killing roughly 1.5 million people; countless others suffered imprisonment, persecution, and forced migration. And during the years 1975–79, Pol Pot's Khmer Rouge regime, motivated by a combination of ideological and ethnopolitical reasons, caused the deaths of approximately 1.7 million people by murder, overwork, and starvation.

The military, political, and social aspects of these events have been studied extensively, and the death tolls have been tallied. This edited volume focuses on the ways people reacted to these horrific past events. It investigates how individuals and communities responded to such traumas; how caregivers, physicians, and spiritual and religious leaders interpreted these calamities; and how, in the aftermath, survivors attempted to restore a sense of psychological normality to their lives and world. The way trauma is experienced, expressed, understood, and reacted to in several countries in Asia is compared and contrasted to what is known about these phenomena in the Western world, particularly with the goal of discovering new insights and approaches relevant to the global study of historical trauma.[1]

The Background to Trauma Studies in Asia

Across Asia, natural disasters—including earthquakes, volcanic eruptions, floods, prolonged droughts, tropical storms, and tsunamis—as well as horrific episodes of warfare, state-sanctioned violence and killing, terrorism, ethnic conflict, genocide, and mass displacement by forced migration have occurred with tragic frequency. These traumatizing events have inevitably left deep physical and mental scars. Large parts of Asia are lower- and middle-income countries; the limited resources available to react to such disasters often prolongs and exacerbates suffering. Like populations exposed to intensely adverse events elsewhere in the world, Koreans, Chinese, Japanese, Taiwanese, Vietnamese, Cambodians, Indonesians, Kashmiris, and Burmese have responded by rebuilding their communities and by developing individual and collective repertoires to overcome trauma, regain a sense of equilibrium, and foster resilience. Drawing on various healing traditions, traditional healers, local caregivers, physicians, and several others have provided ways to address individual suffering and rebuild communities. At times, some of them provided medical, psychological, and psychiatric interpretations of the aftereffects of trauma. These interpretations often blend age-old local practices, religious and spiritual ideas, and psychiatric theories from various medical traditions of the Western world.

Over the past two decades, international humanitarian agencies working in Asia have employed Western psychiatric conceptions of traumatic suffering, in particular the influential concept of Posttraumatic Stress Disorder (PTSD), to diagnose and treat affected individuals. Yet these Western conceptions and therapeutic initiatives are not always congruent with local approaches dealing with disaster, disruption, and trauma. The twelve historical and anthropological case studies in this volume analyze responses to extremely violent and destructive events, disasters, and acts of violence that occurred in a range of Asian settings from the mid-1930s to the present. They examine how individuals and communities reacted to these calamities, and how victims, survivors, and others crafted narratives and coping strategies to render their suffering legible, intelligible, visible, manageable, and legitimate. In addition, some chapters explore how medicine, psychiatry, and psychology played a role in interpreting and managing such acutely stressful experiences and how these approaches interact with local understandings of suffering and trauma, and local cultural repertoires to overcome them.

In the past two generations, Western psychiatry, and particularly Anglo-American diagnostic terminology, has been spreading globally. Perhaps no diagnosis is currently applied more widely in non-Western settings than PTSD. International humanitarian organizations seeking to alleviate the debilitating psychological aftereffects of natural disasters, interstate and intrastate conflicts, and political and ethnic repression, attempt to bring the best of modern mental medicine to populations across Asia.[2] The moral motivations of these organizations are wholly admirable, but their ministrations, recent research indicates, are not without problems. The way Westerners experience trauma is not necessarily the same as it is experienced elsewhere; interpretations of trauma and its effects on individual well-being vary across cultures as well.

A heightened concern with psychological trauma among physicians, social scientists, humanities scholars, and many others originated in North America during the years following the Vietnam War. In 1980, Post-Traumatic Stress Disorder was formally introduced in the third edition of the *Diagnostic and Statistical Manual of Mental Disorders (DSM-III)*.[3] A novel feature of PTSD as compared to earlier stress- and trauma-based diagnoses was the potentially delayed onset of symptoms. Over the past four decades, in North America, and to a lesser extent in the rest of the West, PTSD has become increasingly prominent both as a medical diagnosis and as a popular concept to explain behavior. As Nancy Andreasen, a psychiatrist who was a member of the task force that formulated the criteria for PTSD for the *DSM-III* noted: "The concept of PTSD took off like a rocket, and in ways that had not initially been anticipated."[4]

In the Western world, the number of individuals diagnosed with PTSD has risen steadily. The numbers of self-diagnosed has risen even more. Increases in the use of PTSD can partially be explained by "bracket creep": individuals exposed to increasingly less serious adverse events are currently diagnosed.[5] These include people who have overheard crude jokes in the workplace, watched the collapse of the Twin Towers in New York City on television on 11 September 2001 (or any time thereafter), or have given birth to healthy babies.[6] PTSD diagnoses are also increasingly used in legal contexts, as seemingly objective indicators of mental anguish inflicted upon victims by the negligence of third parties or to exculpate perpetrators of criminal acts.[7] According to some commentators, people in Western countries today are exposed to a panoply of personalized, collectivized, and mediatized forms of psychic trauma on an almost daily basis.[8] As Andreasen commented elsewhere: "It is rare to find a psychiatric diagnosis that anyone likes to have, but PTSD seems to be one of them."[9]

In a parallel development, the idea of post-traumatic mental distress has broken its original disciplinary boundaries in psychological medicine and has spread widely into many other fields of knowledge, including theology, history, anthropology, sociology, Holocaust studies, film studies, and literary criticism as well as popular culture. Especially in North America, trauma has become an important cultural metaphor—it is part and parcel of the way we experience, describe, explain, and manage our own distress and that of others. In a recent history of PTSD, medical sociologist Allan V. Horwitz claims that PTSD has become ubiquitous and that North America has embraced a culture of trauma.[10] Yet the severe intergenerational traumas experienced by the descendants of African slaves and indigenous people, to cite only two prominent but ignored groups, have hardly been addressed thus far.

Asian mental health professionals and lay counselors have adjusted medical and psychotherapeutic approaches to suit local approaches, thereby implicitly or, at times, explicitly critiquing Western psychiatry.[11] Systematic critique of the globalization of PTSD has thus far been fairly circumscribed within Western psychiatric medicine itself; instead, the strongest criticisms have been formulated by anthropologists and sociologists, operating from a wide range of national backgrounds. They have noted that diagnostic categories conceived by and contained in Western psychiatric textbooks capture specifically Western behavioral and mental conditions, despite their aspirations to universality. Psychological trauma, they insist, is culturally and historically situated and cannot be extracted from its complex social, cultural, and political contexts.[12] Others have argued that providing counseling and other forms of psychological assistance merely constitute an affordable way of providing support when substantial aid to rebuild communities is required.[13]

Experiences of trauma vary substantially across place and time.[14] The way individuals and communities experience traumatic events, how anguish is expressed through mental or somatic symptoms, and how emotional pain is interpreted in local frameworks of meaning depend on a variety of political, social, and cultural factors.[15] Similarly, both personal and communal rituals and strategies for coping with and overcoming trauma vary across the world and are not necessarily compatible with individualized, Western-style treatment modalities. The perception of social support—related most often to the degree of family integration and community functioning—appears to be essential in the recovery of traumatized individuals everywhere.[16] Recent research on psychological resilience bears out the same phenomena.[17] Despite the findings by medical anthropologists and others, many Western-trained mental health workers continue to adhere to individualistic perspectives on trauma and its treatment, including one-on-one psychotherapies, even though they at times acknowledge that communities collectively working through adverse experiences are often more successful in alleviating stress and restoring people to their former functioning lives. Developing collective rituals and coping repertoires that draw on familiar cultural practices and religious beliefs appear to be especially common and effective in the non-Western contexts studied below.[18]

These realities lead us to one of the major arguments underpinning *Traumatic Pasts in Asia*: Western concepts of psychological trauma provide a powerful lens of analysis through which to study modern Asian history. The various Asian conceptions of, and rituals and repertoires of working through trauma, in their turn, can broaden and enrich contemporary Western conceptions. However, in extending "historical trauma studies" to Cambodia, China, Indonesia, Japan, Kashmir, Korea, Indonesia, Taiwan, and Vietnam, it is imperative to take Asian experiences of trauma "on their own terms" and not just conceptualize them as instantiations of dominant Western models of traumatic suffering. Time and again, the authors in this volume demonstrate how independent, indigenous perspectives and practices—which may be national, regional, or even local in origin—provided efficacious methods of healing and consolation for survivors. Put differently, in the stories they tell, the observations they make, and the insights they achieve, trauma scholars of Asia (as well as Africa, Latin America, and elsewhere) must be equal partners with their European and North American counterparts. This volume seeks to work toward the construction of a model of psychological trauma that is truly globalized—globalized, not just factually and geographically, but also conceptually and interpretatively.

Back in 2001, Mark Micale and Paul Lerner co-edited a seminal collection of studies entitled *Traumatic Pasts: History, Psychiatry, and Trauma in the Modern Age, 1870–1930*.[19] That volume contained essays on various war-induced disorders and others related to industrial accidents in Europe and North America during the late nineteenth and early twentieth centuries.[20] More recently, Micale has speculated on the possibility of writing a global history of trauma.[21] Hans Pols has extensively researched American military psychiatry during World War II as well as colonial psychiatry in the Dutch East Indies.[22] In his studies, he established contacts with Indonesian mental health professionals and became interested in past and present mental health care in Indonesia, including the reception of Western-based approaches to trauma.

Working independently, Micale and Pols observed the appearance of a new generation of young scholars—often born in Asia but educated in graduate schools in Australia, Canada, Britain, or the United States—who sought to apply approaches from historical trauma studies to various sites of suffering in Asia. The bi-cultural identity of many of these researchers is shedding light and yielding insights on historical phenomena that would otherwise have been missed or somehow inaccessible. Since around 2000, scholars working in the two fields of comparative literature and film studies have to great effect been interrogating trauma in the Asian imaginary, highlighting how it is represented in literature, movies, and other creative art forms.[23] Scholars in other domains, however, have yet to explore the trauma theme to the same extent. As a result, the editors joined forces and decided to organize two workshops, where these previously dispersed early career scholars were able to meet and share their ideas, findings, and works in progress. *Traumatic Pasts in Asia: History, Trauma, and Psychiatry from the 1930s to the Present* is the result.

Twelve Case Studies

As settings of psychological trauma, both World Wars in Europe—especially the trenches of the Western Front during World War I and the Nazi extermination camps of World War II—have unquestionably received the most historical attention. The core patient population in the original diagnostic formulation of PTSD consisted of veterans of the Vietnam War who displayed symptoms of depression and anxiety while suffering from intrusive war-related memories and flashbacks after their return home. But whereas the locus of the original trauma for these ex-servicemen was Southeast Asia, the patient-soldiers and the diagnosing physicians were all Americans, and all patients were treated in US institutional facilities, especially veterans' hospitals.

Several features differentiate traumatic experiences in Asian history from the better-known accounts of psychic trauma in Europe and North America. For instance, natural disasters of various sorts appear much more frequently in Asia. Because of their location along the "Pacific Rim of Fire," with its constant collision of continental and oceanic tectonic plates, Asia-Pacific nations are more prone to earthquakes, volcanic eruptions, and tsunamis than any other region. The geology of the Himalayan region is similarly unstable. Furthermore, many affected nations have dense coastal populations and weak material infrastructures to manage these catastrophes.[24] In chapter 1, Harry Yi-Jui Wu observes that no systematic clinical research on the psychological sequelae to natural disasters had been conducted anywhere in the world before World War II. That situation changed in the early 1940s, Wu demonstrates, when Japanese physicians published the results of the very first research project in psychiatric epidemiology on the long-term aftereffects of an earthquake that occurred five years previously in colonial Taiwan.

Despite the relatively well-developed state of psychiatric medicine in Japan, Japanese physicians had never studied earthquake victims in their own country. Against the backdrop of imperial Japanese nationalism, Japanese psychiatrists in the 1930s were convinced that pathological emotional reactions were more widespread among the Taiwanese people, partly because of their supposedly inferior constitution and partly because of the enervating tropical climate of the island. In fact, only after the devastating Kobe earthquake in 1995 did Japanese medical interest in the nature, symptoms, and treatment of PTSD-like reactions following natural disasters in Asia take off.[25] It has subsequently stimulated attention to the mental health aspects of natural disasters across Asia.[26] Over the past fifteen years, a large number of mental health professionals across Asia have conducted studies of the deadly 2004 Boxing Day tsunami.[27] Since the 11 March 2011 Tōhoku earthquake off Japan's northeastern coast—a devastating triple disaster consisting of an earthquake, a tsunami, and an industrial meltdown—Japan has become a world leader in mental health responses to natural disasters. Wu argues that natural disasters should henceforth be integrated into global historical trauma studies and that trauma as an analytical category has much to offer the field of environmental history.[28]

Several chapters in this volume examine military psychiatry and the potentially traumatic experience of combat—a topic that has received extensive attention in the historical literature in the Western world. The nature of early military psychiatry in Asian countries, it turns out, is closely linked to their colonial histories, to their prevailing political orientations, and to where the nation's physicians and psychiatrists received their medical training.[29] In chapter 2, Eri Nakamura writes that, until the 1940s, Japanese medicine was primarily based on German medical traditions, which were predominantly somatic. In the 1870s, the Japanese government invited German physicians to establish a medical school in Tokyo, and until the middle of the 1930s, many Japanese medical students traveled to Germany for advanced medical training.[30]

Nakamura analyzes the theoretical orientation and therapeutic approaches of Japanese army physicians in diagnosing and treating war neuroses in the Japanese Imperial Army during the Pacific War. She concludes that these corresponded to German (and, to a lesser extent, French) ideas and practices from World War I onward. According to European psychiatrists at that time, hysteria and nervous breakdown were primarily female maladies encountered in civilian, domestic settings. German war doctors officially denied the presence of mental breakdown among their nation's fighting forces and ascribed its occasional and undeniable appearance to constitutional weakness.[31] In 1940s Japan, Nakamura detects a similar militaristic ethos, which, combined with a strong belief in Japanese racial superiority, contributed to widespread ideas on tough emotionless manliness.[32] Japanese physicians and psychiatrists explained nervous breakdowns in soldiers by physical injuries, prior illness, or constitutional deficiencies. The same defensive and gendered attitude toward war neurosis, Nakamura speculates, helps explain the silence about traumatized veterans in postwar Japanese society. Just as in Germany between the two World Wars, the public spectacle of psychologically incapacitated soldiers became a living reminder of the dishonorable national defeat and therefore needed to be avoided or even censured.[33]

Four chapters in this volume deal with Japan, and it is worthwhile to read them comparatively. In Ran Zwigenberg's essay, the source of psychological shock is not traditional warfare or a natural disaster but, instead, the world's first (and to date only) atomic bomb blasts. Targeting civilian populations, these took place over the cities of Hiroshima and Nagasaki in August 1945. In the years and decades following these detonations, Zwigenberg notes, Japanese psychiatrists failed to study the psychological responses of survivors. There are well-known bone-chilling accounts, including firsthand reports, of the atomic explosions as well as extensive follow-up studies of radiation sickness among survivors. In conspicuous contrast, the emotional and psychiatric impact of these events has never constituted a valid subject of study. The mental health needs of survivors were consequently never addressed, at least not until the end of the twentieth century.

Zwigenberg provides several overlapping explanations as to why post-traumatic suffering was not considered a welcome, or even legitimate, topic of study in postwar Japan. Foremost among these factors were the role of psychiatric theories that still dominated Japanese psychiatry post-1945; the general shame and ostracism faced by survivors of the nuclear attacks; and American censorship, especially during the seven postwar years when the Allies occupied the country.[34] Zwigenberg's chapter raises the questions of when, why, in what contexts, and with reference to which populations medicalized explanations of human suffering and trauma are acceptable.[35] He also aims to explain why something failed to take place and the forces that can inhibit particular lines of observation, research, and analysis. The absence of any research on the mental suffering of the survivors of the nuclear bombs is all the more striking today when the subject seems to scream out for attention.

The origins and early history of military psychiatry in Korea have thus far hardly received any historical attention. In chapter 4, Jennifer Yum-Park corrects this omission.[36] According to her account, Korean military psychiatry followed an entirely different path than its Japanese counterpart. During the fifty years when the country was a Japanese colony (1895–1945), Japanese medical traditions were imported into Korea, but when the Asia-Pacific War (1941–1945) broke out, psychiatry was still in its infancy. At that time, psychiatry in Korea ministered only to cases of severe and persistent forms of mental illness and had no experience in treating war-related psychiatric syndromes. This changed dramatically, Yum-Park explains, when just a few months into the war, a group of psychiatrists from the United States arrived in Seoul. These American physicians, led by the well-known military neuropsychiatrist Albert Glass, provided crash courses into the entire subfield of military psychiatry and psychology for a generation of young Korean physicians, who proved unhesitatingly receptive to their teachings. They did so partially because of their political-military alliance, as the US armed forces were their allies in their fight against hostile Communist forces.

In addition, these US army psychiatrists had developed considerable expertise in the clinical management of mental breakdown in battle during World War II, which had ended just five year earlier.[37]

Yum-Park documents the introduction of new concepts of unconscious mentation, psychological repression, and somatic conversion into Korean case-history records as well as neo-Freudian approaches in psychiatric theorizing. Some young, ambitious Korean practitioners traveled to the United States for further training, akin to the earlier generations of Japanese physicians who had journeyed to Germany. The influence of American neo-Freudianism, Yum-Park finds, lingered into the 1960s and 1970s, when newly-founded hospitals, journals, lecture series, and even an institute of child psychology were directly modeled on US precedents.[38] Nevertheless, the implantation of Western psychiatric ideas into Cold War Korea was not just an uncritical adoption of foreign ideas and practices. Reflecting on the wartime situation in his country decades earlier, one retired army psychiatrist recollected in an interview with Yum-Park that, in light of the exigencies of the moment, he and his colleagues in the early 1950s made a conscious decision to diagnose "Yankee style trauma" in their patients.[39]

As mentioned above, PTSD as a diagnostic construct was first formulated by US psychiatrists aiming to capture the psychological condition of US veterans who had returned from the war in Vietnam.[40] In chapter 5, Narquis Barak analyzes the strikingly different medical and psychiatric conceptions of war trauma formulated by physicians on the North Vietnamese side of that conflict, which has thus far received hardly any historical attention. The result is ironic: in North Vietnam, models and treatments of war-traumatized civilians and soldiers were completely different from those found in US-style PTSD medicine. In Vietnamese medicine today, a psychological understanding of war trauma remains rare, and, at least according to its leading psychiatrists, PTSD is virtually absent. Caregivers in North Vietnamese clinics after the war even had separate names for the symptoms manifested by their patients based on the type of US ordnance or chemicals that had struck patients. Barak's chapter illustrates a disturbing but undeniable process: the erasure from the historical record of traumas—even the trauma of millions of people—for contemporary ideological purposes.[41]

Many Asian physicians followed a variety of different European medical traditions. In the case of Indochina, physicians during colonial times had been trained in French medical traditions. Barak relates that during the war years in Vietnam, this was supplemented by Soviet medical perspectives. Both traditions emphasized somatic over psychological causation, and Soviet psychiatry emphasized social determinants of mental illness over individual emotional and intra-psychic ones. Barak notices that this medley of European influences, all of which were the products of colonial and ideological contexts outside Vietnam, blended with a set of local factors in shaping Vietnamese views of trauma. These indigenous sources, she finds, include specifically Vietnamese approaches to mental health and illness; the teachings of Buddhism, Taoism, and other Eastern religious beliefs, especially regarding endurance and resilience in the face of hardship; and the deeply communitarian organization of Vietnamese society.[42]

Barak's chapter highlights another recurrent theme in these Asian-based studies, too: in narratives of trauma that derive from European and US history, science and religion are typically presented antagonistically. Answers to questions of what constitutes mental suffering, how to label it, and where and how to console or cure sufferers differ fundamentally if individuals and their families have secular medical-materialist worldviews or religion-based understandings of life and death, sickness, and suffering. In Barak's study, though, Vietnamese people had little trouble combining religious and other spiritualist practices with medical ideas. For them, Buddhist notions of mindfulness and practices of meditation in overcoming suffering, for instance, chimed with Western psychotherapeutics, in particular those that originated in France and the Soviet Union.[43]

In many Asian countries, Western psychiatric influences have been mostly absent. There are many areas where, in Vikram Patel's words, "there is no psychiatrist," and, concomitantly, where Western psychiatric ways of understanding trauma have hardly influenced public and medical ideas.[44] In much the same way that communities around the world have specific "idioms of distress," some societies have developed remarkably effective rituals for working through trauma, both individually and communally. As anthropologist Catherine Smith has analyzed, groups of women in Aceh, Indonesia, have developed their own means of processing the traumas associated with the 2004 Boxing Day tsunami and the effects of civil war there.[45] Healing rituals, spiritual practices, religious beliefs, and cultural habits have assisted victims and survivors to overcome the shock of such events, rebuild communities, and maintain resilience against violence and torture. Several chapters in this volume analyze the various ways individuals and communities deal with traumatic experience without assistance from mental health professionals and without referring to medical-psychological vocabularies.[46]

Vannessa Hearman's chapter illustrates the relatively mundane sources of psychological assistance sometimes in operation. Following the killings of some half million members and sympathizers of the Indonesian Communist Party, carried out by army units and local militant groups in 1965, many leftists were murdered, imprisoned, or exiled to prison camps, such as the one on remote Buru island.[47] In response, early in the 1970s Amnesty International and the Religious Society of Friends (Quakers) began an extensive campaign of letter writing between members of these two organizations in the Global North and political prisoners. In its 1977 report on Indonesia, Amnesty International estimated that between 55,000 and 100,000 political prisoners were being detained in that country, most of them without trial. These two organizations also hoped to monitor prison conditions, assess the health of prisoners, and report on the incidence of torture in Indonesia. In chapter 6, Hearman investigates the importance of these epistolary exchanges for the mental and emotional well-being of political prisoners.

Most letter writers and recipients in her study were women. Hearman focuses in particular on a remarkable primary source: the rich private archive of Patricia Cleveland-Peck, an English Quaker writer of children's stories and humanitarian activist, who for a decade corresponded with a particularly marginalized group of Indonesian women political detainees as well as prisoners in Asia, Latin America, and Africa. By maintaining this correspondence, prisoners experienced a continuation of exchange and contact with the outside world while their persecution and imprisonment excluded them from everyday social life. Hearman sensitively analyzes the exchange of life stories between these writers from different countries, languages, political cultures, and educational levels. During their long years of hardship, she shows, Cleveland-Peck gave these women an empathic audience; their handwritten correspondence—maintained for years and across great geographical distances—became a writing cure. Here, cross-cultural East-West exchanges involved stories and friendships rather than doctors, drugs, and diagnoses.

Chapter 9, by Dyah Pitaloka and Mohan J. Dutta, examines the same generation in Indonesian history, but in the present time. In addition to being imprisoned, tens of thousands of Indonesian women during the anti-Communist pogroms were assaulted, widowed, orphaned, raped, or left to survive as best they could. To this day, victims are ignored and have limited access to trauma therapy or advocacy, or any kind of support.[48] Pitaloka and Dutta study an extraordinary group of women survivors who have established a choir to perform songs of hope and resilience as a means of coming to terms with their past ordeal.[49] Its name—Dialita Choir—is an acronym for *Di Atas Lima Puluh Tahun* (Above fifty years of age) because the choir is made up entirely of women who themselves, or whose parents, relatives, and friends, were captured, tortured, or exiled during the 1965–66 repression.

In recent years, the group has been performing throughout the country. Its members dress colorfully in traditional Javanese women's outfits. With their performances, they reach young Indonesians who know little about this dark chapter in their country's history. Through the shared expressive medium of song, the Dialita Choir demonstrates how musical narration can be used to make sense of and alleviate distress through public performances. Their very presence on stage challenges the marginalization by successive Indonesian governments of those who survived the 1965–66 violence. By singing and being heard, the women are reclaiming a voice denied them by the stigmatization of the past. Some of the songs they choose challenge the army's repression of ideas associated with former President Sukarno's rule because they are about Afro-Asian solidarity and internationalism. In this way, Indonesia's painful, repressed past is addressed, and new generations of Indonesians are invited to participate in dialogues of hope and strength, and in the act of witnessing.[50]

In so far as historical trauma studies have been gendered, they have paid greater attention to adult men—especially to male combatants either behind the lines or back at home. The related theme of a "crisis in masculinity" in the face of paralyzing physical danger is routinely invoked in this scholarship. Correspondingly, in narratives centered on Europe, women figure mostly as either the occasional collateral victims of male combat or in traditional normative roles as grief-stricken wives, mothers, and sisters.

The chapters by Hearman and Pitaloka and Dutta instead put the historical experiences of women in the center. But, in addition to enduring traumatic events, Hearman's political prisoners and Pitaloka/Dutta's choir members have collaboratively developed sources of shared resilience and recovery. They perform "the work of trauma" for themselves, for other affected women, and for their nation. To a greater extent than previous historical research on trauma, the studies in this volume focus on female choice and agency.[51]

The essay by Pitaloka and Dutta also brings out one of the most important themes running through this volume: the central role of the social and the communal. Their inspiring stories are not about individual women in isolation. It is all about community: they perform as a choir to audiences and try to enlighten the community as a whole in order to bridge the gap between generations, and they express the experience of not only social suffering, but also resilience, survival, and hope. The construction of long-term traumatic memory, too, is a social process.[52]

In the chapters of this volume, the cultural connection between psychic trauma and modern medicine shifts. That relation is most tenuous in chapter 7, Caroline Bennett's powerful study of haunting and burial practices in post-Khmer Rouge Cambodia. One of the worst massacres of the twentieth century was during the Khmer Rouge regime from 1975–79. Dictator Pol Pot's Communist regime caused the deaths of an estimated 1.7 million people (nearly a quarter of the nation's population) as well as the destruction of many state institutions, the aftermath of which continues to affect the country in many ways still today. The damage extended to the treatment of the dead: corpses littered the notorious "killing fields" of Cambodia; the bodily remains of those who were killed are mostly unidentified, and the mass graves of victims remain mostly unexcavated.

Bennett's study explores how Cambodians have sought to reestablish relationships between themselves and those who died during the genocidal violence.[53] Her ethnographic research on mass grave sites across Cambodia reveals that experiences such as haunting (the felt presence of ghosts and other supernatural entities) and encounters with the dead represent ongoing relationships between the living and the dead, relationships that are central to maintaining individual well-being, communal security, and material prosperity. In the cosmology of many Cambodians, the dead are a social presence whose relationship with their living loved ones must be cultivated through specific funerary rituals, shrine building, and caring for their spirits through annual ceremonies. By leaving masses of bodies exposed and unburied, the Khmer Rouge regime dislocated dead individuals from their bodies, communities, and the home landscapes where under normal circumstances they would have received this care.[54]

Bennett's chapter makes clear that the Anglo-American conception of trauma is not compatible with the way most Cambodians understand or narrate pain and suffering. Experiences that within Western clinical settings would be interpreted as markers of trauma (such as dreaming of the dead or having recurrent nightmares of past atrocities) are locally understood within socio-religious frameworks in which the living and the dead continue to share an existence and interact and support each other's daily lives.[55] Bennett contrasts these interactions with the formal memorialization practices of the Cambodian state that focus on documentation and museum display in the cities.[56] Those practices do not share a Western psychological focus either. In conclusion, Bennett argues that it would be a mistake to interpret the concern of many Cambodians in reestablishing harmonious connections with their deceased relatives as a culturally specific expression of psychological trauma.

China remains a fertile field of inquiry because of the many deeply traumatic events that occurred throughout its modern history. As part of Mao Tse Tung's Cultural Revolution, millions of people in their late teens went through state-mandated processes of "rustication" during the decade of 1966–76, which entailed the forced resettlement of people from China's urban centers to the countryside where they were assigned for years to perform agricultural-related activities to realize ideological purification.[57] In chapter 8, Hua Wu is the first scholar to investigate the long-lasting psychological impact of this rustication experience. In 2017, she accompanied and interviewed a group of Chinese men and women, now elderly, who revisited a remote farm in mid-southern China that had been the site of their coerced ideological retraining over forty years earlier. Returning to the physical location of their powerful youthful experiences at a much later period in their lives evoked an uncanny range of responses ranging from breakdown, to introspection, to emotional numbing. Some who took these tours experienced involuntary rushes of sensations and memories. Wu also perceived that visitors' first reactions tended to be private and personal, but that they increasingly used the visitation to reestablish old social ties, share memories, and work through past adversities together. Some returned multiple times in a kind of ongoing effort to master their past.[58] In her analysis, subjective sensory experiences of space and place play key roles in conjuring up, confronting, and eventually transcending trauma.[59]

Wu's story also illustrates the changing, at times erratic, relations between politics and psychiatry in modern China. Under Mao, the psychological sciences were banned as Western ideologies of bourgeois individualism, just as they had been in Stalinist Russia. However, in the immediate post-Mao years (the late 1970s to the early 1980s), the Chinese government actually permitted some people to write and publish about their personal suffering. The literary-autobiographical genre known as *shanghen wenxue* (scar literature) gave writers and readers a way of mourning what they had lost or missed during the Cultural Revolution. By the early 1980s, the government again clamped down on such publications, which were implicitly critical of the Communist state.[60] Since the 1990s, post-socialist China has witnessed a remarkable growth in psychiatric organizations, publications, and services, including the proliferation of psychological counseling.[61] As a native ethnographer, Wu was allowed to pursue her project, and some other Chinese scholars have been granted access to patient interviews, hospital records, and archival sources. According to Vanessa Pupavac and Jie Yang, the Chinese Communist party today deploys these flourishing psychiatric activities to foster social stability, economic productivity, and political order.[62] Nevertheless, the archives of China's Ministry of Foreign Affairs, a fundamental repository for general national history, has opened and closed four times since 2004, each time with different rules about admittance and access to materials.[63] "Therapeutic governance" in contemporary China is an intriguing phenomenon with little counterpart in the United States or Europe—including in formerly Communist Central and Eastern Europe.[64]

Historians, anthropologists, and others have noted that Western conceptions of trauma are increasingly applied to non-Western populations despite incongruences between these conceptions and the way acutely adverse events are experienced and expressed locally. As Didier Fassin and Richard Rechtman have highlighted in *The Empire of Trauma: An Inquiry into the Condition of Victimhood* (2009), humanitarian organizations reacting to wars, natural catastrophes, and the plight of refugees often utilize the PTSD diagnosis as a seemingly objective indication of psychological damage, thereby establishing to international audiences the extent to which certain groups have been the object of oppression, violence, and, at times, genocide.[65] In other words, in an effort to represent traumatic suffering as objectively real, and for it to achieve international currency and moral legitimacy, humanitarian groups seek to locate and document the prevalence of PTSD in affected populations. In doing so, they make their suffering visible to an international audience, even if the concepts and therapeutic interventions are discordant with longstanding local cultural conventions.

The possibilities and the limitations of these practices are illustrated in compelling detail in Seinenu Thein-Lemelson's chapter on discourses of trauma in Myanmar (formerly called Burma) during the early twenty-first century. In her analysis of the brutal repression by Myanmar's military regime, she relates how advocates of reform, many of them journalists, artists, and university students, were able to deal with years of incarceration in the country's extensive penal system, including at times torture and solitary confinement. They did so by enacting a complex cultural system of rites, rituals, and moral beliefs based on the concept of sacrifice (*anitnah*). *Anitnah*, Thein-Lemelson explains, engendered a deep sense of awe from the broader public, which subsequently elevated former political prisoners into national heroes for withstanding hardship, including physical pain, and donating years of their life to a larger, communal purpose. The concept has a respected spiritual and religious lineage, rooted in Theravada Buddhism, and was integral to Burma's political resistance during the colonial era and the struggle for independence. After their release, the community of former political prisoners engaged in elaborate rituals and processes of communal meaning-making that honored their collective sacrifice and narrated the history of their own suffering as having been endured for the betterment of the people and the nation state.

Thein-Lemelson proposes that adherence to *anitnah* among the people of Myanmar should be characterized as "a local idiom of resilience." As part of her research, she conducted ethnography and person-centered interviews with several hundreds of previously imprisoned pro-democracy figures, often following them through their daily political and social activities. She observed that a community organization consisting of female political prisoners incorporated the language of PTSD into its workshops but that, upon closer examination, this appropriation was rather superficial; Western concepts were often embedded in local ideas emphasizing the importance of sacrifice. According to Thein-Lemelson, the dynamic intermixing of the local and the global in repertoires of traumatic coping—or, broadly conceived, medical versus non-medical conceptualizations of suffering, trauma, and resilience—is clearly on display in Myanmar today.

In chapter 11, Saiba Varma demonstrates the importance of local perspectives on the nature of historical trauma. Since the end of the British colonial occupation of greater India in 1947, the agriculturally fertile Kashmir Valley, located southwest of the Himalaya Mountains, has been a territory contested by India, Pakistan, and China. Today, it is one of the most heavily militarized civilian areas in the world. Varma analyzes the Kashmiri concept of *kamzori*, which roughly equates to chronic fatigue and pain, as a condition that physically and symbolically expresses the ongoing anguish of people living in India-occupied Kashmir. For Kashmiris, this condition consists of physical weakness induced by social, political, and economic oppression in daily lives.[66] Western-trained physicians and members of non-profit non-government organizations (NGOs) working in Kashmir continue to acknowledge that the PTSD construct does not adequately describe the ways residents manifest their distress, but they continue using it. Yet clinical data on the prevalence of PTSD among the inhabitants of Kashmir, Varma notes, has proven politically useful as an internationally recognized indictment of the cruelty of long-term Indian occupation.

Varma's study is a good illustration of another signal difference between Euro-American and Asian trauma. American Vietnam War veterans were suffering from the chronic after-effects of traumatic events that had taken place several years earlier on the other side of the globe—a place that bore little, if any, resemblance to their current living environment. Holocaust survivors were, and are, in a similar position. In dramatic contrast, many individuals in Asia today remain in situations that continue to traumatize them; they therefore are not yet *post* their trauma. The harsh political oppression in occupied Kashmir, India's only Muslim-majority state, not only continues unabated but has ratcheted up since August 2019, when Prime Minister Narendra Modi's hardline Hindu nationalist party abrogated the region's autonomy by revoking Article 370 of the Indian Constitution. Analogously, survivors of the 1965 persecutions in Indonesia had to live on the margins of society, where they suffered stigma and exclusion. In addition, government officials and perpetrators remained in positions of power and influence for decades after the killings took place. In other words, because there is little temporal or spatial distance between these individuals and their past traumatic suffering, there exists no psychological "safe space" to process their painful experiences. In certain historically oppressed settings, the stability and security on which contemplation and catharsis are preconditioned simply do not exist.[67]

To make matters worse, the events that traumatized are often officially denied, and culpability is not acknowledged.[68] As Sigmund Freud formulated in *Beyond the Pleasure Principle* (1920), the human psyche experiences trauma *as if* it is in the present, even though it has taken place in the past, sometimes the remote past.[69] When the conditions of the original trauma persist, and the possibility of their recurrence is constant, past and present become indistinguishable. The possibility of working through trauma generally depends on broader social and political factors.[70] If trauma remains unacknowledged in the public sphere, and if the violent events that led to trauma are officially denied, individuals can only work through their past trauma in small communities of like-minded people.[71] For example, the Law of Historical Memory in Spain and the accommodation of Pinochet in Chile led to a split of society into at least two camps in regard to the Franco and Pinochet regimes. After both regimes ended, problematic and ambiguous transitions took place that made ascertaining what happened in the near past essentially contested.

Although access to archives remains relatively straightforward in current-day Japan, the psychological legacies of Japan's wartime history remain fiercely contested. In chapter 12, Maki Kimura considers the many heritage sites and peace parks across Japan today. These sites of memory and mourning are mainly dedicated to Japanese victims of the war, such as those of the nuclear attacks on Hiroshima and Nagasaki, or of allied air raids and assaults (including the firebombing of Tokyo and the battle of Okinawa), or to those who died in service to Japan. Yet, as Kimura notes wryly, the Japanese government has not adequately acknowledged Japanese imperial aggression against its Asian neighbors during the Asia-Pacific War and the preceding China-Japan War. This includes non-recognition of the Nanking Massacre of 1937–38, the locus classicus of a long-ignored atrocity in twentieth-century Asian history.[72] A succession of postwar Japanese governments has clearly preferred to remember and memorialize wartime episodes in which the nation was the victim rather than the victimizer. Nationalist parliamentarians and government officials are more concerned with constructing meta-narratives centered around heroic service and tragic defeat.

Before and during the Asia-Pacific War, tens if not hundreds of thousands of teenage and adult women across Japanese-occupied Asia became the victim of sexual slavery. The largest number of victimized women were from Korea, China, Taiwan, and the Philippines.[73] In the book's final chapter, Kimura describes how the growing activism surrounding these World War II "comfort women" has in recent years found expression in the making of memorials and their strategic placement in symbolically resonant public locations. These sculptures do not merely commemorate past events; their construction, Kimura emphasizes, is also part of a determined campaign to gain full and formal recognition of this past violence against and exploitation of women in Japan's national history.[74]

In 2011, a sculpture of a girl-victim was placed close to the Japanese embassy in Seoul, South Korea, which for years had been the site of weekly protests. The Japanese state persists in downplaying, at times even in denying, the existence of networks of sexual exploitation and violence, rather than entertaining the possibility of apologies, health care, and financial compensation for surviving victims, and including the subject in the high school curriculum to prevent its reoccurrence.[75]

The heinous practice of sexual enslavement by the Japanese military ended with Japan's capitulation in 1945. Apart from a handful of women who came forward with their stories in the 1970s and 1980s, most women remained silent until the 1990s. Debate in the public arena, which emerged then, has been further energized by the involvement of transnational feminism and global human rights activism. In other words, the politics of war memory and memorialization have intensified rather than diminished with the passage of time.[76] The way the past is commemorated is a deeply political process.[77]

According to Kimura, the campaign for official acknowledgement has transformed into something much more than a single issue in Japan's contemporary culture wars. "Comfort women" memorials, whose emotional and aesthetic strategies the author analyzes, have recently been erected in such far-flung locations as Seoul, Busan (South Korea), Nanjing, Shanghai, Sydney, Wiesent (Germany), Palisades Park (New Jersey), and Glendale (California).[78] Kimura's chapter raises the intriguing question of how, in our day and age, terrible events that have occurred generations ago in specific places and times become universal moral exemplars of an entire category of traumatic violence, in this case, the victimization of women in war.[79]

Concluding Reflections

Historical accounts of trauma and the medical reactions to explain and alleviate its destructive psychological effects have thus far mostly focused on Europe (especially the UK, Germany, and France) and North America. Central to these studies have been, on the one hand, war-related mental disorders and those caused by industrial accidents, and, on the other, the Holocaust. Warfare and mental breakdown as a historical subject has also appeared in scholarship on Asia, the Pacific War being the most obvious example. Other types of warfare have been fought in Asia as well, which were motivated by the political dynamics of the Cold War, including wars in Korea and Vietnam, which escalated intensively after the world's superpowers became involved. Several Asian countries have also witnessed the brutal repression of civilian populations under internal dictatorships or one-party states, such as the Communist regimes in China, North Korea, and Cambodia; the military dictatorship in Myanmar; and Suharto's New Order regime in Indonesia. Today, governments in several Asian countries ignore or minimize their country's painful pasts rather than publicly acknowledge and address them. The historical traumas of Franco's Spain, Portugal's Estado Novo regime, the Greek *junta*, and several regimes in formerly Communist Eastern European countries have similar situations, but these have received little attention from scholars. Fortunately, current humanities research on trauma is expanding its geographical horizons.[80]

Many Asian nations have also experienced a colonialized past, which is common with African, South American, and Caribbean countries too. Asia witnessed the long-term military occupation of Korea, Taiwan, and Manchuria by the Japanese Imperial army, but also the oppressive hand of the British, French, Portuguese, and Dutch empires for generations. Furthermore, during the Cold War the influence of the post-World War II empires of the United States, Soviet Union, and China were keenly felt.[81] At the same time, intra-Asian violence has played a considerable role: Japan occupied Taiwan, Korea, and China; and the Indian government still occupies Kashmir. The United States holds a profoundly ambivalent role in this volume—alternately as savior, facilitator, perpetrator, and, at times, victim.[82] It is striking that European and North American scholars have hardly explored the traumatic effects of their historical presence in their former colonies. Frantz Fanon was the first to see specific forms of psychopathology as a critique of colonialism.[83] Because of the (until recently) almost exclusive focus on Western experiences, Peter Leese and Jason Crouthamel have asked "to what extent is 'trauma' a colonizing concept?"[84] And the well-known Holocaust scholar Michael Rothberg has provocatively declared that "trauma is not just for white Westerners."[85]

Even though warfare and trauma is a shared theme in historical research about Europe, North America, and Asia, several types of warfare and military repression in Asia have been distinctive. Current conflicts in Asia, the Middle East, and Africa have led to large refugee and involuntary migrant populations, which often reside in refugee camps for years without clear prospects for permanent relocation.[86] Other factors prominent in this volume have to date also received insufficient attention in earlier historical trauma studies. The effect of natural cataclysms that have plagued and continue to plague Asia is one of these.[87] According to United Nations figures, Asia accounts for 57 percent of the global death toll from natural disasters, principally from earthquakes, storms, and floods.

Another factor is the presence of physical disease—particularly febrile illnesses related to the tropical climate—and endemic malnutrition, which have symptoms that are easily mistaken for those of mental disorders. In this volume, trauma is less about the distressing experiences that army soldiers had in battle zones far from home and more about civilian men, women, and children who are struggling under the devastating impact of systemic violence or natural disasters. One conclusion seems clear: the history of trauma across the Asian continent does not merely duplicate, with a somewhat different chronology, geography, and emphasis, the scenarios found in European- and American-focused scholarship. Common themes present in trauma research on Asia can potentially enrich the study and understanding of trauma in general and in all locations.

What sets discussions about trauma in Asia (and Africa and Latin America?) apart is the dynamic interplay between dominant (Western) psychiatric views on PTSD and various local idioms of distress. Beginning around 2000, spirited interdisciplinary conversations commenced about the globalization of Western psychiatry and its possible drawbacks and dangers. Critics have asked to what degree the theories, diagnoses, and therapeutic interventions of contemporary Anglo-American psychiatry can be exported and applied to individuals living "elsewhere" in the world.[88] More important, in our opinion, are the ways in which mental health professionals and others working in Asia receive these views, what adaptations they think are necessary, and their record of clinical effectiveness. Although we are convinced of the utility of trauma as a broad category of psychological (as well as legal and moral) analysis, the chapters in this volume highlight the necessity of taking various local social, cultural, and political elements into account. Byron J. Good and Devon Hinton have argued that it is more appropriate to speak of "post-traumatic syndromes" with porous cultural boundaries that can incorporate other points of view and reactions.[89]

On another point, the chapters below document a familiar spectrum of emotional reactions following sudden severe trauma, including grief, panic, delirium, acute confusion, and, at times, psychotic agitation. Clinical manifestations of these states are not necessarily consonant across cultures, however.[90] Asian "idioms of distress" may manifest more readily via somatic and physiological symptoms than through the expression of subdued or depressed emotional states as in the psychologized West.[91] In a related thought, it may be possible with these studies to "provincialize Europe" by observing the cultural effects that the lack of a long Freudian heritage exerts on the history of trauma theory and praxis.[92]

Also illustrated in this collection is the key role played by public opinion, governments, and political ideology in determining which traumas are to be acknowledged. A wide diversity of governments is present in Asia today, including one-party Communist states, military juntas, dictatorships based on personality cults, constitutional monarchies, parliamentary republics, and governments in exile. All governments tend to embrace a preferred vision of their national past, granting priority to certain events, heroes, and villains; such self-serving histories often indicate the types and episodes of past suffering to be recognized and memorialized and, conversely, those to be denied and "de-remembered." Conservative nationalist governments often seek to sponsor patriotic histories and are reluctant to elaborate on grave human rights violations.[93] Repressive and authoritarian governments worldwide censor or forbid the study of past atrocities, although some of them may encourage it for a desired political function.

Even in open liberal-democratic societies—as recent anti-racist, anti-immigrant, and anti-colonial sentiments indicate—there is no longer a consensus about whose past suffering matters and whose does not. Internationally supervised tribunals and reconciliation commissions to investigate past wrongdoing that have brought some perpetrators to justice and offered reconciliation and rehabilitation to victims have taken place in South Africa, Yugoslavia, and Rwanda; lamentably, these initiatives have been less common in Asia, with the exception of Cambodia and East Timor, where the tribunals to date have had limited results.

Finally, in chronological terms the preponderance of past historically based research has thus far dwelled on psychological traumas before the 1950s. Most of the research presented in this volume, however, concerns more recent events, and sometimes much more recent. As a result, anthropologists outnumber historians among the contributors, and interviews and participant-observation are commonly employed, which allows investigators to give voice to living research participants.[94] The further integration of historical and anthropological research on trauma appears to us highly promising. Likewise, the research conducted by scholars up to this point needs to incorporate a much broader range of traumatic experiences such as those canvassed in this volume. A European-centered historical template cannot simply be transposed onto other regions in the world, especially when these regions possess deep, rich, and independent histories. The twelve original studies in this book, we believe, establish powerfully that psychological trauma is "a useful category of analysis" in writing Asian history and that critical trauma studies should become a standard part of the analytical armamentarium of scholars in Asian studies.[95]

Hans Pols is Professor at the School of History and Philosophy of Science at the University of Sydney. He is interested in the history of colonial medicine and the transformation medical research and practice underwent during the process of decolonization. His research has focused on the Dutch East Indies and Indonesia, and on psychiatry and mental health. His book *Nurturing Indonesia: Medicine and Decolonisation in the Dutch East Indies* was published by Cambridge University Press in 2018. He is currently involved in several projects that aim to shape the future of mental health care in Indonesia.

Mark S. Micale is Emeritus Professor of History at the University of Illinois in Urbana-Champaign. After receiving his Ph.D. at Yale in 1987, he taught at the Wellcome Institute for the History of Medicine (1988–90), Yale (1990–1996), the University of Manchester (1996–2000), and the University of Illinois (2000–2018). His fields of scholarly interest are modern European intellectual and cultural history; post-revolutionary French history; the history of medicine, especially psychiatry and neurology; the history of the life sciences; psychoanalytic studies; and masculinity studies. The majority of his publications have dealt with the history of the mental sciences; they include *Beyond the Unconscious* (1993), *Discovering the History of Psychiatry* with Roy Porter (1994), *Approaching Hysteria: Disease and Its Interpretations* (1994), *The Mind of Modernism: Medicine, Psychology, and the Cultural Arts in Europe and America, 1880–1940* (2004), *Traumatic Pasts: History, Psychiatry, and Trauma in the Modern Age, 1860–1930* (2001), *Enlightenment, Culture, and Passion: Essays in History in Honor of Peter Gay* (2000); and *Hysterical Men: The Hidden History of Male Nervous Illness* (2008).

Notes

1. We are aware that words like "trauma" and "traumatic" are not part of the various languages that are spoken in Asia, although in several of them the word has been incorporated recently. In this introduction, we refer to "trauma" as a shorthand for horrific, catastrophic, and disastrous events, including natural disasters and violent events by human beings, that have led to the loss of life on a relatively large scale or that include threats to the lives and well-being of individuals, their families, communities, and societies. The after-effects of such events often include unexplained medical disorders or a variety of adverse emotional reactions that interfere with health, well-being, and the ability to work. For reflections on trauma in Asia, see Surin, "Conceptualizing Trauma."

2. This phenomenon has been analyzed and critiqued by Fassin and Rechtman, *Empire of Trauma*. See also Fassin, *Humanitarian Reason*, and Fassin and Pandolfi, *Contemporary States of Emergency*.
3. American Psychiatric Association, *DSM-III*.
4. Andreasen, "Acute and Delayed Posttraumatic Stress Disorders," 1322. For a similar argument, see also Andreasen, "Posttraumatic Stress Disorder: History and Critique."
5. The term "bracket creep" was introduced by Richard McNally in "Progress and Controversy."
6. McNally, "Expanding Empire," 9. See also Horwitz, "PTSD Ubiquitous."
7. Miller, *PTSD Forensic Psychology*; Mullany and Handford, *Tort Liability Psychiatric Damage*; Handford, Mullany, and Mitchell, *Tort Liability Psychiatric Damage*.
8. Riebeling, "Wounds of the Past," Introduction.
9. Andreasen, "Posttraumatic Stress Disorder: False Dichotomies," 964.
10. Horwitz, *PTSD: A Short History*.
11. See, for example, the adjustments counsellors made as analyzed by Varma, "Where There Are Only Doctors." See also Somasundaram, "Collective Trauma Northern Sri Lanka," 5. In the perspective of some people in Asia, a concern with trauma should include the dead. See Caroline Bennett, in this volume, and Kwon, "Can the Dead Suffer Trauma?"
12. Breslau, "Cultures of Trauma." For critical perspectives on this phenomenon, see Watters, *Crazy Like Us*; Mills, *Decolonizing Global Mental Health*; Summerfield, "How Scientifically Valid?"; Summerfield, "Afterword"; and Pupavac, "Psychosocial Interventions."
13. Summerfield, "Childhood, War, Refugeedom"; Summerfield, "How Scientifically Valid?"; and Pupavac, "Psychosocial Interventions."
14. Marsella et al., *Ethnocultural Aspects*; Kirmayer, Lemelson, and Cummings, *Re-Visioning Psychiatry*; Hinton and Good, *Culture and PTSD*.
15. Marsella, "Ethnocultural Aspects"; Stamm and Friedman, "Cultural Diversity"; Argenti-Pillen, "Discourse Trauma."
16. See, for example, the chapters in Hinton and Good, *Culture and PTSD*; and Kirmayer, Lemelson, and Barad, *Understanding Trauma*.
17. Snijders et al., "Resilience."
18. Yehuda and McFarlane, "Conflict Current Knowledge." See also Kirmayer et al., *Understanding Trauma*. See also the chapters in Shalev, Yehuda, and McFarlane, *International Handbook*.
19. See Micale and Lerner, *Traumatic Pasts*. The historical research on Western precursors of PTSD is voluminous. See Lerner, *Hysterical Men*; Leese, *Shell Shock*; Young, *Harmony Illusions*; and Pols, "Tunisian Campaign." Many studies have focused on trauma and war; for overviews, see Jones and Wessely, *Shell Shock to PTSD* and Shephard, *War of Nerves*.
20. Micale and Lerner, *Traumatic Pasts*. See also Micale, "Charcot."
21. Micale, "Toward Global History Trauma"; Micale, "Beyond the Western Front."
22. Pols, "War Neurosis, Adjustment Problems, Ill Nation"; Pols, "Tunisian Campaign"; Pols, "Nature Native Mind"; Pols, "The Psychiatrist as Administrator"; and Edington and Pols, "Building Southeast Asian Psychiatric Expertise."
23. See, for example, Hillenbrand, "Trauma Politics of Identity"; Lin, *Representing Atrocity in Taiwan*; and Berry, *A History of Pain*; Ma, *The Last Isle*; and Choi, *Healing Historical Trauma*.
24. Beginning in 2011, a group of scholars, including historians, started to collect research and teaching/learning materials related to disasters in Asia. The website "Teach311" has become one of the most important databases related to disasters and catastrophes in the region. Recently, it has joined forces with the COVID-19 Collective. See: https://www.teach311.org/. From the website: "Teach311 + COVID-19 is a collective of educators,

Introduction • 23

researchers, artists, students and survivors spanning disciplinary and linguistic boundaries who study and teach about disasters. Our collaborative process encourages empathic inquiry into the past, and shares those stories for the future."

25. This outcome was the combination of the presence of a team of American researchers and internal developments in Japanese psychiatry. A first report was published as Mollica et al., *Invisible Human Crisis*. See also Kokai et al., "Natural Disaster Mental Health" and Breslau, "Globalizing Disaster Trauma." Japan had started to prepare for earthquakes after the Great Kantō Earthquake in 1923, which killed over 100,000 people. See Borland, *Earthquake Children* and Chan, "Bonds and Companionship."
26. See Yang, *Great Exodus from China*, which examines hundreds of thousands of refugees expelled across the Taiwan Strait following the Chinese Communist Revolution in 1949. See also Wu and Cheng, "A History of Mental Healthcare in Taiwan"; and Wu, "Charted Epidemic of Trauma."
27. This literature is by now extensive. See, for example, Kar, Krishnaraaj, and Rameshraj, "Long-Term Mental Health Outcomes"; Good, Good, and Grayman, "PTSD 'Good Enough'?"
28. On the concept of "psychological first aid," see Kim, "Great East Japan Earthquake." See also the Introduction by Micale and Lerner to the Japanese translation of *Traumatic Pasts*. For an analysis of the US response to a national disaster, see Eyerman, *Is This America?*
29. Changes in political power have generally led to adherence to different medical traditions. Political changes can lead to changes in the basic orientation in physicians, often associated with the languages they are taught to speak. This can severely disrupt medical traditions. In Laos, French, Soviet, and American approaches have alternated; in Vietnam, a French medical tradition was replaced by a Soviet one. See Sweet, "Women's Health in Laos"; and Aso, "Learning to Heal the People."
30. Kim, *Doctors of Empire*.
31. Lerner, *Hysterical Men*; Roudebush, "Battle of Nerves."
32. Uchida, "Revival of Military Masculinity." See also Nakamura, "Aftermath of War Trauma"; Nakamura, "'Invisible' War Trauma in Japan." Nakamura lists a number of Japanese-language studies of civilian war trauma following the land battle at Okinawa in footnote 32 of her article.
33. See also Hashimoto, *The Long Defeat*. Contrast these attitudes with those found in a recent publication: McCurry, "Japan Makes Progress."
34. See, for example, Sundram et al., "Psychosocial Responses to Disaster."
35. Similar questions have been raised in a comparative study of pension determinations in Europe after World War II. See Withuis and Mooij, *The Politics of War Trauma*.
36. Yum, "In Sickness and in Health." See also Jones and Palmer, "Army Psychiatry Korean War."
37. See, for example, Pols, "Tunisian Campaign"; see also Min and In-sok, "Mental Health in Korea." See also Menninger and Nemiah, *American Psychiatry after WWII* and Pols, "Waking up to Shell Shock."
38. For US versions of psychoanalysis, see Plant, "William Menninger American Psychoanalysis"; Hale, *Rise Crisis Psychoanalysis US*.
39. Kim, *Memory, Reconciliation, Reunions* studies the emotional trauma of long-term family separations across the North-South divide since the Korean War. Minkyu Sung of the Ulsan National Institute of Science and Technology is researching a book titled *Against the Trauma Claim: A Critique of Re-Humanizing North Korean Defectors in Times of Reconciliation*.
40. Indicative is Kolk, *The Body Keeps the Score*, an intelligent, wide-ranging account by a leading international authority on trauma medicine that opens with a chapter titled

"Lessons from Vietnam Veterans" yet never considers the people of Vietnam themselves, millions of whom perished in the war.
41. For moral and theoretical reflections on this question, see Butler, *Frames of War*, and Modlinger and Sonntag, *Other People's Pain*.
42. For other work on Vietnam, see Tran, "The Anxiety of Well-Being," Kim (Kim Thu Le), *Cultural Expressions of Trauma*, and Nguyen, "Vietnamese Refugee Women." For a comprehensive account of "madness" in Indochina, see Edington, *Beyond the Asylum*.
43. Barak's is also the first chapter in the collection to highlight the disciplinary identity of the studies in *Traumatic Pasts in Asia*. A generation ago, the contributors to the first *Traumatic Pasts* were all historians of modern Europe. Since the global dissemination of North American psychological and psychiatric theories is relatively recent, however, historical analysis in the present project needs to be combined with contemporary on-site anthropological research. In the ensuing chapters, anthropological data gathering methods—including on-site observation, in-depth interviewing, and cultural immersion—supplement, and at times supplant, traditional historical perspectives.
44. Patel, *Where There Is No Psychiatrist*.
45. Smith, *Resilience Localisation of Trauma*.
46. Kohrt and Hruschka, "Nepali Concepts of Psychological Trauma" finds significant variations in idioms of distress even within one "small" country.
47. Lemelson, "40 Years of Silence: An Indonesian Tragedy," a documentary film featuring four survivors and their families from Bali and Java.
48. Schreiner, "Lubang Buaya."
49. Atreyee Sen has described singing as a coping strategy in an Indian prison. See Sen, "Torture and Laughter." For music making as consolatory practice in a European setting, see Rogers, *Resonant Recoveries*.
50. Pitaloka, "Singing the Hope."
51. Joanna Bourke has highlighted the ways women suffer violence during war and conflict. See Bourke, *Rape: Sex, Violence, History*, among several other writings.
52. A point also well-established in regard to Arab culture in Nikro and Hegasy, *Social Life of Memory*, Introduction.
53. See also Bennett, "Living with the Dead."
54. On the representation of dead bodies in the landscape as part of the national imaginary, see Ly, "Broken Body." For comparisons with how other societies mourn, exhume, and re-bury corpses following mass violence, see Robben, *Companion Anthropology Death*.
55. See also Guillou, "Structuration rituelle."
56. For the parallel government-supported program in Cambodia that draws on PTSD medicine, see Schaack, Reicherter, and Chhang, *Cambodia's Hidden Scars*.
57. Rene, *China's Sent-Down Generation*.
58. For complementary studies, see Gao, "Paradoxes of Solidarity"; and Markert, "The Chinese Cultural Revolution," which is based on psychoanalytically informed interviews with survivors and their children. For the impact of the Cultural Revolution on the arts, see Wang, *Illuminations from the Past*.
59. For "the spatial turn" in trauma studies, see Coddington and Micieli-Voutsinas, "On Trauma, Geography, and Mobility."
60. Zhigang, "Scar Literature."
61. Moffic, "Psychiatry China"; Huang, "Emergence Psycho-Boom."
62. Pupavac, "Therapeutic Governance"; Yang, *Mental Health in China*.
63. For example, the archives of the Chinese Ministry of Foreign Affairs closed again, only to re-open one year later. See Minami "China's Foreign Ministry Archive."
64. Marks and Savelli, *Psychiatry Communist Europe*.

65. Fassin and Rechtman, *Empire of Trauma*; and Fassin and Pandolfi, *Contemporary States of Emergency*.
66. Akin to Frantz Fanon on psychopathologies of colonialism in North Africa. See Fanon, *Toward the African Revolution*. See also Varma, *The Occupied Clinic*, especially chapter 3.
67. McEwen and Schmeck, *The Hostage Brain*, documents the permanent neuroendocrinological damage done to the human brain from high levels of chronic stress among historically marginalized people.
68. McFarlane, "On the Social Denial of Trauma"; Herman, "A Forgotten History."
69. Freud, *Beyond the Pleasure Principle*.
70. Herman, "A Forgotten History."
71. For an analysis of the situation in Indonesia refer to Hearman, "Under Duress."
72. Chang, *Rape of Nanking*; Alexander with Rui Gao, "Mass Murder and Trauma."
73. Yoshimi, *Comfort Women*. For the larger story of sexual exploitation in Asia through the first half of the twentieth century, see Tanaka, *Japan's Comfort Women*.
74. On this role of monuments, see Winter, *Sites of Memory, Sites of Mourning*.
75. Kimura, *Unfolding the 'Comfort Women' Debates*. See also Nishino, Kim, and Onozawa, *Denying the Comfort Women*. Two documentary films on the subject, both directed by the Canadian filmmaker Tiffany Hsiung, are *Within Every Woman* (2012) and *The Apology* (2016).
76. Chirot, "World World II Memories."
77. For a comparative perspective, consult Macaluso, *Monument Culture*, especially section 3.
78. Mackie and Crozier-De Rosa, "Remembering the Grandmothers."
79. In chapter 4 of *The Cultural Politics of Emotion*, author Sara Ahmed discusses how pain is used to demand action or shape identities in the political sphere today.
80. See, for example, Casper and Wertheimer, *Critical Trauma Studies*; Kivimäki and Leese, *Trauma, Experience and Narrative*; Leese, Köhne, and Crouthamel, *Languages of Trauma*.
81. See, for example, Westad, *The Global Cold War*; Westad, *The Cold War*.
82. The bombing of Hiroshima and Nagasaki killed between 150,000 and 220,000 people on the day of the bombing; thousands more died later because of radiation exposure. In Vietnam, there were over 1 million Vietnamese (military and civilian) casualties and close to 50,000 American (military) ones. During the Korean war, more than 5 million people died.
83. Fanon, *The Wretched of the Earth*; Fanon, *Black Skin, White Masks*. For a contemporary reworking of the Fanonian critique, see Lazali, *Colonial Trauma*.
84. Leese and Crouthamel, *Traumatic Memories Second World War*, 15.
85. Rothberg, "Beyond Tancred and Clorinda," xi–xviii; Rothberg, "Decolonizing Trauma Studies: A Response."
86. Duncan Pedersen has urged broadening our conception of warfare and focusing our attention in particular on refugees and involuntary migrants. See Pedersen, "Rethinking Trauma Global Challenge."
87. Gordan, "Disaster, Ruin, and Permanent Catastrophe." For a European historical angle on the theme, see Rousso, *The Latest Catastrophe*.
88. Peter, "Experience of 'Mental Trauma'"; Summerfield, "A Critique of Seven Assumptions"; Summerfield, "Invention of Post-Traumatic Stress Disorder." For a response, see de Jong, "Deconstructing Critiques."
89. On interdisciplinarity and the study of trauma, see Kirmayer, Lemelson, and Barad, *Understanding Trauma*.
90. In a classic research project, Harvard psychiatrist Arthur Kleinman argued that somatization—that is, the expression of mental distress through physical conversion symp-

toms—was much more common in certain East Asian populations. See Kleinman and Good, *Culture and Depression*. For updates on the author's thinking on the matter, see Kleinman and Kleinman, "Remembering the Cultural Revolution"; and Lee and Kleinman, "Somatoform Disorders Changing?"
91. For this issue in another Asian country, see Kitanaka, "Reading Emotions in the Body"; Kitanaka, *Depression in Japan*.
92. Chakrabarty, *Provincializing Europe*. For a defense of the traditional psychoanalytic model of trauma in a globalized context, see Davoine and Gaudilliere, *History beyond Trauma*.
93. For Indonesia, this process has been analyzed by Kate McGregor in her *History in Uniform*.
94. A similar observation has been made by Christina Zarowsky on the basis of her research in Ethiopia. See Zarowsky, "Trauma Stories."
95. See, for example, Casper and Wertheimer, *Critical Trauma Studies*. For book-length studies of Asian countries not covered in the book, see Jain and Sarin, *Psychological Impact Partition*; Mookerjea-Leonard, *Literature, Gender, and the Trauma of Partition*; Singh, Iyer, and Gairola, *Revisiting India's Partition*, which examines "partition trauma" in India, Pakistan, and Bangladesh; Winichakul, *Moments of Silence*; and Baral, *Nepal*.

Bibliography

Ahmed, Sara. *The Cultural Politics of Emotion*. Edinburgh: Edinburgh University Press, 2004.
Alexander, Jeffrey C., with Rui Gao. "Mass Murder and Trauma: Nanjing and the Silence of Maoism." In *Trauma: A Social Theory*, edited by Jeffrey C. Alexander, 118–35. Cambridge: Polity Press, 2012.
American Psychiatric Association. *Diagnostic and Statistical Manual of Mental Disorders*. 3rd ed. Washington, DC: American Psychiatric Association, 1980.
Andreasen, Nancy C. "Acute and Delayed Posttraumatic Stress Disorders: A History and Some Issues." *American Journal of Psychiatry* 161, no. 8 (2004): 1321–23.
———. "Posttraumatic Stress Disorder: A History and a Critique." *Annals of the New York Academy of Sciences*, no. 1208 (2010): 67–71.
———. "Posttraumatic Stress Disorder: Psychology, Biology, and the Manichean Warfare between False Dichotomies." *American Journal of Psychiatry* 152, no. 7 (1995): 963–65.
Argenti-Pillen, Alexandra. "The Discourse on Trauma in Non-Western Cultural Contexts: Contributions of an Ethnographic Method." In *International Handbook of Human Response to Trauma*, edited by Arieh Y. Shalev, Rachel Yehuda, and Alexander C. McFarlane, 87–102. Boston, MA: Springer, 2000.
Aso, Michitake. "Learning to Heal the People: Socialist Medicine and Education in Vietnam, 1945–54." In *Translating the Body: Medical Education in Southeast Asia*, edited by Hans Pols, C. Michele Thompson, and John Harley Warner, 146–72. Singapore: NUS Press, 2017.
Baral, Lok Raj. *Nepal, Trauma of Political Development and Stability: Essays on Nepal and South Asia*. New Delhi: Adroit Publishers, 2017.
Bennett, Caroline. "Living with the Dead in the Killing Fields of Cambodia." *Journal of Southeast Asian Studies* 49, no. 2 (2018): 184–203.

Berry, Michael. *A History of Pain: Trauma in Modern Chinese Literature and Film*. New York: Columbia University Press, 2011.
Borland, Janet. *Earthquake Children: Building Resilience from the Ruins of Tokyo*. Cambridge, MA: Harvard University Press, 2020.
Bourke, Joanna. *Rape: Sex, Violence, History*. Berkeley, CA: Counterpoint, 2009.
Breslau, Joshua. "Cultures of Trauma: Anthropological Views of Posttraumatic Stress Disorder in International Health." *Culture, Medicine, & Psychiatry* 28 (2004): 113–26.
———. "Globalizing Disaster Trauma: Psychiatry, Science, and Culture after the Kobe Earthquake." *Ethos* 28, no. 2 (2000): 174–97.
Butler, Judith. *Frames of War: When Is Life Grievable?* London: Verso, 2009.
Casper, Monica J., and Eric Wertheimer, eds. *Critical Trauma Studies: Understanding Violence, Conflict, and Memory in Everyday Life*. New York: New York University Press, 2016.
Chakrabarty, Dipesh. *Provincializing Europe: Postcolonial Thought and Historical Difference*. Princeton: Princeton University Press, 2000.
Chan, Michelle. "Bonds and Companionship: The Healing Efficacy of Picture Books of the 2011 Great East Japan Earthquake." In *Memory, Trauma, Asia: Recall, Affect, and Orientalism in Contemporary Narratives*, edited by Rahul K. Gairola and Sharanya Jayawickrama, chapter 7. New York: Routledge, 2021.
Chang, Iris. *The Rape of Nanking: The Forgotten Holocaust of World War II*. New York: Basic Books, [1997] 2012.
Chirot, Daniel. "Why World World II Memories Remain So Troubled in Europe and East Asia." In *Remembrance, History, and Justice: Coming to Terms with Traumatic Pasts in Democratic Societies*, edited by Vladimir Tismaneanu and Bogdan C. Iacob, 45–68. Budapest: Central European University Press, 2015.
Choi, Chungmoo. *Healing Historical Trauma in South Korean Film and Literature*. Abingdon, Oxon: Routledge, 2021.
Coddington, Kate, and Jacque Micieli-Voutsinas. "On Trauma, Geography, and Mobility: Towards Geographies of Trauma." *Emotion, Space and Society* 24 (2017): 1–112.
Davoine, Françoise, and Jean-Max Gaudillière. *History beyond Trauma*. Translated by Susan Fairfield. New York: Other Press, 2004.
De Jong, Joop T. V. M. "Deconstructing Critiques on the Internationalization of PTSD." *Culture, Medicine & Psychiatry* 29, no. 3 (2005): 361–70.
Edington, Claire E. *Beyond the Asylum: Mental Illness in French Colonial Vietnam*. Ithaca, NY: Cornell University Press, 2019.
Edington, Claire E, and Hans Pols. "Building Southeast Asian Psychiatric Expertise: Site Visits, Scientific Journeys, and Medical Exchanges between French Indochina and the Dutch East Indies, 1898–1937." *Comparative Studies in Society and History* 58, no. 3 (2016): 636–63.
Eyerman, Ron. *Is This America?: Katrina as Cultural Trauma*. Austin: University of Texas Press, 2015.
Fanon, Frantz. *Black Skin, White Masks*. Translated by Charles Lam Markmann. New York: Grove Press, 1967.
———. *Toward the African Revolution: Political Essays*. New York: Grove Press, 1964.
———. *The Wretched of the Earth*. Translated by Constance Farrington. New York: Grove Press, 1965.
Fassin, Didier. *Humanitarian Reason: A Moral History of the Present*. Translated by Rachel Gomme. Berkeley: University of California Press, 2011.
Fassin, Didier, and Mariella Pandolfi, eds. *Contemporary States of Emergency: The Politics of Military and Humanitarian Interventions*. New York: Zone Books, 2010.

Fassin, Didier, and Richard Rechtman. *The Empire of Trauma: An Inquiry into the Condition of Victimhood*. Translated by Rachel Gomme. Princeton, NJ: Princeton University Press 2009.

Freud, Sigmund. *Beyond the Pleasure Principle*. Translated by James Strachey. New York: Norton, [1920] 1989.

Gao, Rui. "The Paradoxes of Solidarity: Cultural Trauma and Collective Identity in Mao's China." *Chinese Journal of Sociology* 1, no. 1 (2015): 108–35.

Good, Byron J., Mary-Jo DelVecchio Good, and Jesse H. Grayman. "Is PTSD a 'Good Enough' Concept for Postconflict Mental Health Care? Reflections on Work in Aceh, Indonesia." In *Culture and PTSD: Trauma in Global and Historical Perspective*, edited by Devon E. Hinton and Byron J. Good, 387–417. Philadelphia: University of Pennsylvania Press, 2016.

Gordan, Lewis R. "Disaster, Ruin, and Permanent Catastrophe." In *The Time of Catastrophe: Multidisciplinary Approaches to the Age of Catastrophe*, edited by Christopher Dole, Robert Hayashi, Andrew Poe, and Austin Sarat, 125–42. London: Routledge, 2015.

Guillou, Anne Yvonne. "Structuration rituelle de la relation défunts-vivants au Cambodge dans les morts individuelles et collectives" [Ritual structuring of the relationship between the dead and the living in Cambodia in individual and collective deaths]. *L'Autre: Revue Transculturelle* 19, no. 3 (2018). Retreived 1 December 2020 from https://revuelautre.com/articles-dossier/structuration-rituelle-de-la-relation-defunts-vivants-au-cambodge-dans-les-morts-individuelles-et-collectives/.

Hale, Nathan G. *The Rise and Crisis of Psychoanalysis in the United States, 1917–1985*. New York: Oxford University Press, 1995.

Handford, Peter R., Nicholas J. Mullany, and Philip B. Mitchell. *Mullany and Handford's Tort Liability for Psychiatric Damage*. 2nd ed. Sydney: Law Book Co., 2006.

Hashimoto, Akiko. *The Long Defeat: Cultural Trauma, Memory, and Identity in Japan*. Oxford: Oxford University Press, 2015.

Hearman, Vannessa. "Under Duress: Suppressing and Recovering Memories of the Indonesian Sixties." *Social Transformations* 1, no. 1 (2013): 5–25.

Herman, Judith Lewis. "A Forgotten History." In *Trauma and Recovery: The Aftermath of Violence, from Domestic Abuse to Political Terror*, 7–32. New York: Basic Books, 1992.

Hillenbrand, Margaret. "Trauma and the Politics of Identity: Form and Function in Fictional Narratives of the February 28th Incident." *Modern Chinese Literature and Culture* 17, no. 2 (2005): 49–89.

Hinton, Devon E., and Byron J. Good, eds. *Culture and PTSD: Trauma in Global and Historical Perspective*. Philadelphia: University of Pennsylvania Press, 2016.

Horwitz, Allan V. *PTSD: A Short History*. Baltimore, MD: Johns Hopkins University Press, 2018.

———. "PTSD Becomes Ubiquitous." In *PTSD: A Short History*, 135–64. Baltimore, MD: Johns Hopkins University Press, 2018.

Hsiung, Tiffany. dir. *Within Every Woman*. Documentary, 24 minutes. Toronto: Gold Nugget Productions, 2012.

———. *The Apology*. Documentary, 104 minutes. Montreal: National Film Board of Canada, 2016.

Huang, Hsuan-Ying. "The Emergence of the Psycho-Boom in Contemporary Urban China." In *Psychiatry and Chinese History*, edited by Howard Chiang, 183–204. London: Routledge, 2015.

Jain, Sanjeev, and Alok Sarin, eds. *The Psychological Impact of the Partition of India*. New Delhi: Sage, 2016.

Jones, Edgar, and Ian P. Palmer. "Army Psychiatry in the Korean War: The Experience of 1 Commonwealth Division." *Military Medicine* 165, no. 4 (2000): 256–60.
Jones, Edgar, and Simon Wessely. *Shell Shock to PTSD: Military Psychiatry from 1900 to the Gulf War*. Hove, East Sussex: Psychology Press, 2005.
Kar, Nilamadhab, Rameshraj Krishnaraaj, and Kavitha Rameshraj. "Long-Term Mental Health Outcomes Following the 2004 Asian Tsunami Disaster: A Comparative Study on Direct and Indirect Exposure." *Disaster Health* 2, no. 1 (2014): 35–45.
Kim (Kim Thu Le). *The Tam-Giao: Cultural Expressions of Trauma in Vietnamese Visual Arts*. Champaign, IL: Common Ground Research Network, 2018.
Kim, Hoi-eun. *Doctors of Empire: Medical and Cultural Encounters between Imperial Germany and Meiji Japan*. Toronto: University of Toronto Press, 2014.
Kim, Nan. *Memory, Reconciliation, and Reunions in South Korea: Crossing the Divide*. Lanham, MD: Lexington Books, 2017.
Kim, Yoshiharu. "Great East Japan Earthquake and Early Mental Health Care Response (Editorial)." *Psychiatry and Clinical Neurosciences* 65 (2011): 539–48.
Kimura, Maki. *Unfolding the 'Comfort Women' Debates: Modernity, Violence, Women's Voices*. New York: Palgrave Macmillan, 2016.
Kirmayer, Laurence J., Robert B. Lemelson, and Mar Barad, eds. *Understanding Trauma: Integrating Biological, Clinical, and Cultural Perspectives*. New York: Cambridge University Press, 2007.
Kirmayer, Laurence J., Robert B. Lemelson, and Constance A. Cummings, eds. *Re-Visioning Psychiatry: Cultural Phenomenology, Critical Neuroscience, and Global Mental Health*. New York: Cambridge University Press, 2015.
Kitanaka, Junko. *Depression in Japan: Psychiatric Cures for a Society in Distress*. Princeton, NJ: Princeton University Press, 2011.
———. "Reading Emotions in the Body: Translating Depression at the Intersections of Japanese and Western Medicines." In *Transnational Psychiatries: Social and Cultural Histories of Psychiatry in Comparative Perspective c.1800–2000*, edited by Waltraud Ernst and Thomas Mueller, 1–23. Newcastle upon Tyne, UK: Cambridge Scholars, 2010.
Kivimäki, Ville, and Peter Leese, eds. *Trauma, Experience and Narrative in Europe after the Second World War*. Cham, Switzerland: Palgrave Macmillan, forthcoming.
Kleinman, Arthur, and Byron Good, eds. *Culture and Depression: Studies in the Anthropology and Cross-Cultural Psychiatry of Affect and Disorder*. Berkeley, CA: University of California Press, 1985.
Kleinman, Arthur, and Joan Kleinman. "Remembering the Cultural Revolution: Alienating Pains and the Pains of Alienation/Transformation." In *Chinese Societies and Mental Health*, edited by Tsung-Yi Lin, Wen-Shing Tseng, and Eng-Kung Yeh, 141–55. Hong Kong: Oxford University Press, 1995.
Kohrt, Brandon A., and Daniel J. Hruschka. "Nepali Concepts of Psychological Trauma." *Culture, Medicine & Psychiatry* 34, no. 2 (2010): 322–52.
Kokai, Masahiro, Senta Fujii, Naotaka Shinfuku, and Glen Edwards. "Natural Disaster and Mental Health in Asia (Review Article)." *Psychiatry and Clinical Neurosciences* 58 (2004): 110–16.
Kolk, Bessel A. van der. *The Body Keeps the Score: Brain, Mind, and Body in the Healing of Trauma*. New York: Penguin, 2015.
Kwon, Heonik. "Can the Dead Suffer Trauma?: Religion and Science after the Vietnam War." In *Religion and Science as Forms of Life: Anthropological Insights into Reason and Unreason*, edited by Carles Salazar and Joan Bestard, 207–20. New York: Berghahn Books, 2015.

Lazali, Karima. *Colonial Trauma: A Study of the Psychic and Political Consequences of Colonial Oppression in Algeria*, translated from the French by Matthew B. Smith. Cambridge: Polity, [2018] 2020.

Lee, Sing, and Arthur Kleinman. "Are Somatoform Disorders Changing with Time? The Case of Neurasthenia in China." *Psychosomatic Medicine* 69, no. 9 (2007): 846–49.

Leese, Peter. *Shell Shock: Traumatic Neurosis and the British Soldiers of the First World War*. New York: Palgrave Macmillan, 2002.

Leese, Peter, and Jason Crouthamel, eds. *Traumatic Memories of the Second World War and After*. Cham, Switzerland: Palgrave Macmillan, 2016.

Leese, Peter, Julia Barbara Köhne, and Jason Crouthamel, eds. *Languages of Trauma: History, Memory, and Media*. Toronto: University of Toronto Press, 2021.

Lemelson, Robert B., dir. *40 Years of Silence: An Indonesian Tragedy*. Documentary, 87 minutes. Los Angeles: Elemental Productions, 2010.

Lerner, Paul. *Hysterical Men: War, Psychiatry, and the Politics of Trauma in Germany, 1890–1930*. Ithaca, NY: Cornell University Press, 2003.

Lin, Sylvia Li-chun. *Representing Atrocity in Taiwan: The 2/28 Incident and White Terror in Fiction and Film*. New York: Columbia University Press, 2007.

Ly, Boreth. "Broken Body: Situating Trauma in the Visual Cultures of Cambodia and Its Diaspora." In *Traces of Trauma: Cambodian Visual Culture and National Identity in the Aftermath of Genocide*, edited by Boreth Ly, 12–36. Honolulu: University of Hawai'i Press, 2019.

Ma, Sheng-mei. *The Last Isle: Contemporary Film, Culture, and Trauma in Global Taiwan*. London: Rowman & Littlefield, 2015.

Macaluso, Laura A., ed. *Monument Culture: International Perspectives on the Future of Monuments in a Changing World*. Lanham, MD: Rowman & Littlefield, 2019.

Mackie, Vera, and Sharon Crozier-De Rosa. "Remembering the Grandmothers: The International Movement to Commemorate the Survivors of Militarized Sexual Abuse in the Asia-Pacific War." *The Asia-Pacific Journal* 17, no. 4 (2019): Article ID 5248. Retrieved 1 December 2020 from https://apjjf.org/2019/04/MackieCrozierDeRosa.html.

Markert, Friedrich. "The Chinese Cultural Revolution: A Traumatic Experience and Its Intergenerational Transmission." In *Landscapes of the Chinese Soul: The Enduring Presence of the Cultural Revolution*, edited by Tomas Plänkers, 143–63. London: Karnac Books, 2014.

Marks, Sarah, and Mat Savelli, eds. *Psychiatry in Communist Europe*. New York: Palgrave Macmillan, 2015.

Marsella, Anthony J. "Ethnocultural Aspects of PTSD: An Overview of Concepts, Issues, and Treatments." *Traumatology* 16, no. 4 (2010): 17–26.

Marsella, Anthony J., Matthew J. Friedman, Ellen T. Gerrity, and Raymond M. Scurfield, eds. *Ethnocultural Aspects of Posttraumatic Stress Disorder: Issues, Research, and Clinical Applications*. Washington, DC: American Psychological Association, 1996.

McCurry, Justin. "Japan Makes Progress in Facing Up to Post-Traumatic Stress." *Lancet* 363 (20 May 2004), 1782.

McEwen, Bruce, and Harold Schmeck. *The Hostage Brain*. New York: Rockefeller University Press, 1994.

McFarlane, Alexander C. "On the Social Denial of Trauma and the Problem of Knowing the Past." In *International Handbook of Human Response to Trauma*, edited by Arieh Y. Shalev, Rachel Yehuda, and Alexander C. McFarlane, 11–26. Boston, MA: Springer, 2000.

McGregor, Katherine E. *History in Uniform: Military Ideology and the Construction of Indonesia's Past*. Singapore: National University of Singapore Press, 2007.

McNally, Richard J. "The Expanding Empire of Posttraumatic Stress Disorder." *Medscape General Medicine* 8, no. 2 (2006): 9.

———. "Progress and Controversy in the Study of Posttraumatic Stress Disorder." *Annual Review of Psychology* 54, no. 1 (2003): 229–52.
Menninger, Roy W., and John C. Nemiah. *American Psychiatry after World War II (1944–1994)*. Washington, DC: American Psychiatric Press, 2000.
Micale, Mark. "Beyond the Western Front." In *Trauma, Experience and Narrative in Europe after the Second World War*, edited by Ville Kivimäki and Peter Leese. Cham, Switzerland: Palgrave Macmillan, forthcoming.
Micale, Mark S. "Charcot and the Idea of Hysteria in the Male: Gender, Mental Science, and Medical Diagnosis in Late Nineteenth-Century France." *Medical History* 34 (1990): 363–411.
———. "Toward a Global History of Trauma." In *Psychological Trauma and the Legacies of the First World War*, edited by Jason Crouthamel and Peter Leese, 289–310. Basingstoke, Hampshire: Palgrave Macmillan, 2017.
Micale, Mark S., and Paul Lerner, eds. *Traumatic Pasts: History, Psychiatry, and Trauma in the Modern Age, 1870–1930*. New York: Cambridge University Press, 2001.
Miller, Laurence. *PTSD and Forensic Psychology: Applications to Civil and Criminal Law*. New York: Springer, 2015.
Mills, China. *Decolonizing Global Mental Health: The Psychiatrization of the Majority World*. Hove, Sussex: Routledge, 2014.
Min, Sung-kil, and Yeo In-sok. "Mental Health in Korea: Past and Present." In *Mental Health in Asia and the Pacific: Historical and Comparative Perspectives*, edited by Milton Lewis and Harry Minas, 79–92. New York: Springer, 2015.
Minami, Kazushi, "China's Foreign Ministry Archive: Open or Closed?," *Wilson Centre*, 28 July 2017. Retreived 2 December 2020 from https://www.wilsoncenter.org/blog-post/chinas-foreign-ministry-archive-open-or-closed.
Modlinger, Martin, and Philipp Sonntag. *Other People's Pain: Narratives of Trauma and the Question of Ethics*. Oxford: Peter Lang AG, Internationaler Verlag der Wissenschaften, 2011.
Moffic, H. Steven. "Psychiatry Comes to China: Will You?". *Psychiatric Times* (5 Nov 2010). Retreived 1 November 2020 from https://www.psychiatrictimes.com/view/psychiatry-comes-china-will-you.
Mollica, Richard, Yasushi Kikuchi, James Lavelle, and Kathleen Appleton. *The Invisible Human Crisis: Mental Health Recommendations for the Care of Persons Evacuated and Displaced by the Hanshin-Awaji (Kobe) Earthquake*. Cambridge, MA: Harvard Program in Refugee Trauma [Harvard School of Public Health] and Tokyo: Waseda University, 1995.
Mookerjea-Leonard, Debali. *Literature, Gender, and the Trauma of Partition: The Paradox of Independence*. London: Routledge, 2017.
Mullany, Nicholas J., and Peter R. Handford. *Tort Liability for Psychiatric Damage: The Law of "Nervous Shock."* Sydney: Law Book Company, 1993.
Nakamura, Eri. "The Aftermath of War Trauma: War Neurosis in Imperial Japanese Army." Ph.D. dissertation. Tokyo: Hitotsubashi University, 2015.
———. "'Invisible' War Trauma in Japan: Medicine, Society and Military Psychiatric Casualties." *Historia Scientiarium* 25, no. 2 (2016): 140–61.
Nguyen, Nathalie Huynh Chau. "Vietnamese Refugee Women: Diasporic Memory and Narratives of Loss and Trauma." In *Gender and Trauma since 1900*, edited by Paula A. Michaels and Christina Twomey, chapter 10. London: Bloomsbury 2021.
Nikro, Norman Saadi, and Sonja Hegasy, eds., *The Social Life of Memory: Violence, Trauma, and Testimony in Lebanon and Morocco*. Cham, Switzerland: Palgrave Macmillan, 2017.
Nishino, Rumiko, Pu-ja Kim, and Akane Onozawa, eds. *Denying the Comfort Women: The Japanese State's Assault on Historical Truth*. Abingdon, UK: Routledge, 2018.

Patel, Vikram. *Where There Is No Psychiatrist: A Mental Health Care Manual.* London: Gaskell, 2003.
Pedersen, Duncan. "Rethinking Trauma as a Global Challenge." In *Trauma and Migration: Cultural Factors in the Diagnosis and Treatment of Traumatised Immigrants,* edited by Meryam Schouler-Ocak, 9–31. New York: Springer, 2015.
Peter, Sebastian von. "The Experience of 'Mental Trauma' and Its Transcultural Application." *Transcultural Psychiatry* 45, no. 4 (2008): 639–51.
Pitaloka, Dyah. "Singing the Hope: Turning Unspoken Trauma into Song in Indonesia." In *Gender and Trauma since 1900,* edited by Paula A. Michaels and Christina Twomey, chapter 13. London: Bloomsbury, 2021.
Plant, Rebecca Jo. "William Menninger and American Psychoanalysis, 1946–1948." *History of Psychiatry* 16, no. 2 (2005): 181–202.
Pols, Hans. "The Nature of the Native Mind: Contested Views of Dutch Colonial Psychiatrists in the Former Dutch East Indies." In *Psychiatry and Empire,* edited by Sloan Mahone and Megan Vaughan, 172–96. London: Palgrave Macmillan, 2007.
———. "The Psychiatrist as Administrator: The Career of W. F. Theunissen in the Dutch East Indies." *Health and History* 14, no. 1 (2012): 143–64.
———. "The Tunisian Campaign, War Neuroses, and the Reorientation of American Psychiatry during World War II." *Harvard Review of Psychiatry* 19, no. 6 (2011): 313–20.
———. "Waking up to Shell Shock: Psychiatry in the US Military during World War II." *Endeavour* 30, no. 4 (2006): 144–49.
———. "War Neurosis, Adjustment Problems in Veterans, and an Ill Nation: The Disciplinary Project of American Psychiatry During and after World War II." *Osiris* 21, no. 1 (2007): 72–92.
Pupavac, Vanessa. "Psychosocial Interventions and the Demoralization of Humanitarianism." *Journal of Biosocial Science* 36, no. 4 (2004): 491–504.
———. "Therapeutic Governance: Psycho-Social Intervention and Trauma Risk Management." *Disasters* 25 (2001): 358–72.
Rene, Helena K. *China's Sent-Down Generation: Public Administration and the Legacies of Mao's Rustication Program.* Washington, DC: Georgetown University Press, 2013.
Riebeling, Zachary. "Wounds of the Past: Trauma and German Historical Thought after 1945." Ph.D. dissertation. Urbana-Champaign: University of Illinois, 2018. Retrieved 1 December 2020 from http://hdl.handle.net/2142/105654.
Robben, Antonius C. G. M. *A Companion to the Anthropology of Death.* Hoboken, NJ: Wiley Blackwell, 2018.
Rogers, Jillian C. *Resonant Recoveries: French Music and Trauma between the World Wars.* New York: Oxford University Press, 2021.
Rothberg, Michael. "Decolonizing Trauma Studies: A Response." *Studies in the Novel* 40, no. 1/2 (2008): 224–34.
———. "Preface: Beyond Tancred and Clorinda—Trauma Studies for Implicated Subjects." In *The Future of Trauma Theory: Contemporary Literary and Cultural Criticism,* edited by Gert Buelens, Sam Durrant and Robert Eaglestone, xi–xviii. London: Routledge, 2013.
Roudebush, Marc. "A Battle of Nerves: Hysteria and Its Treatments in France during World War I." In *Traumatic Pasts: History, Psychiatry, and Trauma in the Modern Age, 1870–1930,* edited by Mark S. Micale and Paul Lerner, 253–79. New York: Cambridge University Press, 2001.
Rousso, Henry. *The Latest Catastrophe: History, the Present, the Contemporary.* Translated by Jane Marie Todd. Chicago: University of Chicago Press, 2016.

Schaack, Beth van, Daryn Reicherter, and Youk Chhang, eds. *Cambodia's Hidden Scars: Trauma Psychology in the Wake of the Khmer Rouge*. Phnom Penh: Documentation Center of Cambodia, 2011.
Schreiner, Klaus H. "Lubang Buaya: Histories of Trauma and Sites of Memory." In *Beginning to Remember: The Past in the Indonesian Present*, edited by Mary S. Zurbuchen, 261–77. Singapore: National University of Singapore Press, 2005.
Sen, Atreyee. "Torture and Laughter: Naxal Insurgency, Custodial Violence and Inmate Resistance in a Women's Correctional Facility in 1970s Calcutta." *Modern Asian Studies* 52, no. 3 (2018): 917–41.
Shalev, Arieh Y., Rachel Yehuda, and Alexander C. McFarlane. *International Handbook of Human Response to Trauma*. Boston, MA: Springer, 2000.
Shephard, Ben. *A War of Nerves: Soldiers and Psychiatrists in the Twentieth Century*. London: Jonathan Cape, 2000.
Singh, Amritjit, Nalini Iyer, and Rahul K. Gairola, eds. *Revisiting India's Partition: New Essays on Memory, Culture, and Politics*. Lanham, MD: Lexington Books, 2016.
Smith, Catherine. *Resilience and the Localisation of Trauma in Aceh, Indonesia*. Singapore: National University of Singapore Press, 2017.
Snijders, Clara, Lotta-Katrin Pries, Noemi Sgammeglia, Ghazi Al Jowf, Nagy A. Youssef, Laurence de Nijs, Sinan Guloksuz, and Bart P. F. Rutten. "Resilience against Traumatic Stress: Current Developments and Future Directions." *Frontiers in Psychiatry* 9, no. 676 (2018): 1–11. https://doi.org/10.3389/fpsyt.2018.00676.
Somasundaram, Daya. "Collective Trauma in Northern Sri Lanka: A Qualitative Psychosocial-Ecological Study." *International Journal of Mental Health Systems* 1, no. 5 (2007). https://doi.org/10.1186/1752-4458-1-5.
Stamm, B. Hudnall, and Matthew J. Friedman. "Cultural Diversity in the Appraisal and Expression of Trauma." In *International Handbook of Human Response to Trauma*, edited by Arieh Y. Shalev, Rachel Yehuda, and Alexander C. McFarlane, 69–85. Boston, MA: Springer, 2000.
Summerfield, Derek. "Afterword: Against 'Global Mental Health'." *Transcultural Psychiatry* 49, no. 3–4 (2012): 519–30.
———. "Childhood, War, Refugeedom and 'Trauma': Three Core Questions for Mental Health Professionals." *Transcultural Psychiatry* 37 (2000): 417–34.
———. "A Critique of Seven Assumptions behind Psychological Trauma Programmes in War-Affected Areas." *Social Science & Medicine* 48, no. 10 (1999): 1449–62.
———. "How Scientifically Valid Is the Base of Global Mental Health?" *British Medical Journal* 336 (2008): 992–94.
———. "The Invention of Post-Traumatic Stress Disorder and the Social Usefulness of a Psychiatric Category." *British Medical Journal* 322 (13 Jan 2001): 95–99.
Sundram, Suresh, M.E. Karim, Lourdes Ladrido-Ignacio, Albert Maramis, Khalid A. Mufti, D. Nagaraja, Naotaka Shinfuku, et al. "Psychosocial Responses to Disaster: An Asian Perspective." *Asian Journal of Psychiatry* 1, no. 1 (2008): 7–14.
Surin, Kenneth. "Conceptualizing Trauma, but What about Asia?" *Positions* 16, no. 1 (2008): 15–37.
Sweet, Kathryn. "Women's Health in Laos: From Colonial Times to the Present." In *Translating the Body: Medical Education in Southeast Asia*, edited by Hans Pols, C. Michele Thompson, and John Harley Warner, 116–45. Singapore: National University of Singapore Press, 2017.
Tanaka, Toshiyuki. *Japan's Comfort Women: Sexual Slavery and Prostitution During World War II and the U.S. Occupation*. New York: Routledge, 2002.

Tran, Allen. "The Anxiety of Well-Being: Medicalizations of Worry in a Vietnamese Psychiatric Hospital." *Medical Anthropology Quarterly* 31, no. 2 (2016): 198–217.
Uchida, Masakatsu. "The Revival of Military Masculinity Presented by Boys' Magazines: Masculinities under the Occupation of the Allied Forces." *Jenda Shigaku* 8 (2012): 75–84.
Varma, Saiba. *The Occupied Clinic: Militarism and Care in Kashmir.* Durham, NC: Duke University Press, 2020.
———. "Where There Are Only Doctors: Counselors as Psychiatrists in Indian Administered Kashmir." *Ethos* 40, no. 4 (2012): 517–35.
Wang, Ban. *Illuminations from the Past: Trauma, Memory, and History in Modern China.* Stanford, CA: Stanford University Press, 2005.
Watters, Ethan. *Crazy Like Us: The Globalization of the American Psyche.* New York: Free Press, 2010.
Westad, Odd Arne. *The Cold War: A World History.* New York: Basic Books, 2017.
———. *The Global Cold War: Third World Interventions and the Making of Our Times.* Cambridge: Cambridge University Press, 2005.
Winichakul, Thongchai. *Moments of Silence: The Unforgetting of the October 6, 1976 Massacre in Bangkok.* Honolulu: University of Hawai'i Press, 2020.
Winter, Jay. *Sites of Memory, Sites of Mourning: The Great War in European Cultural History.* Cambridge: Cambridge University Press, 1995.
Withuis, Jolande, and Annet Mooij, eds. *The Politics of War Trauma: The Aftermath of World War II in Eleven European Countries.* Amsterdam: Aksant Academic Publishing, 2010.
Wu, Harry Yi-Jui. "A Charted Epidemic of Trauma: Case Notes at the Psychiatric Department of National Taiwan University Hospital between 1946 and 1953." In *Psychiatry and Chinese History*, edited by Howard Chiang, 161–82. London: Pickering & Chatto, 2014.
Wu, Harry Yi-Jui, and Andrew Tai-Ann Cheng. "A History of Mental Healthcare in Taiwan." In *Mental Health in Asia and the Pacific: Historical and Cultural Perspectives*, edited by Harry Minas and Milton Lewis, 107–21. New York: Springer, 2017.
Yang, Dominic Meng-Hsuan. *The Great Exodus from China: Trauma, Memory, and Identity in Modern Taiwan.* Cambridge: Cambridge University Press, 2020.
Yang, Jie. *Mental Health in China: Change, Tradition, and Therapeutic Governance.* Newark, NJ: Polity Press, 2017.
Yehuda, Rachel, and Alexander C. McFarlane. "Conflict between Current Knowledge about Posttraumatic Stress Disorder and Its Original Conceptual Basis." *American Journal of Psychiatry* 152, no. 12 (1995): 1705–13.
Yoshimi, Yoshaki. *Comfort Women: Sexual Slavery in the Japanese Military During World War II.* New York: Columbia University Press, 2000.
Young, Allan. *The Harmony of Illusions: Inventing Post-Traumatic Stress Disorder.* Princeton, NJ: Princeton University Press, 1995.
Yum, Jennifer. "In Sickness and in Health: Americans and Psychiatry in Korea." Ph.D. dissertation. Boston, MA: Harvard University, Departments of History and East Asian Languages, 2014.
Zarowsky, Christina. "Trauma Stories: Violence, Emotion and Politics in Somali Ethiopia." *Transcultural Psychiatry* 37, no. 3 (2000): 383–402.
Zhigang, Huang. "Scar Literature and the Memory of Trauma." In *The Columbia Companion to Modern East Asian Literature*, edited by Joshua S. Mostow, 524–28. New York: Columbia University Press, 2003.

Chapter 1

TROPICAL STUPOR?

An Investigation into Patients Affected by Earthquakes and Tropical Weather in Colonial Taiwan

Harry Yi-Jui Wu

Medical historians have extensively explored the history of psychological trauma in industrial and military contexts.[1] Recently, scholars have also begun to focus their attention on the psychiatric aftereffects of major natural disasters, such as cyclones, floods, landslides, forest fires, and earthquakes. With the benefit of hindsight, efforts to look for evidence of psychic trauma associated with natural catastrophes often retrospectively group together a range of heterogeneous psychological conditions.[2] Most historical trauma studies thus far suggest that our understanding of what is today known as PTSD (Posttraumatic Stress Disorder) is also cultural and political. The great majority of this research to date, however, has been related to the aftermath of human-caused atrocities, such as wars and mass killings.[3] Can natural disasters and their severe mental health impacts also carry cultural and political implications? This chapter presents a detailed case study to explore this question and to complicate our knowledge of psychological trauma by studying it in a less discussed setting that still requires historical contextualization in order to fully understand.

Early modern Europeans produced firsthand accounts that attempted to make sense of natural disasters in both rational and emotional ways.[4] Several of these narratives are found in personal and anecdotal recollections rather than in official printed scientific literature. For example, the famous seventeenth-century English diarist Samuel Pepys documented his witnessing of the Great Plague and the Great Fire of London of the 1660s.[5] Voltaire famously wrote poems in response to the cataclysmic Lisbon earthquake of 1755.[6] And, a century and a half later, the American philosopher William James reflected on his personal experience of the San Francisco earthquake in 1911.[7]

The modern medical treatment of trauma resulting from natural disasters emerged alongside the development of the psychiatric and psychological disciplines. Systematic scientific studies of the psychological effects of sudden and extreme natural events did not emerge until the maturation of epidemiology during and after World War II, such as with Adolf Adler's and Erich Lindemann's pioneering research into Boston's Coconut Grove Fire in 1942 and William Menninger's investigation into the Kansas City River flood of 1951.[8] In Asia, too, where discourses of trauma have been incorporated into the metaphorical analysis of its colonial pasts and postcolonial legacies, discussions about psychological trauma have at times been more complicated. Working in a Fanonian tradition, some scholars deemed colonialism itself a pathogenic experience that can produce long-term adverse psychological responses. Other scholarly analyses that look at the history of colonialism focus on memory politics.[9] As for trauma related to natural disasters, historical assessments have thus far been scarce, partially because no observers at the time were available to account for post-disaster emotional and psychological behaviors.

This chapter finds that in a single site-specific Asian colonial setting, investigations of prolonged psychological trauma related to natural disasters was, tellingly, found only among victims of the colonized population, while in foreign colonizers it was absent. This pattern is best exemplified in a unique and quite remarkable psychiatric research project on victims of an earthquake in Taiwan in 1935. In the early morning of 21 April 1935, an extremely powerful earthquake struck central Taiwan, which was then a colony of the Japanese Empire in its last decade of colonization. The earthquake was the second largest calamity to affect Taiwan since its colonization by Japan began in 1895. Records of the number of casualties vary. According to a report published in the National Museum of Natural Science's newsletter, the quake caused 3,276 deaths and 12,053 injuries. It also destroyed more than 50,000 houses.[10] In the following month, the Department of Psychiatry at Taihoku Imperial University in Taipei City sent seventy-nine investigators to study the mental symptoms of five patient groups located in different healthcare institutions and temporary asylums across Taiwan. In 1942, seven years after the earthquake, researchers published their one-of-a-kind study's results in *Taiwan Igaku Sassi*, the precursor of *The Journal of the Formosan Medical Association*, the most prominent medical journal published in colonial Taiwan. Led by psychiatry professor Naka Syuzo, this research team concluded that many of the post-quake patients who they examined presented with something resembling *Emotionslähmung* (emotional paralysis), a condition introduced to the Japanese medical community by German psychiatrist Erwin Bälz, who had spent twenty-seven years teaching at the Medical College of Tokyo Imperial University. Naka Syuzo's team asserted furthermore that some of these patients' neurological symptoms resulted not from the experience of the earthquake but from the island's tropical weather. As the first psychiatric study related to a natural disaster, this research project of the years 1935–1942 was unique in its method, timing of publication, and scientific hypothesis as well as in the role it occupies in the field of colonial medicine.

The Absence of Psychiatric Commentary following the 1937 Earthquake

Human narratives of trauma typically begin to appear soon after the "traumatic" events. Depending on the various social, cultural, and political circumstances in which traumatic memories are formed, these stories emerge in different forms and at their own pace. In a recent scholarly account of the social effect of earthquakes, the Japanese sociologist Wata Yoshikata compared and contrasted Japan's great 1995 Kobe earthquake with Taiwan's 1999 Chichi earthquake, implying that there are similarities between the two East Asian societies and their responses to seismic catastrophes.[11] No such comparison, however, was made in any post–World War II professional accounts until 1995, when Japan started to reconsider the mental health consequences of earthquakes and reflect on the cultural, political, and even scientific dimensions of Japanese society that might determine the psychological reactions of their citizens.[12] It can be argued that this dramatic momentum since the 1990s is a result of the globalization of psychiatry with its focus on Western-style trauma, as well as the networking of psychological professionals who actively link modern psychiatric understandings of disasters with local narratives.[13] Whatever the causes of this new initiative, it has resulted in Japan's government securing more resources for psychological recovery services and searching for foreign expertise on treatment and rehabilitation in the aftermath of natural catastrophes.

However, few studies, either clinical or historical in nature, have examined the long and conspicuous absence of discussions about trauma in Japan before the process of psychiatric globalization in the past generation. National silence on the subject lasted until around 1995, when Japanese psychiatrists began to actively investigate the varied and profound mental impact of the Kobe earthquake. Before that time, there existed a lengthy time lag between the actual occurrence of traumatic phenomena and widespread social recognition of psychological trauma.[14] Medical historians had previously noted the limited discussion of trauma among Japanese military personnel over the past half century. (See, for instance, the essays of Eri Nakamura and Ran Zwigenberg in this volume.) During the years of the Asia-Pacific War (1931–1945), for instance, the Japanese government prevented their own psychiatrists from diagnosing mental disorders among soldiers in order to build a strong, patriotic image of the state and its armed forces.[15] One of the most notable trauma psychiatrists in Japan, Dr. Hisao Nakai, lamented that such ignorance was caused by the *bushido* spirit permeating the entire Japanese educational system, which required students to suppress their emotions, and the fact that most of the psychiatrists practicing before the 1990s were still trained in the spirit of traditional Japanese militarism.[16] Examining today the details of the medical report that Dr. Naka and his colleagues published in 1942, one finds that it too carried a certain level of purposeful analysis in line with Japan's economic and territorial expansion plans, namely the *Nanshin-ron*, or Southern Expansion Doctrine, before and during World War II, which will be discussed later in this chapter.

Historians have previously pointed out the interconnections between colonial medicine and tropical psychiatry. From the late eighteenth century onward, scientists and medical experts began to construct racially-colored, Eurocentric understandings of tropical diseases in various colonies throughout the world. This practice is exemplified in James Johnson's *Influence of Tropical Climates on European Constitutions* (1812), which taught generations of traveling European readers how to preserve their health in faraway hot climates.[17] This early nineteenth-century Anglo-Irish physician wrote his widely circulated book based in part on his personal travels as a naval surgeon to Egypt, India, and China. In Johnson's time, "degenerationists" feared that civilization might be in decline as a result of progressive biological deterioration in the human species. Their theories were often associated with authoritarian political attitudes, including nationalism, militarism, and racial science.[18] In Asia, abundant examples can be found in British India, the American Philippines, and in atypical colonial situations such as the hospitals in Shanghai.[19] In Taiwan, as shown in Yu-Chuan Wu's study of tropical neurasthenia in the late 1930s, the Japanese Southern Medical Society observed that a high proportion of Japanese people residing in Taiwan developed debilitating symptoms including fatigue, lethargy, poor appetite, low mood, and difficulties concentrating. Akin to *netsutai kyoran* (tropical madness) or *Nanyō boke* (Nanyang stupor), these cases mimicked the degenerative symptoms that European individuals could acquire after a long stay in the tropics.[20] Most of these examples revealed how colonizers perceived their own psychiatric burden in the tropics by constructing new value-laden categories of disease.

European and North American psychiatrists working in colonial settings were also known for creating theories of "the native mind." These characterizations described the native minds of indigenous people as immature, child-like, and easily aroused by minimal stimuli.[21] However, unlike how they treated psychiatric patients at home, colonial health care administrations were averse to initiate the sorts of "Great Confinements" found in Europe but rarely observed in the colonies because of their inadequate human and material resources. Without clinical samples for systematic observation, such theories of the native mind were often not supported by organized scientific research. Instead, colonial administrations tended to exercise various forms of social engineering work with ill-trained and under-resourced medical practitioners.[22] In the case of colonial Taiwan, no absolute consensus was found regarding the psychopathology of weather-related neurasthenia before the 1930s.[23] What has yet to be studied is the infrastructure of modern psychiatry and the scientific rationale behind the construction of tropical psychiatric diseases, especially in Taiwan during the last decade of Japanese colonial occupation of the island during the years 1935–1945.

From Statistics to Institutionalization

Colonial psychiatry in Taiwan had deep roots in the Meiji period of Japanese history. From the mid-1800s onward, science and technology in Japan were mobilized under the empire's ideology of modern national building. Japan's aim in developing modern science was to catch up with Western science as rapidly as possible. To this end, Germany was promoted throughout Japanese culture at this time as the ultimate academic model.[24] Not only were German scholars regularly invited to lecture and set up schools in Japan, but Japan also eagerly sent scientists and physicians to Germany for specialized training in psychiatry.[25] This Japanese-German conduit influenced the early construction of modern psychiatry as a profession in Taiwan. Almost all of the major Japanese psychiatrists who worked in Taiwan—including Kure Shūzō (1865–1932), Nakamura Yuzuru, Naka Syuzo, and Ryosuke Kurosawa—had either studied for a certain period in Germany or followed German scientific and intellectual traditions.[26]

Educated first at Tokyo Imperial University, Kure Shūzō studied between 1897 and 1901 in Vienna, Heidelberg, and Munich with renowned German psychiatrists Heinrich Obersteiner, Richard von Krafft-Ebing, and Emil Kraepelin. Many psychiatrists in Germany were criticized for being overly preoccupied with theory and not putting sufficient effort into positivist observation and clinical research.[27] Kraepelin, however, was different. He was recognized for his deep interest in foreign cultures and specifically for his survey trip to the island of Java in the colonial Dutch Indies in 1903.[28] Furthermore, Kraepelin had developed techniques involving diagnostic cards to categorize diseases.[29] In addition to being heavily influenced by German psychiatry, Kure Shūzō's research questions were formed under the influence of his brother, the renowned Kure Bunso (1851–1928), who established the theoretical and methodological foundation of Japan's Kokusei Chōsa (National Survey).[30] As the superintendent working at Tokyo's first psychiatric hospital, Sugamo Byōin, Kure Bunso managed to publish the hospital's annual report based on state-of-the-art statistical studies. Kure Bunso also authored Japan's first theoretical account of medical statistics.[31] Statistical data gathering, therefore, became the method used in constructing the picture of mental disorders in Japanese psychiatry.

The population census designed by the Empire's Cabinet Office, Japan's National Survey, was one of the most important pieces of infrastructure to modernize the Japanese nation. In 1885, with the establishment of the cabinet system, the Statistical Institute became the Statistics Bureau. In 1901, the bureau began to compile the data book of population statistics for the entire Japanese Empire.[32] The statistical census project, however, was delayed until 1920 due to the Russo-Japanese War that broke out in 1904. Instead, the Government-General of Taiwan established the Kanbō Tōkeika (Government Statistical Office) in 1908, overseeing all aspects of survey work in the colony. In addition to these survey works, the Government Statistical Office coordinated academic teams for scientific expeditions and prepared for the establishment of educational institutions related to colonialism in the tropics.[33] In 1910, Kure Shūzō and two assistants traveled to central Taiwan for three months in order to conduct a survey on cretinism.[34] After returning to Japan, he and twelve assistants continued between 1910 and 1916 with this line of research by surveying the condition of *shitaku kanchi* (private confinement) in Japan. Originating in the Edo period, *shitaku kanchi* was one of the most common but dishonorable methods of handling "mad" people in Japan. For more than two centuries before Japan opened up to European and American science in the late 1860s, the empire was characterized by its strict social order and isolationist foreign policies. In 1918, Kure Shūzō and his assistants published a document titled "The State of *Shitaku Kanchi* and Statistical Observations of Insane People." Their report had been celebrated as a key document in transforming psychiatry in Japan from an impoverished and unethical private-confinement practice into a modern and hospital-oriented enterprise.[35] Apart from some Whiggish eulogies of Kure's work, however, few scholarly studies to date have examined the meaning of the abandonment of *shitaku kanchi* in Japan.[36]

In Taiwan, the development of psychiatry as a medical specialty was first based on building new health care institutions. Nakamura Yuzuru had been Kure's assistant during the three-month cretinism survey in 1910. In 1916, the Governor General of Taiwan had invited Nakamura Yuzuru to become the superintendent of Keelung Hospital in Keelung City. Nakamura, who had studied in Germany in 1925, was in effect the first and only hospital-based psychiatrist in Taiwan.[37] At Keelung Hospital, Nakamura began to compile and report cases on various types of mental disorders, especially in the field of forensic psychiatry.[38] In 1922, two specialized asylums—Ninsaiin and Yomeito—both located in the colony's capital Taihoku (modern Taipei), were established to provide custodial care for mental patients. Together, the two facilities had fifty beds. In 1935, Yoshinin, an official mental hospital with a hundred beds, was finally established by the Governor General of Taiwan.[39] As in Korea, mental patients in these newly created hospitals rather quickly became the subjects of scientific studies in addition to receiving treatment and care.[40]

Epidemiological Research from Hospital to Field

With the growth of institutionalization, it became easier for Japanese psychiatrists to conduct systematic observation of cases admitted to hospitals with psychiatric wards. Private or charity-based institutions became convenient venues for Japanese psychiatrists to conduct statistical observations. In 1927, for example, the chief medical officer of the Government-General Office, Takeuchi Yawata, made a speech to the medical community on the statistical analysis of Ninsaiin's inmates.[41] During the 1930s, medical research combining field trips and statistics in Taiwan began to proliferate. At the same time, psychiatric knowledge was also introduced more systematically into Taiwan through the translation of foreign works and via research projects sponsored by the recently founded Taihoku Imperial University. Established in 1928 and located in the capital of the colony, Taihoku Imperial University was founded in order to serve various purposes of the Japanese Empire. At the war's end, in 1945, it was renamed National Taiwan University, and it retains that name today. Because of Taiwan's geographical location, the focus of research at the university covered East Asia, Nanyang in southern coastal China, and the Pacific areas.[42] From 1935 to 1939, Dr. Naka Syuzo conducted an island-wide statistical study and identified 3,484 individuals among different ethnic populations who were suffering from various types of mental disorders.[43] Naka Syuzo's analysis found that in Taiwan, mental health could be connected with physiological responses to the tropical environment and that this association might explain the high prevalence of manic depressive disorders in the colony.[44]

Later, at the beginning of the 1940s, Naka and his five students joined the National University's medical task force of Kinrō Hōkokutai (Labor Service Corps) in order to study the condition of mental disorders on Hainan Island in south China. Starting in 1941, the Japanese colonial government in Taiwan organized various task forces belonging to Kinrō Hōkokutai that were intended to mobilize all kinds of activities supporting the Japanese Empire's ambitions of southward military expansion. Interestingly, during this period a massive amount of medical knowledge on the Dutch East Indies was being translated into Japanese. These newly available foreign texts were either published as textbooks or columns in medical journals and included literature on mental health issues in tropical and sub-tropical climates.[45] As for the psychiatric task force from Taihoku Imperial University, their research covered three areas: ethno-psychiatry among numerous races, tropical neurasthenia among immigrants, and the statistical observation of neurological diseases. In their reports, one can find time and again obvious causal reasoning concerning the relations between torrid weather and psychological and neurological conditions.[46]

The island of Taiwan, for instance, was reported to have a high prevalence of symptoms related to physical discomfort and decreased mental capacity, such as the feeling of a heavy head, headache, dizziness, insomnia, immobility, etc. These collective symptoms were named *Kainan-Boke* (Hainan fog), after the south China province. Researchers convey the impression that these symptoms might have been caused by the hot climate in the region. Among the 112 Japanese people working on Hainan Island, the research team found that their symptoms were mostly caused by psychogenic factors, namely the fear of tropical diseases, homesickness, and the hot, humid climate.[47]

Seismic Shock and Its Psychological Effects

From the eighteenth century onward, theories emerged to explain the association between earthquakes and mental conditions. Toward the closing decades of the nineteenth century, with the emergence of notions such as "psychic shock" and "traumatic shock," observers began to distinguish the mental and emotional effects of a severe earthquake from its physical and physiological impacts.[48] Much of this early medical commentary was influenced by proto-industrialization and technological development. Following an earthquake, it is often difficult to separate intense emotional reactions from physical, especially neurological, injuries. Among various theorists who argued that such responses were in fact totally normal, two physicians' remarks based on their own experiences were renowned. William James, who back in the 1860s had studied in the sciences at Humboldt University in Berlin, observed during the San Francisco earthquake of 1906 that people demonstrated cohesiveness while responding to the catastrophe despite being highly stressed by its demonic, literally earth-shaking power. The German psychiatrist Erwin Bälz (1849–1913) likewise described the "emotional paralysis" (*Emotionslähmung*) that he had experienced during the Tokyo earthquake in 1894.[49]

Bälz, in fact, may well be the first psychiatrist anywhere to have studied the medical implications of an individual's psychological reaction to natural calamities. In 1876, the Meiji Government of the Japanese Empire wished to recruit foreign professionals and appoint them to official governmental positions and university posts. Bälz arrived in Tokyo in 1876 as a lecturer of physiology with a hope to modernize medical education and practice medicine long-term in Japan. Besides lecturing, he also dedicated his career to research during his subsequent thirty-seven years in Japan, including to the physical anthropology of Japanese populations and psychiatric epidemiology.[50] Bälz later received acclaim for his survey of *kitsunetsuki*, a mental condition of "being possessed by a fox" in Japanese folklore.[51]

When a second major earthquake hit the Great Kanto area on 1 September 1923, few observations about immediate human responses to the terrifying experience appeared in the Japanese press. The quake resulted in more than 100,000 deaths and more than 40,000 people missing. Most historical commentaries about any abnormal human behaviors surrounding the event focused on the spread of irrational rumors among survivors and on post-quake aggression between the Japanese and Koreans residing in Tokyo. Minami Orihara and Gregory Clancy have argued that the scale of the earthquake changed the Japanese way of thinking about emergencies.[52]

It was perhaps the scale and urgency of the 1923 disaster that prevented thinkers from documenting and further analyzing possible psychological reactions among victims. Nevertheless, clues about the psychological aftereffects of the Great Kanto earthquake are present in various forms of documentation. Intriguingly, the most common observation about the human reactions concerned the rampant nature of rumors and the efforts of the government to control and disprove these false beliefs. According to some of these hysterical rumors, socialists and Koreans in Japan at the time of the quake were setting buildings on fire, which instigated multiple riots and caused fierce conflicts between Japanese and Koreans.[53] According to Yushio Uchimura, who at that time worked for Matsuzawa Hospital, authorities evacuated the entire hospital; some seven hundred mental patients had to be temporarily moved to safer shelter. In the subsequent days, most of the people who sought psychiatric help suffered from symptoms of acute stress. However, no systematic research into such victims was ever attempted in the chaos of the post-disaster environment.[54] A popular illustrated science magazine, *Kagaku Gahō*, reasoned that the appearance of these rumors was caused by the unscientific mindset among Japanese people.[55] The editor of *Seismological Notes*, published by the Imperial Earthquake Investigation Committee, commented that people at the time were "startled by the shock, realized their helplessness and rushed like sheep in the path of an electrical storm" because of humans' "feeble" minds "in the face of Nature's mighty forces."[56]

In fact, almost all of the post-disaster narratives produced after the Great Kanto earthquake focused on building citizens' morale and rehabilitating the infrastructure of the nation, especially its communication and transportation networks. Across the country, *Shinkou* became the key concept for national recovery. *Shinkou* involves revitalizing the operation of all governmental and civil organizations and society as a whole. The Ministry of Education publicly expressed concerns about the loss of traditional moral values in Japanese society, which was supposedly intensified by the unsettling shock of the earthquake. Accordingly, it designed educational programs targeting Japanese youth that offered moral guidance and physical training to quickly reorder and reinvigorate the nation's morale.[57] The Social Education Division of Tokyo also implemented policies employing sports activities intended to relieve stress among the many victims who were living in temporary shelters and promote citizens' vigor and physical well-being.[58] Besides boosting Japanese citizens' sense of national morale, measures to prevent or respond to future earthquakes or aftershocks were also taken by the national government. While rebuilding Tokyo, apart from the continuing improvement of design techniques for buildings and other structures (which had started in the nineteenth century), urban planners this time also purposefully planted more trees in order to improve citizens' physical and psychological health.[59]

Accounts documenting individuals' lived experiences at the time are relatively rare. Analogous to William James's observations during the 1906 San Francisco earthquake, the Japanese people apparently demonstrated a great humanitarian spirit of help and cooperation. Noel F. Busch, an American journalist who witnessed the Tokyo earthquake in 1923, also documented that more than eighty medical teams were rapidly formed on the day of the earthquake. Furthermore, while reconstruction progressed, the traditional Japanese system of social class stratification was restored to much the same shape as before.[60] Documentation of negative emotions induced by the earthquake appeared mostly in literary works. Apparently, subjective emotional reflection was easier to expression in literary forms. For example, in the poetry anthology *The Collection of Ashes*, writers depicted the cries, fear, anxiety, and uneasiness during and after the disaster.[61] However, as described by Busch, the Japanese confronted the catastrophe with exemplary courage and calm. Busch observed that panic was rare and looting relatively minimal after the event. According to his contemporary account, fear, anxiety, and psychological stress were countered by blithe courage.[62]

The Report on Taiwan Igakku Sassi

The report on the victims of central Taiwan's 1935 earthquake is unique in the rationale behind its research methods, its scholarly references, and the timing of its publication during World War II. Immediately after the earthquake, Taihoku Imperial University organized a research team to investigate the phenomenon. Specifically Dr. Naka and his team conducted what today would be called a "catchment area" study. After the trembling had stopped, the team traveled twice to Miaoli and Taichung, on 27–30 April and 4–8 May in 1935. These two sites were prefectures in central Taiwan close to the quake's epicenter. Naka and his researchers identified five basic categories of patients being treated at various medical institutions, including local hospitals and temporary asylums. The first clinical group consisted of 79 patients being housed in temporary shelters around the Miaoli area. The second group contained 70 patients who were badly injured physically and were admitted to Taichung Hospital. The third group of 55 patients was slightly injured individuals sheltered at a site in the Toufen area. The fourth group of 101 patients was admitted to temporary wards provided by the Red Cross in Miaoli, and the last group of 128 patients was made up of those who were also admitted to Taichung Hospital with miscellaneous complaints.

Tropical Stupor? • 45

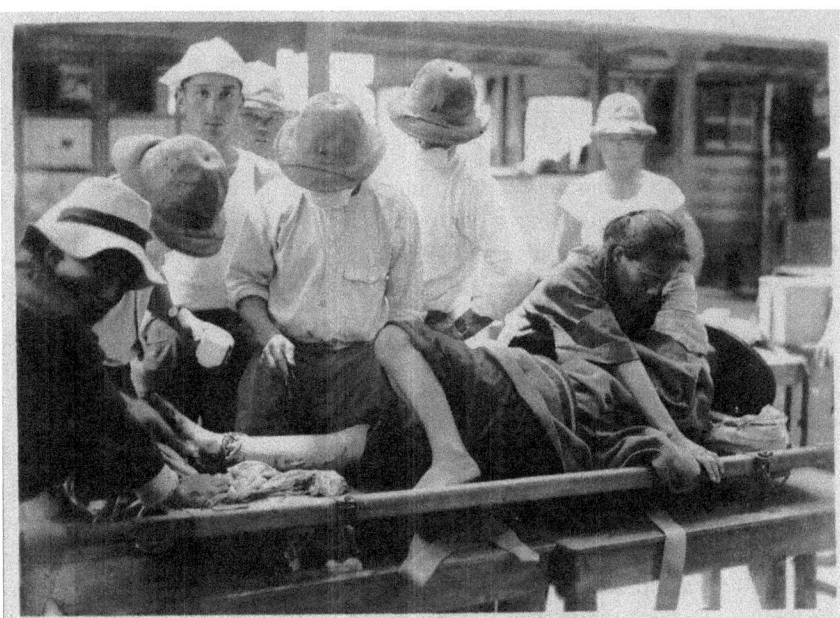

FIGURE 1.1. Patients receiving emergency care. Courtesy Institute of Taiwan Studies, Academia Sinica. Yang Zhaojia photos: LJK_08_01_0150008.

TABLE 1.1. Number of patients presenting symptoms

Symptoms	Number of Patients presenting symptoms	Positive rate
Loss of appetite	340	55.9 percent
Frightening memories	337	49.9 percent
Constipation	345	41.4 percent
Dreams	333	37.5 percent
Dizziness	339	31.9 percent
Headache	344	29.7 percent
Hypersensitivity	293	26.6 percent
Bodily Tremors	277	25.6 percent
Tinnitus (perception of noises or ringing in the ear(s))	341	25.2 percent
Nausea	341	16.1 percent

The researchers carefully numbered, recorded, and classified all 364 patients. They also noted their gender, age, type and location of injuries, and any special psychiatric signs. The above table presents the overall symptom profile of patients in the study.

Researchers interviewed all 364 patients. They also used a standard form with a checklist of general symptoms and neurological examinations. Researchers found that, apart from the frequently observed inability to be emotionally affected (*kankyo funou*)—a condition resembling Erwin Bälz's description of *Emotionslähmung*—two other symptoms manifested frequently: insomnia and anuria, the inability to pass urine. Due to scanty description, it is impossible to determine if the "inability to be emotionally affected" resembled what we would now call emotional numbing or affectlessness. Additionally, more than 65 percent of the patient population reported that they could not fall asleep easily. In Group I and Group V, it was further found that about a tenth of the patients could not sleep well because of physical pain. According to their findings, most of the insomnia symptoms were not psychogenic but neurological in nature. In addition, among all patients, almost a fourth had urinary difficulties. Except for several individuals whose anuric symptoms might have been caused by spinal injuries, the others were assumed to suffer from psychogenic anuria.[63]

Similar to the governmental response to the earlier Great Kanto earthquake in Japan, the colonial government in Taiwan immediately initiated *shinkou* activities. Coincidentally, these activities took place right before the heyday of the *Nanshin-ron* period. The ideology of reform for the empire's political and social structure commenced in the Meiji period right after the nation abolished its closed country policy implemented in the Edo period. The *shinkou* campaign was characterized by the acceleration of economic industrialization and the adoption of a wide range of Western ideas. This initiative corresponded with the Southern Expansion Doctrine, which asserted that imperial Japan should advance into British, French, and Dutch colonial territories in South East Asia. The Southern Expansion Doctrine reached its peak right before the outbreak in the Pacific of World War II in 1941.[64] During these years, university-based academic activities were co-opted to study the society, culture, and economy of Southeast Asia and to formulate scientific justifications for Japan's territorial aspirations.

Post-quake recuperative measures were also incorporated into this Southern Advance ideology. In its rehabilitation work, the colonial government demonstrated its determination to propagandize and support this military-imperial initiative. The colonial government established the Taichou Earthquake Rehabilitation Office to oversee the reconstruction of the island-wide railway system, which took less than a year to be completed. Between 14 and 20 July 1938, the Rehabilitation Office held an exposition at Taichung Kyōka Kaikan, a building in the Asian Renascent style, in order to showcase the government's success and stamina. Nevertheless, not everyone became dutiful subscribers of the new

FIGURE 1.2. Patients waiting at Taichung Hospital. Courtesy Institute of Taiwan Studies, Academia Sinica. Yang Zhaojia photos: LJK_08_01_0160009.

colonial doctrine. Less often found in official records, Taiwanese authors sometimes submitted their own more negative reflections on the earthquake experience to newspapers in poetic form. These were common expressions originating from Han Chinese literary practices that were localized in Taiwan under Japanese colonial rule, reflecting everyday life and the spiritual world of learned people.[65] On 18 June 1935, for example, one author used the pen name Youhuan Yusheng to lament the earthquake.[66] In July of the same year, a poem entitled "Chín-chai Pi-siong Koa" ("Mournful song for the earthquake") also appeared in a newspaper published by the Presbyterian Church in Taiwan.[67]

Under the clinical-statistical gaze of Japanese psychiatrists, earthquake victims in Taiwan presented a very different physical constitution than their Japanese civilian counterparts characterized by paralyzed emotions and confused thinking. Their symptoms, according to the Japanese researchers, were not psychogenic but mostly abnormal autonomous neurological conditions complicated by the tropical weather. Such discourse, however, had not prevailed at the beginning of Japan's colonization of the Taiwanese island in the late 1890s or with the initial introduction of modern psychiatric medicine into Taiwan. The new popularity of the idea that post-disaster psychological trauma and tropical pathologies were related can only be understood if we take into consideration other psychiatric research projects conducted in Taiwan and Hainan in the 1930s. According to the same research report, so-called tropical neurasthenia found among the Japanese residents in colonial Hainan was mostly psychogenic, meaning that their symptoms were reversible as long as suitable treatments, such as psychotherapy, were provided. Conversely, if complicated neurasthenia-like symptoms were non-psychogenic in nature, that meant the conditions were mostly biological, implying that the main cause was an inferior bodily constitution and functioning.

A second striking feature of the 1942 earthquake report by Naka Syuzo and his colleagues is its reliance on Western medical literature. Among the fourteen references cited in the report, thirteen were from German sources. None of these European textual sources made any reference to research conducted on the earthquake in Japan. The literature review cited published research on earthquake victims in the Crimea in 1927, New Zealand in 1933, Los Angeles in 1933, and India in 1934. Apart from earthquake research, some sources also referenced research on traumatic war neuroses. Very interestingly, the authors of the study also perceived clinical similarities between the harmful effects of wartime fighting and this earthquake, if not specifically in relation to psychopathology, then at least with respect to the manifested symptoms from sudden shock and the fear of injury and death. These studies were mostly careful statistical analyses conducted in controlled environments prone to earthquakes.[68] In addition, Naka Syuzo's team referred to several medical studies related to wartime experiences, such as humans' irrational and shock responses to wartime air raids. However, all the medical studies of warfare cited for comparative purposes dated from 1916 to 1936. Although the report appeared in 1942, during World War II, it failed to reference any studies concerning current or recent battlefield experiences. Such exclusion might explain the larger absence of discussions of World War II in Japan's history of mental trauma, as noted at the beginning of this chapter. Moreover, as Deborah Coen has noted, psychiatric professionals had long debated the comparison of neurological or psychogenic responses to earthquakes.[69] In the context of both Japanese colonization in Asia and World War II, such debates became a powerful tool for differentiating between physical constitutions of the Japanese and their supposedly weaker and inferior colonial populations.

Perhaps the most important and interesting finding in the 1942 report involved Erwin Bälz's concept of *Emotionslähmung*. Instead of observing this psychogenic acute psychosis among his patients or study subjects, Bälz detected the psychological phenomenon in himself right after the earthquake in Tokyo. Similar to William James' reflections on the San Francisco quake, Bälz's *Emotionslähmung* was a kind of retrospective self-reflection. Alongside the fear of fires and tsunamis possibly caused by the earthquake, what paralyzed his thinking at the time was the question of whether his family members, back in Germany, were still safe. Such an inability to rationally process these involuntary thoughts at the time of the crisis, according to Bälz, differed from the much more common defunctionalized shock reaction (*Schreckreaktion*), which included an affective element of intense fright.[70] However, while Naka Syuzo and his researchers concluded that the surveyed patients often suffered cognitive disturbances and related signs of momentary stupor, they could not obtain from them the content of specific thoughts that obstructed interviewees' thought patterns, such as Bälz's sudden reminiscence of home and family back in his homeland. For example, the researchers asked one patient, who appeared blank in his facial expressions and unresponsive in speech, "What does your head feel like?" The interviewee answered, "I don't feel anything in my head; I don't feel, I suffer."[71] Such presentations in the hospital setting were interpreted by the on-site psychiatrist as a representation of *Emotionslähmung*.

Interestingly, psychiatrists in Japanese Taiwan did not encourage the earthquake victims in their study to report, much less elaborate on, what was actually going on in their minds. Instead, they only took into consideration what was observed externally without probing the emotional or psychological content of their patients' stupor-like behaviors. In the context explored in this chapter, Japanese psychiatrists described the mental conditions afflicting Taiwanese people solely with reference to colonial medicine, but the mental sufferings of these patients were only deemed deficient in comparison to Western psychiatry.[72] Naka Syuzo's report identified the signs of *Emotionslähmung* in their earthquake patients without exploring the in-depth psychological meaning of such mental expressions. The same symptom checklist approach caused the research team to screen out insomnia and anuria among earthquake victims. Apart from the possible cause of insomnia being physical pain, researchers did not inquire into patients' sleep patterns, nor did they follow up on the cognitive aspects regarding patients' inability to fall asleep. As for anuria, no records were kept of food and water intake and output before researchers advanced the idea of a possible causal connection with the tropical weather on patients' autonomic nervous systems. Uniquely, it was modern statistical science that provided the logical argument behind the racialized construction of tropical psychiatry.

Conclusion

The case study of earthquake-induced psychological trauma presented in this chapter contains a complicated story that weaves together the history of medicine, Japanese colonialism, military history, and environmental history. Led by Dr. Naka Syuzo, one of the leading figures of modern psychiatry in Taiwan under Japanese colonial rule, Taihoku Imperial University's research team conducted a highly significant clinical study that positioned psychiatry on the world map between the European and Japanese Empires. Toward the end of the 1800s, Japan was still a passive recipient of Western science. The first half of the twentieth century saw a much more active stance among Japanese scientists regarding the construction of scientific Japanese theories and practices independent of those of the European powers. In Europe, while theories about the effects of earthquakes were still diverse, the earthquake in central Taiwan in 1935 provided an exceptional opportunity for Japanese psychiatrists to observe and test their hypotheses using the methods and instruments they had gradually acquired during that same time period.

Taihoku Imperial University's investigation into the traumatized victims of the 1935 earthquake in central Taiwan revealed three aspects related to the history of psychotrauma in Asia that have not previously been considered carefully. First, it reveals aspects of the history of military trauma in East Asia, especially in Japan, regarding delayed public and scholarly attention because of the need to construct an idealized strong and healthy mind during the periods of wartime morale construction and post-World War II nation building. In Japan, it was not until 1995, when the Great Hanshin earthquake hit Kobe, that a fuller recognition and a more complete understanding of psychological trauma in Japan was presented. Of course, this was partially because no official psychiatric diagnoses were available until post-traumatic stress disorder was officially described in the *DSM* and *ICD*, two internationally recognized psychiatric nosological systems, both in the 1980s. Before Hisao Nakai and other psychiatrists' efforts at studying trauma after the Great Hanshin earthquake, and in a society that only focused on positive *shinkou* activities, and in which the building of hospitals was given more attention than social infrastructure, the promotion of mental health and social care systems languished.

Second, the report made by Naka's team revealed the Japanese version of colonial psychiatry, which was different from the European one vis-à-vis its approach, namely statistical observation. When tropical psychiatry was still being developed in the various colonies of the European empires, the end of social engineering, including a clear plan to categorize different types of people into distinct social structures for the benefit of empires, stimulated the formation of such theories. In the case of Japan's fifty-year occupation of the island of Taiwan, it was the fieldwork and survey-based statistical method that laid the foundation of science during the Meiji period that expedited Japan's nation building. Such science was conducted to demonstrate the fact that Japan was a modern model empire as distinct from its hegemonic European counterparts. In addition, in colonial Taiwan, while languages were not available for ordinary Taiwanese to express their reactions, numerical figures were represented as the best instrument to account for the earthquake's impact on the colonized. And, evidently, Taiwanese bodily reactions might be as normal as those of any human being struck by an earthquake.

Racialized tropical psychiatry, however, gained its legitimacy as a means for the empire to expand its territory southward, including to seasonal tropical environments like Malaysia and Thailand, albeit for only a short time. When scholars today ask: "What might be a history of psychiatric epidemiology?", this story offers a possible timeline rooted in an East Asian context.[73]

Third, and finally, in the wake of environmental concerns related to the history of medicine, this study urges historians to reappraise what the environment means to the mental wellness of both colonized and colonizer. It also reorients East Asia from the recipient of Western knowledge to a nexus of relations in which various psychiatric theories and practices clash with one another. When PTSD was first introduced in the third edition of the *Diagnostic and Statistical Manual of Mental Disorders* (the *DSM-III*), the diagnostic criteria pointed out a paradox regarding whether trauma should be characterized by the traumatic event itself or by an individual's reactions to it and the ensuing post-traumatic symptoms. In the manual's diagnostic criterion A, the presentation of PTSD was defined by a set of symptoms "following a psychologically distressing event that is outside the range of normal human experience." What constitutes the range of normal human experience, however, is highly variable. In human-inhabited areas of the globe that are constantly prone to natural disasters such as earthquakes, monsoon rains, landslides, and tropical cyclones, do people become more fragile or more resilient? Does the construction of new victim categories by medicine only reveal the anxiety of a seemingly modern society? These questions will not be answerable until a more complete picture of the disaster-related history of the psychological sciences across the world has developed.

Harry Yi-Jui Wu is Associate Professor at the Cross-College Elite Program and Department of Medical Humanities and Social Medicine, National Cheng Kung University. He studied medicine in Taiwan and then obtained a DPhil in Modern History from the University of Oxford in 2012. Before taking up his current post, he taught medical humanities at Nanyang Technological University and The University of Hong Kong. He has written on the transnational history of psychiatry related to the WHO's international social psychiatry projects, the formation of psychiatric disciplines in Taiwan, China, and Hong Kong and he has co-edited several related special issues of journals, including *East Asian Science, Technology and Society: An International Journal* (with Wenji Wang) and *History of Psychology* (with Hans Pols). His first monograph is entitled *Mad by the Millions: Mental Disorder and the Early Years of the World Health Organization* (MIT Press, 2021). Currently, he is writing the history of mental health along the development of trade ports in East and Southeast Asia between the mid-nineteenth century and the mid-twentieth century, focusing on the relationship between migration and empire networks.

Notes

1. See Micale and Lerner, *Traumatic Pasts*; Jones and Wessely, *Shell Shock to PTSD*.
2. DiMauro et al., "Historical Review Trauma-Related Diagnoses."
3. See Hinton and Good, *Culture and PTSD*.
4. See Barnett, *After the Flood*.
5. Daly, "Samuel Pepys and PTSD."
6. See Molesky, *This Gulf of Fire*.
7. James, *Some Mental Effects Earthquake*, 209–26.
8. Adler, "Neuropsychiatric Complications," Cobb and Lindemann, "Symposium," Menninger, "Psychological Reactions."
9. Wang, *Illuminations from the Past*.
10. Chiang, "Huí gù 1935 nián xīn zhú tái zhōng dì zhèn."
11. Wata, *Jishin shakaigaku no bōken*.
12. Nakai, *1995 nen 1 tsuki kōbe*.
13. Breslau, "Globalizing Disaster Trauma."
14. Nakamura, "'Invisible' War Trauma in Japan." Also see Zwigenberg, this volume, and Nakamura, this volume.
15. Matsumura, "State Propaganda and Mental Disorders."
16. Nakai, *Nippon shakai niokeru gaishōsei sutoresu*.
17. Johnson, *Influence Tropical Climates*. See its historiographic analysis in Chakrabarti, *Medicine and Empire*.
18. Pick, *Faces of Degeneration*.
19. Wang, "Tropical Neurasthenia or Oriental Nerves?", Anderson, *Colonial Pathologies*. Also see Anderson, "White Masculinity and Colonial Breakdown."
20. Wu and Teng, "Qì hòu, tǐ zhì yú xiāng chou."
21. See, for example, Hans Pols, "Psychological Knowledge in a Colonial Context."
22. Mahone and Vaughan, eds., *Psychiatry and Empire*.
23. Wu and Teng, "Qì hòu, tǐ zhì yú xiāng chou."
24. Low, *Science Building of a New Japan*, Kim, *Doctors of Empire*.
25. Hashimoto, "Teikoku aigaku to seishinbyōgaku to seishinbyōsha".
26. Wu and Cheng, "History Mental Healthcare Taiwan."
27. Porter, *Madmen*.
28. Engstrom. "'On the Question of Degeneration.'" Also see Pols, "Emil Kraepelin."
29. Weber and Engstrom, "Kraepelin's 'Diagnostic Cards.'"
30. Miyakawa, *Tōkeigaku no nipponshi*.
31. Kaneko, *Kure Shūzō hakase no shōgai to sono kōgyō*.
32. Koch, "History of Demography in Japan."
33. Yeh, *Tái běi dì guó dà xué*.
34. "Kure Shūzō seishinbyō chōsa wo shokutaku su."
35. Hashimoto, "Present State and Statistical Observation."
36. Kanata, "Japanese Mental Health Care."
37. Jin, "Zài zhào hù zhì liáo yú gé lí shōu róng zhī jiān."
38. Yuzuru. "Three So-Called Malaria Psychosis."
39. Wang, "Jīng shén yī xué níng shì xià de fú ěr mó shā."
40. See Yoo, *It's Madness*.
41. Takeuchi, "Ninsaiin seishinbyō kanja no tōkei teki kansatsu."
42. Chou, "Nanyo-shi as Research Chair."
43. Naka and Wakesima, "Study Psycho-Neurotic Diseases."

44. Matsumura, "Politics Manic Depression."
45. Minamizaki, *Nanpō seikatsu hikkei.*
46. Wakesima "Psychiatrische und Neurologische Uebericht."
47. Syuzo et al., "Ueber Neurasthenia Tropica."
48. Coen, *Earthquake Observers.*
49. Bälz, "Über Emotionslähmung."
50. Yasui, *Berutsu no shōgai.*
51. For Bälz's autobiography, see Bälz, *Awakening Japan,* edited by his son Toku Bälz.
52. Orihara and Clancey, "Nature of Emergency."
53. Saigai kyōkun, *1923 kantōdaishinsai hōkokusho.*
54. Uchimura, *Aga ayumishi seishin igaku no michi.*
55. Nakao, "Tenhen chī oaguru kagaku shisō."
56. See Imperial Earthquake Investigation Committee, "Appendix II." The Committee was established in 1891 immediately following the Nobi earthquake to promote earthquake research and disaster prevention. See Hagiwara, "Gravity Changes."
57. Borland, "Capitalising on Catastrophe."
58. Obayashi and Sanada, "Recovery from the Great Kanto Earthquake."
59. Schencking, *Great Kanto Earthquake.*
60. Busch, *Two Minutes to Noon.*
61. Araragi Magazine. *Kaijinshū*
62. Busch, *Two Minutes to Noon.*
63. Surgeons at Taichung Hospital also observed anuria among earthquake victims but no neuropsychiatric explanation was given. Surgeon Lu Qingtu reported 51 out of 332 admissions (13.8 percent) suffered from it. However, no neuropsychiatric reasoning was made. See Lu, "Kankai taishin ni keru kizusha."
64. Schneckling, "Imperial Japanese Navy."
65. See Huang, "Confrontation and Collaboration."
66. Youhuan Yusheng, "Ai zhen zai."
67. Koa, "Chín-chai Pi-siong Koa."
68. For the history of statistical methodologies in the West, see Porter, *Rise Statistical Thinking.* Japanese psychiatrists based in colonial Taiwan actually utilized a combination of statistics and survey studies.
69. Coen, *Earthquake Observers.*
70. Yasui, *Berutsu no shōgai.*
71. Yasui, *Berutsu no shōgai,* 58.
72. Littlewood, "Disease Illness Back Again."
73. Lovell and Susser, "What Might Be a History of Psychiatric Epidemiology?"

Bibliography

Adler, Alexandra. "Neuropsychiatric Complications in Victims of Boston's Cocoanut Grove Disaster." *Journal of the American Medical Association* 123, no. 17 (1943): 1098–101.

Anderson, Warwick. *Colonial Pathologies: American Tropical Medicine, Race, and Hygiene in the Philippines.* Durham, NC: Duke University Press, 2006.

———. "The Trespass Speaks: White Masculinity and Colonial Breakdown." *The American Historical Review* 102, no. 5 (1997): 1343–70.

Araragi Magazine. *Kaijinshū: taishō jūni nen shinsai kashū* [Collection of ashes: Taisho Year 12 songs on the earthquake]. Tokyo: Araragi Hakkōjo, 1924.

Bälz, Erwin. *Awakening Japan: The Diary of a German Doctor*, edited by Toku Bälz. Bloomington, IN: Indiana University Press, 1974.

———. "Über Emotionslähmung" [About emotional paralysis]. *Allgemeine Zeitschrift für Psychiatrie* 58 (1901): 717–27.

Barnett, Lydia. *After the Flood: Imagining the Global Environment in Early Modern Europe*. Baltimore, MD: Johns Hopkins University Press, 2019.

Borland, Janet. "Capitalising on Catastrophe: Reinvigorating the Japanese State with Moral Values through Education Following the 1923 Great Kanto Earthquake." *Modern Asian Studies* 40, no. 4 (2006): 875–907.

Breslau, Joshua. "Globalizing Disaster Trauma: Psychiatry, Science, and Culture after the Kobe Earthquake." *Ethos* 28, no. 2 (2000): 174–97.

Busch, Noel F. *Two Minutes to Noon: The Great Kanto Earthquake of September 1, 1923*. New York: Simon & Schuster, 1962.

Chakrabarti, Pratik. *Medicine and Empire: 1600–1960*. Basingstoke: Palgrave Macmillan, 2014.

Chiang, Cheng-Hsing. "Huí gù 1935 nián xīn zhú tái zhōng dì zhèn" [Review of 1935 Hsinchu and Taichung earthquake]. *National Museum of Natural Science Newsletter* 332 (2016): 1–7.

Chou, Wan-Yao. "Nanyo-shi as Research Chair and as a Major at Taihoku Imperial University and Its Postwar Legacy." *Historical Inquiry* 61 (2018): 17–95.

Cobb, Stanley, and Erich Lindemann. "Symposium on the Management of the Cocoanut Grove Burns at the Massachusetts General Hospital: Neuropsychiatric Observations." *Annals of Surgery* 117, no. 6 (1943): 814–24.

Coen, Deborah R. *The Earthquake Observers: Disaster Science from Lisbon to Richter*. Chicago: University of Chicago Press, 2012.

Daly, R. J. "Samuel Pepys and Post-Traumatic Stress Disorder." *British Journal of Psychiatry* 143, no. 1 (1983): 64–8.

DiMauro, Jennifer, Sarah Carter, Johanna B. Folk, and Todd B. Kashdan. "A Historical Review of Trauma-Related Diagnoses to Reconsider the Heterogeneity of PTSD." *Journal of Anxiety Disorders* 28, no. 8 (2014): 774–86.

Engstrom, Eric J. "'On the Question of Degeneration' by Emil Kraepelin (1908)." *History of Psychiatry* 18, no. 3 (2007): 389–98.

Hagiwara, Yukio. "Gravity Changes Associated with Seismic Activities." *Journal of Physics of the Earth* 25, Suppl. (1977): S137–S146.

Hashimoto, Akira. "'The Present State and Statistical Observation of Mental Patients Under Home Custody,' by Kure Shūzō and Kashida Gorō (1918)." *History of Psychiatry* 30, no. 2 (2018): 240–56.

———. "Teikoku aigaku to seishinbyōgaku to seishinbyōsha: Meiji taishōki niokeru seishinbyō chiryō shisō no keifu" [Imperial universities, psychiatric disciplines and mental patients: Genealogy of psychiatric treatments and thoughts in Meiji and Taisho periods]. In *Meiji taishōki no kagaku shisōshi* [Intellectual history of science in Meiji and Taisho periods], edited by Kamori Osamu, 275–330. Tokyo: Keiso Shobo, 2017.

Hinton, Devon E., and Byron J. Good, eds. *Culture and PTSD: Trauma in Global and Historical Perspective*. Philadelphia: University of Pennsylvania Press, 2015.

Huang, Mei-Er. "Confrontation and Collaboration: Traditional Taiwanese Writers' Canonical Reflection and Cultural Thinking on the New-Old Literatures Debate during the Japanese Colonial Period." In *Taiwan under Japanese Colonial Rule, 1895–1945: History, Culture, Memory*, edited by Ping-hui Liao and David Der-wei Wang, 187–209. New York: Columbia University Press, 2006.

Imperial Earthquake Investigation Committee. "Appendix II." *Seismological Notes* 6 (1924): 15.
James, William. *On Some Mental Effects of the Earthquake: Memories and Studies*. New York: Longmans, Green, 1911.
Jin, Jungwon. "Zài zhào hù zhì liáo yú gé lí shōu róng zhī jiān: Zhí mín dì tái wān de jīng shén bìng yuàn [Between care and custody: Psychiatric hospitals in colonial Taiwan]. In *Kàn bu jiàn de zhí mín biān yuán rì zhì tái wān biān yuán dòu shǐ* [Invisible edges of colonialism: A reader of marginal histories in Taiwan under Japanese colonial rule], edited by Jungwon Jin, 144–59. Taipei: TIPI, 2012.
Johnson, James. *The Influence of Tropical Climates on European Constitutions*. London: Underwood, 1818.
Jones, Edgar, and Simon Wessely. *Shell Shock to PTSD: Military Psychiatry from 1900 to the Gulf War*. Hove: Psychology Press, 2005.
Kanata, Tomoko. "Japanese Mental Health Care in Historical Context: Why Did Japan Become a Country with So Many Psychiatric Care Beds?" *Social Work/Maatskaplike Werk* 52, no 4 (2016): 471–89.
Kaneko, Junji. *Kure Shūzō hakase no shōgai to sono kōgyō* [Dr. Kure Shūzō's career and life achievements]. Tokyo: Japanese Association of Psychiatric Hospitals, 1965.
Kim, Hoi-eun. *Doctors of Empire: Medical and Cultural Encounters between Imperial Germany and Meiji Japan*. Toronto: University of Toronto Press, 2014.
Koa, I-su. "Chín-chai Pi-siong Koa" [Lamentation of the earthquake]. *Taiwan Kau-Hue Kong-Po* [Taiwan church news], *Mustard Seeds Northern Branch Affairs* no. 114 (July 1935): 27.
Koch, Matthias. "History of Demography in Japan." In *The Demographic Challenge: A Handbook about Japan*, edited by Florian Coulmas, Harald Conrad, Annette Schad-Seifert, and Gabriele Vogt, 97–117. Leiden: Brill, 2008.
"Kure Shūzō seishinbyō chōsa wo shokutaku su, 1909 12 28" [Entrusting Kure Shūzō to investigate psychiatric diseases]. In Taiwan Government-General Collections: Taiwan Historical. Call No. 00001569077.
Littlewood, Roland. "From Disease to Illness and Back Again." *The Lancet* 337, no. 8748 (27 April 1991): 1013–16.
Lovell, Anne M., and Ezra Susser. "What Might Be a History of Psychiatric Epidemiology? Towards a Social History and Conceptual Account." *International Journal of Epidemiology* 43 (26 July 2014): i1–i5.
Low, Morris. *Science and the Building of a New Japan*. Basingstoke: Palgrave Macmillan, 2005.
Lu, Ching-Tu. "Kankai taishin ni keru kizusha ni on te [Injured Patients in the Earthquake]." *Taiwan Igakku Sassi* 34 (1935): 1666.
Mahone, Sloan and Megan Vaughan. *Psychiatry and Empire*. Basingstoke: Palgrave Macmillan, 2007.
Matsumura, Janice. "The Politics of Manic Depression in the Japanese Empire." In *Science, Technology and Medicine in the Modern Japanese Empire*, edited by David G. Wittner and Philip C. Brown, 98–116. Abingdon: Routledge, 2016.
———. "State Propaganda and Mental Disorders: The Issue of Psychiatric Casualties among Japanese Soldiers During the Asia-Pacific War." *Bulletin of the History of Medicine* 78, no. 4 (2004): 804–35.
Menninger, William C. "Psychological Reactions in an Emergency (Flood)." *American Journal of Psychiatry* 109, no. 2 (1952): 128–30.
Miyakawa, Tadawa. *Tōkeigaku no nipponshi: Chikoku keisei e no negai* [Historical vignettes of national leaders and statisticians in Japan: Their common desire for enhancing good governance, wealth and welfare of the nation]. Tokyo: University of Tokyo Press, 2017.
Micale, Mark S., and Paul Lerner, eds. *Traumatic Pasts: History, Psychiatry, and Trauma in the Modern Age, 1870–1930*. Cambridge: Cambridge University Press, 2001.

Minamizaki, Yushichi. *Nanpō seikatsu hikkei: igaku to eisei* [Living in the south essentials: medicine and hygiene]. Tokyo: Kyosaisha, 1942.
Molesky, Mark *This Gulf of Fire: The Great Lisbon Earthquake or Apocalypse in the Age of Science and Reason*. New York: Vintage, 2016.
Naka, Syuzo, and Satosi Wakesima. "Study on the Psycho-Neurotic Diseases in Formosa: 1st Report, Statistical Observation." *Journal of the Medical Association of Formosa* 38 (1939): 74–111.
Nakai, Hisao. *1995 nen 1 tsuki kōbe: hanshin daishinsai shita no seishinkaitachi* [January 1995, Kobe: Psychiatry in the Hanshin earthquake]. Tokyo: Misuzu, 1995.
Nakai Hisao, *Nippon shakai niokeru gaishōsei sutoresu* [Traumatic stress in Japanese society]. Tokyo: Misuzu, 2019.
Nakamura, Eri. "'Invisible' War Trauma in Japan: Medicine, Society and Military Psychiatric Casualties." *Historia Scientiarum* 25, no. 2 (2016): 140–60.
Nakao, Maika. "Tenhen chī oaguru kagaku shisō" [Scientific Reasoning on Natural Disasters]. In *Meiji taishōki no kagaku shisōshi* [Intellectual history of science in Meiji and Taisho periods], edited by Kamori Osamu, 331–368 Tokyo: Keiso Shobo, 2017.
Obayashi, Taro, and Hisashi Sanada, "Recovery from the Great Kanto Earthquake of 1923 through Sport Events in Tokyo, Japan." *International Journal of the History of Sport* 33, no. 14 (2016): 1640–51.
Orihara, Minami, and Gregory Clancey. "The Nature of Emergency: The Great Kanto Earthquake and the Crisis of Reason in Late Imperial Japan." *Science in Context* 25, no. 1 (2012): 103–26.
Pick, Daniel. *Faces of Degeneration: A European Disorder, c.1848–c.1918*. Cambridge: Cambridge University Press, 1989.
Pols, Hans. "Emil Kraepelin on Cultural and Ethnic Factors in Mental Illness." *Psychiatric Times* 28, no. 8 (22 June 2011), 1–6.
_____. "Psychological Knowledge in a Colonial Context: Theories on the Nature of the 'Native Mind' in the Former Dutch East Indies." *History of Psychology* 10, no. 2 (2007): 111–31.
Porter, Roy. *Madmen: A Social History of Madhouses, Mad Doctors and Lunatics*. Stroud: Tempus, 2004.
Porter, Theodore M. *The Rise of Statistical Thinking: 1820–1900*. Princeton, NJ: Princeton University Press, 1986.
Saigai kyōkun no keishō nikansuru senmon chōsakai [Investigation Committee of Disaster Lessons], *1923 kantōdaishinsai hōkokusho: Dai ni hen* [2nd edition of 1923 Kanto earthquake report]. Tokyo: Chūō bōsai kaigi, 2008.
Schencking, J. Charles. *The Great Kantō Earthquake and the Chimera of National Reconstruction in Japan*. Cambridge: Cambridge University Press, 2013.
_____. "The Imperial Japanese Navy and the Constructed Consciousness of a South Seas Destiny, 1872–1921." *Modern Asian Studies* 33, no 4 (1999): 769–96.
Syuzo, Naka, Okamoto Hosei, Yamagata Kunibiro, Hamasaki Keiei, Gohara Yukiti, and Sakakibara Katusi. "Ueber Neurasthenia Tropica in Hainan." *Taiwan Igakku Sassi* 40 (1941): 32–58.
Takeuchi, Yawata. "Ninsaiin seishinbyō kanja no tōkei teki kansatsu" [Observational statistics of mental patients at Ninsaiin]. *Taiwan Igakku Sassi* no. 26 (1927): 1203.
Uchimura, Yushio. *Aga ayumishi seishin igaku no michi* [My road and the way of psychiatry]. Tokyo: Misuzu, 1968.
Wakesima, Takasi. "Psychiatrische und Neurologische Uebericht in Hainan" [Psychiatric and neurological review in Hainan]. *Taiwan Igakku Sassi* 41 (1942): 146–52.

Wang, Ban. *Illuminations from the Past: Trauma, Memory and History in Modern China*. Palo Alto, CA: Stanford University Press, 2004.

Wang, Pei-Ying. "Jīng shén yī xué níng shì xià de fú ěr mó shā: Rì zhì zhōng qī (1916–1929) zhōng cūn ràng zhī dì wèi jiàn gòu yú tuì huà lǐ lùn" [Formosa under psychiatric gaze: The Establishment of Nakamura Yuzuru's Career status in the middle of Japanese colonial period (1916–1929) and degeneration theories]. *Xinbeida Shixue* 3 (2005): 89–106.

Wang, Wen-Ji. "Tropical Neurasthenia or Oriental Nerves? White Breakdowns in China." In *Psychiatry and Chinese History*, edited by Howard Chiang, 111–28. London: Pickering & Chatto, 2014.

Wata, Yoshikata. *Jishin shakaigaku no bōken: Taiwan toruko kōbe shinsaichi no fukkō kenkyū* [Adventure of earthquake sociology: Of Taiwan, Turkey, the Kobe earthquake disaster area reconstruction research]. Tokyo: Astra, 2004.

Weber, M. M., and E. J. Engstrom. "Kraepelin's 'Diagnostic Cards': The Confluence of Clinical Research and Preconceived Categories." *History of Psychiatry* 8 (1997): 375–85.

Wu, Harry Yi-Jui, and Andrew Tai-Ann Cheng. "A History of Mental Healthcare in Taiwan." In *Mental Health in Asia and the Pacific: Historical and Cultural Perspectives*, edited by Harry Minas and Milton Lewis, 107–21. New York: Springer, 2017.

Wu, Yu-Chuan and Hui-Wen Teng. "Qì hòu, tǐ zhì yú xiāng chóu—zhí mín wǎn qī zài tái rì rén de rè dài shén jīng shuāi ruò [Tropics, neurasthenia, and Japanese colonizers: The psychiatric discourses in late colonial Taiwan]." *Taiwan: A Radical Quarterly in Social Studies* 54 (2004): 61–103.

Yasui, Yirou. *Berutsu no shōgai: Kindai igaku dōnyū no chichi* [Bälz's life: The father who introduced modern medicine]. Kyoto: Shibunkaku, 1995.

Yeh, Pi-Ling. *Tái běi dì guó dà xué yú rì běn nán jìn zhèng cè zhī yán jiū* [Academic pioneer: Taihoku Imperial University and Japan's Nanshin policy]. Taipei: Dao Shiang Publishing, 2010.

Yoo, Theodore Jun. *It's Madness: The Politics of Mental Health in Colonial Korea*. Berkeley, CA: University of California Press, 2016.

Youhuan Yusheng, "Ai zhen zai" [Mourning the Earthquake]. *Taiwan Nijiniji Shinbo* no. 192649, 18 June 1935, 8.

Yuzuru, Nakamura. "Three So-Called Malaria Psychoses." *Taiwan Igakku Sassi* 17 (1918): 141–49.

Chapter 2

MALE HYSTERIA IN MODERN JAPAN

Trauma, Masculinity, and Military Psychiatry
during the Asia-Pacific War

Eri Nakamura

A number of studies have demonstrated conclusively that modern warfare, and in particular World War I, exerted a significant effect on the male body and psyche, including causing nearly epidemic rates of psychological breakdown (also known as shell shock) and that this phenomenon represented a powerful, if implicit, challenge to historical ideals of heroic masculinity in Western countries. In *The Female Malady: Women, Madness, and English Culture, 1830–1980*, the feminist literary critic Elaine Showalter uncovered historical representations of "feminine madness and masculine rationality." Showalter observed that World War I became "a crisis of masculinity and a trial of the Victorian masculine ideal" as thousands of soldiers reacted to overwhelmingly stressful situations with "symptoms of hysteria," a disorder traditionally regarded as the quintessential "female malady."[1] In 2000, George Mosse, a historian of modern Germany, argued in a similar vein that war as an activity was regarded as the ultimate test of manliness in modern Europe. Masculine will power and emotional self-mastery were essential for defending the homeland in times of war and maintain respectability in peacetime; wartime neurosis represented the deterioration of these essential capabilities. According to Mosse, soldiers afflicted with shell shock were deemed to have failed a basic test of manliness.[2]

In *Hysterical Men: War, Psychiatry, and the Politics of Trauma in Germany, 1890–1930*, published in 2003, Paul Lerner, another Germanist, showed how shell-shocked soldiers in postwar Germany got caught up in national debates about German manhood, military strength, and economic recovery in the interwar period.³ And in 2008, the medical historian Mark Micale tracked conceptualizations of hysteria, in both their female and male incarnations, over the centuries. In *Hysterical Men: The Hidden History of Male Nervous Illness*, Micale highlighted physicians' refusal through the generations to acknowledge male nervous illness despite widespread counterevidence in times of war and peace. The studied silence in the medical community about this clinical reality, Micale proposed, reflected apprehensions in patriarchal society that male hysteria could unveil vulnerable "feminine" elements in the male psyche.⁴

The studies of Showalter, Mosse, Lerner, and Micale have explored the subject of war, psychiatry, and masculinity in significant depth; all of the scholarship to date, however, has been restricted to Western countries, specifically to Britain, France, and Germany. This chapter examines war and masculine nervous illness in one particular time and place in Asian history—namely, in Japanese society during the 1930s and 1940s—a time and period characterized dramatically by rapid modernization, expansionist nationalism, and intensive warfare. After the Second Sino-Japanese War broke out in 1937, the Imperial Japanese Army began to prepare for the treatment of psychiatric patients, while simultaneously concealing the existence of this group of soldiers from the public. In 1938, the army converted Kōnodai Military Hospital—located southeast of Tokyo in the Chiba Prefecture—into an army hospital that specialized in mental and neurological illnesses in soldiers. By the end of the war, Kōnodai Military Hospital had admitted, diagnosed, and treated approximately 10,500 soldier-patients.

In this chapter, I explore how gender, race, and class intersected during this period and how they were interwoven with medical discourses on psychological trauma in soldiers in wartime Japan. I locate an interesting set of similarities to and differences from the more familiar account of twentieth-century wartime trauma in the European West. In the first part of the chapter, I provide an overview of the militarization of the Japanese Empire and the concomitant construction of a notion of ideal, "hegemonic masculinity" in Imperial Japan. In the second part, I analyze both medical-scientific and lay-popular discourses on male hysteria in Japan during the 1930s and 1940s. As in modern Western countries, hysteria in prewar Japanese medicine was regarded essentially as a women's health issue. "Male hysteria," in so far as it was acknowledged to exist in the Japanese context, was simultaneously feminized and racialized during the Asia-Pacific War. In the third and last part of the chapter, I examine the clinical records of the Kōnodai Military Hospital. Contrary to official concealment of war neurotic patients, medical authorities at this facility encountered hundreds of cases of war hysteria in male soldiers. I consider how gender, class, and race, in a wartime militarized setting, combined to shape the theories and practices of physicians and other health care providers at this key institution in the nation's capital.

Masculinity and the Military in Modern Japan

The Imperial Japanese Army played a major, in fact decisive, role in the social and cultural construction of masculinity in modern Japan. All branches of the Japanese armed forces (army and navy) were exclusively male institutions until the surrender of the Japanese Empire in World War II. Way back in 1873, the Conscription Ordinance (*Chōheirei*) and Article 20 of the Constitution of the Empire of Japan (*Dainihon teikoku kenpou*) in 1890 stipulated that all adult male subjects of Japan be enrolled in compulsory military service. In prewar Japan, men were conscripted at the age of twenty with very few exceptions. The conscription examination was considered a fundamental rite of passage in becoming a full-fledged Japanese man. As Teresa Algoso has pointed out, the military entrance examination defined a specific kind of manhood, and it created a new standard and method of evaluating masculinity that could not have existed before establishment of the modern system of universal conscription. The examination in effect established a gendered hierarchy in which the highest status was assigned to healthy, strong, and courageous men who were fighting for the nation, whereas it excluded men who were short in stature, medically unwell, or judged to have permanent physical or mental disabilities.[5] Within Japanese society, soldiers were considered to be "real men," and the ideal role model of mature manhood was propagated in boys' magazines.[6]

During the writing of the Military Service Law (*Heiekihou*), which went into effect on 1 December 1927, a member of the House of Peers raised a question about the relation between this law and the Japanese Constitution. He asserted that Article 1 of the law, which said that *danshi kokumin* (male subjects) were liable for military service, may have been unconstitutional because Article 20 of the Constitution of the Empire of Japan stated that *shinmin* (subjects), which is a gender-neutral term, were liable for military service. In reply, the government declared that "[w]omen have been excluded from military duty since the enactment of Conscription Ordinance, which was before the establishment of the Constitution, and nobody has wondered why [women were excluded from service].... That's why people will accept that this article is constitutional."[7]

Several overlapping discourses in modern Japan contain examples of a naturalized gender dichotomy that assigned soldiering to men and mothering (and related domestic activities) to women. For example, in his speech to educators in August 1911, Inoue Tetsujirō (1856–1944), a professor of philosophy at Tokyo Imperial University, argued as follows:[8]

> Men and women are completely different. Although sometimes we can treat them equally, we must make a distinction between them.... They are different physiologically and mentally. Women are rather emotional, and men are rational.... As a result of longstanding custom, men do hard work today. It's

natural that men become soldiers and there cannot be women soldiers. . . . Women, instead, have to do work which men cannot do. . . . It is only women who can make home and raise children.⁹

Inoue justified a traditional gendered division of "emotional women" versus "rational men" on the basis of natural, biologically grounded differences between "opposite" sexes. On the basis of this unquestioned dichotomy, the Imperial Japanese Army excluded women until 1945.

As in many Western countries at the time, citizenship in Japan at this time was strongly associated with patriotic military service. When on 24 March 1931, a women's civil rights bill was rejected by an overwhelming majority in the House of Peers—after having been passed in the House of Representatives—Baron Kii exclaimed that "[i]f they insist on equal rights between men and women, we will have to discuss women's military service," as if merely calling out this extraordinary possibility would settle the debate.¹⁰ The Japanese newspaper *Yomiuri Shimbun* published a critical cartoon on 25 March 1931, titled "What Shelved the Women's Civil Rights Bill? What Male Members of the House of Peers Were Obsessed with on That Day." The illustration vividly depicts the Japanese male legislators' fear that the existing division of roles between men and women in Japanese society would fall apart if the women's civil rights bill should happen to be passed. In this telling representation, two Japanese lawmakers imagine a "dystopia" in which men clean houses and raise children while women become politicians and soldiers.

The Imperial Japanese construction of masculinity inevitably entailed related constructions of femininity and effeminacy. The Imperial Japanese Army made social bonds between men stronger by excluding women and femininity. Male comradeship in the service of the nation was regarded as the supreme goal. As ex-captain and writer Ijichi Susumu observed, it was "stronger than the bond between lovers" or "family ties."¹¹ In the all-important process of military training, men were required to discipline their emotions in order to become maximally effective fighting soldiers. Shimozawa Zuisei, who in 1913 had conducted research on *Bushidō* (the code of *samurai*) and military psychology after the Russo-Japanese War (1904–05), stated that the armed services were the place to train bodies and minds in the creation of "real men." According to Shimozawa, the hardships that new conscripts would experience were indispensable for their mental training "to be calm and control their feelings." Shimozawa concluded that those who failed to pass this trial were not *nippon danshi* (Japanese men).¹²

A distinctive feature of nervous breakdown among servicemen in the Imperial Japanese Army is that at times it was caused by violence within the military, as well as by more expected sources such as fear of death on the battlefield, the witnessing of comrades dying, guilt associated with killing, and physical overfatigue. Japanese soldiers were strictly disciplined, sometimes by harsh punishment.¹³

New conscripts as well as mentally disabled soldiers were highly susceptible to such violence.

Physically and mentally challenged men had been disqualified from military service under the conscription system, but as the war dragged on for years and the shortage of soldiers became critical, it became necessary to enlist them as well. As a result of the 1940 revision of The Regulation for Physical Examination of the Army (*Rikugun Shintai Kensa Kisoku*), Japanese men with various minor infirmities could pass the conscription examination if they were at least capable of carrying out certain military tasks.[14] For example, a private second class, a peasant born in 1925, was admitted to Kōnodai Military Hospital in 1945 because of his thieving habits and was diagnosed with mild mental retardation; he was not good at memorizing and sometimes disrupted the order of his unit. However, it was reported that the man had a sturdy physique, and his senior officer admired his skill at operating artillery.[15] The number of patients admitted to Kōnodai Military Hospital who were diagnosed with mental retardation increased from 0.9 percent in 1938 to 13.9 percent in 1945.[16] They suffered not only from battlefield trauma, but also from *shiteki seisai*, or bullying and abuse in the barracks. Recruits who could not endure the demanding training regime were regarded as weak, defective, and "effeminate."

The Feminization and Racialization of Male Hysteria

Western psychiatric discourse, including discourses on hysteria, were first introduced to Japan in the middle of the nineteenth century. Indicatively, in several medical books written toward the end of the Edo period (1603–1868) and Meiji period (1868–1912), the word *hysteria* was written using Chinese characters as a phonetic equivalent. However, Kure Shūzō (1865–1932), a professor of psychiatry at Tokyo Imperial University Medical School and the founder of psychiatry in modern Japan, proposed to translate hysteria as *zōsō*. Kure based this proposal on the concept of *fujin* (female) *zōsō*, which had been introduced via an old Chinese medical book, *Jingkui Yaolve*, written by Zhang Zhongjing (150–219), a Chinese physician during the later years of the Han dynasty. According to Kure, *zōsō* was regarded as a manic state caused by a defect in certain bodily organs. But which organs? Akin to medical debates in eighteenth-century Britain and France, Japanese physicians claimed the causative site of the disease to be either the brain, the mind, the lungs, or the abdomen. Kure argued that the old view that *zōsō* was caused by an ischemia (lack of blood supply) of the uterus became influential after Shen Mingzong published his medical commentary on *Jingkui Yaolve* in 1692. Kure also referenced a similar belief that hysteria was caused by a disorder of women's genitalia in contemporaneous medical discourses.[17] Although such an association had a long history in Western countries, tracing back in fact to ancient Greek Hippocratic texts, Kure seemed to emphasize that the Japanese medical community could find important similar ideas in Eastern medicine.

The term *zōsō*, however, was used only by a small segment of psychiatrists in Japan, whereas *hisuterī*, which denotes hysteria in *katakana*, a Japanese syllabary, became much more popular among both psychiatric experts and the public. Since the early twentieth century, many Japanese publications had discussed hysteria, with the number of articles peaking, interestingly, in the 1930s. In these articles, hysteria was frequently connected with criminality.[18] Although hysterical symptoms were usually represented as intrinsically female in popular medical books and mass media, the notion that adult males too could be hysterical was generally accepted among experts in psychiatry and psychology.[19] One influence on this subject was French: in 1907, a translation into Japanese appeared of the clinical lectures of Jean-Martin Charcot (1825–1893), the famous Paris-based "founder of neurology." Charcot's works presented many cases of "traumatic hysteria" in working-class men who had undergone sudden shocks from physical accidents in the workplace.[20]

Learning from case studies in European medicine, Japanese physicians published papers on their own case studies of Japanese patients. The all-male national armed forces were a natural place to conduct such clinical investigations. In 1916, a medical officer named Iijima Shigeru (1868–1953) had published an intriguing series of articles about hysteria in the military.[21] Written during the years of World War I in Europe, Iijima's studies are one of the earliest examples of research on masculine hysteria in the Japanese military. In his preface, Iijima objected to the view that hysteria was exclusively a "female malady":

> "Hysterie"[22] means uterus in Greek. The ancients gave this name to what was equivalent to psychoneurosis today because they thought this illness was caused by [the] uterus. However, not only women who have uterine disease but also those with no disease, children and men often become hysterical. Therefore, I have to say it was wrong that the ancients used "Hysterie" for one of the names of functional disease.[23]

According to Iijima, hysteria, as a formal primary diagnosis among soldiers, was first used in a statistical compilation prepared by the Imperial Japanese Army in 1908. According to this statistical source, Japan had fewer hysterical soldiers but more neurasthenic soldiers than did the German military; Iijima, however, doubted this conclusion. In addition, Iijima discussed the ratio of male-to-female hysteria in both Germany and France. According to him, the army's 1908 report contended that male hysteria was much less common than female hysteria in Germany, whereas there were more cases of male hysteria than cases of female hysteria in France. Iijima was again skeptical of this percentage, but he claimed that "[t]here is less male hysteria in the Anglo-Saxon and the Germanic races than in the Latin races because the Latin people are precocious and oversensitive."[24]

This was a widespread, if tendentious, belief in European medicine from the 1880s onward.

Iijima's claim is disputable because French physicians also claimed that male hysteria was less common than female hysteria. Charcot himself had supported the view espoused by the mid-nineteenth-century French internist Pierre Briquet (1796–1881) that the ratio of male-to-female hysteria was 1 to 20, and he estimated that the ratio was in fact somewhat lower than this in clinical reality.[25] As Micale has pointed out, the charge that French men were more prone to hysteria, and in general were more impressionable psychologically, than men in Germany began to appear after France's humiliating defeat in the Franco-Prussian War (1870–1871).[26]

In 1948, Hosokoshi Masakazu (1914–1991), a psychiatrist and ex-medical officer, wrote a pioneering doctoral thesis "Sensō hisuterī no kenkyū" (Research on war hysteria).[27] Hosokoshi's medical thesis was based on his clinical experience in treating war neurotic patients at Kōnodai Military Hospital during the war. Hosokoshi opens his dissertation on the subject by observing that World War I had been an epoch-making event in modern medicine, which gave rise to many cases of nervous derangement diagnosed as "shell shock," "male hysteria," and "traumatic neurosis," among other things.[28] Although these cases of war-induced male hysteria became well-known among Japanese experts in the psy-sciences, by the outbreak of the Asia-Pacific War, there still prevailed a deep-rooted prejudice among the public that hysteria was by definition a female pathological phenomenon.

In his book *Seishin' byō no kangohō* (How to nurse mental illnesses), Usa Shizuo (1886–1957), a psychiatrist and Buddhist monk, wrote that "[a]lthough many people think that hysteria and neurasthenia are similar and that men get neurasthenia and women get hysteria, that is wrong. . . . Not only women but also men, old people and children get hysteria."[29] Usa nevertheless referred to only women's cases of hysteria in his book, and he claimed that "[p]eople who are oversensitive by nature are prone to get [hysteria] . . ., therefore it is natural that women are more likely to get hysteria."[30] This statement is a typical example of Japanese medical discourse at the time, and it makes clear that experts in the psy-sciences, even while acknowledging the theoretical possibility of individual male cases, still considered hysteria, as a pathological entity, to be gendered feminine. Hysterical symptoms in an adult male were statistical rarities—a freakish abnormality, in more ways than one.

After the advent of the Second Sino-Japanese War in the summer of 1937, military-medical authorities in Japan systematically concealed cases of war neurosis from the general population. The Imperial Japanese Army, which called itself *kōgun* (the Emperor's Army), declared that it was superior to any of the other foreign armies. Against the background of imperial ideology, the military leadership regarded war neurosis in combatants as a form of moral corruption and a degeneration of the national spirit. During the war, even the officials at the

Medical Bureau of the Japanese Army and medical officers at Kōnodai Military Hospital felt the need to publicly deny the existence of war neurosis among the troops.

On 5 April 1939, about two years after the war with China began, an article ran in *Yomiuri Shimbun*. It was declaratively titled "Kōgun ni hōdan byō nashi" (There is no shell shock in the Emperor's Army).[31] The headline was based on the conclusion of clinical research conducted by the medical officer Hayao Torao, who had investigated mental illnesses among the Japanese Army on the battlefield in China. In the article, Hayao reported some cases that might appear on first blush to be shell shock that had in fact revealed previous histories of mental illness before enlistment or were complicated by malaria or head injuries; he never found a single case caused directly or solely by fear of war, Hayao maintained.

Four years later, after war with the United States and Great Britain had commenced, the same newspaper reported that many American soldiers had collapsed from neurasthenia during the battle on Guadalcanal Island.[32] Moreover, in the war years, the directors of both the Kōnodai Military Hospital and the Musashi Military Sanatorium constantly emphasized the mental superiority of the Emperor's Army.[33] These official, publicly expressed opinions were clearly affected by the exigencies of war.

At times, the Emperor's Army demonstrated outright disregard for the lives of its own personnel. The "Imperial Rescript to Soldiers and Sailors" (*Gunjin Chokuyu*, 1882) was an edict that instructed soldiers to die for the emperor and the country. In the same nationalistic spirit, "The Instructions for the Battlefield" (*Senjinkun*, 1941) taught soldiers that becoming a prisoner of war, under any circumstances, was shameful conduct.

Consider the story of a private first class, born as a peasant in 1917, who was dispatched to China in 1938 and who fought in several battles there. According to case records, in February 1940 the private began to develop symptoms of acute nervousness. He became forgetful, would walk around in a daze, and had many disturbing dreams. He also experienced auditory hallucinations in the form of the repetitive sound of a door opening and closing, as if it were the sound of a bullet. The man had witnessed several of his fellow soldiers get killed in battle, and his company commander admonished him for not dying as well. The man blamed himself for the deaths of his comrades and suffered from suicidal thoughts. A month later, he ran away from the barracks several times because it made him feel better to be away from the other soldiers. However, each time he was located and brought back to the barracks. Eventually the private was transported from China to Tokyo, where on 7 February 1940, he was admitted to the Kōnodai Military Hospital.[34] This example illustrates poignantly how the high internalized pressure that Japanese soldiers die for their country intensified soldiers' guilt about surviving. Even Japanese civilians on the home front at times expected soldiers to die for their country. Soldiers who instead faltered psychologically under the excruciating pressures—whose wounds were invisible—were despised by society much more than those who survived but were physically injured.

This judgmental attitude explains why so many soldier-patients diagnosed with war neurosis were ashamed and called themselves *kokuzoku* (traitors). Another private first class from a rural background became neurasthenic during the Manchurian invasion early in 1937. In the initial clinical interview, the soldier told his doctor at the Kōnodai Military Hospital that "I am ashamed of myself to have such an illness. I should have thrown myself into the ocean on the way back to the homeland. Please do not allow any visitors from my hometown because I can't make excuses to them."[35]

Over the course of the Asia-Pacific War, hysteria also became racialized by non-military psychiatrists. In 1931, the year when Japan invaded northeastern China, known as Manchuria, the prominent psychiatrist and eugenicist Sugita Naoki (1887–1949) had warned the nation that in any future battle "degenerate hysterical patients" would bring discredit upon the nation. According to Sugita, Japanese women, for the strength of the nation, were brought up not to express their emotions because by nature women tended to be much more sensitive and emotional than men. As a result of such training, he claimed, women in Japan were less liable to becoming hysterical in the face of adversity than their Western counterparts, who, he imagined, were encouraged to express their emotions extravagantly. However, Sugita continued, "[a]s the ways of living of Japanese women were westernized, it seems people of hysterical disposition are increasing." He went on to criticize feminists and women who were not chaste in their personal lives as examples of these pernicious foreign influences.[36]

At the same time, Sugita was confident that the incidence of war neurosis in the Emperor's Army remained much less frequent than in Western armies during World War I. Sugita's belief was based not on comparative clinical data but rather on the blanket assumption that the "Japanese train for battles harder than people in any other countries from childhood." According to Sugita, Japanese males were introduced to many war stories and played war games from early childhood, which was "proof of being a genuine Japanese man"—an example of bravery and assertiveness as well as evidence of the indomitable "*samurai* spirit."[37] Later he argued that by nature the people of Japan had a strong fighting instinct *yamato damashii* (Japanese spirit). In contrast, he averred, the Chinese lacked such a noble fighting instinct.[38] Sugita also boasted that the Imperial Japanese Army did not need to learn the lessons of Western military psychiatry because Japanese soldiers, due to their *yamato damashii*, simply were not afraid of the enemy's bullets.[39]

During World War II, the Japanese medical profession also observed and commented on neurotic symptoms in civilian women. It is noteworthy that during the war, *yamato minzoku no yūshūsei* (Japanese racial superiority), rather than considerations of gender, was emphasized in Japanese medical discourse. The importance of this dichotomy is best expressed by Shikiba Ryūzaburō (1898–1965), a Tokyo-based psychiatrist, when writing about Japanese women in his 1937 article "Sensō to hisuterī" (War and hysteria): "There are more hysterical women in the Western countries than in Japan. You Japanese women can be proud of that. Japanese women don't become hysterical because they have long trained and have strong nerves."[40] At the same time, Shikiba warned women that they were "easily moved to emotion," so he encouraged them, especially in the current wartime environment, to be tough: "Now, it is the critical moment for our country. We need women's power in times like this. Women are prone to be moved because they are more emotional than men.... Fortunately, there are fewer patients of real hysteria in Japan, but every woman has hysteric symptoms. Don't make the symptom worse."[41] As a result of the heightened feminizing and racializing of male nervous disorders during the war years of 1937–1945, rank-and-file soldiers in Japan who could not control their fear and who broke down emotionally and required medical attention tended to be stereotyped, stigmatized, and "othered." An example of this denigration can be found in a pamphlet written by the office of the Inspectorate General of Military Training: "If the elite Japanese servicemen in their prime cannot fight bravely," the pamphlet stated categorically, "they are inferior to Chinese child soldiers and girl students. That will be a shame to them forever."[42]

The Feminization of Hysterical Soldiers

Although officials at the Medical Bureau of the Japanese Army, including army psychiatrists, denied the existence of hysterical disorders in soldiers, the rate of patients diagnosed with hysteria at Kōnodai Military Hospital during the war was in fact "considerably high." Of the total number of 10,453 patients admitted at the hospital during the war, war neuroses accounted for about 20 percent. Specifically, 1,199 soldiers were diagnosed with hysteria, and 739 were diagnosed with neurasthenia.[43]

At the end of the war, the Japanese military ordered all public institutions to incinerate official war documents, including the clinical records of military hospitals. Suwa Keizaburō, the director of Kōnodai Military Hospital, instead concealed and protected the clinical records at the hospital because they were filled with medically valuable information. As a fortunate consequence, approximately 80 percent of the records have survived. Asai Toshio, who was a medical officer at the hospital, printed, analyzed, and archived these records from the 1980s to the 1990s.[44] Shimizu Hiroshi and his colleagues have conducted historical research into these records since the 1990s and reprinted the records of 486 patients diagnosed with mental retardation, 816 servicemen diagnosed with hysteria, and

353 servicemen diagnosed with neurasthenia. What follows is an examination of several of these case records.[45]

During the war, Hosokoshi Masakazu worked at the Kōnodai Military Hospital as a young medical officer. Decades later, he recollected that the patients categorized with *hisuterī* (hysteria) and *noirōze* (neurosis) were despised and regarded almost as if they were guilty of treason.[46] In addition to the feminizing implications of the diagnosis, hysterical patients were regarded as being self-centered and emotionally immature. Moreover, after the war ended and social solidarity among the people became a more urgent issue, hysteria was increasingly denounced as an illness associated negatively with *seiyō no kojin shugi* (Western individualism). In short, soldiers prone to nervous illness at the time of the national emergency were effectively disqualified both as brave servants of the nation and respectable men.

As a consequence, some soldier-patients were extremely anxious about being so diagnosed. A twenty-two-year-old private second class from the countryside became highly agitated in Manchuria and was admitted to the Kōnodai Military Hospital on 11 September 1940. He confided to the doctor that "[b]efore I came here, a military policeman asked me about the name of my illness, and I answered it was hysteria. He was sorry to hear that, and he said he would see to it that I could receive a war disablement's pension."[47] Nevertheless, the patient did not receive a war disablement's pension in the end. The case file of another private diagnosed with hysteria recounts: "The patient said he could go back home and work in his present physical condition, but he worried that he couldn't be hired by large companies because of his illness. . . . He said he wanted to go home early because his family had difficulty in making a living."[48] Before the war's outbreak, many of these men had been the primary source of income for their family; they were therefore very concerned for the livelihoods of their loved ones back at home. As a result, hysterical patients were fretful about local knowledge of their illnesses; if they became stigmatized in their village or town, how would they secure re-employment?

Possibly because of this concern, medical officers at Kōnodai Military Hospital often replaced the word hysteria with the term *zōsōbyō* as a formal diagnosis. In an article titled "Senji shinkeishō no seishinbyōgakuteki kousatsu daiippen" (Psychiatric analysis of neurosis in wartime, Part 1) in 1941, Sakurai Tonao (1907–1988), a medical officer at Kōnodai Military Hospital, reported that "[h]ysteria is commonly a misleading disease name and has a bad influence on the patients and people around them."[49] For the patient's long-term well-being (and perhaps also for the economic advantage of the nation), medical officers thus quietly preferred the term *zōsōbyō*, which was a compound word consisting of *zōsō* and *byō*. *Zōsō* is a translation of the word hysteria derived from traditional Chinese medicine as stated above, and *byō* in Japanese means simply "illness."

What has to be noted here is that zōsōbyō was far less commonly used than hysteria. Table 2.1 presents the number of articles using *hysteria* or *zōsōbyō* in two major Japanese newspapers, *Yomiuri Shimbun* and *Asahi Shimbun*, that were

TABLE 2.1. The number of newspaper articles using hysteria / *zōsōbyō*.

	Yomiuri Shimbun (1874–1945)	*Asahi Shimbun* (1879–1945)
hysteria:	234	455
zōsōbyō:	0	1

Source of data: online article database of *Yomiuri Shimbun* (https://database.yomiuri.co.jp/rekishi kan/) and *Asahi Shimbun* (https://database.asahi.com/index.shtml). Both accessed on 21 Dec. 2020/

published from the latter half of the nineteenth century to the end of the Asia-Pacific War, which I determined by searching online databases of these newspapers. As this tabulation indicates, unlike hysteria, *zōsōbyō* was almost never used in popular discourse. After the Second Sino-Japanese War broke out, and as the number of such cases multiplied, medical officers at the nation's leading hospital for wartime nervous and psychiatric disorders at times sought to lessen the stigma for hysterical soldier-patients.[50]

Both diagnostic rubrics, however, were class-biased. Table 2.2 below reveals that 816 patients at the Kōnodai Military Hospital were categorized as suffering from war neurosis with hysterical symptoms. Out of these 816 patients, 549 were diagnosed with *zōsōbyō* and 49 with hysteria, whereas the remainder of patients were given other diagnostic labels, such as "dissociative reaction" and "psychogenic reaction." In addition, many of the afflicted men had their diagnoses modified over time from hysteria to *zōsōbyō*. Interestingly, at the time of their final discharge from the hospital, only ten of these patients were still assigned the dishonoring diagnosis of hysteria.

If we organize the figures based on patients' military rank, the diagnostic picture changes further: although 5.3 percent of patients who manifested hysterical symptoms were officers, none of these officers were diagnosed with hysteria, and only 0.5 percent of them were diagnosed with *zōsōbyō*. Both hysteria and *zōsōbyō* were terms likelier to be used as the military rank of the patients decreased and was thus rarely employed for officers. This pattern dovetails with the findings of historians of shell shock in Britain during and after World War I.[51]

In a prewar psychiatric textbook written by Shimoda Mitsuzō and Sugita Naoki, two renowned Japanese psychiatrists, hysteria was categorized as a degenerative psychosis. According to Shimoda and Sugita's book, when people with a "hysterical abnormal personality" (*hisuterī sei ijyō jinkaku*)—that is, a "psychotic character based on inherent degeneration"—are stricken by a psychological breakdown, they also become hysterical.[52] Medical officers at the Kōnodai Military Hospital also often attributed stereotypically feminine "personality" and "character" features to their hysterical patients in their clinical certificates. Out of 638 records, 221 indicated a patient having "changeable emotion," 93 indicated

TABLE 2.2. The number of hysterical patients at Kōnodai Military Hospital by diagnosis and military rank.

	Officer	NCOs	Soldier	Total
hysteria	0 (0%)	1 (2%)	48 (98.0%)	49
zōsōbyō	3 (0.5%)	8 (1.5%)	538 (98.0%)	549
patients with hysterical symptoms	43 (5.3%)	21 (2.6%)	752 (92.2%)	816

"sensitive emotions," 60 indicated "weak will," and 49 indicated that a patient was "suggestible." At times, medical authorities explicitly described patients as being "girlish" or "childish." In a few instances, they even described bodily sensations in the male patient such "pain of breasts" and "pain of ovaries." The idea that "pseudo-ovarian" features occasionally manifested on the bodies of male hysterical patients was a colorful throwback to the Charcotian model of hysteria in the 1880s and 1890s.[53]

Japanese medical authorities during the war also utilized these negative images in treatment. A twenty-five-year-old warrant officer fell ill in August 1943. His file indicates that he had become panicky, delirious, and emotionally volatile. Upon further examination at the 109th Japanese base hospital in Indonesia, the man was also diagnosed with aphasia, a diagnosis that the doctors modified to hysteria in May 1944. After being admitted to the Kōnodai Military Hospital in September 1944, the patient was again re-diagnosed, this time with an unspecified neurological disorder after contracting malaria, a diagnosis that exempted him from military service.[54] At the Kōnodai Military Hospital, the patient received local electrotherapy for his speaking difficulties. According to Sakurai Tonao, who was a medical officer at Kōnodai Military Hospital, the purpose of treatment for war neurosis was to get rid of the patient's desire both for a pension and to return home. For this purpose, Sakurai recommended "coercive" treatment like ECT, cardiazol convulsion treatment, and transfer to a room for psychotic patients.[55] Here is an exchange between the patient and the doctor administering the treatment before the first electrotherapeutic session. The medical officer's military rank was higher than that of the patient, and the physician spoke in a rather arrogant manner. That was because medical officers at Kōnodai thought keeping a strict hierarchy between doctors and patients was especially important for the treatment of war neurosis.[56]

Q: What do you think of your illness?
A: Hysteria.

Q: Is there any hysteria in the Japanese army?
A: No, sir.
Q: Who becomes hysterical, men or women?
A: Women.
Q: Why do women become hysterical?
A: I don't know.
Q: Do you want to cure your illness?
A: Yes, sir.
Q: Are you ready to cure your illness at any costs?
A: Yes, sir.
Q: Ok, I will cure you today.
A: I'm happy, sir.[57]

These leading questions from the attending physician caused the patient to blame himself for his situation because he suffered from an illness that soldiers in the Japanese army, and men in general, were not supposed to experience. After their brief conversation, the electrical current session lasted for two-and-a-half hours, at which time the patient had regained a slight ability to speak again. He finally managed to utter a sound, and the doctor was apparently satisfied. In the final medical report, there is no mention of hysterical symptoms, perhaps because the patient was beginning to improve, had endured the treatment, and passed a test of manliness.[58]

As was the case in Britain during World War I, neurasthenia in the Japanese military context was a less derogatory diagnosis than hysteria. Table 2.3 represents the number of patients who were diagnosed with neurasthenia by their military rank. Throughout the war, 353 patients were diagnosed with neurasthenia at the Kōnodai Military Hospital. Of these 353 patients, 45 were officers, 37 were non-commissioned officers (NCOs), and 271 were rank-and-file soldiers. Generally, 5 percent of personnel of the Imperial Japanese Army were officers, 15 percent were non-commissioned officers, and 80 percent were soldiers.[59] Not unexpectedly, then, soldiers accounted for the majority of patients diagnosed with neurasthenia at the Kōnodai Military Hospital. Most noteworthy, however, is that the percentage of officers diagnosed with neurasthenia is higher than the percentage of officers in the military hierarchy.

Moreover, neurasthenia, it seems, was used as a means of avoiding, or at least lessening, the stigma implied by nervous illness in the case of patients who in their prewar lives were "respectable men." The New York nerve doctor George Miller Beard had published *American Nervousness* back in 1881; by the end of the nineteenth century, Japanese doctors were familiar with the neurasthenia concept as a diagnosis attributed to civilization, urbanization, and modernity. Although in 1930s Japan, the rubric came to be applied to men of all classes,[60] and although some psychiatrists were concerned with the "abuse" of a diagnosis that incorporated so many general symptoms (including fatigue, headache, aches and

TABLE 2.3. The number of patients with neurasthenia at Kōnodai Military Hospital by military rank.

officer	NCOs	soldier	total
45 (12.7%)	37 (10.5%)	271 (76.8%)	353

pains, anxiety, and depression),[61] neurasthenia during the war retained its association with an educated high-class sector of society. Some officers were diagnosed with neurasthenia even if they displayed blatantly "hysterical characteristics." The clinical record of a first lieutenant, an office worker who became incapacitated in 1942 while working in Manchuria, indicates this tendency: "He is controlled by emotion, and says he has gastroenteritis because he has been sick in bed for a year. He thinks he suffers from a severe illness. I think he is controlled by his hysterical characteristics."[62] Likewise, other army officers who suffered more serious psychiatric problems were also diagnosed with neurasthenia in order to save face and preserve their future career prospects. In 1941, for example, a thirty-eight-year-old surgeon became gloomy and depressed after his sister passed. The man developed headaches, anemia, difficulties sleeping, and loss of appetite; twice he tried to kill himself. Although suspected of schizophrenia, the lieutenant received the official diagnosis of neurasthenia at Kōnodai Military Hospital because of "his future prospect as an army surgeon."[63] To similar ends, in 1941 a major in the army required hospitalization in Manchuria and then later Tokyo. His case file reads "it is better for him to modify his diagnosis from schizophrenia to neurasthenia rather than exclude him as a lunatic."[64]

Conclusion

The rigorous male-exclusive conscription program and training regime that prevailed in Japan during the 1930s and 1940s aimed to establish and instill specific ideals of modern warrior manliness into the male population of modern Japan. The Imperial Japanese Army defined national manhood as the state of being strong, brave, and healthy enough to be an effective fighting soldier. The imperial model of masculinity characterized any man who failed the conscription exam or who was unable to handle the stresses and strains of military training as lacking, contemptible, and unmanly.

As an official, government-sanctioned construction, however, Japanese imperial codes of masculinity were inherently unstable and perpetually in need of maintenance. Even in light of these high standards of performance, the horrors and intensities of modern industrialized warfare revealed the vulnerability of men's bodies and minds. It therefore became necessary to formulate a set of official explanations and interpretations of war-induced nervous and mental breakdown among the Emperor's troops: these readings of war neurosis allowed the medical profession to acknowledge the existence of soldiers who required hospitalization while also protecting the honor and heroism of the Empire's fighting force.

After the Second Sino-Japanese War broke out in 1937, both military and civilian psychiatrists asserted the superior mental stamina of the Emperor's Army. They denied the possibility of war neuroses among the national armed forces while simultaneously condemning it. In doing so, the military authorities in Japan sought to differentiate their fighting forces from the shell-shocked soldiers of the West in the 1914–18 war. As a strategy for doing so, they racialized war hysteria and asserted that the enemy's forces were rife with nervous breakdowns and madness. Characteristically, they deemed women in Japan to be more susceptible than men to psychiatric sickness, but nevertheless stronger mentally than Western women for racial-genetic reasons.

Even in time of war, however, racializing, or Westernizing, hysteria was a gesture not without problems. In his book *War Without Mercy*, the historian John Dower has perceptively pointed out that, whereas insulting other categories of people has been a distinguishing feature of racism in Western history, the Japanese have traditionally been eager instead to elevate their own collective value. Accordingly, Japanese government documents repeatedly discouraged the habit of characterizing the war in progress as a "war between the white race and colored race" because such view contradicted the Tripartite Pact of 1940 among Japan, Germany, and Italy.[65] Such racialization was therefore more common during the war against China, in the late 1930s, than the war against the United States and British Empire in the first half of the 1940s.

Nonetheless, Japanese military authorities, for urgent practical purposes, needed to manage their wartime "human resources." As the military situation worsened, these manpower sources included nervously debilitated soldiers who could still perform certain non-combatant duties and who therefore the command sought to distinguish from "lunatics." To that end, medical officers substituted *zōsōbyō* for hysteria in order to avoid diminishing military authority. As in certain Western countries, soldiers who fell prey to "the hysterization of the male body" were overwhelmingly those with a low military rank and a humble, often peasant, class background. Conversely, Japanese physicians tended to apply the face-saving diagnosis of neurasthenia to officers whose social, military, and educational status were higher than the common soldier and in fact whose status in society approximated that of the diagnosing physician. In doing so, the military establishment protected the personal respectability and professional prospects of those victims of the war who were also viewed as more essential for the war effort and the postwar national economy.

Eri Nakamura is associate professor at Hiroshima University, Japan. Her main fields of research include Japanese modern history, the social history of war and medicine, and masculinity and militarism in modern Japan. She is the author of a Japanese monograph entitled *Sensō to torauma: Fukashika sareta nihon'hei no sensō shinkeishō* [War and trauma: Invisible war neurosis within the Imperial Japanese Army] (Tokyo: Yoshikawa Kōbunkan 2018), which examines how Japanese soldiers afflicted with psychological injuries were treated during the Asia-Pacific War and why postwar Japanese society has lacked collective memory of them.

Notes

1. Showalter, *Female Malady*.
2. Mosse, "Shell-Shock as a Social Disease," 103–4.
3. Lerner, *Hysterical Men*.
4. Micale, *Hysterical Men*.
5. Algoso, "Not Suitable as a Man?," 196.
6. Uchida, *Dai nihon teikoku no shōnen to danseisei*.
7. Ōe, *Ten'nō no guntai*, 67.
8. In this chapter, Japanese names are written in accordance with Japanese convention in putting family names first followed by the given name. All translations are my own.
9. Inoue, *Kokumin dōtoku*, 4–5, 7–8.
10. *Kanpō*, 25 March 1931, 631–32.
11. Ijichi, *Kasen ni chiru*, 152.
12. Shimozawa, *Jikken nihongun shinri*, 222.
13. Fujiwara, *Ten'nō no guntai to nicchū sensō*.
14. Yoshida, "Senjyō to heishi," 62–64.
15. Shimizu, *Shiryoushū*, vol. 2, 233–34.
16. Suwa, "Gaikyō," 17.
17. Kure, "Hisuterīkyō wo zōsōkyō to yakusubeshi."
18. Satō, *Seishin shikkan gensetsu*, 186.
19. Funakoshi, "Hisuterī."
20. Charcot, *Sharukō hakase shinkeibyō rinshou kougi*, 12–32, 83–84.
21. Iijima, "Guntai ni okeru hisuterī ni tsuite."
22. Iijima wrote hysteria in German since modern Japanese medicine was strongly influenced by German medicine, and physicians often used German words and phrases in their papers and clinical records. The Germanization of Japanese psychiatry was almost complete by the beginning of the twentieth century. See Hashimoto, "A 'German World' Shared among Doctors," 182.
23. Iijima, "Guntai ni okeru hisuterī," 41.
24. Iijima, "Guntai ni okeru hisuterī," 42.
25. Micale, *Hysterical Men*, 129.
26. Micale, *Hysterical Men*, 201.
27. Hosokoshi, "Sensō hisuterī no kenkyū."
28. Hosokoshi, "Sensō hisuterī no kenkyū," 4.
29. Usa, *Seishinbyō no kangohō*, 116–17.
30. Usa, *Seishinbyō no kangohō*, 118.
31. *Yomiuri Shimbun*, 5 April 1939.
32. *Yomiuri Shimbun*, 1 July 1943.
33. Suwa, "Sensō to seisinbyō," 148; Sekine, "Sensō to seishinbyō," 7.

34. Hosobuchi and Shimizu, *Shiryō shūsei*, vol. 1, 340–44.
35. Hosobuchi and Shimizu, *Shiryō shūsei*, vol. 1, 24–25.
36. Sugita, *Kindai bunka to sei seikatsu*, 506, 10–12.
37. Sugita, "Sensō to seishinbyō," 80–81.
38. Sugita, "Sensō wo meguru seishinbyō," 183.
39. Sugita, "Sensō to seishinbyō," 80–81.
40. Shikiba, "Sensō to hisuterī," 167.
41. Shikiba, "Sensō to hisuterī," 169–70.
42. Kyōiku Sōkanbu, *Senjyō shinri*, 39.
43. Suwa, "Gaikyō," 17–18.
44. Asai, *Uzumoreta taisen no giseisha*.
45. See Shimizu, *Shiryoushū*; Hosobuchi and Shimizu, *Shiryō shūsei*. Private information on patients and their families, such as name, address, date of birth, and unit name, is concealed in these reprinted records.
46. Hosokoshi, "Zoku gaigo naika kaikoroku," 59.
47. Shimizu, *Shiryoushū*, vol. 5, 267–68.
48. Shimizu, *Shiryoushū*, vol. 5, 273.
49. Sakurai, "Kousatsu daiippen," 1,658.
50. Nakamura, *Sensō to torauma*, 77.
51. Showalter, *Female Malady*; Barker, *Regeneration*; Leese, *Shell Shock*.
52. Shimoda and Sugita, *Saishin seishin byōgaku*, 412.
53. Micale, *Hysterical Men*, 155–61.
54. Shimizu, *Shiryoushū*, vol.7, 80–81.
55. Sakurai, "Kousatsu dainihen," 36–38; Sakurai, "Kousatsu daisanpen," 976–77.
56. See Nakamura, *Sensō to Torauma*, 155. In conversations between patients and medical officers, patients usually used honorific expressions, while medical officers spoke in an authoritative and sometimes coercive manner.
57. Shimizu, *Shiryoushū*, vol.7, 81–82.
58. Showalter, *Female Malady*, Showalter, "Rivers and Sassoon," Barker, *Regeneration*, Linden, Jones, and Lees, "Shell Shock at Queen Square."
59. For example, in the case of a unit disposed at Woleai Atoll in the Pacific Ocean, out of 3,205 patients, there were 188 officers (5.9 percent), 39 warrant officers (1.2 percent), 515 NCOs (16.1 percent), and 2,463 soldiers (76.8 percent). See Fujiwara, *Uejini Shita Eirei Tachi*.
60. Satō, *Seishin Shikkan Gensetsu*, 307–17.
61. Kitanaka, "'Shinkei Suijyaku' Seisuishi," 159–61.
62. Hosobuchi and Shimizu, *Shiryō Shūsei*, vol. 1, 320.
63. Hosobuchi and Shimizu, *Shiryō Shūsei*, vol. 2, 275–76.
64. Hosobuchi and Shimizu, *Shiryō Shūsei*, vol. 2, 102.
65. Dower, *War without Mercy*.

Bibliography

Algoso, Teresa A. "Not Suitable as a Man?: Conscription, Masculinity, and Hermaphroditism in Early Twentieth-Century Japan." In *Recreating Japanese Men*, edited by Sabine Frühstück and Anne Walthall, 190–205. Berkeley: University of California Press, 2011.

Asai, Toshio, ed. *Uzumoreta taisen no giseisha: Kōnodai rikugun byōin seishin'ka no kicyōna byōreki to shiryō* [Unrecognized victims of the Second World War: Valuable clinical records of the Department of Psychiatry of Kōnodai Military Hospital and analysis of them]. Tōgane: Kōnodai Rikugun Byōin seishin-ka byoureki bunseki shiryōbunken ronshū kinen kankou iinkai, 1993.

Barker, Pat. *Regeneration*. London: Penguin, 1992.

Charcot, Jean-Martin. *Sharukō hakase shinkeibyō rinshou kougi zenpen gekan* [Dr. Charcot's clinical lectures on certain diseases of the nervous system, vol. 1, part 2]. Translated by Satō Tsunemaru. Tokyo: Iji Shinshi-kyoku, 1907.

Dower, John W. *War without Mercy: Race and Power in the Pacific War*. New York: Pantheon, 1986.

Fujiwara, Akira. *Ten'nō no guntai to nicchū sensō* [The Emperor's Army and the Second Sino-Japanese War]. Tokyo: Otsuki Shoten, 2006.

———. *Uejini shita eirei tachi* [Spirits of soldiers who died of starvation]. Tokyo: Aoki Shoten, 2001.

Funakoshi, Mikio. "Hisuterī: Media no naka no yamai" [Hysteria: Representation of illness in media]. In *Henken to iu manazashi*, edited by Hideto Tsuboi. Tokyo: Seikyūsha, 2001.

Hashimoto, Akira. "A 'German World' Shared among Doctors: A History of the Relationship between German and Japanese Psychiatry before World War II." *History of Psychiatry* 24, no. 2 (2013): 180–95.

Hosobuchi, Tomio, and Hiroshi Shimizu, eds. *Shiryō shūsei seishin shougai heishi byōshō nisshi* [Collection of clinical records of soldiers with mental disability]. 2 vols. Tokyo: Rikka Shuppan, 2016–2017.

Hosokoshi, Masakazu. "Sensō hisuterī no kenkyū" [Research on war hysteria]. Ph.D. dissertation. Sapporo: Hokkaido University, 1948.

———. "Zoku daigo naika kaikoroku" [Memoirs about the days at the 5th medical ward, part 2]. In *Daitōa Sensō Rikugun Eisei-Shi, Vol. 6*, edited by Friendly Association of the Japan Ground Self-Defense Force Medical School, 58–59. Tokyo: JGSDF Medical School, 1968.

Iijima, Shigeru. "Guntai ni okeru hisuterī ni tsuite" [About hysteria in the military]. *Shinkeigaku zasshi* 15, no. 1 (1916): 40–45.

Ijichi, Susumu. *Kcasen ni chiru* [Fall in battle]. Tokyo: Kin'eikaku, 1932.

Inoue, Tetsujirō. *Kokumin dōtoku* [National morality]. Kyoto: Ryūbunkan, 1911.

Kanpō [Stenographic record of the proceedings of the House of Peers, 59th Imperial Diet, No. 38.] Retrieved on 21 December 2020 from https://teikokugikai-i.ndl.go.jp/#/detailPDF?minId=005903242X03819310324&page=8&spkNum=20&current=71.

Kitanaka, Junko. "'Shinkei suijyaku' seisuishi [The rise and fall of 'neurasthenia' in modern Japan]." *Eureka* 36, no.5 (2004): 150–67.

Kure, Shūzō. "Hisuterī wo zōsō to yakushi hisuterīkyō wo zōsōkyō to yakusubeshi" [We should translate hysteria into *zōsō* and hysterical insanity into *zōsōkyō*]. *Chūgai iji shimpō* 289, no. 40 (1892): 16–18.

Kyōiku Sōkanbu ed. *Senjyō shinri to seishin kyōiku* [War psychology and spiritual education]. n.p.: n.p., 1938.

Leese, Peter. *Shell Shock: Traumatic Neurosis and the British Soldiers of the First World War*. New York: Palgrave Macmillan, 2002.

Lerner, Paul. *Hysterical Men: War, Psychiatry, and the Politics of Trauma in Germany, 1890–1930*. Ithaca, NY: Cornell University Press, 2003.

Linden, Stefanie C., Edgar Jones, and Andrew J. Lees. "Shell Shock at Queen Square: Lewis Yealland 100 Years On." *Brain* 136, no. 6 (2013): 1,976–88.

Micale, Mark S. *Hysterical Men: The Hidden History of Male Nervous Illness*. Cambridge MA: Harvard University Press, 2008.

Mosse, George L. "Shell-Shock as a Social Disease." *Journal of Contemporary History* 35, no. 1 (2000): 101–8.
Nakamura, Eri. *Sensō to torauma: Fukashika sareta nihon'hei no sensō shinkeishō* [War and trauma: Invisible war neurosis in the Imperial Japanese Army]. Tokyo: Yoshikawa Kōbunkan, 2018.
Ōe, Shinobu. *Ten'nō no guntai* [The Emperor's Army]. Tokyo: Shōgakukan, 1982.
Sakurai, Tonao. "Senji shinkeishō no seishinbyōgakuteki kousatsu daiippen: Senji shinkeishō no gaisetsu" [Psychiatric analysis of neurosis in wartime, part 1: The outline of neurosis in wartime]. *Gun'i-dan zasshi*, no. 343 (1941): 1,653–67.
———. "Senji shinkeishō no seishinbyōgakuteki kousatsu dainihen: Senji shinkeishō no shori, sono ni" [Psychiatric analysis of neurosis in wartime, part 3: Treatment of neurosis in wartime, no. 2]. *Gun'i-dan zasshi*, no. 344 (1942): 35–42.
———. "Senji shinkeishō no seishinbyōgakuteki kousatsu daisanpen: Senji shinkeishō no shori (sono-ni)" [Psychiatric analysis of neurosis in wartime, part 3: Treatment of neurosis in wartime, no. 2]. *Gun'i-dan zasshi*, no. 350 (1942): 975–985.
Satō, Masahiro. *Seishin shikkan gensetsu no rekishi shakaigaku* [Historical sociology of discourse of mental illness]. Tokyo: Shinyō-sha, 2013.
Sekine, Shin'ichi. "Sensō to seishinbyō" [War and mental illness]. *Iji kōron*, no. 1536 (1942): 7–9.
Shikiba, Ryūzaburō. "Sensō to hisuterī" [War and hysteria]. *Fujin kurabu* 18, no. 4 (1937): 166–70.
Shimizu, Hiroshi, ed. *Jyūgonen sensō gokuhi shiryoushū, Hokan 28* [Collection of classified documents during the Asia-Pacific War, Supplement 28], Vols. 1–2, 5–7. Tokyo: Fujishuppan, 2007–2008.
Shimoda, Mitsuzō, and Sugita Naoki. *Saishin seishin byōgaku* [Contemporary psychiatry]. Tokyo: Kokuseido Shoten, 1922.
Shimozawa, Zuisei. *Jikken nihongun shinri* [Experiment in the psychology of the Japanese army]. Tokyo: Bukyō Kyōkai, 1913.
Showalter, Elaine. *The Female Malady: Women, Madness, and English Culture, 1830–1980*. New York: Pantheon, 1985.
———. "Rivers and Sassoon: The Inscription of Male Gender Anxieties." In *Behind the Lines: Gender and the Two World Wars*, edited by Margaret Randolph Higonnet, Jane Jenson, Sonya Michel and Margaret Collins Weitz, 61–69. New Haven, CT: Yale University Press, 1987.
Sugita, Naoki. *Kindai bunka to sei seikatsu* [Modern life and sex life]. Tokyo: Bukyōsha, 1931.
———. "Sensō to seishinbyō" [War and mental illness]. *Kakushin* 2, no. 2 (1939): 77–84.
———. "Sensō wo meguru seishinbyō" [Mental illness relating to war]." In *Oto: Kagaku Zuihitsu*, edited by Horikawa Toyonaga, 178–90. Tokyo: Jinbunkaku, 1942.
Suwa, Keizaburō. "Konji sensō ni okeru seishin shikkan no gaikyō" [Overview of mental illness in the last war]. *Iryō* 1, no. 4 (1948): 17–20.
———. "Sensō to seisinbyō" [War and mental illness]. *Bungei shunjyū special issue* 17, no. 14 (1939): 144–48.
Uchida, Masakatsu. *Dai nihon teikoku no shōnen to danseisei* [Boys of the Japanese Empire and manliness]. Tokyo: Akashi Shoten, 2010.
Usa, Shizuo. *Seishinbyō no kangohō* [How to nurse mental illnesses]. Kyoto: Jinbun Shoin, 1941.
Yoshida, Yutaka. "Ajia taiheiyō sensō no senjyō to heishi" [The battlefield and soldiers during the Asia-Pacific War]. In *Iwanami kōza ajia taiheiyō sensō, Vol. 5*, edited by Aiko Kurasawa, Tōru Sugihara, Ryūichi Narita, Tessa Morris-Suzuki, Daizaburō Yui, and Yutaka Yoshida, 59–86. Tokyo: Iwanami Shoten, 2005.

Chapter 3

ATOMIC TRAUMA

Japanese Psychiatry in Hiroshima and Nagasaki

Ran Zwigenberg

In February 1946, the *New York Times* reported from Hiroshima that "[medical] officers of the twenty-fourth division now turning over the garrison to arriving British empire troops [discussed] whether the inhabitants of this city have also undergone freakish psychological effects differentiating them from other Japanese."[1] This was not a subject of mere curiosity on behalf of the departing troops. The A-bomb was supposed to produce, according to the target committee that selected Hiroshima, "the greatest psychological effect against Japan."[2] In 1945–46, the United States Strategic Bombing Survey (USSBS) conducted extensive surveys to determine such effects and the ways the bombings impacted morale. This research was only the beginning of efforts by psychiatrists, psychologists, and social scientists to investigate the complex ways minds were affected by the advent of the nuclear age. Such efforts, which I have examined elsewhere, ranged from debates over the problem of human aggression to research into the trauma, panic, anxiety, and other psychological effects of the bomb. In the United States, such research was in line with US military psychiatrists' interest in and handling of battlefield psychological trauma, and it led to the early understanding of the A-bomb as largely a psychological weapon of "mass terror."[3] US psychiatrists, who worked on the subject with nuclear and civil defense research bodies, sought to investigate the bombings of Hiroshima and Nagasaki to demonstrate the ability of civil defense medical personnel to deal adequately with psychological trauma and to keep morale high. The USSBS's findings were central to a new domestic civil defense effort in the United States to teach Americans how to deal with a possible nuclear attack. This was done in the context of broader efforts by psychiatrists and psychologists to harness the psychological sciences in the service of society, or, as the first director-general of the World Health Organization, G. Brock Chisholm, put it, of "healing a sick world."[4]

In Japan, no such body of research was allowed to develop, as hardly any public discussion of nuclear anxiety, civil defense, or even the medical consequences of the bomb were permitted under the occupation. US censorship authorities in Japan actively suppressed research on and discussion of the possible impact of nuclear warfare.[5] The American Atomic Bomb Casualty Commission (ABCC), which was established in Hiroshima and Nagasaki as a permanent research facility to ascertain the A-bomb's medical effects, the US military, and the Atomic Energy Commission (AEC) were quite resistant to admitting the existence of long-term damage, physical or otherwise. This suppression of research was, tragically, also supported by most Japanese psychiatrists, who were not sympathetic to the idea of long-term trauma. As a consequence, there is a peculiar yet telling gap within this body of psychological and psychiatric research—the actual survivors of the bombing of Hiroshima and Nagasaki were hardly studied by Japanese, American, or any other group of researchers. Following the initial studies by the USSBS, only a handful of researchers worked on the long-term psychological impact of the bomb on its survivors. It was not until the mid-1960s with the work of Robert J. Lifton that the first research on survivors was conducted. Even then, it took another three decades, following the Kobe earthquake, for the concept of Posttraumatic Stress Disorder (PTSD) to be introduced into Japan.[6]

As a result, *hibakusha* (A-bomb survivors) faced a dismal lack of care and understanding of the multiple psychological effects caused by their experiences in August 1945. This chapter aims to explain this particular lacuna by focusing on the work of Japanese psychologist Kubo Yoshitoshi and psychiatrist Konuma Mashiho in Hiroshima.[7] The work of Kubo and Konuma is examined within the context of the longer history of research on PTSD and trauma in Japan and elsewhere. The trajectory of research on A-bomb survivors' trauma, I argue, was the result of a confluence of developments, the most important of which were US censorship, Japanese researchers' suspicion of trauma and its victims, and the very complex relationship between radiation damage—then still unknown—and its psychiatric effects. The combination of these factors made research difficult and led to decades of neglect for *hibakusha*'s mental suffering, even as their presence was celebrated by the Japanese public and while their radiation damage was intensely researched both in Japan and the United States.

Konuma Mashiho and Japanese Psychiatry's Attitude toward Trauma

Japanese psychiatry's record of dealing with trauma in general—and the A-bomb in particular—was minimal, and psychiatrists were not sympathetic to the idea of long-term trauma.[8] The first professionals to encounter and write about trauma in Japan were doctors who dealt with military casualties and workplace accidents. The records of work-related injuries have recently been the subject of a large research initiative, the results of which are just now being published.[9] The civilian aspects of trauma are important but, because of the limited space allotted, and the military training of our main protagonist, Konuma Mashiho, I will focus here on the military side of the story. For our current purposes it suffices to say that civilian doctors were as suspicious of civilian claims of mental injury as their military counterparts. As (co-contributor to this volume) Nakamura Eri and others have shown, the Japanese military's reliance on its superior "spirit" made it hard to accept psychiatric suffering.[10] Military psychiatry's status was not very high, and doctors rarely acknowledged psychological injuries.[11] In 1937, for example, military psychiatrist Kamata Shirabe told physicians: "Unlike the Western militaries during the First World War, there has been no neurotic illness called war neurosis in the Japanese military since the present war [the Asia-Pacific War] broke out. I'm proud as a member of the military of the Emperor that the fact shows people of the Japanese Empire have especially high morale."[12]

Japanese psychiatric casualties were significant but without a proper accounting and treatment system—there was only one dedicated psychiatric hospital—it is almost impossible to determine its prevalence. Doctors stressed their own role in preventing psychiatric casualties from weakening the fighting spirit of other troops. Similar to those German doctors who, during World War I, had dismissed combat trauma as hysteria, Japanese military doctors tended to downplay psychological symptoms and tried to return as many shell-shocked soldiers as possible to their units.[13] This was no coincidence, as Japanese psychiatry was heavily influenced by German psychiatry.[14] The German psychiatric establishment was, as Paul Lerner and others have shown, quite resistant to diagnosing trauma. After the war, psychiatrists dismissed trauma as an excuse for receiving a war pension and categorized traumatized soldiers as suffering from "pension neurosis."[15] This was the case beyond Germany as well. As Jolande Withuis and Annet Mooij argued, on the eve of World War II the consensus among psychiatrists was that war-related psychiatric symptoms "were the expression of a disease in the structure or working of the brain . . . [with an] organic basis."[16] Thus, if one could not detect such damage, there was usually a tendency to dismiss patients displaying such symptoms as malingerers. During the Asia-Pacific War, Japanese doctors used the exact same language as German doctors to dismiss traumatized soldiers' claims for compensation; in their opinion, soldiers who claimed to be mentally hurt during their service suffered from a "compensation neurosis" (*hoshō shinkeishō*).[17]

Konuma was exceptional among military doctors in conducting follow-up research on veterans. After the war, only a handful of dedicated long-term studies were conducted on veterans and none, to the best of this author's knowledge, were done on civilian victims of the fire-bombing raids.[18] In 1949–1953, Konuma, who was based at Hiroshima University, conducted research on veterans to determine causes for the persistence of neuropsychiatric and psychiatric "functional disturbances [which] stand stationary in spite of ample surgical viz. orthopaedical treatment, thereby including some vetran [sic] cases of Chino-Japanese (1894–95) and Russo-Japanese (1904–05) wars."[19] Research on war veterans of this type could not have been conducted at the turn of the century. Konuma mentioned "a case of a 26-year-old with a bullet wound," and, given Konuma's age—he graduated from medical school in the early 1930s—it is almost certain this research was conducted in the 1930s or 1940s. Indeed, the original 1949 Japanese language article does not mention this, and later articles refer to soldiers who were shot in 1938.[20] The reference to earlier wars is significant as it shows the very serious limitations faced by Konuma and his colleagues, as, in all probability, he inserted this sentence to evade censorship. In 1948–49, military-related research, similarly to *hibakusha* research, was heavily curtailed. The political atmosphere and the general reluctance to deal with veterans in general was a contributing factor to the paucity of research.[21]

Furthermore, Konuma, following the German precedent and contemporaneous Japanese practice, insisted on providing somatic explanations for his patients' neuroses and related psychiatric problems. As Svenja Goltermann has demonstrated, Wehrmacht veterans were routinely denied pensions in West Germany as doctors insisted on finding physical causes for their psychiatric ailments. As psychiatrist Kurt Schneider wrote in 1947 while conducting a pension evaluation, "under no circumstances do physical impairments that are expressions of emotions, for example, a psychogenic gait impairment following fright, qualify as a pathological physical change [for pension]." German POWs who came back from the USSR and suffered from a range of psychiatric issues were, according to psychiatrists, "being ill without a disease."[22] Konuma, who, like Schneider, also looked for somatic explanations like brain lesions, which he claimed were hard to diagnose, cautioned that "[symptoms] are very often looked upon as simply psychogenetic or neurotic; especially when there is [sic] no foci symptoms with skull fractures."[23] It is noteworthy that Konuma was not satisfied with "simply psychogenetic" explanations, and that he argued for damage to the central nervous system as the cause of latent and persisting psychiatric issues. This damage was caused by "heavy brain concussion, which must in turn cause injuries in the midbrain-hypophyseal system."[24] This was a classic "shell shock" assessment that looked for concussions and damage from shelling or other physical factors as explanations for persistent psychiatric symptomatology. German psychiatrists persisted with such diagnoses well into the 1960s. Konuma reached a similar conclusion in all the research he produced on head injuries and relied on the German psychiatric literature to corroborate his conclusions.

In their work on *hibakusha,* Konuma and other psychiatrists, again in the style of the German psychiatric literature, preferred physical and somatic evidence to mental evidence and were generally hostile to psychological trauma (indeed the word trauma rarely appears in the literature unless it refers to physical injuries). Thus, it is not surprising that psychiatric research on survivors' mental injuries was sporadic and not part of a consistent research effort. The social context in which doctors were operating was not conducive to this type of research. This was the result of a number of factors. First, severe censorship by the Americans in the early years after the war curtailed any research related to the bomb. Second, cultural and social taboos prevented many survivors from seeking help or even openly taking about their suffering. Third, as noted above, Japanese psychiatry, which was heavily influenced by German psychiatric culture, was traditionally hostile to psychological trauma. Fourth, the peculiar nature of radiation damage and its unknown characteristics made it hard to distinguish between physical and mental effects. Fifth, and as a result of all of the above, no reparation schemes were set up for mental injuries, hence there was no institutional incentive to evaluate survivors. This was acknowledged at the time by Konuma (and others) who wrote in 1963: "both in terms of intellectual [pursuit] and [pushing for] financial [compensation], only a few [researchers] have adequately grappled with the psychiatric aftereffects of the Atomic Bomb so far."[25]

Immediately after the bombing, the Japanese military sent a medical and scientific delegation to the two cities, which included two psychiatrists sent by Uchimura Yūshi at Tokyo Imperial University, who was one of the founders of Japanese psychiatry. The two young researchers, Okada Key and Shimizano Yasuo, were sent to perform autopsies and collect samples of brains for the purpose of ascertaining radiation damage, rather than questioning survivors. The somatic approach was typical of researchers at the time. Furthermore, Uchimura, who also went to Hiroshima, was quite dismissive of trauma. Though he experienced the fire-bombing personally, he admitted only "some anxiety for my family," and was actually "thrilled by the danger of bombings."[26] Uchimura "expected that numbness and despair would last only a short time."[27] He had "heard that refugees from bombed-out London had suffered from emotional paralysis and depersonalization," but, like most of his military colleagues, he expected the Japanese to react differently.[28]

According to his memoir, Uchimura's research notes were confiscated by the US authorities and not much seemed to result from his initial research foray into Hiroshima.[29] It is safe to assume that even if doctors had been interested in conducting research, American censorship and the harsh conditions of the early occupation would have made such projects difficult to execute. It took a full four years for Japanese research to begin in earnest. Starting with the first surveys that were conducted in 1949 at Kyushu University by Okumura Nikichi and Hitsuda Heizaburō, a small number of researchers, in separate undertakings, examined *hibakushas'* persistent health problems, but their research was generally not followed up.[30] A concentrated research campaign focusing on *hibakusha* never materialized. Psychiatrists found it very hard to directly link the experience of mass death with that of psychological trauma. This was, again, mostly because patients' syndromes were viewed as related to general bad health, physical trauma, and radiation rather than to psychological injuries. A plausible causative link between symptoms and trauma was very hard to prove scientifically. It was difficult for researchers to isolate the psychological effects of the bomb from the effects of radiation—still an unknown phenomenon at the time.[31]

Like Konuma, many other psychiatrists and psychologists lamented the lack of research on the matter. In 1956, Fujinami Takeshi and his colleagues observed: "ten years after the bomb, although there were no surgical or other medical problems, *hibakusha* still complain of fatigue, memory and other subjective issues."[32] Conducting research on both a *hibakusha* and non-*hibakusha* groups, he found that the *hibakusha*, especially laborers, suffered disproportionally more than non-*hibakusha* from mental illness, but no significant differences were found in urine samples or other physical measurements. The Fujinami team, however, offered no concrete explanation for this and recommended further research. As I have argued elsewhere, this was a typical conclusion for the dozen or so research schemes that were initiated in the 1950s and early 1960s.[33] During 1956, the year when awareness of the plight of *hibakusha* peaked—following the establishment of *hidankyo* (the *hibakusha* relief organization), a number of other studies were conducted. That year, a medical survey found that 7.3 percent of *hibakusha* suffered from nervous disorders, and there were an "overwhelming number of people who suffered from neurasthenia."[34] One of these groups, led by Kondō Toshiyuki and Yoshioka Ichirō, conducted research in Hiroshima and concluded that *hibakusha* indeed had higher rates of memory problems, excitability, and other symptoms in comparison to the general population. Kondō and colleagues did not progress beyond that conclusion.[35] However, it is important to note that, with the exception of Konuma's work, neither the Kondō group nor any of the other studies discussed here cited each other.[36] All Japanese research on *hibakusha* only made reference to radiation or other related studies, and no mention was made of survivors of the Nazi camps or other traumatic experiences.

The longest and most consistent research effort to investigate the *hibakusha* was conducted by Konuma. Starting in 1953, Konuma, in the largest survey of its time, examined hundreds of *hibakusha* in Otake, just outside of Hiroshima. Konuma, significantly, was one of few researchers who worked on long-term issues, such as A-bomb fatigue (known as *bura bura byo*) and made connections between military and *hibakusha* research. In his work with survivors, he found evidence of autonomic ataxia (lack of muscle coordination), dizziness, headaches, sleep disorders, insomnia, vertigo, emotional intolerance, amnesia, difficulties in cognitive tasks, intolerance to mental shocks, and so on. The long list of complaints "appeared after the atomic bomb diseases and remained stationary till now."[37] Again, just like in his research on veterans, Konuma noted that these symptoms were usually the result of brain injury, and that "it was not supposed, that their complaints and symptoms are merely neurotic ones."[38] In his first research articles, he remained ambiguous about the causes of these symptoms. Like his other colleagues in Hiroshima and Nagasaki, Konuma concluded: "It is supposed or recognizable that there lies diencephalic, namely central regulations disturbances of autoatic nervous functions as the after-effects of A.B. [Atomic Bomb] casualties. . . . But it is not yet concluded that the facts have direct relation to A.B. Casualties. As the exact cause of the disorders being not clarified."[39]

In a 1960 article and as part of a symposium on the "psychiatric effects of [the] A-bomb," Konuma noted: "As we [continue] to deepen our understating of 'the symptoms of and distress [caused] by head trauma' [and] neuroses . . . We still cannot [positively] recognize that [these symptoms] are the 'after effects of A-bomb disease.'"[40] Konuma gave an overview of his research including, significantly, his work on military casualties as well as other psychiatrists' work on the topic so far and strongly suggested that (but still refraining from arguing forthrightly) a connection existed between the A-bomb and the varied symptoms suffered by *hibakusha*. Konuma still insisted on physical damage as the main cause of mental disease, but he also included environmental and social elements as contributing factors: "The Atomic bomb is *Noxe*, it has a [harmful] impact socially and personal, on both body and mind. Even if *Noxe* disappears, the mental effect is of [these combined factors]."[41] For Konuma, however, acknowledging the social and economic impact of the A-bomb only further muddied the waters of diagnosis. In a 1963 report, going back to his original Otake research, he noted that the living conditions of *hibakusha* were generally poor, "and he could also see arteriosclerosis, beriberi, stomach disorder, parasites, and intellectual insufficiency [in patients] . . . [and thus] it is difficult to judge whether the cause of the symptoms is due to the living conditions or the impact of the Atomic Bomb."[42]

Konuma did gradually come to see a clearer connection between the A-bomb and mental health issues among *hibakusha*, and even came to attribute some of these issues to non-somatic factors. In the same report from 1963 mentioned above, Konuma argued for the existence of outside factors—"namely the startle response (to the A-bomb) and radiation"—as major contributors to the onset of neurosis.[43] A later report from 1965 listed "psychogenic psychosis" as one of the "A-bomb aftereffects," as well as "anxiety disease at the time of atomic bomb exposure."[44] Konuma then added, significantly, that "those exposed within two kilometers [of ground zero] suffer from psychogenic psychosis, which often lead to suicide attempts. Such psychological symptoms, which [existed] at the time of the bombing, as well as the chronic symptoms [*hibakusha* still suffer from] should be understood as psychogenic reactions."[45] Konuma speculated that what was understood as "A-bomb disease" (*genbaku byō*) was actually schizophrenia.[46] Again, Konuma was conforming to contemporaneous medical trends in which shell shock and other similar conditions were often wrongly diagnosed as schizophrenia or a personality disorder.[47] This was nevertheless a departure of sorts from the usual framework of organic causation. This apparent turn away from somatic explanations, however, was not followed through. Most of the paper stuck to an examination of brain waves, blood circulation, and possible central nervous system damage, but Konuma did speculate that there was an interaction between psychogenic and organic factors that produced the "interbrain syndromes" that his patients suffered from. In the end, Konuma, almost alone among his peers, went beyond conventional somatic explanations for *hibakusha* mental illness. Yet he too did not reach out to psychologists nor coordinate a coherent care program. Konuma published no new research on *hibakusha* after the article mentioned above and moved on to work on alcoholism and other issues.

Kubo Yoshitoshi and the Psychology of War and Peace

Psychologists in Japan, for the most part, were uninterested in nuclear issues. An official history of the Japanese Society for Peace Psychology lamented that "studies [of *hibakusha*] have been on the fringe of Japanese psychological societies, and in addition they have not been paid very much attention to by Western psychologists because of linguistic problems."[48] This can be explained by the same reasons that curtailed psychiatric research. Psychologists, however, were much more socially oriented. While psychiatrists worked in hospitals and wrote mostly to academic and medical audiences, psychologists tended to be more involved with issues outside of their specific professional domain. However, during the US occupation (1945–1952), Japanese "self-censorship" and, later, dependence on government funding, contributed to their silence on the matter well into the 1960s. As Osaka Eiko demonstrated, the occupation also heralded a shift in Japanese psychology toward US methodologies.[49] This shift continued after the occupation ended in 1952 as Japanese researchers tried to integrate themselves into the American-dominated postwar research.[50] During the occupation, the US military administration made use of psychologists to survey Japanese attitudes toward the administration's reforms. Kubo Yoshitoshi, a Hiroshima native and former Imperial Navy doctor, was one of these psychologists.[51] Kubo's work on *hibakusha* represents one of the only sustained efforts to tackle the psychological impact of the bomb. Kubo was alone among Japanese researchers to stick to psychological explanations and did not connect mental health to the impact of radiation or other aspects of *hibakusha* health. Like his American colleagues who worked on civil defense issues—which I have examined at length elsewhere— Kubo's earlier work focused on the issue of panic as well as individual and mass nervous breakdown.⁵² Kubo divided survivors' reactions into four stages in which they went from "instinctive action," to "panic," "quasi panic," and a "blank" (stupefied) stage. None of these stages, however, lasted beyond a week or two after the bomb.⁵³ Kubo's work completely neglected any impact beyond these two weeks. Even though he was writing in 1952, seven years after the bomb, Kubo asserted: "We can hardly estimate the next stage." He concluded: "but perhaps some time after, every respondent succeeded in slowly adjusting to their circumstances."⁵⁴ Kubo's emphasis in his later research was, likewise, on the short-term impact of the bomb, and his writing increasingly tended to emphasize the political implications of his work, namely the promotion of peace.⁵⁵

Although Japanese politics gave rise to an increasing interest in the *hibakusha*'s plight, this did not translate into more research on the matter. This failure can partly be attributed to *hibakusha*'s reluctance to come forward. Also, in 1956, a survey conducted by *hidankyō* reported, somewhat cryptically, that many *hibakusha* "suffer from problems of the heart, which lead to family problems and a-social behavior."⁵⁶ The report did not go beyond this observation, which is not surprising as the subject continued to be taboo. Many *hibakusha* did not even raise the issue within the survivor community, let alone speak about their mental issues publicly, preferring instead to complain, like Holocaust survivors, of more "normal" physical ailments.⁵⁷ *Hidankyō* did not raise the issue of treatment for mental damage when it campaigned for a medical law to be instated. Reparations from the Americans were, of course, out of the question.

Kubo Yoshitoshi, who was one of the principal backers of the compensation movement, was a definite exception to this trend. Kubo's motivation for his research can be tied to his political activities, both with the University Scholars Society and "Japanese Psychologists for Peace." Inspired by American social scientists, the Scholars Society sought to further the "link between psychoanalysis and peace."⁵⁸ Kubo was among the founding members of the society and signed a 1950 "peace appeal to American psychologists," which was written at the fourteenth annual conference of the Japanese Psychological Association. The peace appeal, as well as the peace society as a whole, underscored the Japanese psychologists' unique position as citizens of "the country [which] experienced the terrors of the atomic bombs in Hiroshima and Nagasaki."⁵⁹ However, the society's as well as Kubo's points of intellectual reference were exclusively American. In his 1952 paper, he cited Irving Gitlin's research, the Social Science Research Council (SSRC), a US organization with ties to the USSBS and similar civil defense research institutes, as well as an article on the psychological impacts of Orson Welles's famous "War of the Worlds" scare.⁶⁰ Kubo's political work, together with Nakano Seiichi and his colleagues as well as the main survivor relief organizations, was important in pushing for the publication of white papers and other reports on the state of *hibakusha* that were instrumental in bringing about the medical relief laws for the *hibaksuha*.⁶¹

The same political entanglement that drove Kubo's research, however, was also a reason for the stalling of his research. Lacking funds to pursue his research, Kubo turned to the Atomic Bomb Casualty Commission [ABCC] in search of financial and logistical support. In 1959, Kubo met with Scotty Matsumoto, a medical sociologist in the Hiroshima-ABCC. Matsumoto reported to his superior that Kubo "had spent a great deal of time recounting his past research experiences, probably to convey the great difficulty involved in undertaking a psychological research program in Hiroshima."[62] Kubo had worked with the ABCC before, but, according to his own account, "Dr. [Grant] Taylor called him in midway through the project and asked him to be 'cautious' in using the material [obtained through this cooperation]. According to Kubo, some members of the *gensui-kyo* (anti-nuclear organization) later 'warned' him not 'to be used' by the ABCC. The work, I gather, then came to a standstill."[63] The 1959 project, which supposedly surveyed 10,000 *hibakusha* "as to health status, family conditions, anxieties, etc. for the local *gentai-kyo* (victims' organization)," was also put on hold. Hiroshima City Hall was "non-enthusiastic," and in spite of the ABCC's positive attitude toward the prospects of Kubo's research and their granting of technical support, nothing much came out of the survey in terms of publications or care programs for the *hibakusha*.[64] This setback was the beginning of the end of Kubo's involvement with nuclear issues. Kubo published a number of other articles, but none of these were based on new research and, unlike Konuma, he seemed to be working in isolation with very little impact. In the mid-1960s, Kubo changed research tracks as well and left his *hibakusha* research behind.

Conclusion: (Un)recognition of Trauma in Hiroshima and Beyond

The question remains why Kubo and other psychologists and psychiatrists did not push for the inclusion of mental health provisions in compensation laws and why care was not provided or institutionalized until well into the 1970s. There is no easy answer to this question. A number of possible explanations can be found in the evidence examined above. Japanese psychiatrists and psychologists did not deny *hibakusha* suffering. Unlike their US counterparts, they did not try to downplay it or, as their colleagues in the military did, claim that *hibakusha* were just being lazy and difficult. *Hibakusha* suffering was definitely acknowledged. For psychiatrists preferring physical and organic explanations, the cause of psychiatric symptoms was in doubt, leading to much confusion and little involvement in *hibakusha* relief. Konuma was exceptional in his evolving diagnoses and recognition of psychogenic causes for mental ills, but even he dropped *hibakusha* research by the mid-1960s. For Kubo, the explanation was psychological (in the "stimuli produced by the bomb"), but he was not interested in developing treatment programs and rather more interested in preventing future war and in participating in the peace movement. Kubo did repeatedly try to conduct research, but the political complications of working with both US and Japanese institutions in the 1950s and 1960s frustrated further initiatives.

Furthermore, Konuma and Kubo's research did not differ much from research (or lack thereof) on the psychological impact of World War II in Western institutions.[65] In contrast to the United States, medical research in Western Europe and Israel did not recognize what we now call PTSD. In almost all countries (France being somewhat of an outlier), patients had to prove a causal link between their experiences during the war and current symptoms in order to be recognized as a patient and receive a pension.[66] It took sustained efforts by veterans' organizations and others to attain medical recognition of their suffering. This was the case in the Netherlands, Belgium, Italy, and other countries that had been occupied by the Nazis. In West Germany, *Wehrmacht* veterans, ironically, had to wait until after the recognition of Jewish victims' psychological damages to gain recognition.[67] The United States did provide extensive care to American GIs during and after the war but focused almost entirely on short-term care. The emphasis was on psychiatry's ability to cure combat neurosis. Patients who were not cured were suspected of exaggerating their symptoms. In a peculiar twist during the 1950s, mothers and wives who had failed to raise or nurse their veteran sons or husbands "properly" were blamed—a theory which came to be known as "momism."[68]

In all of Western Europe, the focus of research was on former resistance fighters and veterans. Civilian populations similar to the *hibakusha* were generally not studied. The only exception to this trend was research on Holocaust survivors. Survivors of the Nazi camps present the clearest parallel to the A-bomb survivors' case. Holocaust survivors, unlike *hibakusha,* gained recognition for their psychological suffering. However, it took a long time for Holocaust survivors to gain this recognition, which happened only after concentrated efforts by physicians and survivor-activists in the late 1960s.[69] As late as 1956, the German-Jewish psychiatrist H. H. Fleischhacker wrote that "personality disorders and neuroses were very rare among Jews (in Displaced Persons camps)." In 1961, Victor Frankl, who is otherwise recognized for being an early advocate for psychic trauma in camp survivors, wrote: "Neuroses in the narrower sense . . . were not observable in the concentration camps; neurotics healed there."[70] Even in Israel, it was only following the Eichmann trial and after greater recognition of survivors took place that attitudes started to change.[71] Survivors of the Holocaust and mental patients were both seen at the time as a potential burden: a threat to the newly emerging and still fragile society within the fledgling state of Israel.[72] Psychiatrists saw their role as helping survivors transform into "healthy Israelis," and encouraged patients to look forward to the bright Zionist future rather than backward to the smoldering ruin of their European lives. Fishel Shneerson, who worked in Displaced Persons camps, for instance, emphasized survivors' ability to overcome their suffering. He saw the behavior of some survivors (in particular their eagerness to learn and return to life) as a sign of "immunization from trauma."[73] But it was not merely physicians' attitudes that hindered recognition. As psychiatric researcher Judith Stern has argued, there was "an unspoken agreement between the therapist and the survivor [which] held that the best way to cope was to leave the hellish period behind and deal only with current problems."[74]

In many respects, Holocaust survivors shared much with the *hibakusha* who likewise refrained from coming forward and refrained from consulting psychiatrists. This parallel brings us to the issue of culture. Japanese psychologists and psychiatrists have often commented on the stigma attached to mental health issues in Japanese society.[75] Stigma could probably have played a role in this case as well (the different dynamics in Israel and Japan could still lead to similar outcomes). However, the issue of culture is rarely commented on in research from the period. There was nothing "Asian" about trauma research in Hiroshima. Researchers presented themselves as scientists who were equal in stature and expertise to their American peers. The overwhelming presence of the ABCC in Hiroshima and Nagasaki was a constant reminder of the disparities of power between Japanese and US science, which researchers were trying to overcome through the invocation of universalist tropes and objective scientific methods. This was the result of conscious efforts by researchers to distance themselves from wartime racial thinking as well as from propaganda on the uniqueness of the Japanese "soul." Both had stifled wartime research. When the question of culture was raised it was mostly by Americans with the purpose of dismissing research sympathetic to the *hibakusha*. At a 1948 ABCC conference, American physician Austin M. Brues rejected the idea of long-term psychiatric damage. When challenged by colleagues he answered: "this is difficult to evaluate because of the differences between the Japanese pattern and our own."[76] When Robert J. Lifton came to Hiroshima, George Darling, then the director of the ABCC, wrote in an internal memo that "[there is] a great danger in assuming that the Neo-Freudian interpretations following the psychoanalytic pattern would be misleading in the extreme if used as an explanation of Japanese behavior which presumably responded in a different way to a totally different set of values."[77] Faced with such dismissals, it was no surprise that Japanese researchers chose not to raise cultural differences when writing about mental trauma.

Although I have written mostly on what hindered research, this did not mean that there was no interest in the impact of the A-bomb. The enormity of the suffering caused by the A-bomb prompted physicians across Japan to address this problem. Researchers reported many symptoms that together constituted what came to be called "A-bomb neurosis," but time and again they failed to connect disparate studies, put forward a standard definition of the problem, or propose any sort of program to deal with it. Researchers were acutely aware of the untidy and confusing nature of their findings and struggled to coordinate or make sense of them. In what they did study there was an overwhelming preference for somatic explanations and an equal aversion to psychological ones. This was perhaps due to the stigma attached to mental issues among both patients and doctors. We must remember that, up until 1950, mental patients in Japan were locked up in cages, and that most of the medical researchers had themselves grown up in a system where racialized modes of thinking tied mental defects to racial inferiority. The tragic result of such shortcomings has been that it was only in the period following the Kobe earthquake in the 1990s that thoughts on trauma started to change in Japan.

Ran Zwigenberg is associate professor at Pennsylvania State University. His research focuses on modern Japanese and European history, with a specialization in memory and cultural history. He has taught and lectured in the United States, Europe, Israel, and Japan, and published on issues of war memory, atomic energy, heritage, psychiatry, and survivor politics. Zwigenberg's first book, *Hiroshima: The Origins of Global Memory Culture* (Cambridge University Press, 2014), winner of the 2016 Association for Asian Studies' John W. Hall book award, deals comparatively with the commemoration and the reaction to the Holocaust and the atomic bombing of Hiroshima.

Notes

1. *New York Times*, 26 February 1946. An earlier version of this chapter appeared as Zwigenberg, "Nuclear Minds." I thank Tanaka Yuriko for generously letting me build on that article. I also thank Kubota Akiko for her help.
2. Bernstein, "Atomic Bombings Reconsidered," 138.
3. Zwigenberg, "Healing a Sick World."
4. Zwigenberg, "Healing a Sick World," 28.
5. Braw, *The Atomic Bomb Suppressed*, especially chapter 2.
6. Zwigenberg, *Hiroshima*, 171–72.
7. Here and elsewhere, I follow Japanese convention in putting family name first, followed by given name.
8. Zwigenberg, *Hiroshima*, 147.
9. Tatsuya, *Kindai nihon PTSD*.
10. Matsumura, "State Propaganda and Mental Disorders," 808; Nakamura, "Psychiatrists Gatekeepers War Expenditure."
11. Nakamura, "Rikugun to sensōshinkeibyō."
12. Nakamura, "'Invisible' War Trauma in Japan," 144.
13. Matsumura, "State Propaganda and Mental Disorders," 807. For Germany, see Lerner, *Hysterical Men*.
14. See Bowers and Chi, "Freud's Deshi."
15. Pross, *Paying for the Past*, 93.
16. Withuis and Mooij, *The Politics of War Trauma*, 140.

17. Matsumura, "State Propaganda and Mental Disorders," 828.
18. See Katō, *Noiroza shinkeishō to wa nani ka*. See also Suzuki Akihito's summary of the book (in Japanese) at *History of Medicine and Modern Japan*, "War Neuropathy in Masaaki Kato's *Theory of Neurosis* (1955)," 27 January 2013. Retrieved 25 July 2016 from http://akihitosuzuki.blog.fc2.com/blog-entry-59.html.
19. Konuma, "Studies After-Effects Brain Traumata."
20. Konuma and Koshiba, "Cases of Accessory Nerve Paresis"; Konuma, "Keibu Senshō ni tuite."
21. Yoshikuni, *Homecomings*; Yoshida, *Nihongun heishi*.
22. Both quotes are from Goltermann, *War in Their Minds*, 143.
23. Konuma, "Studies After-Effects Brain Traumata," 364.
24. Konuma, "Studies After-Effects Brain Traumata," 369.
25. Konuma, "Genbakushō kōishō," 388.
26. Yushi, *Waga ayumishi*, 251.
27. Yushi, *Waga ayumishi*, 252.
28. Yushi, *Waga ayumishi*, 251.
29. Yushi, *Waga ayumishi*.
30. Okumura and Hitsuda, "Genbakudan hisai kanja."
31. Okumura and Hitsuda, "Genbakudan hisai kanja," 50.
32. Fujinami et al., "Genbaku hibakusha no kikakuteki hirōshōjō.", 80.
33. Zwigenberg, "'Wounds of the Heart.'"
34. Quoted in Zwigenberg, *Hiroshima*, 180.
35. Kondō et al., "Genbaku higaisha."
36. Konuma, "Seishin keika no matome."
37. Konuma, "Neuropsychiatric Case Studies," 1716.
38. Konuma, Furutani, and Kubo, "Neuropsychiatric Case Studies," 1,717.
39. Konuma, Furutani, and Kubo, "Neuropsychiatric Case Studies," 1,719.
40. Konuma, "Genbakushō no ishō," 158.
41. Konuma, "Genbakushō no ishō," 167. German in the original. Noxe in German is "Noxa": Something that exerts a harmful effect on the body.
42. Konuma, "Genbakushō kōishō," 389.
43. Konuma, "Genbakushō kōishō," 395.
44. Konuma, "Seishin shinkei kagaku," 232.
45. Konuma, "Seishin shinkei kagaku," 232.
46. Konuma, "Seishin shinkei kagaku," 239.
47. Withuis, "Introduction," 2.
48. Heiwa no Tame no Shinrigakusha Kondankai, *Heiwa shinrigaku no ibuki*, x.
49. Osaka, "Senryō nihon shinrigaku," 181.
50. Osaka, "Senryō nihon shinrigaku," 177, 186.
51. Osaka, "Senryō nihon shinrigaku," 177, 186.
52. Zwigenberg, "'Wounds of the Heart,'" 12–13.
53. Osaka, "Senryō nihon shinrigaku"; Kubo, "Hiroshima hibaku chokugo."
54. Kubo, "Hiroshima hibaku chokugo," 109.
55. Zwigenberg, "'Wounds of the Heart,'" 15–17.
56. Gensuibakuikinshi Hiroshima kyōgikai genbaku higaisha kyūen iinkai, *Ge Genbaku Higaisha Jitai Chōsa Hōkoku*, 6.
57. Author interview with a group of *hibakusha* from the HIP (Hiroshima Interpreters for Peace) group, 23 January 2012, Hiroshima Peace Memorial Museum. See also Braw, "Hiroshima and Nagasaki," 157.
58. Heiwa no Tame no Shinrigakusha Kondankai, *Heiwa shinrigaku no ibuki*, 1.

59. Heiwa no Tame no Shinrigakusha Kondankai, *Heiwa shinrigaku no ibuki*, 2.
60. Kubo, "Hiroshima hibaku chokugo;" Kay and Gitlin, "Atomic Energy Atomic Bomb."
61. Hamatani, "Genbaku taiken to 'kokoro no kizu,'" 5–6.
62. Scotty Matsumoto to George Darling, 20 May 1959, Box 23, Folder: Medical sociology, National Academy of Science Archives, Washington DC, USA.
63. Ibid.
64. Ibid.
65. Withuis and Mooij, *The Politics of War Trauma*; Fassin and Rechtman, *Empire of Trauma*; Grob, "World War II and American Psychiatry."
66. Withuis, "Management Victimhood," 287, 289.
67. Goltermann, *War in Their Minds*, 200.
68. Zwigenberg, "'Wounds of the Heart,'" 7.
69. Herzog, "The Obscenity of Objectivity."
70. Quoted in Goltermann, *War in Their Minds*, 181.
71. For a detailed survey and a comparison of both cases, see chapter 5 in Zwigenberg, *Hiroshima*.
72. Zalashik, *Ad Nefesh*, 114.
73. Stern, "The Eichmann Trial," 398.
74. Stern, "The Eichmann Trial," 400.
75. Shuntaro et al., "Review."
76. Zwigenberg, "'Wounds of the Heart,'" 9.
77. George Darling to Herbert Gardner, 1 July 1968, Box 4, Folder: Dr. Lifton: 1963–1968, National Academy of Science Archives, Washington DC, USA.

Bibliography

Bernstein, Barton J. "The Atomic Bombings Reconsidered." *Foreign Affairs* 74, no. 1 (1995): 135–52.

Bowers, Geoffrey H., and Serena Yang Hsuek Chi. "Freud's Deshi: The Coming of Psychoanalysis to Japan." *Journal of the History of the Behavioral Sciences* 33, no. 2 (1997): 115–26.

Braw, Monica. *The Atomic Bomb Suppressed: American Censorship in Occupied Japan*. Armonk, NY: M. E. Sharpe, 1991.

———. "Hiroshima and Nagasaki: The Voluntary Silence." In *Living with the Bomb: American and Japanese Cultural Conflicts in the Nuclear Age*, edited by Laura Elizabeth Hein and Mark Selden, 155–72. Armonk, NY: M. E. Sharpe, 1997.

Fassin, Didier, and Richard Rechtman. *The Empire of Trauma: An Inquiry into the Condition of Victimhood*. Translated by Rachel Gomme. Princeton, NJ: Princeton University Press, 2009.

Fujitani Takeshi, Yunoki Tomomasa, Hosoma Shizuaki, Sakai Tsunemi, Hiroshi Fujii, Yamate MAsatu, Kozo Hirohisa, "Genbaku hibakusha no jikakuteki hirōshōjō chōsa narabi ni nyū do hannō ni yoru hirō chōsa sesaki ni tuite" [Studies of Atomic bomb survivors by subjective fatigue symptoms and examination of the urine by the Daggagio reaction]. *Hiroshima igaku*, Vol. 9, no. 2 (1956): 78–80.

Gensuibakuikinshi Hiroshima kyōgikai genbaku higaisha kyūen iinkai. *Genbaku higaisha jitai chōsa hōkoku* [Fact finding report on victims of the atomic bomb]. Hiroshima: Gensuibakuikinshi Hiroshima kyōgikai genbaku higaisha kyūen iinkai,1956.

Goltermann, Svenja. *The War in Their Minds: German Soldiers and Their Violent Pasts in West Germany.* Translated by Philip Schmitz. Ann Arbor: University of Michigan Press, 2017.
Grob, Gerald N. "World War II and American Psychiatry." *Psychohistory Review* 19 (1990): 41–69.
Hamatani, Maszaharu. "Genbaku taiken to 'kokoro no kizu'" [The experience of the A-bomb and PTSD]. *IPSHU kenkyū hōkoku* no. 41 (2009): 1–38.
Heiwa no Tame no Shinrigakusha Kondankai. *Heiwa shinrigaku no ibuki* [The journey of peace psychology]. Kyoto: Hōsei Shuppan, 1990.
Herzog, Dagmar. "The Obscenity of Objectivity: Post-Holocaust Antisemitism and the Invention-Discovery of Post-Traumatic Stress Disorder." In *Catastrophes: A History and Theory of an Operative Concept*, edited by Nitzan Lebovic and Andreas Killen, 128–55. Berlin: De Gruyter, 2014.
Katō, Masaaki. *Noiroza shinkeishō to ha nani ka* [What is neurosis nerve disease]. Tokyo: Sōgen igaku shinsho, 1955.
Kay, Lillian Ward, and Irving J. Gitlin. "Atomic Energy or the Atomic Bomb: A Problem in the Development of Morale and Opinion." *Journal of Social Psychology* 29, no. 1 (1949): 57–84.
Klein, Hilel, Julius Zellermayer, and Joel Shanan. "Former Concentration Camp Inmates on a Psychiatric Ward: Observations." *Archives of General Psychiatry* 8, no. 4 (1963): 334–42.
Kondō, Toshiyuki, Yoshioka, Ichirō, Kida, Shigeo, and Hayakawa Tomokazu. "Genbaku higaish no shinriteki chōsa [Psychological researches on the cases accompanied 8 years with aftereffects of atomic bombs casuality [*sic* at Hiroshima]." *Hiroshima igaku* Vol. 9, no. 2 (1956): 59–64.
Konuma, Mashiho, "Genbakushō kōishō seishinshinekei kakgaku no mondai [Psychiatric Problems and the Aftereffects of the Atomic Bomb]." In *Genshi igaku*, edited by Koyama Tsuyoshi, Tabuchi Akira, AND Watanabe Susumu . Tokyo: Kanehara Shuppan, 1963.
———. "Seishin shinkei kagaku no matome [Summary of psychiatric science]." *Hiroshima igaku* 20 (1965): 231–36.
Konuma, Masuho, "Keibu Senshō ni tuite [On head injuries]." *Seishin keigaku zashi* 50, no. 6 (1949): 1–3.
———. "Studies on the After-Effects of Brain Traumata Observed during the Last Three Warfares [*sic*] Implying Japan." *Psychiatry and Clinical Neurosciences* 4, no. 4 (1951): 362–70.
———. "Genbakushō ato ishō no kannōshō seikuhashiku narabi ni shōkō rikai ni osamute [Aftereffects of Post Atomic Bomb Syndrome, Understanding encepalopathy complaints and symptoms]." *Nagasaki igaku zashi*, no. 3 (1961): 158–75.
Konuma, M., M. Furutani, and S. Kubo, "Neuropsychiatric Case Studies on the Atomic Bomb Casualties at Hiroshima." In *Research in the Effects and Influences of the Nuclear Bomb Test Explosions*, edited by Committee for Compilation of Report on Research in the Effects of Radioactivity. 1715–20. Tokyo: Japan Society for the Promotion of Science, 1956.
Konuma, M., and K. Koshiba, "Cases of Accessory Nerve Paresis as the After-Effect of Shot Traumata in Battlefield." *Psychiatry and Clinical Neurosciences* 7, no. 3 (1953): 202–8.
Kubo, Yoshitoshi. "Hiroshima hibaku chokugo no ningen Hiroshima hibaku choku go no ningen kōdō no kenkyu" [A Study of A-Bomb Suffers' [*sic*] Behavior in Hiroshima: A Socio-psychological Reserach on A-Bombs and A-Energy]. *Shinrigaku kenyū* 22, no. 2 (1952): 103–10.
Lerner, Paul F. *Hysterical Men: War, Psychiatry, and the Politics of Trauma in Germany, 1890–1930.* Ithaca, NY: Cornell University Press, 2003.

Matsumura, Janice. "State Propaganda and Mental Disorders: The Issue of Psychiatric Casualties among Japanese Soldiers During the Asia-Pacific War." *Bulletin of the History of Medicine* 78, no. 4 (2005): 804–35
Nakamura, Eri. "'Invisible' War Trauma in Japan: Medicine, Society and Military Psychiatric Casualties." *Historia Scientiarium* 25, no. 2 (2016): 140–61.
———. "Nihon teikoku rikugun to sensōshinkeibyō: senshōbyōsha o meguru shakai kūkan ni okeru 'kokoro no kaze'" [The japanese imperial army and war neurosis: 'Mental Injury' and the Position of War Wounded in Societal Space (Special Feature: War and Trauma)]. *Sensō sekinin kenkyu* 81 (2013): 52–61.
———. "Psychiatrists as Gatekeepers of War Expenditure: Diagnosis and Distribution of Military Pensions in Japan During the Asia-Pacific War." *East Asian Science, Technology and Society: An International Journal* 13 no. 13 (2019): 57–75.
Okumura, Nikichi, and Heizaburo Hitsuda. "Genbakudan hisai kanja seishinkei byōgakuteki chōsa seiseki" [Survey results of the mental health of patients affected by atomic bomb damage]. *Kyushu shinkeiseishin igaku* 1, no. 50 (1949): 50–52.
Osaka, Eiko. "Senryōka nihon no shinrigaku" [Psychology in Occupied Japan]." *Surugadai Daigaku kyuyō kenkyūsho* 1 (2011): 177–91.
Pross, Christian. *Paying for the Past: The Struggle over Reparations for Surviving Victims of the Nazi Terror.* Baltimore, MD: Johns Hopkins University Press, 1998.
Shuntaro, Ando, Sosei Yamaguchi, Yuta Aoki, and Graham Thornicroft. "Review of Mental-Health-Related Stigma in Japan." *Psychiatry and Clinical Neurosciences* 67, no. 7 (2013): 471–82.
Stern, Judith. "The Eichmann Trial and Its Influence on Psychiatry and Psychology." *Theoretical Inquiries in Law* 1, no. 2 (2000): 393–428.
Tatsuya, Satō. *Kindai nihon PTSD kankei shiryō shūsei: 1–2* [A compilation of primary sources related to PTSD in Japan]. Tokyo: Rikkashuppan, 2019.
Withuis, Jolande. "The Management of Victimhood: Long Term Health Damage from Asthenia to PTSD." In *Politics of War Trauma: The Aftermath of World War II in Eleven European Countries*, edited by Jolande Withuis and Annet Mooij, 287–322. Amsterdam: Aksant Academic Publishers, 2010.
Withuis, Jolande. "Introduction: The Politics of War Trauma." In *The Politics of War Trauma: The Aftermath of World War II in Eleven European Countries*, edited by Jolande Withuis and Annet Mooij, 1–11. Amsterdam: Aksant Academic Publishers, 2010.
Withuis, Jolande, and Annet Mooij, eds. *The Politics of War Trauma: The Aftermath of World War II in Eleven European Countries.* Amsterdam: Aksant Academic Publishers, 2010.
Yoshida, Yutaka. *Nihongun heishi: Ajia taiheiyō sensō no genjitsu* [The soldiers of the Japanese Army: The reality of the Asia Pacific War]. Tokyo: Chūō Kōron Shinsha, 2017.
Yoshikuni, Igarashi. *Homecomings: The Belated Return of Japan's Lost Soldiers.* New York: Columbia University Press, 2016.
Yushi, Uchimura. *Waga ayumishi seishin igaku no michi* [My walk on the path of psychiatry]. Tokyo: Misuzu Shobo, 1968.
Zalashik, Rakefet. *Ad Nefesh: Mehagrim, Olim, Plitim, Ve-Ha-Mimsad Ha-Pschiatri Be-Yisrael* [Till the soul: Immigrants, refugees, and the psychiatric establishmnet in Israel]. Tel-Aviv: Ha-kibutz ha-mehuhad, 2008.
Zwigenberg, Ran. "Healing a Sick World: Psychiatric Medicine and the Atomic Age." *Medical History* 62, no. 1 (2018): 27–49.
———. *Hiroshima: The Origins of Global Memory Culture.* Cambridge: Cambridge University Press, 2014.
———. "Nuclear Minds: Japanese Psychiatry's Encounter with the Atom Bomb." *Zinbun Kagaku Kenkyusho* 49 (2019): 1–9.

———. "'Wounds of the Heart': Psychiatric Trauma and Denial in Hiroshima." *History Workshop Journal* 84 (2017): 67–88.

Chapter 4

"Yankee-Style Trauma"

The Korean War and the Americanization of Psychiatry in the Republic of Korea

Jennifer Yum-Park

Throughout the fall and winter months of 1954, psychiatrists at the Capital Army Hospital (*Kunjin Chŏngsin Ŭihak Chiptamhoe*) in Seoul, South Korea, prepared a series of psychological case studies and presented their findings in December of that year at a meeting of the Military Psychiatry Association (*Kunjin Chŏngsin Ŭihak Chiptamhoe*).[1] In their study, they analyzed five male soldiers who complained of a variety of ailments, including headaches, seizures, and back pain, which prevented them from performing their military duties. None of the afflicted patients, however, showed any signs of a war-related physical injury.

These case studies hold immense significance for the history of Korean psychiatry. Specifically, they shed light on how the South Korean army responded to psychiatric casualties during the Korean War (1950–1953). Unlike Western countries with a long tradition of handling mental breakdown among military troops, the South Koreans had no experience in military psychiatry. In fact, the Korean War was the first modern war Koreans fought after having been liberated from Japan just five years earlier. In a time and place before Posttraumatic Stress Disorder (PTSD) had been labeled, Korean army psychiatrists, like their counterparts worldwide, struggled to diagnose and treat, as best they could, the psychiatric victims of war. A close reading of these case studies yields clues to important questions that have yet to be addressed by scholars.[2] For example: what types of symptoms captured the interest of Korean psychiatrists? Which theoretical frameworks did the Koreans adopt? And how did the environment of war and militarization affect the doctors' approach to their patients?[3]

The significance of the patient cases from 1954 does not end here, however. These cases constitute a starting point for discussing the rise of the discipline of psychiatry in South Korea. According to my research, two factors—the Korean War and the United States/Republic of Korea military alliance—facilitated the simultaneous birth and Americanization of psychiatry in this East Asian country during wartime. First, the war created a pressing, practical need for mental health programs throughout Korea. The Korean War decimated the Korean population, killing approximately 3 million people out of a total population of 30 million at the time. The psychological toll this demographic loss took on soldiers and civilians alike was nothing short of catastrophic.[4] Second, the partnership between the US and South Korean armies created a professional pathway for US physicians and psychiatrists to address this urgent need. A cross-cultural partnership between the military psychiatrists of the Republic of Korea (ROK) and the Eighth US Army effectively resulted in the transfer of an entire medical discipline from one country to another with remarkable speed and efficiency. Indeed, it is difficult to think of another instance in which the origins of a nation's psychiatric profession were so closely tied to wartime circumstances. The birth of South Korean psychiatry highlights the role of war in facilitating the global exchange of medical ideas and practices during the twentieth century. As a historical case study, it also serves as a way of examining the dynamics at play in the exportation of Western ideas of mental health and illness to non-Western countries.

Psychiatry in Colonial Korea

Psychiatry did have a limited prewar history in Korea, albeit one that also relied on foreign powers. During the colonial period in Korea's history (1910–1945), Japanese physicians imported their version of psychiatry as part of a larger program of modernizing Korea's medical system.[5] The Korean word for mental illness, *chŏngsinpyŏng*, is in fact a direct translation of the Japanese term *seisinbyō*. The first clinical department of psychiatry in Korea was established in 1913 at the Governor General Hospital (*Chosŏn Ch'ongdokpu Ŭiwŏn*), located in the northern part of the city of Kyŏngsŏng, now known as Seoul. From 1916–1927, a modest system for teaching psychiatry developed at Kyŏngsŏng Medical College.[6] A key development came in 1928 with the founding of Kyŏngsŏng Imperial University, which became the epicenter of psychiatric research and education in Korea for the remainder of the colonial period.[7] Accounts of Japanese and Korean students and professors from the first psychology (*siminihak*) department at Kyŏngsŏng Imperial University during the late 1920s confirm that the quality of its research facilities competed with those in Tokyo.[8]

We should not, however, overstate the influence of these developments on the local population. In the words of Theodore Jun Yoo: "Discrimination against

Korean medical students and the monopoly of psychiatry by Japanese doctors meant that there would be very few trained Korean psychiatrists at the end of the colonial occupation."[9] Koreans may have been introduced to various subfields of Western medicine by the Japanese, but they comprised only a small minority of the student body at these educational institutions.[10] Opportunities for academic and social advancement within the imperial medical system were likewise rare. Still, we cannot completely overlook these early developments because it was at this time that the future leaders of Korean mental health programs first entered the world of psychiatry.

The intellectual foundations of Japanese, and hence Korean, psychiatry relied heavily on European medicine. Discussing the "Germanization" of Japanese medicine during the early twentieth century, Akira Hashimoto has written about the strong influence of biological psychiatrists such as Emil Kraepelin (1856–1926) on the early formation of Japan's mental health programs.[11] Experts throughout the Japanese empire considered brain disease and bad heredity to be the main causes of mental illness. While celebrated psychoanalysts like Sigmund Freud (1856–1939), with his ideas about the psychogenic origins of mental and nervous disorders, caught the attention of East Asian intellectuals, this alternative German-language framework for psychiatry failed to gain traction in the Korean university and hospital systems.[12] Interestingly, during the Korean War, Korean psychiatrists were again confronted with this profoundly different approach to diagnosing and treating mental and nervous illness.

The introduction of Western psychiatric theories and practices during the colonial era minimally influenced the thinking of average Koreans. Analyzing newspaper reports from the 1920s and 1930s yields thousands of references to the mentally ill. Suicide, depression, and crimes committed under fits of insanity were part of the popular discourse.[13] But access to anything that we would recognize today as modern psychiatric care was very limited and prohibitively expensive. In 1928, the colonial Korean government applied for assistance from Japan to build a large-scale mental hospital. Mounting economic pressure on the Japanese Treasury as Japan mobilized for total war, however, meant that funds could not be allocated for a new type of public health care institution.[14] The burden of caring for the mentally ill thus fell on families, who often resorted to measures such as home confinement to manage their deranged relatives.[15] Consequently, traditional ways of understanding mental illness as a form of possession prevailed. The field work of Japanese ethnographer Maruyama Chijun in 1929 depicts folk rituals in which shamans (*mudang*) performed local exorcisms on the mad through a process that involved the beating of drums and whippings with a peach-wood branch (*toji*).[16]

Before 1945, psychiatry in Korea lacked sufficient financial support, professional manpower, and social clout to become a viable medical discipline. It is not surprising that the *Tonga ilbo* (*East Asia Daily*), the nation's largest newspaper, published an article during the fall of 1949 with the headline: "Nine psychiatrists in the Republic of Korea with an estimated mentally ill population of 200,000." Much to the author's lament, the Korean government had no official policy to deal with the mentally ill. Lacking proper treatment facilities, insane men and women could be seen roaming the streets, if they had not already been locked away by family members in their homes.[17] On the eve of the war in 1950, Korea was essentially a nation without psychiatry.

US Psychiatry on the Eve of the Korean War (1945–1950)

The situation could not have been more different in the United States at the time war erupted on the Korean peninsula. The team of army psychiatrists that arrived there in 1950 had experienced a momentous turn in the reputation of their profession as a consequence of their participation in World War II. The story of US psychiatry during World War II is quite well-known, but a few key details are worth restating. When the United States entered the war in 1941, the American Psychiatric Association (APA) offered its advice and assistance to the US Army, only to be ignored initially.[18] At that time, the US Army had appointed thirty-five psychiatrists, only four of whom were board certified.[19] This disregard for mental health in the Army reflected general attitudes toward the discipline in the United States at the time. In the early 1940s, psychiatry was a "marginalized and despised specialty" with its practitioners "trapped within the walls of custodial asylums."[20] By the time the Allied forces declared victory, this had all changed.

In the words of historian Ben Shephard, "it might seem paradoxical that American psychiatry should have emerged from the war with its reputation enhanced when its wartime record was so poor."[21] After high numbers of US soldiers in the North African theater of operations broke down psychologically and emotionally, fears of a mental health crisis were thrust into the spotlight. Throughout the war, Army hospitals admitted approximately 1.1 million US soldiers for neuropsychiatric disorders, of whom nearly 40 percent were discharged unrecovered.[22] Equally disturbing was the fact that mental health screenings had rendered nearly 2 million men unfit for service even before they set foot into a combat environment.[23] Efforts at recruitment screening had been entirely ineffective.

In an attempt to remedy this disastrous situation, the United States Army appointed William Menninger—a "personable and convivial" figure with a "remarkable capacity to inspire confidence among military officers"—as chief psychiatrist of the Armed Forces in December 1943.[24] This change in leadership heralded a very different perspective on the psychological health of US soldiers. Menninger and his team were dynamic psychiatrists who shied away from explanations of mental disease as organic brain dysfunction, adhering instead to a more Freudian-oriented approach. But unlike Freud, the American "neo-Freudians," as they came to be called, did not focus on the "sexual secrets of the unconscious," but rather on a new culprit—high levels of anxiety.[25] Tailoring their diagnostic approach to the current pressing needs of the army, they attributed mental breakdown to pre-existing "psychological and interpersonal" disturbances afflicting soldiers since their early childhood.[26] In effect, it was the ability of the neo-Freudians to explain to military big wigs why some men broke down while others did not that caused respect for and interest in the discipline of psychiatry to surge.[27]

By 1945, these assumptions about nervous and mental breakdown were codified in a landmark document. Menninger and his team prepared "War Department Technical Bulletin, Medical 203," later referred to as "Nomenclature and Method of Recording Psychiatric Conditions," which became the official diagnostic manual for psychiatrists in the US Joint Armed Forces.[28] In the words of Menninger's brother, Karl, this classification finally "cut the Gordian knot of tradition-bound terms and obsolete concepts by formulating de novo a classification . . . largely based on psychodynamic principles."[29]

In addition to re-casting mental illnesses like schizophrenia as a series of psychogenic "reactions" (i.e., schizophrenic reaction),[30] key sections of the "Technical Bulletin, Medical 203" reflected the US psychiatrists' mission to make sense of a critical issue plaguing their troops, namely, chronic somatic pain without any organic pathological trace. Capturing a widespread concern among army leaders about the lack of morale and mental fortitude among US troops, Menninger expressed the mantra of GI Joe: "Oh my aching back."[31] The category of "Psychoneurotic Disorders" in this new document also contained a list of "somatization reactions" that were said to be caused by "the visceral expression of anxiety."[32] Although the conditions outlined in this new manual were to its authors entirely medical in nature, contemporary observers would be struck by the moralistic, if not downright judgmental, undertones that appear throughout. Nowhere was this attitude more apparent than in a section headed "Character and Behavior Disorders." Whether driven by "immaturity" or "passive-aggression," the individuals who fell within this category were said to exhibit "pathological trends in the personality structure, with minimal subjective anxiety, and little or no sense of distress." Interestingly, while Menninger and his colleagues accepted such "developmental defects" as a mental disorder, the patients they diagnosed with it were not cleared of blame. As "Medical 203" stated: "None of the conditions included in the disorder group is acceptable as the cause of separation from the service for disability."[33]

In the postwar era, neo-Freudian theories made their way into mainstream American society, garnering the attention of the nation's most respected news outlets. It was the neo-Freudians after all who now claimed to hold the key to unsettling questions raised by the war. To quote historian Anne Harrington: "What was wrong with America's young men? Why were they so weak, immature and unstable?"[34] Assuming top positions at university medical schools, the new neo-Freudians used their growing professional influence to secure funding for research through the Mental Health Act, which, among other initiatives, authorized the establishment of the National Institute of Mental Health in 1946.[35] A testament to the dominance of neo-Freudians in the world of general psychiatry at the time, "Technical Bulletin, Medical 203" also served as the foundation for the American Psychiatric Association's first *Diagnostics and Statistical Manual of Mental Disorders* (*DSM-I*) published in 1952. By the end of the 1940s, this previously relegated community of psychiatrists had "won the war" within their own profession.[36] It is during this golden era of US psychiatry and "high point of psychoanalytic hegemony" that the war in Korea broke out.[37]

The Beginning of the War on the Korean Peninsula

As far as psychiatry during the Korean War is concerned, its involvement in the conflict can be divided into two phases. During the first phase, Korean psychiatrists responded to the mental health crisis on the battlefield without outside assistance. The second phase began in August 1951 when two Korean medical officers—Yu Sŏk-chin (Yoo Suckjin)[38] and his work partner O Sŏk-hwan—initiated contact with US military psychiatrists, leading to the birth of a US-style military psychiatry program in Korea.

It is difficult to elaborate on the state of mental health in the ROK Army, especially early in the war. Medical record keeping remained poor throughout the war, and the constant shifting of battle lines during the first year of combat compounded the problem. Psychiatric casualties of battle were not accurately registered because the relevant diagnostic categories, nomenclature, methods, and administrative protocols had not yet been established. The information I have collected on this early period is primarily based on interviews with Korea's first military psychiatrists.[39]

Most of the conversations I have had with these figures indicate how quickly and completely the Korean government re-focused its civilian resources to meet military demands. "All medical personnel, including students who had yet to complete their premedical requirements, were drafted into the army," recalled Min Pyŏng-gŭn, who was among the handful of medical students majoring in psychiatry at Seoul National University in 1950.[40] Another psychiatrist, Yi Pong-gi, who was only in his first year of study at the same institution, recalled boarding a train alongside nurses and medical students at Seoul Station to leave for Pusan where they, alongside every other able-bodied male with medical training, became Medical Corps Officers (*wisaengpyŏng*).[41]

The most influential psychiatrist to emerge out of this early situation was the ambitious thirty-year-old named Yu Sŏk-chin, who was later recognized as the founder of Korean military psychiatry.[42] It was Yu who first initiated contact with psychiatrists of the Eighth US Army, an action that turned out to have enormous far-reaching consequences. Born in 1920 in North Kyŏngsang province, Yu graduated from Kyŏngsŏng Imperial University's Medical School in 1944, making him a member of the last graduating class under Japanese colonial rule. In 1949, he had earned his Master's degree in psychiatry at Seoul National University and served as assistant professor at the same institution until the war broke out.[43] In addition to his training, one of the qualities that propelled Yu's career was his ability to speak English. Often going by his English name, "Petrus," Yu hailed from a Catholic family and had been around English speakers since his childhood.[44]

All of the psychiatrists I interviewed acknowledged a dire mental health emergency in the military, which was exacerbated by a lack of resources to address it. That significant numbers of soldiers in the Republic of Korea Army (ROKA) broke down in the face of battle is not surprising. Several factors known to cause high rates of psychiatric casualties were present during the initial phase of the war. First, the ROKA grew quickly. By December 1950, its size had reached 242,000 soldiers.[45] At the high point of the war, 1 million Korean men were enlisted.[46] As a firsthand observer wrote about the challenges of such rapid expansion, "The problem of obtaining men was in itself simple to overcome, but time could not be so easily won, as long as the heavy pressure of battle continued. All too frequently the new replacements were thrown into combat after but a few days of training."[47] In contrast to US troops who had undergone supervised mental hygiene programs for at least three months before deployment, ROK soldiers made the shift from civilian to combatant almost overnight. Officers were similarly undertrained when the war broke out. Any Korean male over the age of twenty-one with an eleventh-grade education could join the Officer Candidate School (OCS). Even at this select institution, however, the training lasted only about six weeks.[48] Both military training and mental preparation were wholly inadequate for the challenge ahead.

Exacerbating this situation was an exceptionally high degree of violence during the first year of the war. In the words of one army medical surgeon, it would be difficult to match the "tactical mobility and intensity of combat in the annals of military history."[49] Studies in military psychiatry have shown that soldiers are most vulnerable psychologically during the "initial severe battle experiences with combat units new to battle before the acquisition and development of group cohesiveness, and the removal of less effective immediate combat leaders."[50]

Unlike their Western allies, the newly formed ROK Army had never fought a modern war. The phenomenon of wartime psychiatric impairment was unknown to them.[51] As Pak In-ho, who began training with the US Army as a psychiatrist in 1953, recalled, "I hadn't even heard of the concept of battle neurosis until I was introduced to it by my American supervisors during the war."[52] A telling sign of the ROKA's unpreparedness in this regard lay in the absence of psychological screenings, a critical tool used by military psychiatrists of the Allied nations during both world wars. As Min Pyŏng-gŭn recalled, "The ROK Army faced a desperate situation, and almost anyone without clear physical disabilities put on a military uniform."[53] As conceptions of mental illness and psychiatry remained outside the purview of ordinary Koreans at this time, even those men who had previously suffered from mental illness had not been diagnosed and could therefore join the armed forces. Yi Chŏng-gyun, a psychiatrist who graduated from Seoul National University in 1952, noted in an interview: "Soldiers were at an age when conditions like schizophrenia were most likely to surface, so the ROK Army was confronted with a combination of war-induced breakdown and everything else."[54] In effect, the absence of screening procedures at recruitment centers meant that anyone who had experienced mental illness—those with pre-existing dormant conditions and those who broke down in battle due to environmental stresses—were grouped under the same category of psychologically malfunctioning South Korean soldiers. For most of these young men, the military provided them with their first encounters with psychiatry.

Lastly, a general bias against mental illness within the ROKA's leadership heightened the early struggles of Korean psychiatrists. Initial efforts to recognize and rehabilitate mentally ill soldiers ranged from indifference to outright antagonism. As Yu recalled: "There clearly were soldiers showing signs of mental illness who had to be treated, but because the psychiatrists were all assigned to other duties, like dressing wounds, these patients were simply discharged without receiving the care they needed."[55] Without a plan to treat psychiatric casualties, most medical authorities considered the treatment of mental illness a luxury that the military could not afford in these urgent circumstances. Yu observed the marginalization encountered by psychiatry at that time in Korea: "To most officers, non-medical officers, enlisted men, and responsible civilians whose energy and interest were absorbed in their own busy work, psychiatry and its role in the organization were new and strange."[56] "Soldiers," Yu continued, "also saw those exhibiting mental abnormalities as threats, fearing that they would commit arson and other acts of violence. . . . [T]he first suggestions made by psychiatrists to create a program for military mental hygiene, a plan to address combat neurosis (*chŏnjaeng sin'gyŏngjŭng*), were laughed off."[57]

Several months into the war in 1951, a group of novice psychiatrists in a rapidly expanding yet still undertrained Korean army grappled with a number of challenges, ranging from a shortage of resources to a sharp rise in cases of mental illness. Reflecting on the hardships that he and his colleagues encountered during this early phase, Yu commented in 1955 that "The tides of psychiatry lay at its lowest point in the months following the beginning of war." The events that followed, however, set the discipline on an entirely new path. According to Yu, "It was at this low-point that the Americans entered the picture."[58]

A Medical Alliance Forms

> In the midst of this struggle and difficulty, psychiatry gained hope and courage because of the American military psychiatrists who came to Korea under the flag of the UN to defend our liberty. We began to see a change in tides initiated by the United States.
>
> —Yu Sŏk-chin (1960)[59]

The birth of psychiatry in Korea may have been sparked by a simple conversation. In August 1951, Yu Sŏk-chin and O Sŏk-hwan established contact with psychiatrists in the Eighth US Army. Yu had served at the head of the Department of Psychiatry at the Capital Army Hospital (Sudo Yukkun Pyŏngwŏn) since its inception in December 1950, He was assisted by O Sŏk-hwan, his junior colleague.[60] In an interview, O Sŏk-hwan explained how the contact with their American colleagues first occurred: "It all began with Colonel Albert Glass, who, as NP (Neuropsychiatric) Consultant for the US forces, came to realize early on during his stay in Korea that there was a clear absence of a psychiatry program for the ROK Army." In O's words: "We practically had nothing," and "Glass realized that psychiatric casualties were soaring among Korean troops."[61]

Glass's arrival in East Asia in the fall of 1950 was the US Army's response to early setbacks by US fighting forces on the battlefield. For the first three months, accounts from the peninsula reported dire mental health conditions among troops. Most likely guided by the false assumption that the war would end quickly, the United States initially "ignored the lessons of the World Wars" and "tried to do without psychiatrists altogether."[62] Specifically, the US military had failed to implement "division psychiatry," which had proven critical in World War II. Soon after Glass's arrival, the main tenets of division psychiatry were synthesized in Korea as PIE (Proximity, Immediacy, and Expectancy), which meant that soldiers had to be treated near the frontlines as soon as symptoms manifested in a simple but authoritative style that encouraged these men to return as soon as possible to their posts.[63] Glass and his team of psychiatrists gained great acclaim in Korea for implementing this program because "he did not only reinstate the World War Two frameworks, he improved upon them."[64] Within three months of Glass's appearance on the job, accounts suggest that "psychiatric casualties fell to almost nothing."[65] Glass and his American medical colleagues used their time in Korea to acquaint the Koreans with this approach.

The 121 Evacuation Hospital and the 212 Neuropsychiatric Detachment

Glass is a well-known figure in the history of US military psychiatry. A colonel in the US Army, he had served in World War II and would later be co-editor of the classic two-volume work *Neuropsychiatry in World War II* (1966–73). Glass's reformist goals in assisting his Korean colleagues were realized after a key structural change in March 1951. As US forces led by General Ridgeway reclaimed the city of Seoul, the 121 Evacuation Hospital, which was first located in Taejŏn and then in Taegu, moved north to its permanent location in the capital city. For the remainder of the war, the 121 in the Yŏngdŭngp'o district of Seoul served as the central army hospital for the entire Eighth US Army. With this newfound institutional stability came opportunities for training and educating medical officers. Removed from areas of direct combat, the 121 received the bulk of psychiatric cases that had proven unresponsive to treatment near the frontlines.[66]

According to official reports filed by the US Army at the time, the physical facilities of the 121 Evacuation Hospital were "excellent." The hospital could house up to a hundred inpatients at a time. A new Director of Neuropsychiatry, Major Henry Segal, assumed his post at the hospital in March 1951. Described by Glass as "resourceful and energetic," Segal used his experience in military psychiatry to re-organize the psychiatry program in Seoul.[67] As the war continued into its second bloody year, 121 Evacuation Hospital expanded and diversified its personnel by also appointing psychiatric social workers and clinical psychologists in August 1951.[68]

When asked how he and Yu Sŏk-chin were chosen to receive training at the 121 as part of their duties to the ROKA, O mentioned their background and good fortune. Both men had been stationed at the 36 Army Hospital and the Capital Army Hospital because of their affiliation with Seoul National University. They consequently were in an opportune position to take the reins of army psychiatry in Korea.[69] They also stood out because of their proficiency in English. O and Yu stayed at the 121 Evacuation Hospital a full year. Even though they also performed their duties at the Capital Army Hospital, they were completely immersed. O recalled that he hardly left the compound, eating all his meals there alongside the Americans. According to O, both Glass and Segal played pivotal roles in allowing the program to gain momentum. Both American physicians showed a high degree of enthusiasm and commitment to teach the principles of division psychiatry and general psychiatry to their Korean colleagues.[70]

In addition to the 121 Evacuation Hospital, the Eighth US Army opened a new medical unit in February 1952 in the It'aewŏn district of Seoul. The 212 Neuropsychiatric Detachment operated out of a "cluster of tents and Quonset huts."[71] Nevertheless, its operations were critical, serving as a middle-ground for those soldier-patients who were being triaged in the combat zone and those being evacuated to the rear.[72] According to a US Army Command Report published in June 1953, more than 5,200 patients were evaluated and treated at this new facility.[73]

The 212 Neuropsychiatric Detachment also served for the remainder of the war as a training site for military psychiatrists. As a "main supply source to divisions for psychiatrists in the US Army," members of the 212 worked closely with psychiatrists at the 121 Evacuation Hospital in order to provide training to "newly arrived psychiatric officers, technicians and wardmen."[74] As the Command Report went on to note: "All psychiatrists coming to the Eighth US Army are first assigned to this unit for training and after completion of training continue to work here until needed by a division."[75] Given its vital role, the army staffed the site with its most accomplished instructors: "Therefore, in order to make full utilization of abilities a possibility, it is suggested that the most highly trained psychiatrists be assigned at this installation."[76]

Most relevant to the Korean side of the story is this comment: "This unit conducts a program of psychiatric education for selected ROKA officers. Each training cycle runs for a six-month period and *helps meet the need for Korean psychiatrists*."[77] Memories of training at the 212 Neuropsychiatric Detachment came up in nearly all of my interviews with Korean psychiatrists. They spoke about the importance of this training (*yangsŏng*) program in producing the first wave of Korean officers who provided psychiatric treatment to their own troops. When asked to recall specific events during his training program, one psychiatrist, Yi Pong-gi, cited lectures by acclaimed psychoanalysts, such as Hugh T. Carmichael of the Chicago Institute of Psychoanalysis, which further sparked his interest in US psychiatry. To the young, budding Korean psychiatrists, "these were like meetings with stars."[78]

Medical Study Abroad: *Tomi Yuhak*

Apart from participating in training programs at US facilities in Korea, Korean psychiatrists also took part in a new program that was instituted in the fall of 1952. Referred to simply as "Study in America" (*Tomi yuhak*), this program brought Korean medical officers to army hospitals throughout the United States for training. Records show that four individuals were selected from each department of medicine in Korea, including prominent figures such as Kim Sŏng-jin, the future Surgeon General of the Army.[79] The first four Korean psychiatrists sent to the United States from Korea for additional medical education were Yu Sŏk-chin, Kang Chun-Sang, O Sŏk-hwan, and Chin Sŏng-gi. For all four of these figures, their training in Seoul greatly assisted them in acclimating to the new foreign setting. In O's words, "I was also fortunate to have received ten months of training at the 121 prior to leaving for the United States. Compared to others, I was able to communicate well and felt that I had a substantial orientation process behind me."[80] According to Pak In-ho, who was included in the next group of psychiatrists who traveled abroad, the Americans made sure that Korean medical officers had plenty of opportunities to prepare for their time overseas. Three months prior to departure, Pak In-ho participated in a program at the 121 Evacuation Hospital in which "daytime activities, ward rounds, and patient interviews were all performed in English alongside the Americans."[81]

Once in the United States, Yu and Kang were sent to Fitzsimons Army Hospital in Denver, Colorado. According to a pamphlet distributed to new military officers that Yu retained in his personal files, Fitzsimons Army Hospital, also known as US Army Hospital No. 21, was the Army's largest general hospital at the time.[82] Yu also preserved a list of all participants in the first six-month training program at Fitzsimons. Of the sixty-one participants listed as of 12 September 1952, six were listed as "Korean Army"; study specialties included Medicine, Surgery, and Neuropsychiatry.[83] He also saved an envelope from the Menninger Foundation, indicating that the most iconic neo-Freudian training facility in the nation in the 1950s had also reached out to the Korean guests during their time in the United States.[84]

Meanwhile, O and Chin made their way to Brooke General Hospital in San Antonio, Texas. There, they had the opportunity to train directly under Albert Glass who had just been appointed head of psychiatry at the Army Medical School adjoining the hospital grounds. Having been reunited with his first American medical mentor, O spent the next seven months working under Glass's tutelage. In O's words: "I and the others considered it nothing short of a blessing (*haengun*) to have Colonel Albert Glass as our supervisor."[85] Using Glass's connections, O enrolled at the Brooke General Hospital in the Army Psychiatry training (*yangsŏng*) course entitled the "8-0-10" class. Interestingly, after completion of this course the US Army issued a credit that certified O to practice psychiatry in Korea as well as the United States.[86] While studying in San Antonio, O had seen venerable psychiatrists lecture, including Franz Alexander, William Borden, and William Menninger. It is not surprising that O referred to his time in Texas as nothing short of a "life-changing experience."[87]

The Triumph of Military Psychiatry

After their remarkable half-year tour in the United States came to an end in the early months of 1953, the group of four returned to Korea equipped with new knowledge and insights as well as renewed conviction about how to develop a state-of-the-art program in military psychiatry in their own country. Compared to the previous year, Korean army leaders were now far less skeptical of their suggestions and seemed much more open to hearing about their travel experiences abroad. "Other Medical Corps members had toured hospitals in the US as well during this time, and this exposure to American standards of mental health care made our work more tolerable to them," noted O. Furthermore, the promotion of former Lt. Colonel Kim to the post of Surgeon General of the country, coupled with Yu and O's personal ties to Kim Sŏng-jin, decisively influenced the army's attitudes and policies.[88] On 8 February 1954, the ROK Army Headquarters (Yukkun Ponbu) issued Regulation 490, which permanently established the role of military psychiatrists in the South Korean armed forces.[89]

According to a study conducted by the Korean Neuropsychiatric Association, a total of forty-five Korean psychiatrists were trained by the visiting Americans during the war.[90] In spite of this modest overall number, it is difficult to overemphasize the importance of this fact for the subsequent history of psychiatry in Korea. The highly successful wartime alliance between the US and South Korean armies created unprecedented opportunities for training and cooperation between psychiatrists from radically different cultures and backgrounds. Because the military was then the only place for aspiring medics to receive medical training, information circulated quickly and efficiently. At the same time, the rigid army hierarchy ensured that the education they received was centralized and uniform.

With the armistice on 27 June 1953, the three-year Korean War came to a close, although political tensions would continue to grow on the peninsula during the following years. With both sides of the conflict maintaining full-scale armies capable of striking at any given moment, the importance of military psychiatry in Korea only increased. As their US supervisors gradually withdrew from the country, the newly trained Korean psychiatrists strove to maintain the momentum of their discipline. Let us now turn to the condition of Korean military psychiatry in the immediate postwar period by analyzing a set of case studies that clearly indicate why US approaches to mental illness appealed to and endured with Koreans psychiatrists after the war's end.

Three Case Studies

Just before Yu Sŏk-chin passed away in 2008, he donated his personal archive of over 30,000 items to Seoul National University's Museum of Medicine. As a visiting researcher at this institution in 2010, I came across a box in this collection marked "Military." It contained all manner of manuals, textbooks, letters, meeting agendas, maps, and unpublished research papers from the 1950s. The materials in this box proved to be illuminating in my quest to explore the foundational years of Korea's mental health system.

One document immediately caught my attention. Labeled "Eunuchoidism," it contained multipage case studies of five patients who had been under the care of Yu and Yi Pong-gi, his colleague, at the Capital Army Hospital in 1954.[91] Each soldier deemed "eunuchoid" showed no signs of physical injury but was nevertheless unable to perform their assigned duties because of unexplained somatoform complaints. After a thorough evaluation of their physiological and psychological profiles, Yu and Yi shared the results of their examinations at the fifth meeting of the Military Psychiatry Association (*Kunjin Chŏngsin Ŭihak Chiptamhoe*) in December 1954.

Aside from its curious title, this text intrigued me for a number of reasons. Most of the study was written in English, even though the audience for Yu and Yi's presentation was Korean. The presence of several "Psychiatric Screening Reports" provided some insight as to why this was the case. The words "121st Evacuation Hospital" appeared at the top of the page with a list of people who had been involved in the study. Alongside the names of the Korean doctors there appeared a certain "First Lt. Arthur C. Robbins, MSC" who had approved all the reports. For these reasons, I assumed that these case studies were a collaborative exercise between the Korean physicians and the Americans who oversaw them. However, the "Psychological Screening Reports" were in fact penned by the Americans themselves. By sharing their diagnostic interpretations with their Korean colleagues, they offered a template for how to conduct this type of analysis.

The venue and timing of these presentations were also significant. The Military Psychiatric Society was formed in January 1954, at a time when the civilian university and hospital system in Korea were still recovering from the war. Held at the Capital Army Hospital, these meetings were critical in keeping the newly minted practitioners up to date with the advances in their profession.[92] In effect, these case studies tell us much more than about how these two Korean doctors thought about the clinical issues at hand. They grant us invaluable glimpses into the state of psychiatry in postwar Korea at a critical juncture in its medical and political history.

A Note on "Eunuchoidism"

The current-day equivalent to "eunuchoidism" is most likely "hypogonadism," a condition thought to be caused by testosterone deficiency. Understanding why the Koreans fixated on this diagnosis requires a consideration of the prewar era. European medical literature from the early twentieth century contained numerous discussions about this condition, which could afflict both sexes but was more common in men. In their introduction to these clinical reports, Yu and Yi cited endocrinologists "Landler [*sic*] and Gross,"[93] who earlier had defined the "eunuchoid" as "someone who may appear castrated, but whose sex glands are not removed." Their footnotes suggest that they in turn relied on the work of Hermann Zondek (1887–1979), a German-Jewish endocrinologist who had served as the head of the Berlin Hospital prior to World War II, quoting Tandler and Gross directly from *The Diseases of the Endocrine Glands*, which Zondek had published in German in 1923.[94] Yu's interest in this topic is understandable if we consider that he had received his medical degree from Kyŏngsŏng Imperial University in 1944. Physicians in Japan and colonial Korea drew heavily on German models from the late nineteenth century onward.[95] Apparently, Yu and his colleagues had been influenced by German sexology and endocrinology that circulated prior to the war's outbreak when Korea was still under Japanese colonial rule.

At the same time, their longstanding interest in eunuchoidism seems to have been re-ignited and reshaped in the 1950s by their American contacts. Hugh T. Carmichael, who delivered lectures on psychoanalytic theory in Korea during the war, had in 1941 published an article titled "A Psychoanalytic Study of a Case of Eunuchoidism."[96] Carmichael's publication indicates that American psychiatrists had put a Freudian spin on this pre-existing medical topic.[97]

In the following section of the case file entitled "Physical Examination," Yu and Yi provide detailed bodily descriptions of the soldiers in question. One soldier, for example, had testicles that had not descended, while his gonads were the "size of a cherry." Another patient had a face that was "edematous" (swollen), while his body was "obese." The doctors ordered a "spermatogensis examination," although the results of such a test were not recorded.[98] In spite of the genital irregularities, Yu concluded that a "simple causal relationship" could not be traced to hormonal disturbances despite the assumed correlations between "endocrine anomalies" and "psychical disturbances."

The remainder of the study sought to locate the cause of these patients' mental dysfunction not in biology but rather in family dynamics. As the following excerpts express, the Korean doctors took a keen interest in mother-son relationships. They also inquired into the sexual relations between their subjects and their spouses. A key point to note is that none of the men diagnosed with eunuchoidism had been castrated, but the psychiatrists' characterizations of them indicate their belief that these patients had been psychologically castrated in childhood. In effect, the failed soldier, upon examination by a multinational medical team, became a metaphorical "eunuchoid" in 1950s Korea.

Patient 1: Lower Back Pain

Private First Class Sin Yu-hŭi came to the Capital Army Hospital on 27 November 1954 with the chief complaint of "lumbago," a medical term for lower back pain. For the entire past year Private Sin had suffered from spastic sensations of the extremities. The pain debilitated him to a point that he was no longer able to fulfill his military assignments, leading army physicians to refer him for evaluation by army psychiatrists.

In an overview of the patient's family history, Yu and Yi noted that Private Sin had been the only child in a financially struggling household. Sin's father had suffered from lung disease for the past three years while his mother died immediately after his birth due to complications with food poisoning. Economic hardship kept him from attending school regularly. Around the age of ten, his father attempted to teach his son the first thousand Chinese characters and orient him to the *Myŏngsim pokam*, a classic handbook of proverbs from the Koryo period (918–1392) of Korean history. The patient soon abandoned these lessons, however, due to a lack of interest and never resumed his studies. The report continues: "Currently he is able to read Korean language, but he has forgotten nearly all Chinese characters. He claims that he wanted to study more but that it was not possible because of a lack of money." Despite his lack of formal education, Sin managed to rise to the status of private first class within six months after being enlisted. Before being hospitalized, his main role had been transporting ammunition. In their evaluation, Yu and Yi described the patient's mental state as "dull and apathetic." "Memory and orientation with person, time, and place is not intact," they wrote. Yu and Yi issued a two-part diagnosis: (1) "Oligophrenia," a medical term for mental retardation, and (2) "Eunuchoidism."

Interestingly, a diagnosis of mental deficiency might have sufficed to explain the patient's inability to perform his duties. Instead, however, the doctors placed greater diagnostic weight on the patient's interpersonal and psychological history, which they presumed would cast light on the most important clinical question: what was causing Sin's chronic back pain? Yu and Yi specifically highlighted aberrations in Sin's sexual biography, stressing his inexperience with intercourse. They noted that apparently he had never had intercourse with his wife of three years. They explained this unusual fact as the outcome of abnormal relationships with his parents: "The patient's mother passed away early on and there was a stepmother with whom relations were poor. Meanwhile, his father was always sick. From age 7 to 9, he was kicked out of the home by his stepmother, so he went to live at his sister's house."

Following this meticulous patient history was the "Psychological Screening Report" that aimed to analyze Sin's condition further. According to his examiners, the patient exhibited an "emotional void" and seemed to have "no understanding of himself and little ability to relate to others. His thinking processes have as their main characteristics a lack of depth, an inability to integrate and organize, and a tendency to be concerted [*sic*]." According to them, however, Sin's inability to have sexual relations with a woman was not attributed to "Eunuchoidism" but rather a longstanding personality defect:

> There seems to be a considerable amount of repressed hostility in this patient, most of this appears to be directed toward the female who apparently is viewed as a threatening ungiving individual who is to be avoided. The test [*sic*] of the world also seems to be thought of by the patient as being hostile, and he appears to passively countour [*sic*] this withdrawn negativistic approach to life.

One may hypothesis [*sic*] that his ability to relate genitally to the woman is a product of both his generally low level of development and intense repressed rage directed toward the woman.

Yu and Yi's medical evaluation concluded with an acknowledgment of his intellectual limitations, although this "mental retardation" was not a cited reason for the soldier's failure to perform his duties. "In summary," the report concludes, "it would seem that due to the patient's inability to comprehend and adjust to the vicissitudes of life, he has withdrawn his already meager personal resources so as to appear even more defective than is apparently the case." The "vicissitudes of life" in this setting referred to his work as a soldier. Yu and Yi's term "appear even more defective" is telling, as it framed the patient's inability to carry out his duties as a decision that originated from the patient's psychological and emotional weaknesses. Medicalization and moral judgment here went hand in hand.

Patient 2: Headache

In contrast to Private Sin Yu-hŭi, a second soldier discussed in Yu Sŏk-chin's archive possessed intellectual capabilities described as "average with a potential in the Bright Normal, or possible superior range." Recently administered tests had determined the unnamed patient's IQ to be 91. For unknown reasons, the "Psychological Screening Report," completed on 11 November 1954, appeared without any background information about the patient. The report itself, however, includes much interesting material.

The opening line reads: "The pt. exhibits a passive aggressive character as manifested by a hostile, ungiving, obstructionist attitude towards life along with a partial conversion of aggression into bodily complaints." The author then re-emphasized the patient's relatively high level of intellectual functioning: "There are no evidences of psychosis, impairment of reality testing, breaks in association, or unconventional modes of thinking." Claiming that the patient's ill-health stemmed from psychological causes, the case history continues, "Similarly, there are no indications of organicity." In the following passage, the attending physicians revealed what they believed to be the true causes of the problems:

> Controlled by an early instilled personality pattern of passive acception [*sic*] love and affection, it became difficult for the pt. to develop the ability to actively and independently seek out his emotional needs. This has resulted in two separate but interrelated problem areas. The first has to do with the internal conflict between the pt's unconscious desire to sit back and be waited on and his more conscious desire to fulfill the culturally accepted role of the self assertive dominant male. . . . The second problem is also an outgrowth of the

pt's passivity in that when a person adopts as his major approach to life the role of meek acceptance, he cannot help but being frustrated many, many times.

It is only at the end of the report that the examiners reveal the source of the patient's initial complaints. They write:

> As a result, there is considerable rage generated toward the world which is viewed as ungiving and threatening. Being passive in orientation, however, it is too dangerous for the pt. to less obvious means. In this case the pt developed a chronic headache which serves both as a successful and at the same time acceptable excuse for refusing to assume his responsibilities. In light of the above factors, it is unlikely that the pt will change his passive aggressiveness toward the world. Prognosis for therapy is poor, because of the long-standing characteristic [sic] nature of the pt's problem.

In this case, too, the observation regarding the patient's desire to "sit back and be waited on" exemplified a dual tendency in the approach of these neo-Freudian trained psychiatrists to medicalize and criticize. Embedded in their tone are a series of moral judgments about the soldier's character. Their references to the patient's alleged impulse to carry out his "culturally accepted role" of the "dominant male" may allude to traditional, Korean expectations of masculinity as well as the type of "warrior" ideal demanded by military life.

Patient 3: Epilepsy

In the last of these three wartime cases, a patient was hospitalized for recurring seizures. Yi Tong-u, a 22-year-old private first class in the ROK Army, was hospitalized just a month before the completion of the study. The patient came from a family of six children. No immediate family members suffered from mental illness. Prior to enlisting, Yi Tong-u had received limited schooling. At home, he worked as a farmer, assisting his parents in the fields. In the military, his primary task was transporting supplies.

From the "mental examination," Yu and Yi noted that the patient's voice and "stream of talk and activity" were "female like." All of his actions, in fact, struck Yi's examiners as feminine and childish. Thought and affect appeared to be normal, but his intelligence was "infantile." Results of the "physical examination" showed that the patient was tall although with a narrow chest. His legs and arms were relatively large. His skin color was described as "female-like," his neck "longer than average." His extremities were "very long" while his testicles showed signs of "atrophy." The doctors continued in their case report by revealing detailed information about the patient's genitalia, noting that they were underdeveloped. Given their findings, Yu and his team diagnosed the patient with eunuchoidism and grand mal epilepsy. They then ordered three additional tests: "1) X-ray for chest and head; 2) Seman [*sic*]; 3) P.E.G."[99]

The "Psychological Screening Report" for this third patient contained rhetoric similar to that used in the previous cases. The examiners characterized Yi as follows:

> This is a depressed dysphoric individual who presents a façade of extreme passivity. Beneath the outer layer, however, are feelings of repressed rage. Fearful of his own hostility, he has withdrawn much of his energy from social interaction. Much repressed hostility is directed toward the parents for the lack of primal love and nurturance; the dominant, punitive, castrative, castrating mother is hated because of her unwillingness to give, and his epileptic episodes appear to represent the punishment he desired.

Only at the end of the Screening Report do the doctors entertain the possibility of a physiological problem causing the patient's seizures: "The patient has a tendency to reverse figure and ground; furthermore there is some impairment in visual-poor control [*sic*]. The possibility of organic brain damage, while not clearly indicated, should certainly be investigated."

The Non-Effective Soldier in Korea

In addition to demonstrating American neo-Freudian ideas in action in Korea, the Psychological Screening Reports I presented above contain a few critical excerpts worthy of further elaboration. The following quote is striking: "The patient's perception of reality is weakened by a morbid concern with corpses, deceasing bodies, and deteriorating anatomy." Given the timing of this study, it is quite possible that the ubiquitous sight of fallen soldiers and injured civilians may, quite understandably, have given rise to this patient's preoccupations. The report did not mention whether the subject had enlisted in the army prior to or after the ceasefire, but, given his age, it is not unlikely that he developed this particular problem while participating in combat. Nowhere in the report do the physicians consider that his health preoccupations could be related to traumatic experiences in battle.

Furthermore, in this report, the supervising Americans write: "It is to be stressed that findings based on best results for this patient are extremely tentative, since techniques used have not been validated for a Korean population. Within the limits imposed by language barriers and cultural differences, however, a schizophrenic character appears in evidence, as manifested by rigid, perserverative [*sic*] alogical thinking, morbidity and defective reality testing." This passage captures a fundamental issue in the unique cross-cultural partnership between American and South Korean psychiatrists: Were these US-based, neo-Freudian theories applicable to foreigners and, specifically, to the Koreans?[100] At times, the medical Americans seem to express some doubts. However, their passing concerns did not halt the transmission of US psychiatry, as their Korean protégés eagerly applied the new theories and terminology that they had acquired.

The somewhat haphazard injection of psychoanalytic theory into the Korean military's handling of psychiatric casualties was seemingly widespread during the Korean War. In 1954, *The American Journal of Psychiatry* published the results of a study conducted at a "neuropsychiatric center in Seoul." It was co-written by a Dr. Edwards from Australia and his associate, Dr. Peterson, from the United States, who had taken over Albert Glass's post after Glass returned to the United States. Their patient was a 25-year-old male soldier referred to simply as "Sargent L." In Edwards and Peterson's study, the patient's complaints included severe headaches and spells of passing out that had begun several months earlier after a "grenade exploded in his vicinity." From the outset, Edwards and Peterson excluded the possibility that Sargent L's condition originated from "organic causes," attributing his symptoms instead to "emotional factors." "Major dynamics" evidenced by the patient's symptoms included "self-conscious doubts of his masculinity with reactive over-assertiveness; efforts to outdo his brother, a sibling rival; feelings of failure as a husband." The final diagnosis of this patient was "emotional instability reaction."[101]

Looking through Yu's rich archival collection, it is possible to reconstruct the background of this study. Included in the collection is an original copy of the "Nomenclature and Method for Recording Psychiatric Disorders"—the World War II creation also known as War Department Technical Bulletin, Medical 203.[102] After receiving it from his American mentors, Yu annotated parts of the text and shared it with his colleagues. The cover page contains the seal of the Capital Army Hospital (Sudo Yukkun Pyŏngwŏn) and a handwritten note by Yu asking that sixty copies be made. Included in the passages that he underlined is the discussion of "Character and Behavior Disorders" and the various "pathological personality types" that fell under this diagnostic umbrella. The Korean subjects in Yu's study were among the first East Asians to be evaluated through this American psychiatric lens.

Yu also appears to have taken a keen interest in a document penned in 1951 by Colonel Albert Glass. The document is titled "The Medical Treatment of a Non-Effective Soldier," and Yu included it in his Korean War collection. A handwritten request on the cover page of Glass's text again asks that fifty copies be made for his fellow Korean military psychiatrists training at the Capital Army Hospital. "The Medical Treatment of the Non-Effective Soldier" contained Glass's observations and ideas on soldiers deemed unable to follow their duties due to psychological breakdown in Korea.[103]

According to Glass in this text, the non-effective soldier was an individual "without physical and mental disease but who demonstrated inadequate duty

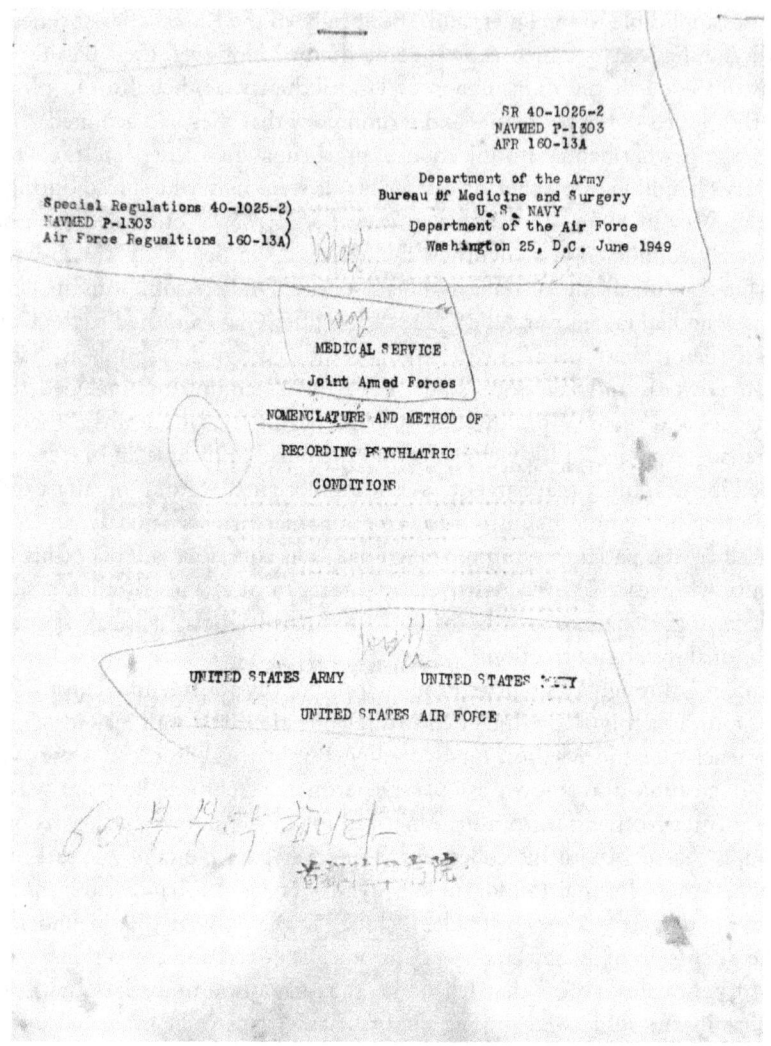

FIGURE 4.1. Cover page of "Nomenclature and Method of Recording Psychiatric Conditions" issued by the United States Joint Armed Forces. An original copy was found in Yu's personal archive. © Jennifer Yum-Park.

performance," a description that referred not only to disabled soldiers "but to individuals who either by virtue of poor attitude and motivation or personality disorders posed disciplinary problems" or who presented a "handicap to their organization." The presumption that psychological disturbances were at the root of a long list of somatic complaints can be seen in Glass's usage of terms such as "unwilling" and "immature." Glass asserted further that "the unwilling soldier often presents himself as being unable to perform duty because of physical complaints." Such an unwilling soldier had "definite character flaws" and suffered from "self-pride" that deprived him of the "inner demand to conform." "Basically," Glass wrote, "the personality defect lies in the inability of the immature individual to either mobilize or adequately discharge aggression when such an adaptation is necessary for effective action." Headaches and backaches were dismissed as "fake" impediments, a conclusion reiterated in Glass's discussion of "immaturity" manifested in the "passive aggressive individual." "He is also conspicuous by the absence of outward manifestations of aggressiveness but demonstrates some degree of hostility in the form of stubbornness, procrastination, and obstructionism. This type of person," the document adds, "may appear resentful but denies such feelings, usually stating that he cannot work because of headache or backache."

The American Neo-Freudian Foundations of Korean Psychiatry

I conclude that Korean psychiatrists adopted the neo-Freudian ideas that their American mentors had brought with them so readily partly because the symptoms of mental breakdown among soldiers transcended culture and geography. Retired military psychiatrist Min Pyŏng-gŭn, who was part of Yu's team at the Capital Army Hospital in 1954, expressed this reality very aptly to me in an interview when I inquired about their mind set and motivations all those years ago: "These soldiers were suffering from Yankee-style trauma (*Yangkisik tŭrauma*), so we figured they should be evaluated in psychodynamic ways."[104] Quite possibly, the "Yankee-style trauma" that Korean psychiatrists encountered during the first half of the 1950s, and which they were then inclined to brush off as the personality dysfunctions of a "Non-Effective Soldier," would today merit the diagnosis of Posttraumatic Stress Disorder. Chronic pain of unexplained origin is indeed one of the signature symptoms associated with the condition. But this was a different time and place, some thirty years before the coining of the term PTSD and the coming of our current "age of trauma." The Koreans struggled to understand symptoms that they had never encountered before, and they were not alone.

Despite many cultural and linguistic barriers, Korean military psychiatrists eagerly and somewhat uncritically accepted the lessons espoused to them by their American counterparts. The power of the US military, the acuteness of the wartime mental health crisis throughout the peninsula, and the career ambitions of doctors on both the US and Korean sides gave this synthesis of neo-Freudian ideas real sticking power. Psychological trauma may or may not be timeless and universal; as the case of mid-twentieth-century Korea clearly illustrates, however, understandings and approaches to it are very much historically situated.

There is an instructive postscript to my story. The cadre of Korean medics who had practiced under the visiting Americans during the 1950–1953 period would go on to become pioneers in postwar civilian psychiatry in Korea. Viewed historically, this is a rare instance in which the emergence of military psychiatry in a given country or culture preceded the development of civilian psychiatry. In fact, after the war's end, this small but highly influential group of military psychiatrists remained united and formed the Korean Neuropsychiatric Association (KNPA) (Taehan Sin'gyŏng Chŏngsin Ŭihakhoe), consciously fashioning themselves after the American Psychiatric Association (APA). The first issue of their academic journal *Neuropsychiatry* (*Singyŏng chŏngsinŭihak*) contained a section called "Academic Terminology," in which key Freudian terminology was translated from English to Korean.[105]

On 6 June 1957, dozens of Korean psychiatrists who now held prominent academic positions at the nation's top hospitals gathered at Seoul National University to celebrate the centennial of Freud. Looking at the proceedings from the event, we see the names of military psychiatrists who are now familiar to us: Min Pyŏng-gŭn of the Capital Army Hospital spoke on "Freud's Concept of Hysteria." Yu Sŏk-chin chose "Freud's Theory on Religion" as his topic. Kang Chun-sang, who had studied in the United States with Yu during the war and who had risen to a high-ranking position in the Office of the Surgeon General (Ŭimu kamsil), lectured on "Freud's Theory on the Arts."[106] The explanation for why a select circle of professional Koreans, many of whom a decade earlier had scarcely heard of Sigmund Freud, orchestrated such an event can only be found in the events that transpired during the Korean War.

Wartime US influences in the field of psychological medicine lingered into the 1960s when the South Korean government founded the first national mental hospital, the National Mental Hospital (Kungnip Chŏngsin Pyŏngwŏn) in Chunggok-dong, in the eastern part of Seoul. If today we examine the early medical records of the National Mental Hospital, we find that they are recorded in English, and that the diagnoses used in the clinical files often derive from a mid-century neo-Freudian paradigm of psychopathology. This heritage is discernible in the ubiquitous use of the term "schizophrenic reaction," which appears to have been a leading cause of hospitalization throughout the 1960s.[107] Moreover, the first wave of patients admitted to the hospital in Chunggok-dong were veterans who had been treated up until that point at army hospitals. Today, the hospital grounds serve as a reminder of this distinctive history. In the lobby of the hospital, a plaque commemorating US-Korean cooperation greets visitors, alongside a painting of a handshake between Koreans and Americans, symbolizing the fundamental importance of the US-ROK alliance of the 1950s for the foundation of the nation's state mental hospital program.[108]

The legacy of the Korean American encounter extended into the world of non-medical mental health care providers, too. We learned above that social

FIGURE 4.2. Yi Pong-gi, co-author of *Eunuchoidism: A Clinical Case Study*, is pictured with Matthew Parrish MD, a US Army psychiatrist who was Yi's mentor at the 121 Evacuation Hospital in 1954. Parrish was chief psychiatric consultant to the Surgeon General of the Army during his time in Korea. Image courtesy of Yi Pong-gi.

workers and clinical psychologists from the United States also made their marks in Korea during the war. The psychologists introduced Rorschach ink blot tests, among other diagnostic screening techniques, into Korean psychology.[109] Social workers, whose professional roots traced back to the child guidance centers of the Progressive Era, had discussed psychoprophylactic programs aimed at rehabilitating wayward youth before they descended too far down the path of mental illness.[110] Not surprisingly, after the war Yu and his team followed the US model in the field of child psychiatry by founding the Seoul Child Guidance Clinic (Sŏul Adong Sangdamso) for "juvenile delinquents" (*pihaeng sonyŏn*) in 1958. The establishment of the Child Guidance Clinic was in fact a perfect occasion to bridge the gap between military and civilian applications of psychiatry since the number of children distraught by their sobering encounters with death, displacement, and crippling poverty skyrocketed in the postwar period.[111]

In South Korea's psychiatric history, then, ideas preceded institutions, and discourses came before buildings. The textual origins of Korean psychiatry track back to the Psychological Screening Reports discussed above; diagnostically, Korean psychiatric medicine traces to "Yankee-style trauma," which was a North American Cold War import.

Lastly, my study, I believe, urges scholars to examine more closely how wars, including international wartime medical alliances, can operate as a mechanism for the transfer of knowledge as well as for the institutionalization of medical-scientific paradigms. Previous books such as Ethan Watters' *Crazy Like Us: The Globalization of the American Psyche* (2011) tap into the theme of the global spread of US psychiatric ideas and practices. "Our definitions have become the international standards," the author writes.[112] Watters's widely-discussed work, however, focuses on a later era, beginning in the 1980s, when the object of internationalization was psychotropic drugs and the institutional agent of psychiatric dissemination was the pharmaceutical companies that market these medications globally. Circumstances surrounding the origins and rise of psychiatry in Korea, however, show that this globalization process goes back in fact at least as early as the middle of the twentieth century. In particular, the Americanization of Asian mental health is a much older story, which has its roots in the trauma of war.

Jennifer Yum-Park received her Ph.D. in History and East Asian Languages from Harvard University in 2014. Since then, she has been affiliated with Harvard as a Research Fellow at the Korea Institute (2018–19) and a Teaching Fellow in the Department of the History of Science. Her dissertation examined the role of the Korean War and the US Army in the rise of South Korean psychiatry during the 1950s and 1960s. She is the author of "Suicide, 'New Women,' and Media Sensation in Colonial Korea" in *Transgression in Korea: Beyond Resistance and Control,* edited by Juhn Y. Ahn (University of Michigan Press, 2018). Her research has been supported by the Korea Foundation, Harvard University, and Wellesley College. From 2011 to 2012, she was a research associate at the Seoul National University Hospital Center for History and Culture and Seoul National Hospital's Department of Mental Health Research. Her scholarly interests include the history of psychiatry, medicine, gender, and popular culture in twentieth century East Asia. She resides in Boston with her husband and two daughters.

Notes

1. Korean words in this chapter have been transliterated according to the McCune-Reischauer system.
2. For comprehensive historical overviews of Western military psychiatry, see Shephard, *War of Nerves* and Jones and Wessely, *Shell Shock to PTSD.*
3. This book chapter is the only published English-language study of psychiatry during the Korean War written from the Korean perspective. Although there are a few Korean-language accounts that touch upon this topic, they were composed by Korean psychiatrists who had a personal stake in their profession's history. While helpful factually, their

writings tend to lack historical contextualization and analytical rigor. Yi Pu-yŏng (Rhi Bou-Yong) is the most prolific among these scholars. Other authors include Chŏng Wŏn-yong (Chung Wonyong), Yi Na-mi (Lee NaMi), and Yi Pang-hyŏn. In 2009, the Korean Neuropsychiatric Association also published its own history: Han'guk chŏngsin ŭihak 100-yŏnsa p'yonch'an wiwŏnhoe, *Han'guk chŏngsinŭihak 100-nyŏn sa.*
4. Fulton, *Red Room*, ix.
5. For a detailed institutional history of hospitals in colonial Korea, see Pak Hyŏng-u, *Chejungwŏn.*
6. During the 1920s, Severance Union Medical College in Seoul also offered a limited psychiatry training-course led by Western missionaries.
7. Yi Pu-yŏng [Rhi Bou-Yong], "Roots Korean Psychiatry," 99.
8. Personal accounts of students' and professors' experiences in the Department of Psychology at Keijo Imperial University can be found in Chŏng Han-t'aek, *Han'guk simnihak 60-yŏnsa*, 21–43.
9. Yoo, *It's Madness*, 52.
10. Chŏng Wŏn-yong, "Kŭndae sŏyang chŏngsin ŭihak ŭi chŏn'gaewa pyŏnch'ŏn' kwajŏng," 124–42.
11. Yu Sŏk-chin, *Kŏn'guk 10yŏn ŭi Han'guk chŏngsin ŭihak*, Unpublished account, personal papers of Yu Sŏk-jin, at Seoul National University Center for Hospital History and Culture. Here, Yu provides an overview of the history of psychiatry in Korea. For an account of Japanese psychiatry in the late nineteenth to early twentieth century, see Hashimoto, "A 'German World' Shared among Doctors."
12. On Kraepelin's commitment to degenerationism, see Engstrom, "'On the Question of Degeneration.'" For a discussion of Freud in colonial Korea, see Yoo, *It's Madness*, xxx.
13. Information obtained from my keyword search of "mental illness" (*chŏngsinpyŏng*) in the *Chosŏn ilbo* (*The Chosun Daily*) and *Tonga ilbo* (*Dong-a Daily*) between 1920 and 1935.
14. Yi Pang-hyŏn, "Singminji chosŏn eso ŭi chŏngsinbyŏngja ŭi taehan kŭndaejŏk chŏpkŭn," 547.
15. Yi Pang-hyŏn, "Singminji chosŏn esoŭi chŏngsin pyŏngja e taehan kŭndaejŏk chŏpkŭn," 546.
16. Maruyama Chijun, *Chosŏn ŭi kwisin*, 218–23. In pre-modern Korea, peach wood was thought to be the strongest wood.
17. *Tonga ilbo*, 26 Sept 1949. The figure of 200,000 is not shocking, given that 1 to 3 percent of people of any society are considered mentally ill and in need of treatment at any given time. The figure of 9 percent, however, is surprising.
18. Glass and Jones, *Psychiatry US Army*, 739–40.
19. Barton, *History Influence APA*, 133.
20. Scull, *Hysteria*, 179.
21. Shephard, *War of Nerves*, 332.
22. Pols, "Tunisian Campaign."
23. Hale, *Rise Crisis Psychoanalysis US*, 188, Harrington, "Mother Love."
24. Shephard, *War of Nerves*, 203.
25. Harrington, *Mind Fixers*, 82.
26. Hale, *Rise Crisis Psychoanalysis US*, 245.
27. Burnham, *Paths into American Culture*, 101.
28. "Psychiatric Disorders and Reactions." This issue of the *Journal of Mental Science* contained a full copy of the War Department Technical Bulletin, Medical 203.
29. Menninger, "Discussion."
30. "Psychiatric Disorders and Reactions," 433.
31. "Notes."

32. "Psychiatric Disorders and Reactions," 433.
33. "Psychiatric Disorders and Reactions," 430.
34. Anne Harrington, "Mother Love."
35. Menninger and Nemiah, *American Psychiatry after WWII*, 203–4.
36. For an extensive discussion of the neo-Freudians in postwar United States, consult Hale, *Rise Crisis Psychoanalysis US*, chapters 13–16.
37. Lunbeck, "Psychiatry," 665.
38. Yu Sŏk-chin Romanized his name as Yoo Suckjin. For the sake of consistency, his name and all other Koreans names mentioned in this chapter have been transliterated using the McCune-Reischauer system.
39. I was able to speak in person with more than a dozen of Korea's first wave of military psychiatrists during my time in Korea between 2011 and 2012. When I interviewed these gentlemen, they were all in their eighties and nineties.
40. Min Pyŏng-gŭn in discussion with the author, 7 March 2011.
41. Yi Pong-gi in discussion with the author, 27 February 2011. For the history of Korean military medicine during the war, see Ch'oe Che-ch'ang, *Han-mi ŭihaksa: ŭisa ŭi kil 60-nyŏn ŭl torabomyŏ*, 268.
42. Yu referred to himself in English as Yoo Suckjin.
43. Yu Sŏk-chin, "Han'guk chŏngsin ŭihakkye ŭi kŏmok: Yu Sŏk-chin Paksa nonmunjip" [Hero of Korean psychiatry: The works of Yu Sŏk-jin]. Unpublished manuscript given by Min Pyŏng-gŭn to the author.
44. In conversation with Yu Sŏk-chin's wife, Kim Myŏng-hŭi, 25 March 2011.
45. Brazinsky, *Nation Building in South Korea*, 79.
46. Huer, *Marching Orders*, 52.
47. Sawyer, *Military Advisors in Korea*, 148.
48. Huer, *Marching Orders*, 52.
49. Apel and Apel, *MASH*, xii.
50. Jones and Wessely, *Shell Shock to PTSD*, 106.
51. It should be noted that during World War II the Japanese army relied on the services of psychiatrists to deal with mental breakdown among their troops. Military psychiatry in Japan, however, did not comprise its own specialized field. Interestingly, there was a military hospital in Seoul during World War II called Keijo Military Hospital that was shut down after the Japanese surrender in August 1945. The Neuropsychiatry Section of Keijo Military Hospital had a normal capacity of 50 beds with a maximum of 120 mentally ill soldiers able to be cared for at one time. A US military psychiatrist's account of the Japanese facility suggests that both the conditions in which patients were kept and the medical treatments used there were different from those in US hospitals. The Japanese primarily relied on administering frequent rounds of electro-shock treatment with machines "far simpler" than what were used in the United States. No Koreans were involved in these Japanese psychiatric practices; apparently, there was a lingering assumption that Korean medical staff would not be loyal to the Japanese in a wartime situation. See Berger, "Japanese Military Psychiatry Korea."
52. Pak In-ho in discussion with the author, 18 April 2011.
53. Min Pyŏng-gŭn in discussion with the author, 27 February 2011.
54. Yi Chŏng-gyun in discussion with the author, 12 May 2011.
55. Yu Sŏk-chin, "Kŏn'guk 10yŏn ŭi Han'guk chŏngsin ŭihak" [Korean psychiatry 10 Years after its founding]. Unpublished essay, found in personal papers of Yu Sŏk-chin.
56. Yu Sŏk-jin, "Division Psychiatry." Unpublished essay, in personal papers of Yu Sŏk-jin. The publication is not dated, but the document was filed under the section that con-

tained materials from the Korean War, so we can assume that it was written in the early to mid-1950s.
57. Yu Sŏk-chin, "Division Psychiatry."
58. Yu Sŏk-chin, "Kŏn'guk 10yŏn ŭi Han'guk chŏngsin ŭihak."
59. Yu Sŏk-chin, "Kŏn'guk 10yŏn ŭi Han'guk chŏngsin ŭihak."
60. O Sŏk-hwan in discussion with the author, 4 November 2012. The Sudo Yukkun Pyŏngwŏn (Capital Army Hospital) opened in 1949, moved down to Pusan where it was temporarily renamed the 36 Army Hospital, and then re-located permanently to Seoul in 1951.
61. O Sŏk-hwan in discussion with the author, 4 November 2012.
62. Shephard, *War of Nerves*, 342. The Chinese intervention in October 1950, which intensified and prolonged the war, came as a surprise to the Eighth Army.
63. Shephard, *War of Nerves*, 343.
64. Shephard, *War of Nerves*, 342.
65. Shephard, *War of Nerves*, 342.
66. Glass, "Introduction," 202.
67. Glass, "Introduction," 202.
68. Glass, "Introduction," 202.
69. Seoul National University's medical school was taken over by the Korean Army as the war broke out; when it moved south to Pusan in December 1950 in order to flee the fighting up north in the capital city, it was temporarily called the 36 Army Hospital. In 1953, the hospital was once again renamed the Capital Army Hospital.
70. O Sŏk-hwan in discussion with the author, 4 November 2012.
71. Cowdrey, *Medics' War*, 205.
72. Cowdrey, *Medics' War*.
73. "Command Report for May 1953," dated 1 June 1953. Department of Defense, Department of the Army, the Adjutant General's Office. Record Group 407: Records of the Adjutant General's Office, 1905 – 1981; Series: Command Reports, 1949 – 1954; File: "212th Medical Detachment (Psychiatric): Command Report, 1953 May - August 1953." . US National Archives at College Park, MD, USA.
74. Glass, "Introduction."
75. "Command Report May 1953," dated 1 June 1953.Record Group 469: Records of U.S. Foreign Assistance Agencies, 1942–1963. US National Archives at College Park, MD, USA.
76. "Command Report," Series from Record Group 469: Records of U.S. Foreign Assistance Agencies, 1942–1963.
77. Emphasis added.
78. Yi Pong-gi in discussion with the author, 27 February 2011.
79. Kim was trained as a surgeon.
80. Han'guk Chŏngsinŭihak 100-nyŏn sa P'yonch'an Wiwŏnhoe, *Han'guk chŏngsinŭihak 100-nyŏn sa*, 90.
81. Pak In-ho in discussion with the author, 18 April 2011.
82. Unpublished pamphlet found in the personal papers of Yu Sŏk-jin.
83. Ibid.
84. Found in the personal papers of Yu Sŏk-jin.
85. Han'guk Chŏngsin ŭihak 100-yŏnsa P'yonch'an Wiwŏnhoe, *Han'guk chŏngsin ŭihak 100-yŏnsa*, 90.
86. Interestingly, most Korean military psychiatrists who had trained and certified in the United States at army hospitals returned to the United States at some point after the war in order to obtain further medical education and eventually to work for several years at

US state hospitals treating the mentally ill. As Pak In-ho explained during our interview, the US government needed more psychiatrists to address the growing population of Americans hospitalized at mental institutions in the 1950s. South Koreans and other foreigners who had earlier trained in American theories and methods were invited to come to the US with their families under the condition that they would work at these hospitals. Pak was one of the military psychiatrists of the ROK Army who accepted this offer. He worked in the New York state hospital system until the 1980s when he retired and returned to Korea.

87. O Sŏk-hwan in discussion with the author, 4 November 2012.
88. O Sŏk-hwan in discussion with the author, 4 November 2012.
89. Yu Sŏk-jin, "Division Psychiatry."
90. Kim Chang-kyu (Kim Jang Kyu) and Yi Pu-yŏng (Rhi Bou Yong), "Psychiatric Care Korea," 345.
91. These case studies were assembled and published in 2001 in a collection of Yu's works. Only a few copies are in circulation today. Min Pyŏng-gŭn lent me his personal copy in 2012; I relied on this publication as well as the original documents in Yu's archive while preparing this chapter: Yu Sŏk-chin, *Han'guk chŏngsin ŭihakkye ŭi kŏmok*.
92. In 1962, this same organization changed its name to the Korean Neuropsychiatric Association, shedding its military identity and becoming the first professional organization dedicated to general psychiatry in South Korea. Among the activities undertaken by its members was to publish an academic journal titled *Neuropsychiatry* (*Singyŏng chŏngsinŭihak*). (Back in the United States, Albert Glass served as editor of the American journal *Neuropsychiatry*.) The first issue of the Korean periodical, published in its founding year, contains a list of presentations made at the meeting of military psychiatrists throughout the 1950s.
93. The authors mistake the name "Tandler" for "Landler." The full names of the German endocrinologists they reference are Julius Tandler and Siegfried Gross. Throughout the 1910s and 1920s, they had contributed to medical discussions about the physiological consequences of castration on males. See Medvei, *History Clinical Endocrinology*, 384.
94. Zondek, *Diseases Endocrine Glands*. It was translated into English in 1935.
95. For an account of Japanese psychiatry in colonial Korea, see Chŏng Wŏn-yong, Yi Na-mi, and Yi Pu-yŏng, "Introduction Western Psychiatry Korea."
96. Carmichael, "A Psychoanalytic Study of a Case of Eunuchoidism."
97. Yi Pong-gi cited Hugh T. Carmichael as an American neo-Freudian he had met during the course of his training in Korea during wartime.
98. It is possible that the test was never conducted given the army's limited medical resources at the time.
99. In the context of World War II, Jarvis notes that "mentally-wounded veterans" challenged the "warrior ideal predicated upon bravery, self-mastery, control, and courage under fire." See Jarvis, "'If He Comes Home Nervous.'"
100. I remain unclear about what P.E.G. stands for. One possibility is the Pneumoencephalogram, also known as an "air test" in which an air bubble is inserted into the spinal canal. The bubble then floats up to the brain ventricles, allowing an x-ray to visualize the cavities of the brain. The procedure is meant to reveal large-scale brain abnormalities and tumors. This invasive procedure went out of vogue after the invention of neuroimaging techniques in the 1970s.
101. For more background on the 1950s as the heyday of personality tests and the rise of clinical psychiatry more generally, see Herman, *Romance American Psychology*.
102. Edwards and Peterson, "Korea."
103. Medical Service, *Nomenclature and Method*.

104. The document indicates that it was first published in the *Surgeon General's Circular* in 1951.
105. Min Pyŏng-gŭn in discussion with the author, 7 March 2011.
106. Complete transcript of the proceedings of the Freud Symposium offered to the author by psychiatrist O Sŭng-hwan who attended the event and kept a personal copy of the program.
107. As a researcher at the National Mental Hospital (now referred to as Seoul National Hospital in an effort to remove the stigma attached to the institution), I was able to sort through and catalog hundreds of patient files from the first decade of the hospital's history.
108. Yum, "In Sickness and in Health." The fourth chapter of my dissertation discusses the founding of the National Mental Hospital in 1962.
109. I learned this information as a result of my conversation with Arthur Robbins who in 1954 served as a "psychology consultant" for the US Army in Korea. Robbins was also the US military psychologist who signed off on "Eunuchoidism." Arthur Robbins in discussion with the author, 21 November 2011.
110. See Harrington, "Mother Love," 6–8, for discussion of Progressive Era child guidance clinics. I wish to acknowledge the insights gleaned from Anne Harrington and her Harvard undergraduate course Madness and Medicine, which helped me place my historical findings about Korean psychiatry in an international framework.
111. See chapter 3 of my dissertation for a discussion of psychiatry's efforts to tackle the problem of juvenile delinquents in postwar Korea. Yum, "In Sickness and in Health."
112. Watters, *Crazy Like Us*, 3.

Bibliography

Apel, Otto, and Pat Apel. *MASH: An Army Surgeon in Korea*. Lexington: University Press of Kentucky, 1998.

Barton, Walter E. *The History and Influence of the American Psychiatric Association*. Washington, DC: American Psychiatric Press, 1987.

Berger, Milton Miles. "Japanese Military Psychiatry in Korea." *American Journal of Psychiatry* 103 (1946): 214–16.

Brazinsky, Gregg. *Nation Building in South Korea: Koreans, Americans, and the Making of a Democracy*. Chapel Hill: University of North Carolina Press, 2007.

Burnham, John C. *Paths into American Culture: Psychology, Medicine, and Morals*. Philadelphia, PA: Temple University Press, 1988.

Carmichael, Hugh T. "A Psychoanalytic Study of a Case of Eunuchoidism." *Psychoanalytic Quarterly* 10, no. 2 (1941): 243–66.

Ch'oe Che-ch'ang. *Han-mi ŭihaksa: ŭisa ŭi kil 60-yŏn ŭl torabomyŏ* [Looking Back at 60 Years of American Medicine in Korea]. Seoul: Yŏngrim K'adinŏl, 1996.

Chŏng Han-t'aek. *Han'guk simnihak 60-yŏnsa* [A 60-year history of Korean psychology]. Seoul: Pagyŏngsa, 1982.

Chŏng Wŏn-yong (Chung Wonyong). "Kŭndae sŏyang chŏngsin ŭihak ŭi chŏn'gae wa pyŏnch'ŏn kwajŏng [The introduction and transformation of modern Western psychiatry]." Ph.D. dissertation. Seoul: Seoul National Universtiy 2003.

Chŏng Wŏn-yong (Chung Wonyong), Yi Na-mi (Lee NaMi), and Yi Pu-yŏng (Rhi Bou-Yong). "The Introduction of Western Psychiatry into Korea (II): Psychiatric Education in

Korea during the Forced Japanese Annexation of Korea (1910–1945)." *Ŭisahak: Korean Journal of Medical History* 15, no. 2 (2006): 157–87.

Cowdrey, Albert E. *The Medics' War*. Washington, DC: Center of Military History, U.S. Army, 1987.

Edwards, Robert M., and Donald B. Peterson. "Korea: Current Psychiatric Procedure and Communication in the Combat Zone." *American Journal of Psychiatry* 110 (1954): 721–24.

Engstrom, Eric J. "'On the Question of Degeneration' by Emil Kraepelin (1908)." *History of Psychiatry* 18, no. 3 (2007): 389–98.

Fulton, Bruce, ed. *The Red Room: Stories of Trauma in Contemporary Korea*. Honolulu: University of Hawai'i Press, 2009.

Glass, Albert J. "An Introduction to Psychiatry in the Korean War." In *Psychiatry in the US Army: Lessons for Community Psychiatry*, edited by Albert J. Glass and Franklin D. Jones, 103-108. Bethesda, MD: Uniformed Services University of the Health Sciences, 2005.

Glass, Albert Julius, and Franklin D. Jones, eds. *Psychiatry in the US Army: Lessons for Community Psychiatry*. Bethesda, MD: Uniformed Services University of the Health Sciences, 2005.

Hale, Nathan G. *The Rise and Crisis of Psychoanalysis in the United States. Freud and the Americans 1917–1985*, vol. 2. New York: Oxford University Press, 1995.

Han'guk Chŏngsinŭihak 100-nyŏn sa Pyonch'an Wiwŏnhoe (The council on the 100-year history of Korean psychiatry). *Han'guk chŏngsinŭihak 100-yŏnsa* [100 years of psychiatry in Korea]. Seoul: Taehan Sin'gyŏng Chŏngsin Ŭihakhoe, 2009.

Harrington, Anne. *Mind Fixers: Psychiatry's Troubled Search for the Biology of Illness*. New York: Norton, 2019.

———. "Mother Love and Mental Illness: An Emotional History." *Osiris* 31, no. 1 (2016): 94–115.

Hashimoto, Akira. "A 'German World' Shared among Doctors: A History of the Relationship between German and Japanese Psychiatry before World War II." *History of Psychiatry* 24, no. 2 (2013): 180–95.

Herman, Ellen. *The Romance of American Psychology: Political Culture in the Age of Experts*. Berkeley: University of California Press, 1995.

Huer, Jon. *Marching Orders: The Role of the Military in South Korea's "Economic Miracle," 1961–1971*. New York: Greenwood, 1989.

Jarvis, Christina. "'If He Comes Home Nervous': World War II Neuropsychiatric Casualties and Postwar Masculinities." *Journal of Men's Studies* 17, no. 2 (2010): 97–115.

Jones, Edgar, and Simon Wessely. *Shell Shock to PTSD: Military Psychiatry from 1900 to the Gulf War*. Hove, East Sussex: Psychology Press, 2005.

Kim Chang-kyu (Kim Jang Kyu) and Yi Pu-yŏng (Rhi Bou-Yong). "Psychiatric Care in Korea between 1945–1955." *Journal of the Korean Neuropsychiatric Association* 35, no. 2 (1996): 342–55.

Lunbeck, Elizabeth. "Psychiatry." In *The Cambridge History of Science*, vol. 7: *The Modern Social Sciences*, edited by Theodore M. Porter and Dorothy Ross, 663–77. Cambridge: Cambridge University Press, 2003.

Maruyama Chijun. *Chosŏn ŭi kwisin* [The Spirits of Korea]. Translated by Kim Hui-Kyŏng. Seoul: Tongmunsŏn, 1990.

Medical Service, Joint Armed Forces. *Nomenclature and Method of Recording Psychiatric Conditions*. Washington, DC: US Army, US Navy, and US Air Force, 1949.

Medvei, V. C. *History of Clinical Endocrinology: A Comprehensive Account of Endocrinology from Earliest Times to the Present*. Boca Raton, LA: CRC Press, 1993.

Menninger, Karl A. "Discussion of Dr. Sandor Rado's Academic Lecture." *American Journal of Psychiatry* 110, no. 6 (1953): 417–19.

Menninger, Roy W., and John C. Nemiah. *American Psychiatry after World War II (1944–1994)*. Washington, DC: American Psychiatric Press, 2000.
"Notes." *Psychoanalytic Quarterly* 15, no. 2 (1946): 274–77.
Pak Hyŏng-u. *Chejungwŏn*. Seoul: Mom kwa ma'ŭm, 2002.
Pols, Hans. "The Tunisian Campaign, War Neuroses, and the Reorientation of American Psychiatry During World War II." *Harvard Review of Psychiatry* 19, no. 6 (2011): 313–20.
"Psychiatric Disorders and Reactions: Definitions and Manner of Recording." *Journal of Mental Science* 92, no. 387 (1946): 425–41.
Sawyer, Robert K. *Military Advisors in Korea: KMAG in Peace and War*. Washington, DC: Center of Military History, United States Army, 1988.
Scull, Andrew. *Hysteria: The Disturbing History*. Oxford: Oxford University Press, 2011.
Shephard, Ben. *A War of Nerves: Soldiers and Psychiatrists in the Twentieth Century*. London: Jonathan Cape, 2000.
Watters, Ethan. *Crazy Like Us: The Globalization of the American Psyche*. New York: Free Press, 2010.
Yi Pang-hyŏn (Bang Hyun Lee). "Singminji chosŏn esoŭi chŏngsin pyŏngja e taehan kŭndaej ŏk chŏpkŭn [Modern Approach to Treating Mental Patients in Colonial Korea]." *Korean Journal of Medical History* 22 (2013): 529–578.
Yi Pu-yŏng (Rhi Bou-Yong). "The Roots of Korean Psychiatry and Its Development before and after WWII." In *Two Millennia of Psychiatry in West and East*, edited by Toshihiko Hamanaka and German E. Berrios, 95–106. Tokyo: Gakuju Shoin Publishers, 2003.
Yoo, Theodore Jun. *It's Madness: The Politics of Mental Health in Colonial Korea*. Berkeley: University of California Press, 2016.
Yu Sŏk-chin, *Han'guk chŏngsin ŭihakkye ŭi kŏmok: Yu Sŏk-jin paksa nonmunjip* (Hero of Korean Psychiatry: The Works of Yu Sŏk-jin). Seoul: Hakjisa, 2001.
Yum, Jennifer. "In Sickness and in Health: Americans and Psychiatry in Korea, 1950–1962." Ph.D. dissertation. Cambridge, MA: Harvard University, 2014.
Zondek, Hermann. *The Diseases of the Endocrine Glands*. Translated from the German by Carl Prausnitz Giles. Baltimore, MD: W. Wood & Co, 1935.

Chapter 5

"No PTSD in Vietnam"

Psychological Trauma, Psychic Shock, and the Biology of War Suffering in the Context of the American War

Narquis Barak

In 1992, Nguyen Van Siem, director of Thuong Tin Central Psychiatric Hospital, one of the main psychiatric facilities in northern Vietnam, was invited to speak to an international group of psychiatrists in Amsterdam about the prevalence and treatment of Posttraumatic Stress Disorder (PTSD) in his home country. He began with a personal story:

> In 1947, when I was 11, a French expedition unit raided my native village. The Legionnaires arrested about twenty people, including me, and brought us to the village entrance where five of us were shot and killed right on the spot, one after the other. At that moment, I experienced both the terrifying event of witnessing my villagers killed and the terrible thought that I might share their same destiny. It was not until the company sergeant-major sounded a retreat that I knew I had safely averted disaster.
>
> Several years later, there were no PTSD-related problems among the survivors. Why so? To this condition two reactions could be postulated: People have developed a kind of coping mechanism characterized by a well-trained ability to suffer and a strong capability for resignation. Distressing events have become so common that they can no longer act as a pathogenic factor for a personality trained unconsciously or by education.[1]

Siem went on to tell the audience that PTSD was also not seen among survivors of the American War, the appellation used in Vietnam for the war involving the United States from 1955 to 1975. He posited that its absence in Vietnam may be connected to particular cultural attributes of Vietnamese society that have a protective influence on the population, such as the widespread belief in Fate (số phận), Buddhism (Đạo Phật), and multigenerational social networks. "Three generations living under the same roof have shared together gladness and bad luck. . . . Vulnerability to serious stressors," he suggested, "is generally more precarious in people living in an individualistic society than in those living within close social and family relationships."

Siem gave me his original typewritten speech in the summer of 1996, the first year of my thirty-two-month ethnographic study in urban and rural psychiatric facilities, district health centers, and village health stations in and around Hanoi and throughout Phu Tho province. After eighteen months in Hanoi, I spent fourteen months in Phu Tho province, where I conducted simultaneous ethnographies: one in Tho Van commune, a rural village in Tam Thanh district, which entailed extensive interviewing and participant observation of the everyday lives of veterans and civilians as they farmed rice and lacquer trees, took part in funerals and reburial ceremonies, visited spirit mediums, and sought medical and psychiatric care; and one at Phu Tho Provincial Psychiatric Hospital, observing everyday clinical interactions and following clinicians and patients back to their home villages located throughout the province.

A major part of my study involved collecting oral histories of psychiatrists and primary historical materials, such as personal military journals, army field reports, and hundreds of medical records from hospitals in Hanoi and Phu Tho as well as from veterans themselves. Some of these had been pulled directly from the pockets of their old army uniforms and others from nylon bags hung from roof rafters or tucked away behind framed photos of the dead high up on ancestral altars, kept safe from tropical elements and flood waters. During the summer of 1996, I had tasked myself with the grueling project of pulling thousands of records dating back to the 1960s and in various stages of decomposition, from plastic trash bags stored in Thuong Tin hospital's basement.[2]

When Siem shared his speech with me to add to my growing archive, I was already familiar with the themes. I had been shadowing psychiatrists at Bach Mai and Thuong Tin for months, observing clinical interactions, and speaking with hundreds of patients who had served in the North Vietnamese Army. Accompanying Siem often involved following him on tours he led for foreign visitors, which had become increasingly frequent. That summer, health officials, psychiatrists, psychologists, social workers, and journalists from the United States, Australia, England, Israel, Sweden, and other Western European countries were arriving in droves to the psychiatric wards at Bach Mai and Thuong Tin on organized "missions" and investigative trips, funded by their home governments, universities, churches, and NGOs. They were invariably interested in PTSD. It was as if the recent lifting of the US embargo and the co-occurring explosion of interest in the global excavation of PTSD had suddenly unleashed a torrent of psychiatric tourists.

At Thuong Tin, the tours would always begin at the giant banyan tree that drooped over the main entrance. Siem would draw guests' attention to the three-foot casing of a detonated 250-pound American bomb dangling by a rope from one of its branches. Dropped by a US F-105 during the Christmas bombings of 1972, it had been stripped of its deadly innards and mounted on the tree by some clever hospital workers to be used as a bell signaling lunch and dinner breaks for patients. He would explain how similar bombs along with the powerful blast waves they unleashed resulted in many of the chronic problems observed in their veteran population, such as epileptic seizures, cognitive dysfunction, and mood disorders. Many visitors assumed he was referring to the obsolescent notion of shell shock from World War I.

I wince reading back through my notes of remarks made to me on the tours. My liminal status, as a person familiar with the Vietnamese staff and proficient in Vietnamese, yet also an American, invited a certain level of comfort on the part of the visitors to relay opinions that they would not necessarily share directly with their hosts. "I was pulled aside today and asked if I thought the Vietnamese psychiatrists were telling the truth." "A psychologist from the US grabbed my arm and told me she couldn't believe they still use shell shock. I tried to explain that it was not the shell shock of World War I, but she wasn't having it." "Another psychiatrist, an Australian, said, clearly, they don't understand that there are psychological factors that cause mental illness." "An Israeli psychologist commented to me in Hebrew, their psychiatry is very primitive, isn't it?"[3] "It's obvious they're over-sedating their patients."

Although visitors rarely spent more than an hour on the wards, had no access to patient records, and could not communicate in Vietnamese, I was struck by the confidence with which they communicated their impressions to me. Some even contended that, contrary to what the Vietnamese were claiming, they had themselves observed Vietnamese patients with their own eyes who had PTSD and "obviously they are being misdiagnosed." I recalled such an instance in my journal: "Someone whose group brought their own translator pulled aside a male patient today and asked him if he has flashbacks of the war. The translator used the term 'sống lại chiến tranh'—*relive* the war. The patient pointed to the sky and said he remembers the bombs. I didn't recognize the patient as a veteran and Siem later confirmed that he had never served." The patient was also too young to have experienced the war and was diagnosed with schizophrenia with visual and auditory hallucinations.

Years later, back in the United States, I would come across American accounts of such tours online, featuring vivid, almost outlandish descriptions of patients whom the authors alleged were exhibiting flashbacks of the war. In one, the author notes that his group had discovered "the presence of all three symptom clusters of PTSD."[4] One female patient, upon seeing them, "fell to the floor with epileptoid movements, screaming out in Vietnamese, 'don't beat me!

I'll do what you say!'" Another patient, asked by the tour group if he was "visited by dead buddies," "burst into tears and replied, 'yes they come every day.'" In the account, the Vietnamese doctor leading their tour expressed surprise, which indicated to the author "his lack of knowledge about the psychological dimensions of the disorder." In a separate account, patients are described as "barking orders to imaginary soldiers," marching in "illusory drills," and firing "nonexistent rifles."[5]

Siem took visitors' armchair diagnoses about the lack of PTSD in stride, but others did not necessarily share his patience with visitors' unabating preoccupation with PTSD. At times tensions would boil to the surface, as on one occasion, when a delegation arrived led by a psychiatrist from Ohio. Faculty and residents were called to the main meeting room at Bach Mai. After brief introductions, the Ohio doctor, an enthusiastic, short stocky man with glasses, who ran treatment programs for US veterans, briskly moved to the head of the table, asking: "What do we know about Posttraumatic Stress Disorder?" He flipped on the switch to the overhead screen light revealing a human brain, its anatomical structures labeled in black bold letters. Indicating the diagram with a laser pointer, he responded to his own question: "We know a lot. We know 6 percent of Americans have PTSD." The audience followed the dot as it flitted from thalamus to cortex to hippocampus and back, while he cited studies that found hippocampus sizes to be smaller in people who have PTSD: "This would explain problems with memory, but the question still remains, are they abnormal to begin with in these people or do the changes occur after the trauma?"

At this point, a young psychiatric resident sitting across the table interjected that they do not yet have a PET scanner in the department. The one they borrow costs $5,000 per use. Other Vietnamese psychiatrists chuckled at his exaggerated estimate. The presenter looked confused, but continued. He explained that the cortisol system is abnormal in people with PTSD and described studies in which the cortisol levels of US veterans were measured before and after they were shown films about the Vietnam War—"like *Apocalypse Now* for example." He paused and looked around. None of the Vietnamese recognized the film title. The speaker continued to describe experiments in which catheters were inserted in veterans' cerebral spinal fluid, to measure cortisol levels, while their "trauma transcripts" were read back to them: "Why do some people get PTSD and not others? Big trauma more likely. Psychotherapy strengthens cortical control. More education is needed before soldiers are sent over, so they have less chance of getting PTSD. Maturity and education enable coping skills."

Suddenly, one of the few female psychiatrists on the faculty, known for being soft-spoken, forcefully shoved her chair back, stood up, and addressed the speaker directly: "A lot of us here at Bach Mai had to undergo horrible events—the bombing of this hospital in 1972. Hanoi was most severely bombed." She gestured toward the hallway outside of the meeting room.

I witnessed people dying, trying to get patients out, right here. The dead bodies were strewn in the corridors amid debris. I and other hospital workers attempted to rescue patients and colleagues from the ruins. In us, stress was very big (*stes rất lớn*). In around 1,000 staff members, we found no PTSD. No one I know who was there has developed Posttraumatic Stress Disorder (*rối loạn sang chấn sau stes*). All Vietnamese of this generation have experienced trauma. With so many people having gone through this, why don't we see PTSD?

There ensued an uneasy silence in the room. The speaker, clearly caught off guard, paused and then picked up on the tangential theme in her comment of training medical personnel to deal with emergency situations: "We have a crisis intervention technique for emergency personnel. They talk about the event—everything is well thought out— . . ." Another Vietnamese psychiatrist interrupted: "But no one came to us with these problems." Siem joined in pointing out Vietnam's long history of wars and the importance of extended family support.

Everyone sat silently for a moment. The American psychiatrist hesitated for a while, before speaking: "For us the Vietnam War was very toxic. What soldiers expected to find was not what they found. They were terribly confused. 500,000 veterans sick with PTSD after the war—a bad thing to suffer and not understand why."

That evening the delegation hosted an informal banquet at the Saigon Hotel. After dinner, the Ohio doctor passed out typewritten sheets to all the Vietnamese present, with the words to Neil Young's "Old Man" and Billy Joel's "Goodnight Saigon," which he played on a tape recorder set up in the center of the room. The members of his delegation sang along, while the Vietnamese psychiatrists looked on. When they were done, Siem took the podium, thanked the visitors, stating that Vietnamese do not have much time to dwell upon the past, but that his hope was that the guests would be able to help the Vietnamese in the future.

Orientations

I was not aware of the tensions surrounding PTSD in Vietnam when I first arrived in Hanoi. Rather, I stumbled upon the situation in the first few months of my research. However, I was not entirely surprised because questions about the cross-cultural applicability of PTSD had formed the initial impetus for my study. In the mid-1990s, PTSD was featuring quite prominently in international humanitarian efforts, and I was interested in the palpable urgency on the part of PTSD proponents to disseminate PTSD criteria, diagnostic instruments, and concomitant therapies to countries all over the world. This mission to globalize PTSD presented a conundrum from an anthropological standpoint, because research about PTSD until then was almost exclusively limited to US veterans of the war in Vietnam and more specifically to a rarified sample of cases being treated in the Veteran Administration's (VA)medical system for whom the diagnosis was a key factor in service-related compensation.[6] The rationale behind the urgency was that contemporary society was being "exposed to" an inordinate amount of high-magnitude stressors: "high rates of war, natural disaster, ethnic conflict, and technological disaster."[7] Yet, there was limited knowledge about war trauma more generally in non-Euro-American cultures.

Particularly influential in the formulation of my initial questions was Allan Young's seminal analysis of PTSD in an American VA psychiatric unit. Young demonstrated that PTSD, including its origination, codification, and the concepts that undergird the disorder, is a cultural product, inextricably linked to the social and political climate of post-Vietnam war America. He traced how PTSD emerged as the result of efforts on the part of clinicians, politicians, and veterans' advocates who were eager to establish and promote a disorder, which could provide a definitive causal link between veterans' delayed psychiatric symptoms—features of which were already included in pre-existing DSM classifications—and their war-related service. Central to this etiological link, Young argued, was the concept of "traumatic memory," a "parasitic" memory, often times repressed, and capable of causing a wide range of symptoms, including flashbacks, avoidance behaviors, changes in cognition and mood, and heightened startle reactions. Furthermore, Young made the case that the etiological basis of PTSD and its treatment methods, which require the help of a trained expert who can extricate the memory and assist in its emotional processing, were not rooted in valid scientific findings, but were drawn from and predicated on philosophies of mind, self, and personhood that had a long history in American religion, society, and political thought: in Christianity where memory is the hiding place of sins and the object of ritual confession, in the writings of John Locke, David Hume, and Théodule Ribot, and, most importantly, in Freudian psychoanalytic thought, which enjoyed prominence in the United States during the two decades leading up to the war in Vietnam.[8]

My study in northern Vietnam was both a response to Young's cultural argument and an attempt to fill a gap in the historical literature on military psychiatry and war trauma, which until then had been exclusively focused on the Euro-American experience, a trend that has continued until today.[9] As I wrote in applications for grants that funded my research, I wanted to understand the longstanding effects of war and other critical events on the psyche, in a culture with a very different moral, political, religious, and economic context than the United States. I mentioned Buddhism, Taoism, Communism, and Confucianism, even though I did not know at the time what these "isms" really meant to Vietnamese psychiatry or to Vietnamese veterans and their families.[10]

My initial year of research focused only on how war trauma was conceptualized and treated at psychiatric facilities around Hanoi. However, I quickly discovered that the structure of veterans' health care in northern Vietnam was vastly different from the American VA medical system and that I would have to expand my research. Most North Vietnamese Army (NVA) soldiers had hailed from the countryside and after the war most of them returned to the same villages, where their parents, wives, and children had remained and where their family lineages were traced, often not in decades, but in centuries. If veterans suffered from chronic problems or if they developed symptoms after the war, their most frequent interaction with the medical community would have taken place at the village level, the lowest tier within the three-tiered health system that had been established after the war—one that served veterans and civilians alike. If psychiatrists treated veterans at all, they would have been seen at their province's psychiatric hospital and sent back to their villages once their symptoms were stabilized. If I wanted to learn how people dealt with the war and its aftermath, how veterans fared, the countryside would give me a more accurate picture.

In this chapter I provide a snapshot of the Vietnamese experience—the other side of the war, as it were. In weaving together interviews with Vietnamese psychiatrists and war veterans, as well as data gleaned from heretofore unexamined Vietnamese language materials—I demonstrate, contrary to visitors claims, that psychological trauma had always been identified as an important etiological factor by northern Vietnamese clinicians, but that the definition of trauma and its role in causality reflected their own particular culture, socio-political history, and environmental conditions. The unique biology of war suffering that emerged in the battlefields of northern Vietnam and in the aftermath of the war evolved from an epistemological foundation that differed substantially from that which birthed PTSD. I describe how foreign theories and categories, mainly French and Soviet, were adapted and interpreted locally through the combined lens of traditional Vietnamese medicine, Buddhism, Taoism, and other cultural frameworks. Markedly different from the US narrative of PTSD, these distinctively North Vietnamese theories and practices emphasized the somatic and social over the intrapsychic and individual, and rather than plumbing the depths of memory and the unconscious, specialized in techniques of forgetting.

French Foundations

After the Viet Minh took control over North Vietnam in 1954, Prime Minister Le Duan appointed Nguyen Quoc Anh in 1957 to lead the establishment of a department of psychiatry and neurology (*khoa tinh thần kinh*) at Bach Mai Hospital in Hanoi.[11] Anh was a native of Hanoi and a French national. Under Anh, French theory, diagnostic categories, and treatment methods predominated. French was the main language used in clinical settings until 1962, when the first official Vietnamese psychiatric lexicon was established.[12] Trained in the neurologically oriented French tradition that flourished in Paris in the 1940s and early 1950s, Anh leaned toward theorists and treatment methods that were part of that tradition, such as Jean Delay and Pierre Deniker, Jacques Rondepierre, and Manfred Sakel whose treatment of patients using chlorpromazine, electroshock, and insulin-induced coma were emulated at Bach Mai.

During these early years, Anh emphasized the importance of recognizing multiple etiologies in the development of psychiatric disorders, including organic, social, and psychological dimensions. He exposed his trainees to the work of Jean-Martin Charcot, Georges Gilles de la Tourette, Joseph Babinski, Henri Baruk, and Henri Ey. In addition to pharmacological treatments and electroshock, students were trained in the psychological technique (*liệu pháp tâm lý*) of suggestion therapy (*điều trị bằng ám thị*), non-hypnotic "verbal" suggestion, which entailed verbal encouragement by the physician to help patients will away their symptoms, while injecting placebo medication to convince them that the illness (*bệnh*) was leaving their bodies. The most popular form of placebo was the injection of calcium, which induced a physical sensation that the physician could refer to as "evidence" of the drug's success in attacking the disease.

It is clear from the earliest years that North Vietnamese psychiatrists were not accepting imported theories, nosologies, and therapeutic methods wholesale, but were engaging them with a critical eye. One notable critique concerned the theoretical shift in French psychiatry at the time from a neurological tradition toward a psychoanalytically oriented understanding of mental illness. For Vietnamese psychiatrists, working with a patient population among whom malaria, encephalitis, measles, typhoid, and malnutrition were still endemic and in which febrile psychosis was not unusual, an exclusive reliance on psychoanalytic theory to explain symptoms was incommensurate with their own clinical experiences. Furthermore, Anh and his students' early attempts to use psychoanalysis (*phân tâm học*) with patients led them to question the applicability of the technique in the Vietnamese context. From a cultural standpoint, behavioral norms that limited intimate one-to-one interactions between people of different stature, age, and gender, rendered this kind of individual-focused therapy almost impossible. Additionally, patients' families could not accept it as a valid form of medical treatment and so were reluctant to try it. The notion of "talking therapy" was altogether culturally dissonant.[13]

The Appeal of Soviet Psychiatry and the Cultural Logic of Pavlov

The turn to Soviet psychiatry in the early 1960s was, in part, a function of geopolitical circumstances. The Vietnamese Workers' Party's embrace of Communist ideology and its commitment to building a society according to Marxist-Leninist ideals had placed it squarely on the side of the Soviet Union in the Cold War. The strengthening relationship between the two countries facilitated the flow of Soviet psychiatric texts into the Democratic Republic of Vietnam and also resulted in an influx of Soviet specialists in mental health. This fed an already growing dissatisfaction with aspects of contemporary French theory. Soviet psychiatry, during the decades following World War II, had followed a very different theoretical trajectory from its French and US counterparts. In the Soviet Union, the theoretical pendulum between psychology and biology had swung in quite the opposite direction. Whereas psychoanalytic theory had flourished in the Soviet Union in the early 1930s—psychoanalysis was "in vogue" among Moscow intellectuals—after World War II, Soviet psychiatry became more heavily grounded in neurophysiology and organic etiological factors were given considerably more attention.[14]

By the 1960s, the prevailing etiological model of psychopathology in the Soviet Union was multifactorial. In line with dialectical principles, psychiatric disorder was considered to result from the interaction of exogenous factors, such as viruses and distressing life events, and endogenous factors, such as genetic predispositions, vascular disease, and brain damage.[15] The relative importance of particular factors was considered to vary depending on the individual and disorder. For example, a distressing life event might provoke a disorder, but it does so opportunistically, owing to biological vulnerabilities peculiar to an individual. The lack of a strict division between psychogenic and organic mental illness appealed to the North Vietnamese.

By the 1960s, the Soviets had produced a sizable body of literature on the neuropsychiatric effects of infectious diseases, for example. They had identified a range of psychiatric symptoms and disorders that could be linked either directly or indirectly to viral infections. This literature was considered of particular relevance in the North Vietnamese clinical setting where the incidence of psychotic symptoms following viral infection and prolonged fever was notably high.[16] During the war against the United States, infectious diseases, including malaria, Japanese encephalitis, and various forms of hemorrhagic infections along with endemic malnutrition among soldiers would become the most common causes of incapacitation among People's Army troops and youth brigade volunteers.

The Soviet emphasis on environmental organic factors was also reflected in an extensive body of research on head trauma and nerve injuries. After World War II, the Soviet government sponsored many longitudinal studies on the long-term psychiatric effects of bomb blasts, land mine explosions, and artillery fire. In addition to tracking the direct effects of traumatic injuries, these studies also examined how other factors such as vascular disease and immune system dysfunction, as well as psychological shock exacerbated the development and course of symptoms and disorders. The findings of this body of research yielded a whole set of new classifications specifically applied to postwar symptoms, some which would be adapted by North Vietnamese psychiatrists in treating veterans of the American and Cambodian Wars.

Additionally, the Soviet emphasis on manifest social and interpersonal factors rather than the unconscious made cultural sense to Vietnamese psychiatrists, many of whom had grown up in villages, where collectivist traditions and extended family networks thrived long before the shift to socialism. The focus in Soviet psychiatry on the inextricability of the individual from his or her social environment was considered to be far more culturally resonant in North Vietnam than the Western preoccupation with intrapsychic processes. Furthermore, Freud's notion of the unconscious was considered to lack any basis in material reality.[17]

Most importantly, North Vietnamese psychiatrists found an epistemological kinship, a kind of cultural logic, in the theoretical vision of Ivan P. Pavlov. "The West had Freud and Vietnam had Pavlov," psychiatrists would often say. Among the Soviet theorists, Pavlov was certainly the most influential and, similar to Freud, penetrated beyond psychiatry into other disciplines as well as into popular culture. Pavlov was quoted, referred to, and cited more often than any other theorist in psychiatric texts published during the period. The number of his works translated into Vietnamese probably exceeds that of any other single theorist to this day. Pavlov's work on reflexology, in particular, became a core theoretical framework through which a wide spectrum of psychiatric disorders was understood.

North Vietnamese psychiatrists were drawn to Pavlovian theory for a number of reasons, but the main one is that the nature of the physiological system Pavlov describes in his work resonated, almost uncannily, with core conceptions of the body and illness in indigenous Vietnamese medical epistemologies. Psychiatrists today still invoke the similarities between Pavlov's theories of reflexology and aspects of traditional medical theory to explain the apparent ease with which his concepts and ideas were taken up and adapted in the 1960s. Pavlov's vision of the higher nervous system, his theory of functional equilibrium, and his contention that mental illness results from the body's inability to maintain balance between opposing processes of excitation and inhibition were considered similar to the Vietnamese traditional medical theory of *âm dương*. Similar to the Taoist theory of "yin and yang," *âm dương* is a theory of oppositional forces that make up the body/mind/universe. According to the theory of *âm dương*, similar to the Pavlovian schema, these two forces must be held in balance in order to avoid illness. *Âm* (yin) is the negative principle, associated with femininity, darkness, cold, the moon, and wetness, for example, whereas *dương* (yang) is the positive principle and is associated with masculinity, light, heat, the sun, and dryness. Both principles are necessary for life and sustenance, but an overabundance in the body of one or the other may manifest in a whole range of illnesses, symptoms, and disorders.

Pavlov's theoretical focus on adaptability to changing environmental stimuli through regulation of neural processes also touched upon essential ideas concerning maintenance of equilibrium and health in traditional medicine. In describing Pavlov's notion of adaptation, one North Vietnamese scholar wrote: "The way in which higher nervous activity enables the body to adapt to complex changes in the outer world is not a process that is difficult for us to understand, because it is a dialectical phenomenon that is described in our own medical regulations."[18] Unlike Pavlov's notion of adaptation, however, which refers to a regulatory process that is, for the most part, beyond an individual's conscious control, the notion of adaptation (*thích nghi*) in Vietnamese traditional medicine refers to conscious self-management of the body. Traditional medicine stipulates preventative, or prophylactic measures, such as avoidance of extremes, whether extremes of temperatures, foods, emotions, or social interactions. Once a loss of equilibrium has occurred, the ingestion of particular medicines and foods, characterized as having "cooling" or "heating" effects (*tính nóng lạnh*), can function to re-regulate (*điều hòa*) the body. The emphasis on conscious self-management and assistance in self-management by close family members in re-regulating the loss of equilibrium inherent in psychiatric disorder would become a central feature of psychiatric praxis.

Another aspect of Vietnamese medicine, which aligned with Soviet psychiatry, was a nominalist approach to disease. In traditional medicine, disease was considered a group of phenomena representing a spectrum of dysfunction in the body/mind, referred to as flow of *khí*. The Soviets espoused a continuum theory of mental illness more in line with the Hippocratic tradition, which was more concerned with prognosis than diagnosis and rejected notions of disease as independent entities that exist in their own right. Rather, disease was an arbitrary concept, simply a name for a group of phenomena.[19] This was in contrast to the Platonic tradition characterized by American and Western European psychiatry, which emphasized classification and diagnosis. North Vietnamese psychiatrists placed less emphasis on diagnostic classifications and more on symptom clusters, often using French, Soviet, and, eventually, ICD classifications interchangeably.

Early Conceptions of Psychological Trauma

The North Vietnamese term for "psychological trauma" (*chấn thương tâm lý*) was coined from the French *traumatisme psychologique* in the late 1950s. Although the medical term was new, the ideas that formed around it were not. The notion that certain life experiences could induce emotional responses, which have pathological effects on one's health was not a novel concept in North Vietnam. It was a commonly held explanation for madness (*điên rồ*) in popular culture and constituted a core theory of pathogenesis in Vietnamese traditional medicine, in which psychiatric residents were formally trained beginning in 1960.[20]

Vietnamese traditional medicine delineates seven categories of emotion (*thất tình*), all of them considered to be potentially harmful to the body: happiness (*vui*), sadness (*buồn*), grief (*bi*), anger (*giận*), worry (*nghi ngợi*), anxiety (*lo lắng*), and fear (*sợ hãi*). Each is associated with a particular organ of the body and directly affects the flow of "life energy" (*khí*) through this organ. Any emotion in excess results in dysfunctionality and imbalance between *âm* (yin) and *dương* (yang). Intense fear (*sợ hãi*), for example, could cause severe dysfunction in its corresponding organ, the kidneys, manifesting in excessive sweat and fainting. The reverse takes place as well: trauma or pathology in a particular organ could manifest in particular emotions or mood changes.

The theory of *Thất Tình* influenced how psychiatrists conceptualized the mechanism by which traumatic experiences affected the development of psychiatric disorder. Unlike Western psychiatry at the time, which held that the pathological effects of trauma resided in cognitive functions of the brain, specifically in an individual's capacity to remember and "assimilate" memories of a traumatic event, North Vietnamese psychiatry located the effects of psychological trauma throughout the central nervous system and hence regarded them as affecting the balance of an individual's neural processes as a whole, or in traditional medical terms—affecting the balance of *âm dương*.[21] Cognitive dysfunction, such as loss of memory, or obsessive preoccupation (*ám ảnh*) with a life event or situation, also referred to commonly and in psychiatry as the idiom "thinking too much" (*suy nghĩ nhiều quá*), would be considered just some among many possible kinds of symptoms of this loss of equilibrium, not inherent to a particular disorder. "Thinking too much," when it appears in medical narratives did not necessarily refer to thinking about a specific traumatic event. The focus was not on the content, but on the act.[22]

The North Vietnamese recognized nothing resembling the core Western notion of "traumatic memory." In fact, a review of northern Vietnamese psychiatric literature from the early 1960s to the 1980s reveals that memory is rarely discussed in relation to disorders associated with psychological trauma. Rather, their conceptualization of the effects of trauma were more reminiscent of the neurologically oriented ideas proposed by George W. Crile, Walter B. Cannon, and, not surprisingly, Pavlov. In *The Harmony of Illusions*, Allan Young distinguishes their neurologically oriented theories of trauma from the "psychological" and memory-focused theories of Pierre Janet and Freud. Culturally, the notion of pathogenic memory—the assertion that memories can be concealed from an individual's consciousness—was culturally alien in the North Vietnamese context.

Another implication of the influence of *Thất Tình* is that the term "psychological trauma," as used by North Vietnamese psychiatrists, had a much broader meaning than has traditionally been the case in Western psychiatry. Unlike in the West, where historically traumatogenic disorders are typically associated with extreme etiological events inducing fear or terror, within the North Vietnamese context, any events, experiences, conflicts, or situations resulting in an overabundance of negative and sometimes even positive emotions, such as love, could fall under the rubric of "psychological trauma." Rather than fear or terror, medical biographies in patient records more often noted that the psychological trauma induced feelings of grief, sadness, shame, and loss.

The emphasis on grief and death, in particular, as a significant etiological event in trauma-related disorders can be considered a salient characteristic of North Vietnamese psychiatry. The Soviets did not consider grief experiences to be significant in this regard, nor has grief historically fallen under the rubric of trauma in the West.[23] Patient charts from Hanoi Military Hospital 103 in the early 1960s reveal that the most-often-noted traumas involve the death of a parent or child and circumstances of emotional abandonment by a spouse or a lover. Interestingly, with respect to "fear-inducing" experiences, the act of being hospitalized itself for a non-psychiatric health problem is identified as a common psychological trauma. Psychiatrists believed that fear of having a mortal illness could cause patients to develop psychiatric symptoms.

In the pre-war literature, three disorders are specifically mentioned in which distressing life events and circumstances are thought to play a more central etiological role. The first, neurasthenia (*suy nhược thần kinh*), was associated with insomnia, thinking too much, headaches, fatigue, generalized physical pain, and the inability to deal with daily activities. As in the Soviet Union, the North Vietnamese considered neurasthenia to be related to ongoing or prolonged social tensions and interpersonal conflicts endured by an individual in the context of his or her home or work environment.

Hysteria (*ixteria*), referred to as a "disease of suggestion" (*bệnh ám thị*), was associated with relatively mild (*nhẹ*) traumas or traumatic contexts—an argument with a spouse, being ridiculed by coworkers, unrequited love, or emotional neglect by a parent. The psychological trauma coupled with personality characteristics made one susceptible to autosuggestion. Literature on hysteria published immediately before the war reveals that North Vietnamese psychiatrists drew from both French and Soviet epistemology in their conceptualization of the disorder.[24] Because its main criterion was that the patient's symptoms could be manipulated through means of persuasive suggestion and hypnosis, North Vietnamese psychiatrists considered replacing hysteria with Babinski's term "pithiatism."[25]

Unlike hysteria or neurasthenia, reaction psychosis (*loạn thần phản ứng*) was almost exclusively associated with short-term, sudden, and severe traumas and the intensity of symptoms correlated with the intensity of the trauma.[26] Adopted from Soviet nosology just before the war, the disorder was considered to be a form of acute psychosis that developed in direct response and immediately following trauma. Hysteria and reaction psychosis were referred to as "reaction states" (*trạng thái phản ứng*). They were considered to be curable with no residual symptoms. The notion of a latency period, the idea that someone could develop symptoms years after a psychological trauma as is recognized in PTSD, did not exist. Research on reaction states at Bach Mai Hospital had just begun when US bombing started in 1964.[27]

Thirty-Seven Ways of Dying

According to accounts of North Vietnamese soldiers, descending onto the Ho Chi Minh Trail was a forbidding experience. Soldiers often referred to "thirty-seven ways of dying" to describe the appalling conditions on the Trail.[28] Da, who worked as an engineer in a state factory when he was drafted in 1965, recalled passing scores of soldiers lying in tattered hammocks strung between trees, moaning and feverish. Makeshift graves dotted the landscape; men had been buried where they fell dead. On the way south, they encountered lines of men returning on foot with stumps for arms, deep infections, and napalm burns. In the backs of trucks were "men who resembled corpses, but were still breathing," and men who had lost their legs, "staring at us."

Aside from multiple ways of dying by bombs—shrapnel, blast injuries, and penetrating fragments—these accounts detail death by exhaustion, freak accidents during the course of building and repairing roads, and drowning in flash floods. One Lieutenant Colonel would warn his new recruits before they left for the Trail: "We have to cope not only with the enemy but also with a fierce trail, a harsh climate, and wild beasts."[29] The Truong Son jungles were home to Bu Phien tigers, pit vipers, and cobras.[30] Veterans recalled having witnessed fellow unit members mauled by tigers[31] or having to guard their corpses, because the smell attracted tigers.[32]

Many units were decimated by malaria even before they made it to the frontlines. Next to bombs, malaria was the most common cause of death among North Vietnamese soldiers and volunteers. Some units lost as many as 50 percent of their new recruits to malaria. Sometimes, whole units had to be replaced.[33] Spleen and liver inflammation, a direct effect of both malaria and the overdosing of anti-malarial medication, were widespread. It was commonplace to see soldiers and volunteers go about their daily lives with fevers of 40°C (104°F), dark yellow skin, and bellies so swollen they looked pregnant.[34] Because the soldiers and youth brigade often lacked a clean water supply, water-borne diseases such as dysentery, rickettsia, typhus, and enteritis were also endemic as were hunger and malnutrition.

> To fill their stomachs the men had to eat rats, bats, and the few fish that had not been swept along by the mighty current. But after a while rats, bats, and fish became scarce, and hunger was felt even more acutely. When we finally

reached them, the men were thin and pale, their eyes sunken, their lips bloodless. Some were in an advanced state of beriberi.[35]

Beriberi, a vitamin B deficiency, was so common that in pension claims after the war, the diagnosis was often the stated basis of pensions. Reports were sent from officers in the field warning that whole units were being incapacitated by hunger. In one, a propaganda cadre wrote: "Many times they had nothing to eat, nothing to exchange for food so they had to ask the advisers to ask the Lao people for some cassava. They were so skinny, no muscles left. Clothes were tattered. No more toothpaste and toothbrushes."[36] Documents from the period report "lagging" of troops on the Trail owing to hunger[37] and mass defections when the hunger became unbearable.[38]

Such conditions formed the backdrop to the most intense and continuous aerial bombardment ever experienced by any one country in terms of sheer tonnage of bombs. US forces dropped aerial bombs that ranged in weight from 500 to 2,000 pounds, some preset to detonate on impact, others at an altitude of several feet to several yards above ground, and still others were rigged to detonate six or seven days after impact. The US military also dropped artillery rockets—rigged with fuel-air-explosive (FAE) warheads designed to enhance their blast effects. Unlike aerial bombs, which propelled fragments and emitted waves on a linear trajectory, the FAE's blast wave could make its way around corners and penetrate bunker openings and foxholes. The effects were deadly in enclosed areas, such as caves and tunnels, where the NVA hid.

North Vietnamese troops referred to bombs and land mines by their local names. "Lake bombs" (*bom dia*) blew gigantic ten-meter-deep craters in the ground that resembled small lakes. "Beehive bombs" (*bom tổ ong*) were cluster bombs, the most feared because they were fitted with warheads that released around three hundred "bomblets" (*bom bi*) upon impact. The bomblets, also called "pineapple bombs" (*bom dứa*) for their resemblance to a pineapple, would subsequently explode like delayed-action landmines, spurting hundreds of high-velocity steel pellets that would mow down everything in their path. The shower of projectiles would penetrate victims' bodies, their abdominal walls, organs, and travel in the bloodstream to other organs. They were purposely designed not only to injure but also to cause injuries that required labor-intensive care from medical personnel.

Another antipersonnel munition that figured prominently in patient memoirs was what the North Vietnamese called "leaf mines" (*bom lá*), resembling harmless tropical plants.[39]

> The thing looked almost like a leaf. It was green, veined, but much thicker and heavier. Millions of such mines had been dropped from the air, each designed to cause sufficient damage to a human foot to render it completely useless. A

man with a damaged foot would have to be carried off by two stretcher-bearers. Altogether, three men would thus be put out of action, one way or another.[40]

Napalm bombs, delivered by air, flame throwers, or warheads fired from rocket launchers, were some of the most feared. While the MK79 (Model 1) 1,000-pound fire bomb, used in Vietnam, did not produce as many casualties as an equivalent weight of high-explosive or cluster munitions, the psychological implications of disfigurement were viewed as an effective technique of intimidation.[41] Officers wrote of massive panic over napalm among NVA truck drivers who were ordered to cross the border to Laos and their desperate efforts to procure medical records that would prove they were not healthy enough to work as drivers; or they would try to convince their superiors that they were the only sons in their families.[42]

Reaction States in the American War

Tai, a 23-year-old NVA infantryman who had been serving in the battlefields for three years, was carried into a field clinic in Quang Tri one day in July 1967. He was described by health workers at the clinic as being in a state of severe agitation (*kích động quá*) following a skirmish with US Marines.[43] Discovered by support troops standing in a trench with his gun still poised speaking nonsense (*nói linh tinh*), he was transported to field medics who described him as panicked (*hoảng hốt*), speaking too fast (*nói nhanh quá*), and unconscious (*không có ý thức*) of his surroundings. A physical exam revealed no apparent injuries. He was given injections of chlorpromazine and morphine, enough to put him to sleep for three days.

Conditions such as Tai's, diagnosed as reaction psychosis, were routinely treated on the frontlines with an intramuscular injection of chlorpromazine or a solution of morphine or Lidol mixed with Thorazine, what was referred to as a "cocktail-lytique."[44] Its main purpose was to induce a deep prolonged sleep, which was considered to be therapeutic. As one medic recalled, "the cocktail would knock a man out for three days. He would wake up having forgotten everything."[45]

The "sleep cure," an adaptation of a Soviet technique, was premised on the Pavlovian theory that experiences of intense fear resulted in disturbances of the regulatory processes of the nervous system, with wide ranging effects on circulation, respiration, thermoregulation, and metabolism. It was seen as the reverse of electroshock treatment, commonly used at the time to treat depression. Sleep, in North Vietnamese psychiatry, as in Soviet psychiatry, was considered to have restorative powers for the nervous system. A proponent of the treatment was Nguyen Viet, who would go on to lead the Vietnamese National Institute of

Mental Health after the war. Viet spent two years in Moscow in the early 1960s, where he was exposed to the vast literature on the neuropsychiatric effects of war trauma on the Red Army. By the late 1960s, Viet had become known for his expertise on the topic of reaction states among civilians who were victims of US air attacks and in 1968 was asked to investigate mass occurrences of hysteria along the Ho Chi Minh Trail.

The sleep cure, as the North Vietnamese utilized it, was different in key aspects from the "deep-sleep" induction methods used by William Sargent with British soldiers during World War II and by United States' military psychiatrists stationed in South Vietnam during the 1960s and 1970s. Sargent, also influenced by the work of Pavlov, similarly viewed war neurosis to be a conditioned response and theorized that the key to prevention was to disallow initial symptoms to become "ingrained" in the soldier's personality.[46] Underlying his methods, however, was also the psychoanalytic concept of abreaction and catharsis, for sedation was used with the intent of enabling patients to speak freely of their memories of traumatic incidents, as a means of preventing such memories from becoming fixed thoughts that could further lead to neurotic symptoms.[47]

US psychiatrists, similarly, aimed to use deep-sleep to facilitate abreaction and catharsis immediately upon waking, through means of individual counseling or group therapy, in which the soldier would be encouraged to relate his or her memories of trauma and uncover "repressed" memories. This psychoanalytic component was absent in the context of North Vietnam and was not considered beneficial by psychiatrists back in Hanoi, who had already determined that the use of psychoanalytic methods of oral catharsis to be culturally inappropriate. As soon as patients woke up from their deep sleep and were determined to be in stable condition, they were immediately sent back to their units. Patients who did not improve or whose symptoms deteriorated were evacuated back to Hanoi for further evaluation and treatment.

One of the difficulties Vietnamese psychiatrists faced in treating such conditions was that soldiers who were evacuated were often not brought immediately to the attention of psychiatrists. Comorbid injuries and infections further complicated their clinical picture and psychiatrists, often times, only received these cases after they had already spent some time being transferred from specialty to specialty. When patients finally did arrive, they were often in worse states than they had been upon initial evacuation. This was particularly the case with patients who were suffering from psycho-traumatic forms of paralysis, deafness, and muteness, whose symptoms were exacerbated by unwitting suggestion by doctors who treated them as if their problems were the effects of physical injuries.

The majority of military patients who arrived in psychiatry departments during the war were diagnosed with either reaction psychosis or hysteria. Both disorders were thought to manifest in a polymorphous array of symptoms, ranging from psychosomatic deafness, muteness, paralysis of the legs or the whole body, and difficulties breathing to symptoms that "mimicked" those of more severe psychiatric illnesses such as mania, delusional thoughts, and hallucinations. The two disorders were distinguished from each other in key ways. For one, while trauma played a role in both, the types of traumas associated with each differed. Reaction psychosis was triggered by events that were circumscribed (*cấp dẫn*) and severe—events that provoked extreme fear, such as encounters with extreme violence, terrifying forms of death, or large-scale disasters on the battlefields. Hysteria was the outcome of prolonged traumatic conditions (*sang chấn tâm lý mãn tính*) and the intensity of symptoms was disproportionate to the severity of trauma. The development of hysteria was also considered to be correlated to age. Towards the end of the war, a large-scale study of women tortured in two South Vietnamese prisons, controlling for the type and intensity of torture, concluded that younger prisoners were more likely to develop the disorder than their older counterparts.[48]

The main psychotherapeutic techniques used were suggestion, hypnosis, relaxation, and placebo, sometimes supplemented with psychotropic medications and acupuncture. Suggestion may involve explaining to patients that their symptoms were not the result of real injuries and that they could will their symptoms away. They might assist the patient with hypnosis or sedation while instructing them to engage in activities that involved the body part that was paralyzed. The goal of hypnosis and sedation was to make the patient more amenable to the doctor's suggestions by weakening the patient's own critical faculties.

In instances of recalcitrant symptoms, North Vietnamese psychiatrists would often supplement their treatments with placebo injections, explaining to the patient that the "medication" being injected would assist them in regaining whatever bodily function had been lost. Because many of the placebo compounds injected into the patients, such as calcium chloride, induced their own bodily sensations, the doctor would refer to the new sensations as evidence that the medication was efficacious. To enhance the effect of injections, they were usually conducted in a special exam room at the hospital, with nurses assisting, to give the impression of a real medical procedure.

The point of suggestion was to make the patient believe that he and the doctor could get his body working again. In one case, an army journalist who had been transferred to four different hospitals before he was referred to Thuong Tin, had become deaf and mute after covering a particularly violent battle in the South. Nguyen Van Siem conducted suggestion with the patient fully conscious. He explained that his symptoms were not indicative of any internal physical injuries, but of a state of "inhibition" (*ức chế*) that could easily be overcome through willful activity.

I examined his ears, nose, and throat and then applied heat and spicy powder to his tongue to stimulate it. The tongue would contract so we knew that all the senses were working and I told him that all of his senses were completely normal. I explained: "You are just inhibited. I will stimulate you to get rid of the inhibition so that you can speak." I would tell him to say "A" only. He would say "A" and from there slowly, slowly he would speak more.[49]

Techniques like suggestion and acupuncture, which were utilized both as a means of assisting in suggestion as placebo and in helping to induce relaxation, were not introduced to the frontlines until 1968, the year of the Tet Offensive, in response to an outbreak of collective hysteria (*ixteria tập thể*) in female units of the Volunteer Youth Brigade. The incidents, involving 20 to 30 women per unit, exhibiting uniform psychomotor disorders, had caught the attention of President Ho Chi Minh. Nguyen Viet was sent to investigate whether the epidemic indicated that conditions had become too violent for women to endure.[50] Viet assuaged the government's concerns, theorizing that the heightened suggestibility of the women was not linked to their gender or the level of violence, but, rather, to chronic social isolation, which male units were not facing to the same degree. Viet spearheaded the first systematic training of medical personnel in suggestion and hypnosis, instructing that patients be isolated using underground bomb shelters, to prevent further spread.

Although there are no reports of collective hysteria among male units, the disorder was diagnosed quite frequently in men. In fact, a common concern back in Hanoi was whether medical personnel were over-diagnosing hysteria on the battlefields, mistaking symptoms of malarial-induced psychosis for symptoms of hysteria. In 1966, a military medical report warned: "people are being given a lot of anti-psychotic medication when they should be receiving quinine."[51] Unable to conduct necessary blood tests and unfamiliar with the clinical symptoms of severe types of malaria that were endemic in the central and southern jungles, health workers had trouble distinguishing symptoms of malarial psychosis from reactive states. Concern led the government to commission research by doctors at Military Hospital 103 to formulate a functional set of criteria for diagnosing malaria-induced psychosis at the battlefront.[52]

Confusion about causation was a constant reality in the battlefields, but also back in Hanoi and malaria was not the only confounding factor. As one psychiatrist, who had served as a physician's assistant during the war, described it: "the effects of hunger could induce symptoms that could be misconstrued as hysteria or psychosis." Advanced stages of beriberi, a thiamine deficiency, could manifest as partial paralysis of the extremities. Chemical poisoning, physical blows to the skull during combat, lingering bomb fragments, left behind by overwhelmed field surgeons who lacked basic radiological instruments, and blast waves could result in amnesia, seizures, paralysis, delusional states, and mania.

The Neuropsychiatric Effects of Bombs

Lieu was brought into a field clinic deaf and mute after his infantry unit was ambushed and almost entirely wiped out by US Marines and fighter planes along Route 9. Field personnel observed no physical injuries that could explain his symptoms. He was treated for psychological shock (*sóc tâm lý*) with a cocktail of morphine and Thorazine. He was eventually evacuated to Military Hospital 103 in Hanoi. Psychiatrists there asked Lieu a series of routine questions about his circumstances on the battlefield. What happened to you in the ambush? What weapons were used against you? Was there an explosion? How far away were you from the explosion? They learned he had been near a rocket explosion, the force of which killed his trench mate and knocked Lieu backwards causing him to bleed from his ears, eyes, and nose. "Organic pathology," they noted, "resulting from blast waves" (*sức ép bom*), which was listed as the cause of what was recorded as hysterical syndrome (*hội chứng hysteria*).[53]

The majority of casualties among NVA resulted from explosive munitions—mines, rockets, and bombs. Aside from penetrating wounds caused by shrapnel and cluster fragments, blast injuries (*tổn thương sức nổ*), from the pressure caused by the rapid expansion and release of gas during an explosion, also referred to as blast wave syndromes (*hội chứng sức nổ*) were common. Blast wave syndromes comprised 11 percent of casualties at the Battle of Quang Tri in 1972, 42 percent of civilian and non-civilian casualties during the Christmas Bombings in Hanoi the same year, and 11 to 14 percent at the Xuan Battle in 1975.[54] In the late 1990s, most of the veterans I encountered who were treated at Bach Mai and in other psychiatric hospitals in northern Vietnam for chronic or delayed symptoms linked to the war were diagnosed with disorders attributed at least in part to blast waves.

Foreign visitors who likened the designation of *sức ép bom* to shell shock were mistaken, however, for the research behind it was unrelated to shell shock. Military medicine in Western Europe had not only dropped the diagnosis of shell shock by 1920, but also, for the most part, discontinued research on psychiatric effects of blast waves.[55] The Vietnamese understanding of blast wave syndromes was mainly influenced by Russian research on Red Army veterans after World War II. Blast wave syndromes, as they were understood in Vietnam, were more akin to the neuropsychiatric consequences that are today associated with blast-related mild Traumatic Brain Injuries (mTBI) in veterans of wars in Iraq and Afghanistan or Chronic Traumatic Encephalopathy (CTE) in professional football players, formally recognized by the American scientific community after 2005.

North Vietnamese psychiatrists held that the effects of blast waves could mimic symptoms associated with a wide range of psychiatric disorders, such as psychosis, mania, depressed affect, accelerated neurological degeneration that looked like dementia, and seizures. The Vietnamese adapted a Soviet classification system, which delineated four types of neuropsychiatric disorder caused by blast waves, the mildest being "traumatic asthenia" (*suy nhược chấn thương*), characterized by general weakness, insomnia, and headaches; traumatic neurasthenia (*suy nhão chấn thương*), associated with deterioration of cognitive functions like memory and logic tasks; traumatic epilepsy (*chấn thương động kinh*); and traumatic amnesia (*mất trí chấn thương*).

Configurations of Trauma at Phu Tho Psychiatric Hospital

In the late 1990s, Phu Tho Provincial Hospital served 235 villages, where the majority of adult males above the age of thirty-five had served in one to three wars.[56] In Tho Van, 80 percent of men between the ages of thirty-five and seventy were veterans.[57] Of the patients admitted to the hospital, 70 percent were classified in medical records as peasants (*nông dân*). They resided in close extended family networks, engaged in ancestor worship and espoused ideas rooted in Taoist/Buddhist syncretic traditions. Clinicians were keenly aware that psychiatry represented only one of a number of modalities that patients drew on to make sense of and mediate the ruptures of experience that brought them to the hospital. "Five words of advice" (*năm thuốc lá*) was a common saying in Phu Tho, referring to the order of whom people turned to in their villages for answers—family, neighbors, ancestors, traditional medicine, and finally the doctor.

The heavy presence of families was the most striking aspect of the hospital. They outnumbered patients and clinicians, day and night. Mothers in black silk pants and cotton tops accompanied their sons and daughters. Fathers perched on cots with their arms around their wives or attending to their children. Hospital policy required that family members stay during the entire course of treatment. It was not a matter of relieving staff burden. The ratio of staff to patients was high, with ten psychiatrists to no more than eighty patients. Their involvement was considered crucial to healing and social reintegration. As was instructed in a hospital pamphlet, "the presence of family prevents patients from developing an emotional complex (*mặc cảm*) over feeling abandoned."[58] Psychiatrists also viewed families, as important purveyors of information and insight into the psychological factors (*căn nguyên tâm lý*) affecting their patients.

Family involvement in the treatment process began with the construction of a patient biography, which involved "identifying psychological trauma" (*khai thác sang chấn tâm lý*). Clinicians did not use structured questionnaires. They directed open-ended questions to family members: "Was there any conflict (*mâu thuẫn*) in the family?" "Did anything happen at home or at work?" "Are they scared of anything?" The number of people involved in answering these questions sometimes made the assessment quite chaotic, when everyone who made the journey wanted to tell their version of events with others interjecting additional details. In this way psychiatrists reconstructed the everyday tensions at home, including spiritual matters that came up in the lives of patients, such as burial rituals gone awry, problems with hungry and thirsty ghosts (*ma khát ma đói*), and spirit possession.

As Phạm Minh Tuấn, lead psychiatrist of the acute male unit, explained it, the world of beliefs (*duy tâm*) played a functionally important role in helping his patients deal with the suffering (*khổ tâm*) that was an ineradicable aspect of life for people whom psychiatrists described as "laboring with their legs and arms" (*lao động bằng chân tay*): farming rice, manioc, corn, and growing cash crops such as lacquer trees. High child mortality, poverty, and the chronic physical pain resulting from backbreaking work comprised the backdrop of their psychiatric disorders. Believing in the afterlife, the existence of spirits, and making offerings to the dead, he contended, was often the only way to make grief bearable. Although most clinicians like Dr. Tuấn were self-described atheists, they did not engage in any systematic effort to disabuse patients and families of alternative etiological frameworks, so long as they adhered to their medication regimens, for they recognized that the moral underpinnings of these belief systems also strengthened family bonds.

Underlying the group interviewing process was an assumption by clinicians that regardless of who said it, information would be forthcoming, including information that in other cultural contexts might be considered very private, because families lived in close quarters, worked together, slept in the same rooms, and were intimately involved in each other's daily lives. Indeed, I was often surprised not only by the detail of observations that family members could supply, but how candid they were. I heard husbands reveal the affairs they were having, which they thought were related to their wives' conditions. People spoke bluntly about violence in the home, gambling away their savings, even rape. The longer I lived in a village, the more these candid exchanges made sense to me, as I realized the extent to which "private" information was known and openly discussed, not only by relatives, but by neighbors, and village health workers. During my hikes up the mountains at three o'clock in the morning to harvest lacquer, the women I accompanied would discuss intimate details about the lives of their neighbors. They knew that Thang and her husband fought, that Huong's mother-in-law was "rotten" to her, that Sau regularly slept in a coffin he had purchased for himself years ago with money he had stolen from his wife, and that Lung's wife left him after he came back from the war, because of his incontinence. Secrets were not easy to keep.

Clinicians took their cues about what was significant from families and the psychological traumas they mentioned fell broadly into five main categories: family conflict, loss of property or money, conflicts at work, life threatening events, and deaths of family members, including the anguish surrounding burial

FIGURE 5.1. Reburial Ceremony in Tho Van, 1998. © Narquis Barak.

rituals or the inability to provide proper reburials—a ceremony in which bones were disinterred and ritually cleaned individually three years after burial.

When these factors were noted, clinicians did not analyze them with their patients. Rather, their concern was with preventing patients from thinking too much, which was viewed as a manifestation of imbalance (*mất cân bằng*). Healing did not necessitate discussing or processing of the content of their thoughts concerning their experiences. If the trauma was acute and sudden, treatment was almost exclusively pharmacological, and consisted of low doses of an antipsychotic and antihistamines, mainly to sedate, along with vitamins to boost immunity and counteract side effects. Sedation was considered the first step in regaining balance.

If the patient was diagnosed with a "lighter illness" (*bệnh nhẹ*) falling under the umbrella term of "neuroses" (*suy nhược tâm căn*), which had resulted from ongoing situations at home or work that caused them tension, they were given the option of staying at the hospital for a month or so to enable them to be removed from the situation that distressed them, obtain respite through sedation, and give the clinicians opportunities to suggest changes in the family and work environment. Suggestion therapy, used in cases of both acute and mild trauma, took a number of forms, including administering placebo injections, hypnotherapy, and positive verbal encouragement that, at times, involved spiritual reinforcement. In one case I witnessed, a doctor told a woman haunted by her sister's death that he was able to communicate with her sister in the afterworld (*âm phủ*) and that she was sending her a message that she was safe and that her sister did not need to worry.

The psychological factors that both families and clinicians considered to be relevant were for the most part recent. Hence, the emotional experiences of battlefield trauma were not considered to be integral to understanding veterans' disorders. The notion that soldiers had returned home and, years later, developed symptoms attributable solely to the traumas experienced in the battlefields or to the memories of those experiences was simply not present inside the hospital or outside. In other words, the key concept of latency that is an integral part of PTSD—the effects of traumatic memory, can reveal themselves long after the traumatic experience occurred—was absent. When horrifying battlefield experiences came up, it was usually in the course of discussing physical injuries sustained during war. Chau, who was 68 years old and had served in the Volunteer Youth Brigade for 14 years, from 1959 to 1973, was such a case.

Chau, her husband, and her son described to clinicians her experience witnessing the incremental obliteration of her whole unit of 350 youth brigade volunteers in 1966, losing more than ten people a day: "There were nights I went to work, smelled something stinking, went to look and found the head of a person. Put it in a plastic bag and took it to bury." She witnessed up close the death of a good friend from her own village, whose head flew into a tree branch, while her legs and intestines were blown onto the road. Chau removed her own clothes to wrap the pieces of her friend's body to bury these herself. The doctors noted the experiences in her medical record and also that Chau had been treated in field clinics for reaction psychosis, but the clinicians did not consider these aspects of her military service to be of importance to understanding her current symptoms. What they highlighted as significant to her condition were the physical injuries she sustained in Quang Binh and Hue, where she had surgery on five separate occasions to remove fragments from pineapple bombs, some of which were still buried in her arms and legs, exposure to blast waves, napalm, and exposure to chemical defoliants. Her diagnosis was dementia caused by progressive neurological damage.

Harrowing stories such as Chau's, psychiatrists explained, were so common as to be expected from veterans. Đỗ Kim Lan, the hospital director, who was in charge of residents at a rescue area near the Battle of Quang Tri, treated many men terror-struck from witnessing gruesome deaths. Most of the psychiatrists had served in battle themselves. Dr. Tuan was seventeen in 1968, when he was ambushed by "enemy rangers" while guarding a munitions storage facility. During the faceoff, shrapnel from artillery fire shattered his elbow, leaving his arm disfigured and of little practical use. Only days before the injury, he had been laid up in a field hospital with cerebral malaria while the rest of his unit was killed by aerial bombs. That someone had experienced shock, hysteria, or psychosis on the battlefield was not only common, it was also not pathologized. Their experiences were considered part and parcel of the emotional landscape of war, one shared by many fellow villagers who had sacrificed husbands and children, their hand-colored grainy black and white photos in army fatigues poised on ancestor altars in homes throughout the province.

Veterans' Postwar Conditions

In the late 1990s, American mental health professionals searching for war-related PTSD arrived with certain assumptions. One preconception was that there was parity in the battlefield experiences of their own patients and those of the Vietnamese, but the war was not the same for the two sides. As shown above, the everyday conditions were far more severe for the NVA than for the Americans, for whom the "Vietnam War" was the least physically demanding and combat intense compared to previous wars.[59] Conditions for the NVA were more akin to those experienced by Union and Confederate soldiers in the US Civil War: rampant disease, endemic malnutrition, indefinite terms of service, long marches and heavy labor on a daily basis, an impoverished medical infrastructure that could hardly support the massive casualties in its care, and, in addition, massive aerial bombardment, which constituted the main reason for the vast disparities in casualty and fatality rates between the two sides.

This physical reality was reflected in the complexity and severity of veterans' conditions. Most veterans who came to psychiatric facilities during the years I conducted research were suffering from seizures or serious cognitive deficits. Cases such as that of Hong, a 47-year-old decorated captain of a radar unit, where he served for four years with no anti-radiation clothing, were typical. Hong had severe beriberi and radar poisoning when I met him at Phu Tho Psychiatric Hospital. He was certain that his death was imminent, because epileptic seizures had become an almost daily occurrence for him and he had recently suffered severe burns to his arm, when he fell unconscious on his stove. Before setting out to the hospital, he had invited his unit mates to bid final farewells and had hired a photographer to commemorate the occasion. Brain damage from the seizures had addled his memory. Hong was diagnosed with "epilepsy with psychotic features" caused by exposure to radar.[60]

Aside from epilepsy, veterans' diagnoses included a wide gamut of disorders, such as neurasthenia, dementia, schizophrenia, and mood disorders, similar to those of civilian patients. However, there was an important difference. In veterans' records, the disorders were always, at least in part, ascribed to neurological damage from contusion injuries, blast waves, chemical poisoning, severe infections, and vitamin deficiencies sustained in the battlefields. Many physicians noted multiple etiological factors, such as in the case of Khanh, a 48-year-old veteran, who was treated for neurasthenia. Khanh's symptoms, listed in his medical record, were "headaches, insomnia, and general pain." The causes noted were malaria, shell fragment injuries to his arms and legs, a paralyzed arm, five battlefield surgeries, a bladder injury, and "exposure to Agent Orange in the Truong Son forest."

Another important difference between veterans and civilians in Vietnam was that veterans' diagnoses often changed over time. Lung, who shared twenty years' worth of medical records with me, which he kept on his ancestor altar near a pillbox filled with neuroleptics and anti-psychotics, was first diagnosed with hysteria straight after arriving from the battlefields, then with hysterical syndrome caused by *sức ép bom*, which was later changed to schizophrenia combined with organically caused amnesia from "extensive firing of an M79 grenade and Katyusha rocket launchers."[61] In these cases, the delayed onset or intensification of symptoms many years following military service were often viewed as the combined effect of the initial wounding and subsequent brain deterioration caused by natural aging. Unlike in the United States, diagnostic categories were not essential to pension classification. Rather, what mattered were causal attributions and the degree of functional loss of health, which was a subjective determination.

Many veterans I met in villages viewed their symptoms through a complex lens of somatic, psycho-social, and even spiritual factors, but when psycho-social factors came into play in this weave, they did not refer to the emotional traumas of war. Worries about finances, sick family members, fears related to the limitations posed by their physical deterioration, and, in some cases, traumatic experiences that occurred long after the war—most commonly the deaths of close family members or the birth and care of children with serious disabilities. Nguyen Thi Dung, who spent close to a decade fighting against the United States in Vietnam and against Pol Pot's army in Cambodia operating anti-aircraft guns, related his *thinking too much*, his sadness, his heavy mood, to his emotional pain for his family (*đau sót cho gia đình*) caused by the drowning of his two daughters, aged fifteen and seventeen, in the Red River when their boat sank coming back from harvesting peanuts. He had experienced shock in the battlefields—seeing corpses of dead soldiers—but, as he put it, nothing compared to losing his daughters.

Tuy, a veteran of both the French and American wars, documented his experiences in detail in a journal, in which he described surviving a French massacre of his village and mass starvation under the Japanese occupation before he volunteered for the army in fourth grade when he would have been between twelve and fourteen years of age. After thirteen years in combat, in 1971, he was diagnosed with blast wave syndrome by military doctors and sent home. According to his family and Tuy himself, he went mad (*lên rô*) seven years later, accusing his wife of cheating on him and threatening to stab her with a knife. The neighbors ran up from the paddy fields to confront Tuy as he held on to his crying infant son, cursing his wife while waving a knife over his head. Kien, who headed the

FIGURE 5.2. Tuy reading from his battlefield journal, Tho Van 1998. © Narquis Barak.

village health station, was able to overpower Tuy, inject him with a sedative to calm him down long enough for the ride to the psychiatric hospital. When I met Tuy in the fall of 1998, he had not been to the hospital in years and had long ago stopped all medication. He and his family ascribed his temporary madness to his mother's death and his inability to give her a proper burial. His wife started taking him to a spirit medium and his condition improved.

Tai served eleven years, from 1965 to 1976, returning home only once to wed in 1975. Over the course of getting to know him, I learned that the range of symptoms he associated with his condition held complex layers of meaning. To him, the ravages of Agent Orange on his body and mind were inextricably related to the effects of years of labor-intensive rice farming and the tensions he felt

FIGURE 5.3. Tai and his daughter, Tho Van, 1998. © Narquis Barak.

regarding his family's chronic economic insecurity, since they could no longer produce enough rice for themselves and had to purchase it from neighbors. He had become too weak to plow. Most importantly, though, were his worries about his 5-year-old daughter Hue who was paralyzed over half her body and suffered from seizures, sometimes five times a night. Tai, Hue's primary caretaker since she was weaned at age three, often woke up scared that his daughter would fall off the bed. His habit was to remain awake, next to her, watching her, *thinking too much,* and worrying about the future, when there would be no one to care for her. All of these postwar aspects of his life coalesced into his understanding of his condition.

Conclusion

> Certain forms of knowledge and control require a narrowing of vision. The great advantage of such tunnel vision is that it brings into sharp focus certain limited aspects of an otherwise far more complex and unwieldy reality.[62]

In "Psychological Responses to War and Atrocity" (1995), Bracken, Giller, and Summerfield write that PTSD has rested on three fundamental suppositions within the American discourse on trauma: an individualist approach to human life, an emphasis on an "intrapsychic" world, and an understanding of society as a collection of separate individuals.[63] I would add one more assumption, an atomistic view of suffering. The focus on identifying a singular trauma in PTSD, isolating one trauma and processing its associated memories in particular kinds of therapy, such as prolonged exposure therapy and cognitive processing therapy—still the only two forms reimbursable by the VA—requires a kind of narrowing of vision. This constriction of view may be convenient for the purpose of the US Veterans' Administration, private insurance systems, and for the courts, but in many ways it is antithetical to the frameworks that undergirded northern Vietnamese psychiatry, with its dialectical emphasis and its Buddhist and Taoist ideas about the changeability and fluidity of experience.

Knowledge and practice at Phu Tho Psychiatric Hospital was predicated on a view of human subjectivity that was quite distinct from these suppositions. The intersubjective was prioritized over the intrapsychic and individuals were treated as inextricable from their social units, to whom doctors deferred to when appropriating meaning. Maintaining equilibrium is a lifelong process that required family agency. The nature of clinical interactions was therefore fundamentally different. These aspects of psychiatry were not just an outgrowth of the theoretical streams that historically dominated the field, but were also rooted in psychiatrists' subjective understandings of the social, cultural, and economic realities of their patients. The impasse over PTSD, described at the beginning of this chapter, can be viewed another way. Perhaps it is better understood, not only as a reflection of these differences, but also more specifically as a resistance to a particular vision of the meaning of the war and veterans' experiences of the war—a rejection of the narrow framework insisted on by their foreign visitors.

When presented with facts of high PTSD prevalence among US veterans, Vietnamese psychiatrists did not deny the medical legitimacy of PTSD as a psychiatric disorder. Traumatogenic syndromes and disorders were well-established in Vietnamese psychiatry, observed and treated in the battlefields, as illustrated above. It was the persistence of symptoms associated with PTSD—long after the United States' involvement in the war ended—that was of salience to them. Unlike foreign visitors, who were determined to view the high prevalence of PTSD among US veterans as one indication of the disorder's universal biological inevitability, Vietnamese doctors understood it as a result of the Americans' specific social and cultural experience of the war and postwar life. Their focus on social bonds and communal belief systems as deterrents to the development or persistence of PTSD is indeed reminiscent of ideas put forth by the American psychiatrist, Jonathan Shay, who has urged that PTSD be viewed as a set of behaviors that are not inherently pathological. Many of the symptoms of PTSD, Shay argues, are in fact adaptive in the combat environment, but become problematic only if they are exacerbated and persist after soldiers' return to civilian life.[64] Shay views PTSD as a moral injury, a rupture in one's relationship to society. Healing, he suggests, requires the "communalization of trauma" and a reestablishment of social trust, meaning, and belonging.[65]

In the late 1990s and early 2000s, my findings that NVA veterans did not exhibit symptoms of PTSD and that psychiatrists were mainly treating people with brain damage from blast waves and other organic causes were waved off by researchers at the VA centers in Boston, where I was then attending graduate school. Similar to the foreign visitors to Vietnam, they could not see beyond the conceptual prism of PTSD. An aspect of this view was likely related to the enduring stigma surrounding shell shock. Part of it was a matter of having only the perspective of what they observed in the US veterans they studied coupled with the psychoanalytic legacy in the United States, which continues today. However, a large part of it may have been that Americans did not experience battlefield conditions in the same way the Vietnamese did. The gap in knowledge is similar to what Richard Kagan describes regarding American literature on the Vietnam War: "The Americans," he states, "despite their skillfulness, lit up only the part of Vietnam they understood. Their cultural baggage, when unpacked and worn, allowed them to discern and walk through a limited part of the war and of Vietnam."[66]

The wars in Afghanistan and Iraq have changed much of this. Since 2005, there has been a slow paradigmatic shift in US military medicine as more and more Americans were exposed to Improvised Explosive Devices (IEDs).[67] After 2008, the VA began to recognize that blast wave induced mTBI can produce long-term neuropsychiatric symptoms. Currently, there are estimates of over 300,000 military personnel with mTBI.[68] It has been referred to as the "signature injury" of the conflicts in Iraq and Afghanistan.[69] Currently, reports indicate that Iran's missile strike on Al Asad Air Base in western Iraq on 8 January 2020 resulted in more than a hundred troops being diagnosed with TBI.[70] Might the US medical establishment have been more prepared for these kinds of casualties if it had looked to the war experiences of other countries? The chapters in this volume highlight the importance of crossing cultural boundaries. Historically, such crossings, particularly in the field of psychiatry, have been uni-directional, with the United States and European countries doing most of the exporting of "international" standards, definitions, and treatments.[71] The northern

Vietnamese case presented here problematizes this trend, and disrupts what Byron Good, Subandi, and Mary-Jo DelVecchio Good refer to as psychiatry's transnational project of "biologization" and "medicalization" through forums such as psychiatric education and pharmaceutical industry-sponsored conferences.[72] The historical trajectory of psychiatric theory, the social-environmental aspects of the war experience, the subjectivities of psychiatrists, and their understandings of their patients' subjectivities, resulted in what Mark Micale and Paul Lerner describe as a very different "medico-cultural milieu," one in which PTSD may not be an ideal framework for understanding traumatic suffering in the context of war.[73]

Narquis Barak is Prevention Research Manager at CrescentCare, a Federally Qualified Health Clinic in New Orleans, Louisiana. She has coordinated the CDC funded National HIV Behavioral Surveillance program in New Orleans for more than eleven years. She conducts large-scale ethnographic and survey research on populations at high risk for HIV and Hepatitis C, including Men Who Have Sex with Men, People Who Inject Drugs, Transgender Women, and High Risk Heterosexuals in the New Orleans metropolitan area, a component of which examines how factors such as exposure to violence, trauma, and stigma affect risk behaviors and exposure to HIV and Hepatitis C. Barak is also Project Director and co-designer of +LOVE, a Ryan White funded intervention to improve health outcomes for Black Men Who Have Sex with Men living with HIV, which provides behavioral health therapy that is trauma-focused. Her research in New Orleans, Louisiana, northern Vietnam, southwestern Nigeria, and southern India has focused on social and cultural factors that shape the practice of medicine, disease experience, and disease etiology and transmission. Barak has an MA in social anthropology from Harvard University and completed all coursework and requirements for her PhD except the dissertation. She has designed and taught courses focused on cross-cultural mental health and violence at Harvard and Stanford University.

Notes

1. Nguyễn Văn Siêm, "Some Considerations about Post Traumatic Stress Disorder in Vietnam," Speech presented in Amsterdam, 1992, manuscript shared with author.
2. I interviewed both formally and informally more than a hundred clinicians who worked directly with soldiers and veterans and reviewed more than 400 case records of psychiatric disorder in soldiers and veterans spanning the years of 1965 to 1999.
3. Hebrew is my first language.
4. Johnson and Lubin, "Uncovering PTSD Republic Vietnam."

5. William Branigin, "Vietnam Asylums: War Never Ended," *Washington Post,* 23 October 1993. Retrieved 28 February 2020 from https://www.washingtonpost.com/archive/politics/1993/10/23/vietnam-asylums-war-never-end/8d1b24e3-7715-4bac-b438-020ecf910a32/.
6. Young, *Harmony Illusions,* 111.
7. Keane, Kaloupek, and Weathers, "Ethnocultural Considerations Assessment PTSD," 184.
8. Other scholars have traced a similar lineage. See Hacking, *Rewriting the Soul*; Merskey, "PTSD and Shell Shock"; and Jones and Wessely, "Paradigm Shift."
9. Micale, "Toward Global History Trauma."
10. James M. Olin Foundation Research Grant, Social Science Research Council Pre-Dissertation Fellowship; Wenner Gren Foundation Research Grant; Social Science Research Council Dissertation Research Fellowship; Kennedy, Knox, Sheldon Travelling Fellowship; Fulbright-Hays Dissertations Research Fellowship; National Science Foundation Research Grant; National Institute of Mental Health Pre-Doctoral Fellowship.
11. The history of northern Vietnamese psychiatry is based on personal communication with Nguyễn Việt (1996–1997), Nguyễn Văn Siêm (1996–1997), Đỗ Kim Lan (1998–2000), Phạm Minh Tuấn (1998–2000), and with numerous other psychiatrists at Thuong Tin Central Psychiatric Hospital, Bach Mai Hospital, Military Hospital 103, and Phu Tho Provincial Psychiatric Hospital, as well as by consulting Nguyễn Việt, *Tâm Thần Học.*
12. Nguyễn, "Xây Dựng Danh Từ."
13. Personal communication with Nguyễn Việt, who studied under Anh.
14. Wortis, *Soviet Psychiatry,* 74.
15. Calloway, *Soviet and Western Psychiatry,* 77.
16. Thái, "Tổng Kết Tình Hình Tử Vong Của Bệnh Nhân Tinh Thần."
17. Nguyễn, *Pháp Y Tâm Thần,* 81.
18. Nguyễn, *Những Kiến Thức Chung Về Chứng Loạn Thần Kinh Chức Năng,* 8.
19. Paul Calloway, *Soviet and Western Psychiatry,* 77.
20. Nguyen, "Renovation of Traditional Medicine."
21. Young, *Harmony Illusions*; Bracken, "Hidden Agendas"; Leys, *Trauma.*
22. Personal communication from Nguyễn Việt, Professor of Psychiatry at Bach Mai Hospital and Director of the Vietnamese National Institute of Mental Health, and Hoàng Bào Châu, Director of the National Institute of Traditional Medicine in Hanoi.
23. Figley, Bride, and Mazza, *Death and Trauma.*
24. Tran and Nguyễn, "Qua Nhận Xét Chẩn Đoán Loạn Thần Hysteria," 62.
25. Nguyễn, "Xây Dựng Danh Từ," 35.
26. Tran and Nguyễn, "Qua Nhận Xét Chẩn Đoán Loạn Thần Hysteria," 71.
27. Nguyễn Việt, *Tâm Thần Học,* 13.
28. Journal of Mission #2 1965 (211), in a collection of memoirs and reports written by military and civilian personnel who participated in events on the Ho Chi Minh Trail during the American War. Originally published in *Tập Chí Văn Nghệ Quân Đội* [Military literature and art review] (Hanoi: Military Publishing House, 1990), courtesy of the William Joiner Center for the Study of War and Social Consequences). When I refer to Journal of Mission, Field Report, or Memoirs it is to these translated manuscripts.
29. Field Report #1 Ch.1 p. 6, Lt. Colonel Nguyen Thanh explaining the situation to new recruits.
30. Field Report #1 Ch. 5, 25.
31. Field Report #1 Ch. 1, 9, and personal communication with several veterans.
32. Personal communication with several veterans of NVA.

33. Journal of Mission #2 1965 (109). Major General Phan Trong Tue was former Minister of Communications and Transport Commander and Political Commissar of Army 559. He had previously been a prisoner at Con Dao prison of the French in colonial times.
34. Dat, *The Maiden Stars*, 124.
35. Memoirs 1990 (86).
36. Journal of Mission 1965 #1 (66).
37. Field Report #1, Ch. 5, 25.
38. Journal of Mission #1, 56.
39. Memoirs 1990 (24).
40. Memoirs 1990, 24.
41. Jones, "Military Psychiatry," 48.
42. Journal of Mission 1965 #1 (43).
43. Medical records provided by Ta.
44. Nguyễn, "Hồi Sức và Chống Sốc Nặng Do Vết Thương," 47.
45. Personal communication with Đức Phức Nguyễn.
46. Shephard, *War of Nerves*, 331.
47. Shephard, *War of Nerves*, 226.
48. Đoàn et al., Điều Tra Về Bệnh Tâm Thần Của Phụ Nữ, 43–49.
49. Personal communication with Nguyễn Văn Siêm.
50. Personal communication with Nguyễn Việt, Nguyễn Văn Siêm, Đỗ Kim Lan. The short story by Vo Thi Hao, "The Remaining Person of the Laughing Jungle," a Vietnamese veteran herself, draws on cases of collective hysteria among the Volunteer Youth Brigade. A rendition of her short story was made into a film titled, *The Jungle of Laughter*, which aired on Vietnamese television in the late 1980s.
51. Trần Văn Chín, "Vài Suy Nghĩ về Sốt Rét," 36.
52. Bích and Lợi, "Mấy Nhân Xét Về Loạn Tâm Thần Sốt Rét," 62–72.
53. Medical record provided by Lieu.
54. Trung, "Đặc Điểm Các Tổn Thương Trong Chiến Tranh."
55. Shephard, *War of Nerves*, 31–41.
56. Đỗ Kim Lan, *Bệnh Viện Tâm Thần Phú Thọ*, 5.
57. Personal communication with Đinh Văn Liễu, Chủ Tịch Xã, Head of the Tho Van Commune.
58. Đỗ Kim Lan, *Bệnh Viện Tâm Thần Phú Thọ*, 5.
59. Jones, "Military Psychiatry."
60. Medical record shared with author by Hong.
61. Medical record shared with author by Lung.
62. Scott, *Seeing Like a State*, 11.
63. Bracken, Giller, and Summerfield, "Psychological Responses War Atrocity."
64. Shay, *Achilles in Vietnam*.
65. Shay, *Achilles in Vietnam*, 194.
66. Kagan, "Disarming Memories," 26.
67. Robert F. Worth, "What if PTSD is More Physical than Psychological?" *New York Times Magazine,* 10 June 2016.
68. McKee and Robinson, "Military-Related Traumatic Brain Injury."
69. Hayward, "Traumatic Brain Injury."
70. Loren DeJonge Schulman and Paul Scharre, "The Iranian Missile Strike Did Far More Damage than Trump Admits," *New York Times,* 12 February 2020.
71. Watters, *Crazy Like Us*, 2.
72. Good, Subandi, and DelVecchio Good, "Subject Mental Illness," 257.
73. Lerner and Micale, "Trauma, Psychiatry, and History," 22.

Bibliography

Bích, Vũ Quang, and Đường Trung Lợi. "Mấy Nhân Xết Về 17 Trường Hợp Loạn Tâm Thần Sốt Rết [A few observations regarding 17 cases of malarial psychosis]." *Nội San Thần Kinh Tinh Thần và Phẫu Thuật* [Journal of Psychiatry, Neurology, and Surgery], no. 197 (1974–75): 62–72.

Bracken, Patrick J. "Hidden Agendas: Deconstructing Post-Traumatic Stress Disorder." In *Rethinking the Trauma of War*, edited by Patrick J. Bracken and Celia Petty, 38–59. London: Free Association Books, 1998.

Bracken, Peter J., Joan E. Giller, and Derek Summerfield. "Psychological Responses to War and Atrocity: The Limitations of Current Concepts." *Social Science and Medicine* 40, no. 8 (1995): 1073–82.

Calloway, Paul. *Soviet and Western Psychiatry: A Comparative Study.* Yorkshire: Moor Press, 1992.

Dat, Duong Trong. *The Maiden Stars.* Ho Chi Minh City: Pham Thanh Hao, 1985.

Đoàn, Phạm Văn, Bình An, Lan Thủy Ai, and Ngọc Bích. Điều Tra Cơ Bản Về Bệnh Tâm Thần Của Phụ Nữ Bị Giam Tại Các Nhà Lao Mỹ Ngụy Sau Khi Tao Trả [Preliminary investigation of psychiatric illness among women tortured in American prisons after return]. *(Khu an Đường T72, 7/1973-9/1973).* Hanoi: Bệnh Viện Tâm Thần, 1975.

Đỗ Kim Lan, *Bệnh Viện Tâm Thần Phú Thọ 20 Năm Xây Dựng và Trưởng Thành* (11-1977-11-1997) [Establishment and development of Phu Tho Psychiatric Hospital (11-1977-11-1997)], 5. Published by Phu Tho Psychiatric Hospital.

Figley, Charles R., Brian E. Bride, and Nicholas Mazza. *Death and Trauma: The Traumatology of Grieving.* Washington, DC: Taylor & Francis, 1997.

Good, Byron, Subandi, and Mary-Jo DelVecchio Good. "The Subject of Mental Illness: Psychosis, Mad Violence, and Subjectivity in Indonesia." In *Subjectivity: Ethnographic Investigations*, edited by João Biehl, Byron Good, and Arthur Kleinman, 243–72. Berkeley: University of California Press, 2007.

Hacking, Ian. *Rewriting the Soul: Multiple Personality and the Sciences of Memory.* Princeton, NJ: Princeton University Press, 1995.

Hayward, Peter. "Traumatic Brain Injury: The Signature of Modern Conflicts." *Lancet Neurology* 7, no. 3 (2008): 200–1.

Johnson, David Read, and Hadar Lubin. "Uncovering PTSD in the Republic of Vietnam." *National Center for PTSD Quarterly* 5, no. 4 (1995): 7–10.

Jones, Edgar, and Simon Wessely. "A Paradigm Shift in the Conceptualization of Psychological Trauma in the 20th Century." *Journal of Anxiety Disorders* 21 (2007): 164–75.

Jones, Franklin D. "Military Psychiatry: Preparing in Peace for War." *Textbook of Military Medicine*, Part I: *Warfare, Weaponry, and the Casualty.* Washington, DC: Department of the Army, 1996.

Kagan, Richard C. "Disarming Memories: Japanese, Korean, and American Literature on the Vietnam War." *Bulletin of Concerned Asian Scholars* 32, no. 4 (2000): 25–32.

Keane, Terence M., Danny G. Kaloupek, and Frank W. Weathers. "Ethnocultural Considerations in the Assessment of PTSD." In *Ethnocultural Aspects of Posttraumatic Stress Disorder: Issues, Research, and Clinical Applications*, edited by Anthony J. Marsella, Matthew J. Friedman, Ellen T. Gerrity and Raymond M. Scurfield, 183–205. Washington, DC: American Psychological Association, 1996.

Lerner, Paul, and Mark Micale. "Trauma, Psychiatry, and History: A Conceptual and Historiographical Introduction." In *Traumatic Pasts: History, Psychiatry, and Trauma in the Modern Age, 1870–1930*, edited by Mark S. Micale and Paul Lerner, 1–28. New York: Cambridge University Press, 2001.

Leys, Ruth. *Trauma: A Genealogy.* Chicago: University of Chicago Press, 2000.
McKee, Ann C., and Meghan E. Robinson. "Military-Related Traumatic Brain Injury and Neurodegeneration." *Alzheimer's and Dementia* 10, no. 3 (2014): S242–S253.
Merskey, Harold. "Post-Traumatic Stress Disorder and Shell Shock: Clinical Section." In *A History of Clinical Psychiatry*, edited by German E. Berrios and Roy Porter, 490–500. London: Athlone Press, 1995.
Micale, Mark S. "Toward a Global History of Trauma." In *Psychological Trauma and the Legacies of the First World War*, edited by Jason Crouthamel and Peter Leese, 289–310. Basingstoke, Hampshire: Palgrave Mcmillan, 2017.
Nguyễn, Đăng Dung. *Pháp Y Tâm Thần* [French psychiatry]. Hanoi: Bệnh Viện Tâm Thần, 1975.
Nguyễn, Đức Phức. "Hồi Sức và Chống Sốc Nặng Do Vết Thương" [Rehabilitating and preventing severe shock caused by injuries]. *Y Học Giải Phóng* Số 1 [Liberation Medicine No. 1], edited by Trần Văn Chín, 9/1966: 46–51.
Nguyễn, Văn Bình. *Những Kiến Thức Chung Về Chứng Loạn Thần Kinh Chức Năng. Lịch Sử Của Vấn Đề: Chứng Loạn Thần Kinh Chức Năng Thực Nghiệm* [General Knowledge About Symptoms of Neurosis. History of the Problem: Experimental Philosophy of Symptoms of Neurosis]. Hanoi: Đại Học Y Học, 1969.
Nguyen, Van Duong. "Renovation of Traditional Medicine." *Vietnamese Studies* 6 (1965): 49–50.
Nguyễn, Việt. "Xây Dựng Danh Từ Tinh Thánh Học" [Establishing psychiatric terminology]. *Nội San Thần Kinh Tinh Thần và Phẫu Thuật* [Journal of psychiatry, neurology, and surgery] (1965–1966): 31–36.
———. *Tâm Thần Học* [Psychiatry]. Hanoi: Nhà Xuất Bản Y Học [Medical Press], 1984.
Scott, James C. *Seeing Like a State: How Certain Schemes to Improve the Human Condition Have Failed.* New Haven, CT: Yale University Press, 1998.
Shay, Jonathan. *Achilles in Vietnam: Combat Trauma and the Undoing of Character.* New York: Simon & Schuster, 1995.
Shephard, Ben. *A War of Nerves: Soldiers and Psychiatrists in the Twentieth Century.* London: Jonathan Cape, 2000.
Tập Chí Văn Nghệ Quân Đội [Military Literature and Art Review]. *Journal of Mission, Field Report* and *Memoirs* Hanoi: Military Publishing House, 1990.
Thái Phục Hanh. "Tổng Kết Tình Hình Tử Vong Của Bệnh Nhân Tinh Thần Trong 10 Nam Qua (1955–1964)" [Summary of Situation of Psychiatric Patients over Ten Years (1955–1964)]. *Nội San Thần Kinh Tinh Thần và Phẫu Thuật* [Journal of psychiatry, neurology, and surgery] No. 2 (1964): 94–109.
Tran, Nam Hung, and Khắc Lung Nguyên. "Qua Nhận Xét Sơ Bộ 45 Cá Chẩn Đoán Là Loạn Thần Hysteria Dạnh Gia Một Bằng 6 Tiêu Chuẩn Chẩn Đoán Loạn Thần Hysteria" [Preliminary basic observations of 45 separate diagnoses of hysteria to form a set of 6 criteria to diagnose hysteria]. *Nội San Thần Kinh Tinh Thần và Phẫu Thuật* [Journal of psychiatry, neurology, and surgery] no. 2 (1964): 62–72.
Trần, Văn Chín. "Vài Suy Nghĩ về Sốt Rét và Gan, Thận, Thần Kinh [Some thoughts on malaria and the liver, heart, and neurological disorder]." *Y Học Giải Phóng* Số 1 [Liberation medicine no. 1], edited by Trần Văn Chín, 9/1966: 35–39.
Trung, Lê Thế. "Đặc Điểm Các Tổn Thương Trong Chiến Tranh Hiện Đại [Characteristics of Contemporary War Injuries]." In *Bài Giảng Về Bệnh Ngoại Khoa Sau Đại Học Tập II* [Lessons in surgical illnesses after university volume II]. Hanoi: Học Viện Quân Y, 1993.
Watters, Ethan. *Crazy Like Us: The Globalization of the American Psyche.* New York: Free Press, 2010.

Wortis, Joseph. *Soviet Psychiatry.* Baltimore, MD: Williams & Wilkins, 1950.
Young, Allan. *The Harmony of Illusions: Inventing Post-Traumatic Stress Disorder.* Princeton, NJ: Princeton University Press, 1995.

Chapter 6

Psychological Trauma and Suffering in Long Distance Friendships Involving Political Prisoners in Indonesia

Vannessa Hearman

> From [Pudji Aswati] I learned so much I realised I was being given insight into the life and thoughts of an exceptional woman.
> —Patricia Cleveland-Peck (1987)[1]

> I am separated for such a long time with the world which is naturally more advanced [from] when I saw it fourteen years ago. . . . Oh, how I am longing very much for my release!
> —Pudji Aswati to Patricia Cleveland-Peck (1982)

By its very nature, letter writing is conventionally understood in Western contexts as an act that takes place between two people in private in the first instance. As a deeply private endeavor, letters and other items of correspondence are a legally protected form of communication, with their theft or misappropriation carrying a penalty in many countries. This chapter discusses a form of letter writing that, while mainly private, reflects the collective traumatic experiences of a group of Indonesian women imprisoned as part of the anti-communist purges in Indonesia of the mid- to late 1960s. Drawing on theoretical literature on trauma and life stories, and cross-cultural dimensions of trauma, this chapter argues that an epistolary friendship, a friendship based on letters, can provide a form of therapeutic intervention in instances of complex and ongoing trauma as that suffered by these prisoners. The findings of this chapter are based predominantly on an analysis of personal letters exchanged between a British author and activist, Patricia Cleveland-Peck, and her Indonesian political prisoner pen pal, Pudji Aswati.[2] This chapter contends that, under certain conditions, letter writing provided a vital outlet for self-expression and relief in a setting in which the women prisoners were still undergoing traumatic experiences and receiving little care for their past suffering. In the hands of women letter writers who were motivated by ideas of social and gender justice, writing became a collective activity to regain a sense of self and re-establish social connections and worth after undergoing psychologically traumatic events.

The Letters and the Archive

The correspondence between Patricia Cleveland-Peck and Pudji Aswati began as part of anti-torture campaigns run by Amnesty International (AI) and the Religious Society of Friends (Quakers) that were launched in the 1970s.[3] In 1979, Quakers in the UK formed the Quaker Abolition of Torture group, inspired by a similar campaign by AI for which the latter was awarded the 1977 Nobel Peace Prize.[4] The Quaker and AI campaigns against torture from the early 1970s onward were initiated by Eric Baker, a co-founder of AI who was himself a Quaker.[5] The Quaker's anti-torture campaign deployed an approach not dissimilar to AI, of engaging in outward information politics that had proven so successful for the latter organization.[6] A part of the campaign was the Prisoner Befriending Scheme in which Quakers wrote letters and cards to political prisoners.[7] Befriending was framed as "an act of faith" for members of the religious congregation.[8] By 1982, the year in which Cleveland-Peck and Pudji began corresponding, Quakers in Britain had befriended a hundred political prisoners, half of them from Chile, and the rest from Argentina, Indonesia, and the Soviet Union.[9] The scheme also enabled the organization to gain insights into the conditions of individual prisoners, with such information being the bedrock of its campaign work.

Many Quakers, including Cleveland-Peck, comprised those who corresponded with Pudji and her husband, Gatot Lestario, who was on death row in a prison in Pamekasan, on the island of Madura, off the north coast of East Java. In 1982, Cleveland-Peck was in her early forties, married, and raising three children on a hobby farm in East Sussex, England. After working as a lawyer for a period, she had decided to take up freelance writing. She recalled hearing and being inspired by Quaker leader George Gorman's address about helping others. As a stay-at-home mum, though, she wondered how she could put this into practice. She recounted, "One thing I could do was to write letters, and there was already a Quaker initiative which found penfriends for prisoners," referring to the Prisoner Befriending Scheme.[10] After receiving Pudji's details through this

FIGURE 6.1. Patricia Cleveland-Peck's collection of Pudji Aswati's letters and a copy of the article she wrote to raise funds for former political prisoners in the Quaker newsletter, *The Friend*. © Vannessa Hearman.

Quaker initiative, Cleveland-Peck recalled, "I began to write to her and learn her story." Cleveland-Peck learned that her new Indonesian pen pal, Pudji, was a convicted political prisoner serving a fifteen-year sentence in a women's prison in the East Javanese town of Malang.

For ten years, from mid-1982 to 1992, Cleveland-Peck and Pudji wrote one another in English approximately once a month. The Englishwoman also sent Pudji small items such as knitting wool, books, magazines, dictionaries, and international reply coupons to enable her to send replies. The archive on which this chapter is based, and which was sent to the author in 2018, contains around 150 letters written by Pudji and copies of replies from Cleveland-Peck. Pudji relied on official prison channels to process, including to censor, and post her letters to her pen pals. The letters sent officially from the prison were usually handwritten in her cursive script on very thin paper to reduce the cost of postage. From approximately 1984, Pudji began writing through unofficial channels, those she termed "NCAs" (non-censored addresses), which allowed greater possibilities for self-expression. NCA letters were those given to prison visitors and mailed from outside prison. Such letters were written on various kinds of paper, mostly lined paper torn out of small cheap exercise books that were then widely available in newsagents and bookshops in Malang. The correspondence between the two women, however, became less regular after Pudji's release in 1989, when she had to adjust to a new life outside, while suffering a serious illness and having to undergo surgeries and hospitalization.

Along with the letters between the two women, the extensive private archive contains dozens of letters that Cleveland-Peck received from other correspondents who were also sympathetic to Pudji and Gatot, including other pen pals, members of the clergy, and supporters in Indonesia and abroad. These letters showed how epistolary relationships drew in wider and wider circles of people as they progressed. Liz Stanley has discussed the capacity for epistolary relationships to develop in this way in her analysis of South African activist Olive Schreiner's networks of correspondence.[11] The letters in Cleveland-Peck's archive showed efforts made to provide physical and moral support to Indonesian prisoners, as well as international campaigns being run in the 1980s by a number of pen pals in the United Kingdom, Canada, and the Netherlands for their release. These campaigns involved petitions and letters to Indonesian government officials. The archive also includes voluminous correspondence on the "Pudji Fund" established by Cleveland-Peck in 1986 to assist her friend financially upon her release from prison.[12] Coordinated by Cleveland-Peck for twenty-two years, the Pudji fund supported former political prisoners in Mexico, South Africa, Philippines, Indonesia, and Australia. The letters in Cleveland-Peck's archives attest to the complexity of the web of support woven around Gatot and Pudji, and the capacity of letter writing, when centered on tragedy and traumatic experiences, to nurture deep emotional connections and entanglements between correspondents.

Political Lives Turned Upside Down

Pudji's imprisonment and her traumatic experiences stemmed from dramatic political changes occurring in Indonesia. She was born in Semarang, Central Java, in 1929. She was working as a teacher in the city of Yogyakarta when she met and later married Gatot Lestario, a teacher and member of the Indonesian Communist Party (Partai Komunis Indonesia, PKI) in 1952. The couple moved to the port city of Surabaya, capital of the province of East Java, two years later, in 1954, when Gatot became more involved in party activities and assumed the role of secretary of the PKI provincial committee. In Surabaya, Pudji was very active in the leftist women's organization, Indonesian Women's Movement (Gerakan Wanita Indonesia, Gerwani), writing articles on international women's movements for its newsletter. From 1955, she began teaching English at a high school where the medium of instruction was Chinese, which was designed to cater to the Indonesian-Chinese community in Surabaya.

Her life changed irrevocably when, on 30 September 1965, a group calling itself the Thirtieth of September Movement (Gerakan 30 September, G30S, hereafter the "Movement"), consisting mainly of military officers and soldiers supportive of President Sukarno, kidnapped and killed six army generals and a lieutenant in Jakarta.[13] Senior army officer Major General Suharto, who was the commander of the Army Strategic Command (Komando Strategis Angkatan Darat, Kostrad), portrayed these actions by the Movement as a "coup attempt," masterminded by the PKI in order to rid the army of a longstanding, irksome political rival. Suharto oversaw the process of purging leftists in many parts of Indonesia in bloody pogroms that started in early October 1965. Half a million people were killed between October 1965 and approximately March 1966 in anti-communist operations.

Some of the worst killings took place in East Java, about 1,000 km from Jakarta, where Pudji and her family lived. In fear for their lives, Gerwani women went on the run and lived underground with relatives or fellow activists.[14] Like so many others, Pudji and Gatot also went into hiding and left their children, Daryanti and Pramono (pseudonyms), in the care of relatives. In preparing to flee, their daughter, Daryanti, recollected how the family's house was burned down by an aggressive mob.[15]

As Suharto amassed more power from March 1966, and the PKI's ally, President Sukarno, became increasingly sidelined, the anti-communist operations intensified. In response, from early 1967 onwards, surviving PKI members retreated to the southern parts of East Java. They began constructing a rural base in South Blitar as a place to wait out the violence and attempted to rebuild the party in secret. Pudji and Gatot were both in these southern parts of the province as part of this base-building. For a short time, she was able to live with her children again and to have Gatot visit them clandestinely at night, as Daryanti recalled.[16]

By 1968, an army-dominated regime, the New Order, with Suharto at the helm, had come to power and the rural PKI bases were destroyed by a large-scale military operation, called the Trisula (Trident) operation, that lasted from June to September 1968. Involving some 5,000 military personnel, army sources estimated that 2,000 people were captured and killed during this operation.[17] According to army documents, Pudji was captured on 28 June 1968.[18] She was transported to the women's prison in the town of Malang, a regional center in East Java, about 100 km away, along with seven other women who had also been captured in the operation. I have interviewed two of these seven women as part of my earlier research on the anti-communist violence in East Java.

Political imprisonment became Indonesia's key human rights issue of the 1970s. In its 1977 report on Indonesia, AI estimated that between 55,000 and 100,000 political detainees were being held in that country, most of them without trial, following the Indonesian army's extremely violent anti-communist pogroms in 1965–66.[19] Although most political prisoners had been released by 1978, a few hundred remained in long-term imprisonment or on death row. Pudji spent ten years in prison before she was tried in court for subversion and sentenced in 1978 to fifteen years imprisonment, without regard for the time already served.[20]

Gendered Suffering and Experiences of Trauma

Prior to their capture in South Blitar, the women detainees discussed in this chapter had already spent up to three years in hiding since October 1965 and experienced terrible suffering and traumatic events. The anti-communist operations of the mid- to late 1960s in Indonesia had an explicitly gendered dimension that affected leftist women like Pudji. Early army propaganda portrayed women who were members of Gerwani as particularly depraved killers and torturers of the seven slain army officers. The army circulated completely fabricated stories that Gerwani women, barely clothed, had performed a lewd dance, the Fragrant Flowers Dance, while sexually pleasuring themselves and torturing the officers. Prison and army authorities forced women and girls in Bukit Duri prison in Jakarta to perform some kind of dance and filmed this performance, as if reenacting these scenes. The killings, in which Gerwani women were supposed to have taken part, according to the propaganda, were so brutal that the army officers had been castrated and their eyes gouged out.[21] Official autopsy reports showed, however, that they had not suffered any genital mutilation, castration, or eye gouging.[22] It is unclear whether the army drew on particular psychological theories to create and disseminate its propaganda. More likely, in crafting black propaganda against the Left, the army drew on its repertoire of psychological warfare concepts, developed out of its experience of counter-insurgency operations in the 1950s and 1960s, and in cooperation with Western intelligence and military bodies.[23] The Gerwani propaganda is permanently displayed in wall reliefs at the monument commemorating these officers, the Sacred Pancasila Monument at Lubang Buaya, Jakarta.

While the inspiration for the propaganda is difficult to trace definitively, its effects were horrendous on the Indonesian Left, particularly on leftist women. In conflicts, women are already affected differently than men by the same acts of violence or are subjected to acts of violence specific to their gender such as rape, sexual harassment, and militarized prostitution.[24] For example, in preparing fifty-eight files on the charge of sexual violence as torture for the 2015 International People's Tribunal on 1965, Annie Pohlman found that 72 percent of victims of rape were women.[25] The aftermath of violence also affects women disproportionately, for example, they may be displaced and suffer increased vulnerability following the loss of family members, social status, and employment.[26]

The army's deeply gendered propaganda provided a perverse legitimation for sexual and other violence that was then committed against leftist women, such as Pudji and her fellow inmates, by members of the security forces and armed militias.[27] They were tortured, killed, raped, and sexually degraded in prisons and army-sponsored detention camps, and even out in public, as if punished for their supposed sexual deviance.[28] Gerwani women were, following Helen Fein, subjected to moral exclusion and placed "outside the universe of obligation of the perpetrator," by supposedly having committed gruesome acts against revered Indonesian army leaders.[29]

The women prisoners in this particular case study, like Gerwani women in general, were targeted and stigmatized for being members of a group, the Indonesian Left, from October 1965. They were subjected to "humiliation memory," where perpetrators of genocide and political violence foster negative self-image and shame among members of a targeted group.[30] Though no two individuals will have the same reactions, even to the same event, it is possible to conclude that these experiences would have constituted events that triggered traumatic reactions. Such reactions, as defined by Judith Herman, occur "when action is of no avail," when neither escape nor resistance is possible, and "the human self defence system becomes overwhelmed or disorganized."[31] Traumatic reactions produce long-term changes to physiological and physical responses to events.

When they were captured, most of the women had been hiding in the forest for several weeks since the beginning of the Trisula Operation in June 1968. They were suffering extreme hunger and exhaustion. Photographs taken by army photographers and published in a military account of the operation showed evidence of what might have been torture and mistreatment of the arrestees, male and female.[32] A photograph of Pudji, which was likely taken shortly after she was caught, showed bruising and swelling to her face and eyes.[33] While we do not know precisely how the injuries were sustained, the circumstances of her capture suggest that it was a harrowing experience, with a fugitive in hiding with Pudji being shot as he tried to escape.[34] Some captives, especially those seen as militants with some influence, were interrogated, tortured in some instances, and pressured to betray their cause and their comrades.[35] In an account to their daughter, which had been translated and copied to Cleveland-Peck, Gatot Lestario might have been alluding to sexual violence committed against Pudji at the time of her arrest, when he referred to the "bestial way" in which Pudji had been treated, and that following her protests, "the involved persons were dismissed."[36] It was only in 2012 that her close friend and fellow inmate Lestari told a journalist that Pudji was gang-raped by seven men, members of the civil guards (*hansip, pertahanan sipil*) following her arrest.[37] The brutality of the Trisula operation in 1968, brought to bear in the arrest of the South Blitar political fugitives, were thus likely to have aroused further traumatic reactions, in addition to events witnessed and experienced at the start of the anti-communist pogroms in 1965.

The women's conditions in prison were, at first, extremely deprived. They received very little food to eat, resulting in extreme malnutrition.[38] One woman recalled her friend and fellow inmate Lestari's repeated screams in her efforts to get the attention of the prison authorities to be provided with more food.[39] Concerned with their physical state, they supplemented their meagre diets by mixing thinly sliced papaya leaves, gleaned from the prison yard, into their rice. They shared a woven mat on the floor on which to sleep. Formal legal proceedings did not begin for some years, leading to a great deal of uncertainty. In terms of psychological and psychiatric care following the traumatic events of 1965–68, care workers and academics worked with the repressive Indonesian state security apparatus to conduct testing on detainees.[40] These tests were designed to gauge the extent of detainees' political convictions and their readiness for release. The psychological and medical professions were, therefore, deeply compromised and of questionable assistance to political prisoners.

As a result of their long imprisonment, the women prisoners discussed in this chapter suffered prolonged and repeated trauma, where the circumstances of captivity led to the loss of control over one's life and surroundings.[41] The women were also likely to have suffered social loss trauma, defined by Devon Hinton and Byron Good as trauma arising from the "loss of significant others owing to death or separation by distance," as well as a fall in social status and economic well-being.[42] The conviction and long-term imprisonment of both Gatot and Pudji led to their children having to reinvent their identities to distance themselves from their prisoner parents and to rely on their relatives for emotional and financial support. Considering these circumstances, it was likely that Pudji and her fellow prisoners suffered complex trauma, defined as the experience of a severe trauma or multiple traumas over an extended period of time.[43]

Recounting Traumatic and Painful Events in Letters

Despite the likelihood that Pudji suffered complex trauma, she never deployed the term "trauma" in her writings. In a criticism against the universalization of the trauma concept, literary scholar Kenneth Surin has argued that the notion of trauma is the outcome of a specific cultural and political production or construction of knowledge.[44] To illustrate this point, he argues that the 1965–66 anticommunist violence was not regarded as a trauma-inducing event in comparison to Cambodia's Khmer Rouge rule of the later 1970s or the 2004 Indian Ocean tsunami because of the lack of a political epistemology to explain the events in Indonesia and Western approval of Suharto's actions.[45] Over the last ten years, however, more scholars and practitioners in psychology, psychiatry, and the neurosciences have turned serious attention to examining a broader array of symptoms and responses to pervasive and complex trauma to take into account "the great cultural diversity of human experience."⁴⁶ Let us now turn to analyze a selection of the letters between Pudji and Cleveland-Peck to examine how difficult experiences were discussed, in the absence of an explicit mention of trauma in the letters.

It was unlikely for Pudji to discuss, early on, many details of her life story, let alone trauma in her correspondence, given the constraints of letters sent from prison. The letters were obviously censored, with each of Pudji's letters bearing the initials of the prison censor. Thus, at the beginning, Pudji first established areas of common ground with her pen pal. Discussions about knitting, wools and yarns, books, family, and a common love of language and reading grounded their burgeoning epistolary friendship. This focus on the ordinary can also be therapeutic, as Janet Maybin has shown in her study of correspondences between prisoners on death row in the United States and pen pals in the UK. Maybin's case study shows that prisoners were fascinated by hearing from their pen pals about everyday activities, activities in which the prisoners could no longer take part.⁴⁷ Therefore, Cleveland-Peck's accounts of her everyday life, such as this one from 14 September 1982, was possibly a source of comfort and an item of interest for the Indonesian prisoners:

> My daughter will soon be home from her violin lesson. She is progressing and can now play a Chopin Prelude quite sweetly. Now in this part of the country, we are having glorious weather, the summer is almost over and the chill of autumn gives a sense of excitement but meanwhile for a short time, the golden sun floods the fields from which the crops have been harvested and in the evenings the long shadows make one feel like walking farther and farther into the lovely evening air. We gather blackberries from the hedges to make into "bramble jeely" [sic] to eat in the winter.⁴⁸

Early in their correspondence, the women began to warm to one another, as evidenced in this quote from one of Cleveland-Peck's letters to Pudji: "I am very happy with our correspondence and so delighted that I have you, such a brave and intelligent woman as my penfriend. I do feel lucky in that, for although many miles separate us geographically, in spirit, in love of literature and in the fact that we are wives and mothers, we are close to each other."⁴⁹ Nonetheless, it was inevitable that discussion would also turn to the differences in the two women's circumstances. Cleveland-Peck went on, in the same letter: "Only you have had many trials and bitter things to bear in your life, whereas, so far, I have had a happy life with my family around me, so of course, I must help you in every way I can."⁵⁰

Even though they discussed seemingly innocuous topics, such as needlework and knitting, books, family, and learning languages, these discussions are suffused by Pudji's grief at the loss of her family and of life opportunities. As Cleveland-Peck empathized with Pudji's long years of involuntary estrangement from her children, and encouraged Pudji to write children's stories, she wrote, "I know that this must be a painful area for you, not having seen your children grow to

FIGURE 6.2. Four former political prisoners meeting Patricia Cleveland-Peck in Malang in 1989. Pudji is seated next to Cleveland-Peck. Image courtesy of Dennis Cleveland-Peck.

adults in your charge, but the memories of their young years must be precious and writing about them may celebrate this in a way."[51] The two women were separated by a vast gulf of difference, of which they were keenly aware. Cleveland-Peck's freedom to travel and earn her own income contrasted, for example, with Pudji's regime of imprisonment and what lay beyond, a life of discrimination and stigmatization as a former leftist prisoner.

Given her long prison sentence, Pudji could not avoid altogether discussing her suffering in her letters, but such discussion occurred only in scraps of memories and confessions about her feelings in relation to other topics. For example, in 1982, she wrote to Cleveland-Peck: "I do all this [language learning] to prepare my future living and I hope that the condition will be parallel with my ideas. This is only the best way I think, as I don't possess anything, but my two children and my husband."[52] Her pen pal replied, "I too think you very brave to keep studying throughout the long years, but of course it is the best way . . . it is preparation for when you resume your life outside."[53] Cleveland-Peck acknowledged Pudji's grief and fears about the future but kept her responses practical to ensure her friend remained hopeful during her imprisonment. This practical response is evident also in an earlier letter: "When you are released (which I pray will be soon) I want to support you in your idea of teaching English. I know you will be good at this and I will, I hope, get those [English] books to you soon."[54] Despite the looming shadow of the prison censor, or perhaps because of it, Pudji's letters to Cleveland-Peck provide the reader with glimpses into her world of suffering, by sharing only snippets of her life, a life of long-term confinement and an inability to plan very far into the future.

Collective Frameworks and Cultural Factors

The epistolary friendship, by its very nature, seems at first to be highly individualistic, however, collective experiences of trauma were also collectively retold in Pudji's letters. The correspondence attracted growing circles of supporters leading to campaigns for the release of Indonesian political prisoners, including a specific focus on Gatot and Pudji, conducted through AI and the UK-based TAPOL Indonesian Human Rights Campaign.[55] Conversant in English and Dutch, Gatot wrote letters to about a dozen pen pals in Canada, the United States, Netherlands, Italy, and the UK that he obtained through Pudji's connections with Cleveland-Peck. In trying to understand how a highly personalized medium such as letter writing can serve a collective purpose, historian Heather Goodall's reflection on her collaborative life story writing with Australian Aboriginal activists can shed light on this interplay between the collective and the individual. Goodall argues that, in writing life stories, Indigenous people are using a written genre that has been developed "in a colonizing culture and focusing on the individual" to relate life stories derived from a setting in which there existed overlapping communities and networks, and "where individual identities are less often the focus of the effort."[56] Similarly, while the medium of the letter seems to be individualistic, with letters being intended for particular addressees, the medium also holds significant collective potential, particularly in instances where letters are shared, read, and responded to by more than one person, as is the case here.

Cleveland-Peck's collection includes letters from other women inmates who had been captured at South Blitar like Pudji. Four women, all of whom had been Gerwani and PKI activists and leaders, also wrote to Cleveland-Peck. The women most importantly took up the correspondence, if, for some reason, Pudji was unable to write or receive letters. Prison regulations, from time to time, prohibited the women from receiving letters or parcels from abroad, usually related to a security issue or the political situation, such as around the time of national elections. The women inmates, in their letters, cross-referenced one another's stories about the army operations in South Blitar and the resulting separation from their children. By showing that more than one woman had survived these experiences, they set out to convey the magnitude of their suffering and the injustice of their situation.

What role can we accord to cultural factors in the way that trauma and difficult experiences are discussed and regarded in these letters and between the women inmates? Robert Lemelson and Annie Tucker argue that "culture structures the events that . . . shapes the personal narratives and embodied experiences that organise and express suffering."[57] The relevant cultural frameworks in this case study are those of female social and political activists of a lower middle-class background who were born in the 1920s and 30s in East and Central Java, two provinces on Indonesia's most populous island. They were of Javanese ethnicity, Indonesia's largest ethnic group. It is difficult to generalize about the Javanese, as there are even distinctions between those hailing from Central Java and those from East Java. One general consideration we can make, however, is about the reticence of women to disclose traumatic events as these may be deemed to be socially and culturally shameful.

This group of women was also shaped by their involvement in significant political and social events in the mid-twentieth century. As a generation, they had lived through, and some participated in, Indonesia's struggle for independence from the Dutch, following the end of the Japanese occupation and World War II. These events left a deep historical imprint on Indonesians of this generation.[58] The women had also all been drawn into social and political activism before their imprisonment, often driven by a sense of nationalism and the excitement of a new nation-state. They shared certain ideas, bonds, and understandings, which included valuing self-sufficiency, autonomy, and independence in the framework of a collective struggle. With the outbreak of anti-communist persecution, they shared the collective experience of being hunted, persecuted, captured, and imprisoned, with all the losses that such experiences brought. The women's background, as well as their shared traumatic experiences, led them to emphasize the collective and the importance of social justice, attitudes they brought to bear to their letter writing.

Aside from the references to other women's suffering, the collective framework of understanding and interpreting suffering and dealing with "bitter things" is also expressed in how Pudji sought meaning and purpose in her confined life by connecting with and helping others. She engaged in solitary pursuits, such as writing and learning French and English, which were important for her emotional well-being and self-esteem. These pursuits also kept her hopes alive about being released and living a normal, productive life. But, in her letters, Pudji especially emphasized to her pen pal her social contribution in prison and the pleasure and contentment she usually derived from such activities. Herman argues that the response of the community in helping with undoing trauma is very important, such as by public acknowledgment of the traumatic event or by allowing the survivor to participate in some form of collective community action.[59] Pudji recounted to Cleveland-Peck that these activities consisted, for example, of working with other women to make handicrafts to sell, attending

Catholic mass, and teaching other inmates to read and write and improve their needlework skills.

The social sphere is an important arena for challenging stigma. By utilizing her knowledge and skills, Pudji hoped to restore her sense of connection with the wider community and to promote her own potential healing by being accepted by others and denying the regime's social stigmatization. If in relating their stories, the women relied on collective frameworks of telling, similarly in trying to overcome their trauma in the absence of medical care in prison, they participated in group activities, such as classes and rituals of religious worship, and in connecting with others through personal letters and visits.

It is more difficult to map the relevant frameworks for analyzing the relationship between Cleveland-Peck and Pudji, given the differences in their cultural and personal backgrounds. It is evident, though, that their shared identity of being a mother, a wife, and a practicing Christian, with a keen interest in their surroundings, underpinned the world that they created through their letters. The word "trauma" was never used in the two women's letters to one another, possibly because they were not readily familiar or comfortable with using such a concept. Instead, comfort and understanding, "an ethics of care," were provided through making and discussing future plans, exchanging information about their different religious rituals and beliefs, and common experiences such as mothering.[60]

Letters as Safe Spaces: Openings and Limitations

Letters, such as those exchanged between Cleveland-Peck and Pudji, provide space for trauma witnessing and testimony. The difficulties of narrating traumatic experiences in a way that is meaningful for those who had not suffered the trauma themselves, as well as the constraints of writing from inside prison reduced the likelihood of Pudji being able to easily tell her story to Cleveland-Peck. Caruth's concept of the crisis of truth, "the historical enigma betrayed by trauma," relates to the impossibility of telling and witnessing about major cataclysms that lead to trauma.[61] Van der Kolk and van der Hart characterize traumatic memories as "unassimilated scraps of overwhelming experiences, which need to be integrated with existing mental schemes, and be transformed into narrative language."[62] In order for this integration to occur, they observe that the traumatized person has to return often to the memory "in order to complete it." However, in practical terms, the return is often a difficult process, and so, the traumatized person continues to live in two worlds of the before and after of the traumatic events.[63]

Storytelling is often promoted in the fields of human rights practice and transitional justice as a way for women to overcome traumatic experiences, for trauma survivors to regain their capacity to speak.[64] However, the task of trauma witnessing and the act of testimony are highly complex and cannot be simplified as consisting primarily of storytelling and an agentic silence, a silence that is being actively practiced by a survivor as a chosen strategy to deal with past events.⁶⁵ It is simplistic to describe survivors of the anti-communist violence in Indonesia as completely silent during the thirty-two years of the New Order regime, but there was an absence of a safe space for the sharing of traumatic experiences or bearing witness to the violence.⁶⁶ There was a society that was reluctant to hear, because of fear, trauma, or a sense of triumphalism on the part of New Order supporters.

Leftist political prisoners were heavily discriminated against under the regime, both in prison and following their release, thus also reducing their capacity or willingness to narrate their life story and traumatic experiences. Anton Lucas describes the challenges that leftists, victimized in the 1965–66 violence, must confront, even beyond their immediate term of detention and imprisonment:

> Those who survived the massacres of 1965–69 have never been "liberated" in the way that, say, concentration camp victims in Europe were liberated at the end of World War II. Survival was difficult in the immediate aftermath of the coup attempt of 30 September 1965, but life after survival was also difficult. Whether inside or outside prison, former members and associates of the PKI saw their families scattered, their health broken, their careers blighted.⁶⁷

Former political prisoners were nominally free but continued to suffer as pariahs. They could not gain a sense of liberation, as they were forced to comply with a raft of rules and regulations, such as where to live, what fields of employment to take up, and what to do to prove they were no longer a danger to society. In some cases, internally, they had lost confidence in themselves and their capacity to function as human beings. These factors, in an environment that remained hostile and dangerous to them, did not contribute to the free and open sharing of a traumatic experience. Such sharing requires a safe space, but such space was absent in Indonesia.

The difficulty of integrating traumatic memories, and thus the opening up of possibilities to begin to speak about these memories, is compounded, in Pudji's case, by the fact that at the time of the correspondence with Cleveland-Peck, her traumatic experiences had not even ended. She was still in prison, worrying about when she would be released and wondering if she would see her mother and other members of her family again.⁶⁸ Physically, she suffered shortages in even the most basic necessities of life, such as soap, medicines, and adequate and nutritious food. Her most significant blow was when her husband, Gatot, was executed along with two other prisoners in July 1985. While he escaped the operation in South Blitar and made his way to Jakarta, he was captured in January 1969 and sentenced to death for subversion in January 1976. Her continued suffering reduced the likelihood of a full and immediate disclosure of one's political pasts, particularly to those abroad who may be suspected by the government of being human rights activists.

Nonetheless, the inaccessibility of trauma, while allowing the traumatized person to survive, also leads to the possibility of engaging "different modes of therapeutic, literary and pedagogical encounter," according to Cathy Caruth.[69] The process of giving testimony through a literary encounter, in this case letter writing, can engage the traumatic experience in certain cultural and gender settings. Drawing on Dori Laub and others, I argue that the process of testimony gives "birth" to the event or makes it known, and the cognizance of this event depends on who listens and who witnesses as the "event" is projected for the first time.[70] Accordingly, such encounters, involving the narrativization of past traumatic experience, may be marked by silences and elisions, thus dislocating, though not eliminating, history altogether.[71]

For Pudji, the audience to her witnessing, and therefore her "safe space" was largely located outside of Indonesia. This space was made safer after she was able to circumvent the prison censor by using "safe addresses" from 1984 onward. As a result, she grew bolder in disclosing her life story. Cleveland-Peck received a lengthy handwritten account from Pudji, likely to have been written in or after 1984, entitled "The Memories of Prison Life," eleven foolscap pages in length. In it, she wrote of what had happened to her and her fellow inmates after they were captured in South Blitar and their conditions in Malang Women's Prison. Drawing on the women's collective experiences, Pudji wrote:

> We left [South Blitar] with a distressed heart . . . because some of us must leave her son, daughters, in this desolate battlefield. How must someone flee in peace when accompanied by little children? So Mrs C, E and G must leave their children in the hands of the people. Mrs C left her 6 years old son, Mrs G her one-year-old daughter, while Mrs E her two children, a suckling and a girl of 5 years old. . . . None of these children were found back again by their parents.[72]

She, however, omitted any suggestion of having experienced sexual violence directly. Pudji's trauma and fear of rejection might have contributed to her unwillingness or inability to narrate the more painful experiences, buried more deeply beneath accounts of the loss suffered by others and of the physical conditions they faced in the prison.

The limitations of an epistolary friendship's capacity to act as a forum in which traumatic experiences can be shared and discussed with another person must, however, also be acknowledged. A relationship between a political prisoner and correspondents living in Western countries is inherently unequal. A prisoner's confinement limits their capacity. Pudji relied on family members, prison authorities, and her pen pals for writing paper, stamps, International Reply Coupons, and envelopes. She relied on them to send the letters she wrote and for her pen pals to reply to her. Prison censors read the letters officially sent from prison.

These constraints reduced the likelihood of these epistolary friendships being relationships of equality.

Despite these difficulties, letter writing, by its very nature relational, intimate, and reciprocal, shares many common characteristics with the spaces required for disclosure of trauma and suffering, for the process of engaging with and in testimony. Although the Freud-based "talking cure" has dominated as a Western psycho-therapeutic method in the twentieth and twenty-first centuries, letter writing "can create a kind of personal haven for prisoners, a space for reparation and for expressions of affection, care, and gentleness" that are often accorded little space in prison.[73] One of the ways letter writing does this, according to Maybin, is by reconfiguring space and time and working dialogically "as a kind of slowed-down, disembodied conversation," by, for example, creating a private enclave while also transforming "distance into immediacy and absence into presence."[74] Within this slowed down conversation, certain spaces are opened up to the process and action of testimony.

The testimony, as Dori Laub writes, "is inherently a process of facing loss—of going through the pain of the act of witnessing, and of the ending of the act of witnessing—which entails yet another repetition of the experience of separation and loss," allowing perhaps "a certain repossession of it."[75] Like letter writing, disclosure requires a witness, a sense of mutual trust and a response. Through an engagement in literary practice, women political prisoners were able to testify about their experiences, within the constraints of the prison environment, writing of the terrible marginalization of leftist prisoners in and after prison, as well as revealing the possible impact of trauma on their testimonies. In this way, writing, receiving and reading personal letters, particularly embodied within a strong social context such as this one, are demonstrated as an important part of the repertoire for dealing with trauma.[76]

What was the value of an epistolary friendship such as this to a long-term prisoner? Maybin argues that letter writing allows prisoners on death row the ability to create virtual families and to develop a sense of inner life and self-esteem. Letter writing provides prisoners with emotional support and allows them, in turn, to express care, affection, and intimacy.[77] An epistolary friendship allows the prisoner to maintain a sense of autonomy in the face of loss. For this reason, according to Herman, political prisoners make strenuous efforts to preserve connections with the outside world, including by placing great importance on "transitional objects," such as letters and mementos as symbols of their attachment and connection to others.[78] Letters also constitute a gift that entails mutual obligations and connections. Drawing on Marcel Mauss's theory on the system of the gift, Liz Stanley argues that the letter is a gift in itself. But the letter also represents and symbolizes "the ongoing social bond between writer-giver and addressee-receiver."[79] The creation of a sense of obligation and the desire for reciprocity through the form of the letter builds an environment of trust in which pain and suffering can be conveyed through personal correspondences.

Conclusion

Letters are more than simply a medium of communication; they are also a medium to express and share trauma and traumatic experiences. With the deep stigmatization of Indonesia's leftist political prisoners, it seemed that this group of people who had suffered great traumatic events were silenced. However, the traces that remain in institutional and personal archives, of years of correspondence taking place between them and Western letter writers and activists, challenge this image of the total silencing of the Indonesian Left. The letters show the struggles of individuals to fashion new modes of presentation to attain and maintain the possibilities of making connections with strangers in foreign countries, in a process in which trauma and stigma loom large over the whole process. Through their letters, prisoners fought for acceptance, for the possibility of gaining and giving sufficient trust and to be able to narrate aspects of their often-traumatic life stories to strangers abroad. Within the epistolary friendships that developed, such as that between Pudji and Patricia Cleveland-Peck, there were challenges for both parties in how to convey, comprehend, and respond adequately to the revelation of traumatic experiences in such a way that bridged the span of time, space, and cultures. While letter writing appears to be an inherently individualistic mode of communication, as educated women of their generation, the prisoners used this method of literary encounter to communicate collective experiences of trauma. Based on their shared cultural and ideological backgrounds, the women deployed extensive letter writing as a means to recount their past painful experiences, to overcome their marginalization in Indonesian society, and to reclaim their status as valued social beings. They may have been vastly disempowered, but by no means were they silent.

Vannessa Hearman is Senior Lecturer in History at Curtin University, Western Australia. A historian of Southeast Asia, she is the author of the book *Unmarked Graves: Death and Survival in the Anti-Communist Killings in East Java, Indonesia* (Singapore: NUS Press, 2018). Her research deals with the Indonesian 1965-66 anti-communist violence, the politics of memory and human rights, and transnational activism related to Indonesia and East Timor.

Notes

1. Epigraphs: Cleveland-Peck, "Return Harsh World," 546; Letter, Pudji Aswati to Patricia Cleveland-Peck, dated 29 September 1982.
   Patricia Cleveland-Peck Papers, held by author (CPP in subsequent notes). The Cleveland-Peck Papers, in addition to the letters between Pudji and Cleveland-Peck, contain correspondence and documents related to the Fund and more generally to advocacy for Indonesian political prisoners. All references to the CPP refer to this collection of letters and documents that are in the author's possession at the time of writing. At the conclusion of the research, Cleveland-Peck has requested that the author deposits these papers in a library or archival institution in Australia or Europe.
2. Patricia Cleveland-Peck, email to author, 23 April 2018. As many Indonesians do not use surnames, hereafter Pudji Aswati is referred to as Pudji while Patricia Cleveland-Peck is referred to by her surnames Cleveland-Peck.
3. Amnesty International, for example, drew up lists containing names of political prisoners to whom members were encouraged to send season's greetings cards. See Amnesty International, "Greeting Cards for Prisoners."
4. See "Quaker Action against Torture," *Quakers in the World*. Retrieved 1 December 2019 from http://www.quakersintheworld.org/quakers-in-action/334/Quaker-Action-Against-Torture.
5. For a biographical note on Eric Baker, see "Influential Quakers in Crime and Justice in the UK in Recent Times (1)," *Quakers in the World*. Retrieved 1 December 2019 from http://www.quakersintheworld.org/quakers-in-action/214/Influential-Quakers-in-crime-and-Justice-in-the-UK-in-recent-times-1.
6. Eckel, "International League Rights of Man," 195.
7. Amnesty International, for example, drew up lists containing names of political prisoners to whom members were encouraged to send season's greetings cards. See Amnesty International, "Greeting Cards for Prisoners."
8. Andrew Clark, General Secretary of Quaker Peace and Service, July 1982 (letter inserted in a copy of Birtles, *Letters from Prison*.
9. Birtles, *Letters from Prison*, 3.
10. Cleveland-Peck, email to author, 23 April 2018.
11. Stanley, "Epistolary Gift."
12. Hearman, "From Indonesia with Love."
13. See Roosa, *Pretext for Mass Murder* for an account of the events surrounding the Thirtieth September Movement.
14. See Hearman, *Unmarked Graves*, 122–24 for accounts of Gerwani women living on the run.
15. "Catatan Bocah Blitar Selatan."
16. "Catatan Bocah Blitar Selatan."
17. "Reds Renew Campaign in Indonesia."
18. Semdam VIII Brawidjaja, *Operasi Trisula*, 231.
19. Amnesty International, *Indonesia*, 9.
20. Case notes on women political prisoners by Kartini, Jeanne van Ammers-Douwes papers, held at the International Institute of Social History, Amsterdam, ARCH02325.
21. Extending this propaganda beyond the immediate events of October 1965, the army portrayed these techniques as being typically deployed by communists. See illustration "How to Gouge an Eye: Demonstration by a Captured Member of the Pemuda Rakyat,"

in Cribb, *The Indonesian Killings*, 36. Pemuda Rakyat [People's Youth] was the PKI's youth wing.
22. Anderson, "How Did the Generals Die?" 111.
23. Prior to October 1965, army officers cooperated and trained with US army personnel and at US training facilities, such as the Command and General Staff College at Fort Leavenworth in Kansas. Some 2,800 Indonesian officers were trained in the United States between 1950 and 1965, most of those after 1958, representing about one-fifth to a quarter of all army officers. See Evans, "Influence United States Army." On US influencing of Indonesian army officers through training and cooperation programs, see Roosa, *Pretext for Mass Murder*, 183–84. On US and British intelligence agencies in Indonesia, see Simpson, *Economists with Guns*, 181.
24. Turpin, "Many Faces," 5.
25. Pohlman, "Sexual Violence as Torture," 580, and Pohlman, *Women, Sexual Violence*.
26. Turpin, "Many Faces," 7–8.
27. Pohlman, *Women, Sexual Violence*, 68.
28. Pohlman, "Sexual Violence as Torture," 583.
29. Helen Fein, 'Revolutionary and Antirevolutionary Genocides," 799.
30. Hinton and Good, "Culturally Sensitive Assessment," 55.
31. Herman, *Trauma and Recovery*, 34.
32. Semdam VIII Brawidjaja, *Operasi Trisula*, 289–310.
33. Semdam VIII Brawidjaja, *Operasi Trisula*, 306.
34. Semdam VIII Brawidjaja, *Operasi Trisula*, 107.
35. Semdam VIII Brawidjaja, *Operasi Trisula*, 91–92 on the arrest of Suwandi, PKI provincial leader, and see *Briefing Panglima Daerah Militer VIII*, 13 on the army's mistreatment of this detainee.
36. Gatot Lestario, "Part II Memoires," unpublished manuscript, CPP.
37. Hansip were civilians who served as auxiliaries to the military. Fadillah, "Peristiwa Gerwani."
38. Anonymous interview with the author, 16 February 2008.
39. Tuti (pseudonym), interview with the author, Surabaya, 2 August 2008.
40. *TAPOL Bulletin*, "Psycho-deception: Enquiry Ends in Cover Up," No. 34 (1979), 15. See also Wieringa and Katjasungkana, *Propaganda and the Genocide in Indonesia*, 133–38.
41. Herman, *Trauma and Recovery*, 74.
42. Hinton and Good, "Culturally Sensitive Assessment," 56.
43. Good and Hinton, "Introduction," 6.
44. Surin, "Conceptualizing Trauma," 24.
45. Surin, "Conceptualizing Trauma," 24.
46. Kirmayer, Lemelson, and Cummings, "Introduction," 16.
47. Maybin, "Death Row Penfriends: Effects," 159.
48. Cleveland-Peck to Pudji, 14 September 1982. CPP.
49. Cleveland-Peck to Pudji, 14 September 1982. CPP.
50. Cleveland-Peck to Pudji, 14 September 1982. CPP.
51. Cleveland-Peck to Pudji, 22 July 1983. CPP.
52. Pudji to Cleveland-Peck, 29 September 1982. CPP.
53. Cleveland-Peck to Pudji, 4 December 1982. CPP.
54. Cleveland-Peck to Pudji, 20 August 1982. CPP.
55. TAPOL was co-founded in London in 1973. The organization was led by the British woman Carmel Budiardjo, who had herself been a political prisoner of the Indonesian New Order regime. McGregor, "Making Transnational Activist," 184.

56. Goodall, "Writing Life with Isabel Flick," 73.
57. Lemelson and Tucker, "Afflictions," 484.
58. Rodgers, *Telling Lives,* 4.
59. Herman, *Trauma and Recovery*, 70.
60. On the concept of ethics of care, see Jolly, *In Love and Struggle*, 12.
61. Caruth, "Trauma and Experience," 6.
62. Van der Kolk and van der Hart, "The Intrusive Past," 176.
63. Van der Kolk and van der Hart, "The Intrusive Past," 176.
64. See, for example, Porter. "Gendered Narratives."
65. Agentic silence is a complex concept with the possibility that such silence has multiple meanings rather than just an absence of voice. See Clark, "Finding a Voice," 6.
66. Leydesdorff et al., "Introduction," 10.
67. Lucas, "Survival," 227.
68. Pudji to Cleveland-Peck, 2 September 1982. CPP.
69. Caruth, "Trauma and Experience," 10.
70. Laub, "Bearing Witness or the Vicissitudes of Listening," 57, and Crownshaw and Leydesdorff, "Introduction," viii.
71. Crownshaw and Leydesdorff, "Introduction," viii.
72. Pudji Aswati, "The Memories of Prison Life," Notes to Cleveland-Peck, no date.
73. Maybin, "Death Row Penfriends: Configuring," 63.
74. Maybin, "Death Row Penfriends: Configuring," 63–64.
75. Laub, "Truth and Testimony," 74.
76. On the importance of the social embeddedness of personal correspondences, see Jolly, "What I Never Wanted to Tell You."
77. Maybin, "Death Row Penfriends: Effects," 160.
78. Herman, *Trauma and Recovery*, 80–81.
79. Stanley, "Epistolary Gift," 140.

Bibliography

Amnesty International, "Greeting Cards for Prisoners," ACT-71-000-74. London: Amnesty International, 1974. Retrieved 1 December 2019 from https://www.indonesia1965.org/wordpress/?attachment_id=66.

———. *Indonesia: An Amnesty International Report.* London: Amnesty International Publications, 1977.

Anderson, Benedict. "How Did the Generals Die?" *Indonesia* no. 43 (1987): 109–34.

Birtles, Dorothy. *Letters from Prison: 100 Political Prisoners Befriended by Quakers.* London: Quaker Peace & Service, 1982.

Briefing Panglima Daerah Militer VIII Brawidjaja Maj. Djen. Moh. Djasin dimuka sidang Paripurna Istimewa ke-II/1968DPRD-GR Propinsi Djawa Timur [Briefing of the Brawidjaja Regional Commander Major General Moh. Jasin before the Special Plenary Session of the Provisional Parliament of the Province of East Java]. Surabaya: Sekretariat DPRD-GR Djawa Timur, 1968.

Caruth, Cathy. "Trauma and Experience: An Introduction." In *Trauma: Explorations in Memory*, 3–12. Baltimore, MD: Johns Hopkins University Press, 1995.

"Catatan Bocah Blitar Selatan [Notes of a South Blitar Child]." Retrieved 1 December 2019 from http://www.wirantaprawira.de/pakorba/teil_7.html.

"Reds Renew Campaign in Indonesia." *New York Times,* 11 August 1968.

Clark, Janine Natalya. "Finding a Voice: Silence and Its Significance for Transitional Justice," *Social & Legal Studies* (Jun. 2019): 355–78.

Cleveland-Peck, Patricia. "A Return to a Harsh World." *The Friend,* 1 May 1987, 546.

Cribb, Robert, ed. *The Indonesian Killings 1965–1966: Studies from Java and Bali.* Melbourne: Centre of Southeast Asian Studies, Monash University, 1990.

Crownshaw, Richard, and Selma Leydesdorff. "Introduction to the Transaction Edition." In *Memory & Totalitarianism,* edited by Luisa Passerini, vii–xviii. New Brunswick, NJ: Transaction Publishers, 2005.

Evans III, Bryan. "The Influence of the United States Army on the Development of the Indonesian Army (1954–1964)." *Indonesia* no. 47 (1989): 25–48.

Eckel, Jan. "The International League for the Rights of Man, Amnesty International, and the Changing Fate of Human Rights Activism from the 1940s through the 1970s." *Humanity: An International Journal of Human Rights, Humanitarianism, and Development* 4, no. 2 (2013): 183–214.

Fadillah. "Peristiwa Gerwani dan Propaganda Tari Harum Bunga yang Erotis [The Gerwani event and the erotic Fragrant Flowers dance]." *Merdeka,* 24 September 2012. Retrieved 1 December 2019 from https://m.merdeka.com/peristiwa/gerwani-dan-propaganda-tari-harum-bunga-yang-erotis.html.

Fein, Helen. "Revolutionary and Antirevolutionary Genocides: A Comparison of State Murders in Democratic Kampuchea, 1975 to 1979, and in Indonesia, 1965 to 1966," *Comparative Studies in Society and History* 35, no. 4 (1993): 796–823.

Good, Byron J., and Devon E. Hinton. "Introduction: Culture, Trauma, and PTSD." In *Culture and PTSD: Trauma in Global and Historical Perspective,* edited by Devon E. Hinton and Byron J. Good, 3–49. Philadelphia: University of Pennsylvania Press, 2016.

Goodall, Heather. "Writing a Life with Isabel Flick: An Exploration in Cross-Cultural Collaboration," *Public Historian* 27, no. 4 (2005): 65–82.

Hearman, Vannessa. "From Indonesia with Love: Friendships between Political Prisoners and Their Pen Pals and the Creation of Human Rights Activist Networks." *Histoire sociale/Social History* 53, no. 108 (2020): 415–34.

———. *Unmarked Graves: Death and Survival in the Anti-Communist Violence in East Java, Indonesia.* Singapore: National University of Singapore Press, 2018.

Herman, Judith. *Trauma and Recovery: The Aftermath of Violence—From Domestic Abuse to Political Terror.* New York: Basic Books, 2015.

Hinton, Devon E., and Byron J. Good. "The Culturally Sensitive Assessment of Trauma: Eleven Analytic Perspectives, a Typology of Errors, and the Multiplex Models of Distress Generation." In *Culture and PTSD: Trauma in Global and Historical Perspective,* edited by Devon E. Hinton and Byron J. Good, 50–113. Philadelphia: University of Pennsylvania Press, 2016.

Jolly, Margaretta. *In Love and Struggle: Letters in Contemporary Feminism.* New York: Columbia University Press, 2008.

———. "What I Never Wanted to Tell You: Therapeutic Letter Writing in Cultural Context." *Journal of Medical Humanities* 32, no. 1 (2011): 47–59.

Kirmayer, Laurence J., Robert Lemelson, and Constance A. Cummings. "Introduction." In *Re-Visioning Psychiatry: Cultural Phenomenology, Critical Neuroscience and Global Mental Health,* edited by Laurence J. Kirmayer, Robert Lemelson, and Constance A. Cummings, 1–40. New York: Cambridge University Press, 2015.

Kolk, Bessel A. van der, and Onno van der Hart. "The Intrusive Past: The Flexibility of Memory and the Engraving of Trauma." In *Trauma: Explorations in Memory,* edited by Cathy Caruth, 158–82. Baltimore, MD: Johns Hopkins University Press, 1995.

Laub, Dori, "Bearing Witness or the Vicissitudes of Listening." In *Testimony: Crises of Witnessing in Literature, Psychoanalysis, and History*, edited by Shoshana Felman and Dori Laub, 57–74. New York: Routledge, 1992.

Laub, Dori. "Truth and Testimony: The Process and the Struggle." In *Trauma: Explorations in Memory*, edited by Cathy Caruth, 61–75. Baltimore, MD: Johns Hopkins University Press, 1995.

Lemelson, Robert, and Annie Tucker. "Afflictions: Psychopathology and Recovery in Cultural Context." In *Re-Visioning Psychiatry: Cultural Phenomenology, Critical Neuroscience and Global Mental Health*, edited by Lawrence Kirmayer, Robert Lemelson, and Constance A. Cummings, 483–514. New York: Cambridge University Press, 2015.

Leydesdorff, Selma, Graham Dawson, Natasha Burchardt, and T.G. Ashplant. "Introduction: Trauma and Life Stories." In *Trauma and Life Stories: International Perspectives*, edited by Kim Lacy Rogers, Selma Leydesdorff, and Graham Dawson, 1–26. Abingdon, Oxon: Routledge, 1999.

Lucas, Anton. "Survival: Bu Yeti's Story." In *The Indonesian Killings 1965–1966: Studies from Java and Bali*, edited by Robert Cribb, 227–39. Melbourne: Centre of Southeast Asian Studies, Monash University.

Maybin, Janet. "Death Row Penfriends: Configuring Time, Space, and Selves." *a/b: Auto/ Biography Studies* 21, no. 1 (2006): 58–69.

———. "Death Row Penfriends: Some Effects of Letter Writing on Identity and Relationships." In *Letter Writing as a Social Practice*, edited by David Barton and Nigel Hall, 151–77. Philadelphia, PA: John Benjamins, 2000.

McGregor, Katharine. "The Making of a Transnational Activist." In *The Transnational Activist: Transformations and Comparisons in the Anglo-World since the Nineteenth Century*, edited by Stefan Berger and Sean Scalmer, 165–91. Cham, Switzerland: Palgrave Macmillan, 2018.

Pohlman, Annie. "Sexual Violence as Torture: Crimes against Humanity during the 1965–66 Killings in Indonesia." *Journal of Genocide Research* 19, no. 4 (2017): 574–93.

———. *Women, Sexual Violence and the Indonesian Killings of 1965–66*. Abingdon, Oxon: Routledge, 2015.

Porter, Elisabeth. "Gendered Narratives: Stories and Silences in Transitional Justice." *Human Rights Review* 17, no. 1 (2016): 35–50.

Rodgers, Susan, ed. *Telling Lives, Telling History: Autobiography and Historical Imagination in Modern Indonesia*. Berkeley, CA: University of California Press, 1995.

Roosa, John. *Pretext for Mass Murder: The September 30th Movement and Suharto's Coup d'Etat in Indonesia*. Madison: University of Wisconsin Press, 2006.

Semdam VIII Brawidjaja. *Operasi Trisula Kodam VIII Brawidjaja* [The Trisula Operation of the Brawidjaja 8th Regional Command]. Surabaya: Jajasan Taman Tjandrawilwatikta, 1969.

Simpson, Bradley R. *Economists with Guns: Authoritarian Development and U.S.-Indonesian Relations, 1960–1968*. Stanford, CA: Stanford University Press, 2008.

Stanley, Liz. "The Epistolary Gift, the Editorial Third-Party, Counter-Epistolaria: Rethinking the Epistolarium." *Life Writing* 8, no. 2 (2011): 135–52.

Surin, Kenneth. "Conceptualizing Trauma, but What about Asia?" *Positions* 16, no. 1 (2008): 15–37.

Turpin, Jennifer. "Many Faces: Women Confronting War." In *The Women and War Reader*, edited by Lois Ann Lorentzen and Jennifer Turpin, 3–18. New York: New York University Press, 1998.

Wieringa, Saskia, and Nursyahbani Katjasungkana. *Propaganda and the Genocide in Indonesia: Imagined Evil*. Abingdon, Oxon: Routledge, 2019.

Chapter 7

HAUNTING AND RECOVERY IN POST-KHMER ROUGE CAMBODIA

Caroline Bennett

This chapter considers haunting in Cambodia after the genocide that occurred under the Khmer Rouge regime from 1975–1979. Although often used as historical metaphor, traces of memory, or indices of psychological trauma, in this chapter I argue that haunting can provide a means for people to understand and negotiate the violent past as it interjects in the present. In Cambodia, the dead are socially salient beings who interact with the living and are the cause of much social action. Their well-being is integral to the well-being of the living. However, the Khmer Rouge regime ruptured relations between the living and the dead, as well as causing an excess of death. In its aftermath, therefore, re-establishing relations between the living and the dead was a key aspect of reasserting control and security. Based on ongoing ethnographic research into mass graves and their human remains in Cambodia, I examine how relations with the dead, and specifically the experience of haunting, provided ways for people to rebuild sociality and community in the post-genocide environment.

This is not an attempt to present a model of absolute relativism or radical constructivism—as Dominic LaCapra has shown, in the writing of histories of violence, such an approach can undermine the horrors that many have experienced.[1] Rather, this chapter is an attempt to provide a counter-narrative or alternative approach to totalizing approaches that consider the aftermath of the Khmer Rouge in Cambodia as a naturalized national trauma, and as such pathologize both the people and the place. I do this by following Rita Atsuti's approach to "taking people seriously" by "paying resolute attention to the multiplicity of ways in which people create and deploy their knowledge in different contexts" and thus engaging with alternative modes of dealing with violent histories.[2]

Cambodia's Killing Fields and the Dead of the Khmer Rouge

Initially celebrated for its potential end to years of conflict, the Khmer Rouge regime (Democratic Kampuchea) devastated Cambodia. The Maoist revolution they instigated, aimed at creating a self-sufficient and independent country, included urban evacuation, collectivization, and the attempted destruction of all state institutions. Following their seizure of power in April 1975, the Khmer Rouge immediately emptied the cities, sending people into the countryside to work on massive projects designed to bring about an idealized agrarian nation: to make way for this they disbanded the old life, attempting to destroy customary forms of family life, religion, education, healthcare, and law.[3] To deal with opposition, they executed anyone deemed a threat to the new regime—former government officials and military, those educated abroad, the intelligentsia, and other influential community figures. They also set up a system of prisons across the country, where those considered to oppose the new rule were imprisoned, tortured, and sentenced to death. Each had an associated killing site—usually within one kilometer of the prison, where prisoners who "confessed" to crimes were sent for execution.[4]

The killings spread far beyond these sites, however. With rations reduced to one watery cup of rice per day, hospitals closed down, doctors killed or forced into exile, and working days that ran from sunrise to sunset, hundreds of thousands of people succumbed to the Khmer Rouge regime. Between 1975 and 1979, between 1 and 3 million people died from disease, starvation, or execution.[5] Hundreds of thousands of others suffered from malnutrition and chronic illness, which impacted them for years after the regime.[6] This was genocide by attrition,[7] as well as by design.[8] The bodies of those who died were buried in mass graves, dumped in wells, rivers, or caves; or simply abandoned where they were killed. These were the killing fields[9] of Cambodia. Koh Sap[10] was one such location.

A small island in the Bassac river, not far from Cambodia's capital, Phnom Penh, Koh Sap, like many of its neighbors, was used as a prison, workcamp, and killing site during the Khmer Rouge regime.[11] Islands were the perfect materialization of the regime's *kuk et chonhcheang* (prison without walls). Before the regime it had been a village and farming site, but during the regime, prisoners and their guards occupied the island, and large parts of it were farmed as part of the Khmer Rouge agrarian project. People were killed every day: some because they did not work hard enough, others because they disobeyed the guards, or did something that was seen as resistant—complaining too much, taking too long to respond to the guards, or eating insects or other small creatures to supplement their rations, for example. It was known in the area that if you were sent to Koh Sap you would likely not return. People were killed where they stood, or taken to the bamboo grove at the end of the island and executed there. Others died of starvation, disease, or exhaustion. Some bodies were buried, others left to rot where they fell. An elderly woman I interviewed, who had worked downriver, said they saw bodies floating in the river: though they wanted to retrieve them, they could not leave their workstations, and the bodies soon washed away.

The Khmer Rouge was deposed in 1979 when, tired of border skirmishes and raids in their country, Vietnam invaded with a group of Khmer defectors, who they put into power as the People's Republic of Kampuchea (PRK).[12] After the regime fell, Koh Sap was slowly transformed back into living and farming space. This took some time: houses had been dismantled and the materials used to build prison facilities, and the farming areas had grown wild. Graves covered one end of the land and piles of dead lay in other areas. According to Samnang, who moved to the island in the early 1980s, the streams that ran through one end of the island were littered with rotting cadavers—*kmoac* in Khmer. Some families who had lived there before the regime returned straight away, but many were initially afraid.

The treatment of the dead is a vital aspect of social control, as well as central to building culture and meaning in all societies (as Thomas Laqueur writes, in his book *The Work of the Dead*: "the dead make civilization").[13] After genocide, conflict, or disaster, their management is of practical, political, and social concern: practical because piles of rotting dead can be disturbing to those who survive;[14] political because the harnessing of the symbolic power of the dead enables their use for all manner of projects from nation building to community recognition;[15] and social because inappropriate treatment of the dead ruptures the norms of treatment and paths of existence, causing the potential production of grievous/unhappy dead—dead who disturb the living in all manner of ways, from illness to death. This is especially true in cases of conflict and genocide, where an excess of death has the potential to cause many unhappy dead, the potency of which can be dangerous for the living.[16]

Cambodia is home to a plethora of ghosts and spirits, many of which are socially active, and, like the living, are organized into hierarchies of power and belonging.[17] They are vital entities that share the largely (Theravada) Buddhist cosmology of Cambodia,[18] and as such exist in *dukkha* (suffering) alongside humans, in the eternal cycle of *samsara* (death and rebirth) until they attain *nibbana* (Sanskrit: nirvana). The dead in all their forms have similar foibles as living humans—they retain attachments to people and places—and must be freed from these for successful rebirth. Sharing the human plane of existence means that they are subject to the same disjuncture, chaos, and disorder as the living, and as emotional and vital entities, they need care and attention to ensure their comfort.

As social agents, the dead have the potential to influence the lives of the living. They interfere in everyday life by demanding certain actions, or haunting in ways that require attention. The annual ritual cycle of Cambodia, which revolves around providing consolation to the dead, is punctuated by the fifteen-day

Pchum Benh festival, a ritual aimed specifically at providing offerings to the dead, particularly *preta* (hungry ghosts—pitiful beings with large, distended bellies and tiny mouths that cannot feed), to help them escape this incarnation and move on to the next.

Because they are social and vital entities, the dead in all their forms need material engagement and must be cared for in Cambodia.[19] Without the living to feed them during Democratic Kampuchea, many were extinguished, and thus there were fewer ghosts than usual.[20] Indeed, the potential expiration of the dead has been the cause of much distress for some in the Cambodian diaspora, as Richard Rechtman has shown from his long-term psychiatric work with Khmer Rouge survivors living in France. Because the Khmer Rouge fractured the relationship continuum between the living and the dead (where the living must pay attention to the dead in order for them to survive), some survivors have become trapped in a "rhetoric of extermination": feeling an obligation to care for the many thousands of nameless dead who died during the regime, but being unable to do so—equating in the minds of some Rechtman worked with, to a second death of the massacred.[21]

Immediately after Democratic Kampuchea, however, *kmoac* were widespread in many areas, and some killing sites were referred to as *prei kmoac* (forest of the dead/forest of ghosts). Although often translated as ghosts, the word *kmoac* has an ambiguous meaning; it can be used to mean the corpse of the recently deceased, ghosts from the recently deceased, or as a generic term referring to other supernatural entities that haunt the living. This ambiguity reflects the liminal status of the dead as well as the living. In fracturing relationships between the living and the dead, the dead were negated as social beings, threatening their viability and, by doing so, that of the living as well. Thus after the fall of Democratic Kampuchea their care became essential.[22]

Haunting at this time was reported by research participants at several field sites I visited across Cambodia. When people first returned to Koh Sap, some reported seeing lights (*far*) moving across the land, indicating the presence of haunting ghosts (*kmoac lorng*). Soldiers were seen marching long after the forces on both sides had left. An elderly woman told me that when she first moved to the island in the 1980s, she would catch glimpses of people walking around, or see shadows, but when she looked again they had disappeared. Others told me of hearing noises—drumming under the mango tree or splashes in a pond when no one was there. This was not only the case at Koh Sap; an employee at Choeung Ek Genocidal Center, just outside Phnom Penh, said that while guarding the site one night, he and another guard heard footsteps in the rain, but when they went to look, they could see no evidence of footprints. Others in villages nearby heard chains dragging or children and babies crying at night.

Some people at Koh Sap had specific encounters with the dead. Yei Malis felt hands grabbing at her legs as she transplanted rice one morning; she crawled back to her house, and passed out for several hours after feeling the dead pinning her to the bed.[23] Yei Touch had to dismantle her house[24] and move it because she and her children were haunted—at night she felt the house spinning and the children began sleepwalking.

Sometimes the dead asked the living for specific acts of care. After finding a gold tooth while planting turmeric, Yei Mean was visited in a dream by the person whose tooth it was—he asked her to take offerings for him to the pagoda in exchange for his tooth (although she did not know the ghost, she thought perhaps they were biologically related). In another case, a middle-aged woman who lives close to Choeung Ek was visited in a dream by her father. He told her that he and two others had been killed one day while they were returning from work, and asked her to come and find his bones. He told her they were next to an irrigation canal in front of a pagoda between two other graves. When her sister visited the spot he had described, she found three graves, but the bodies had been removed some time before, so she could not take the bones as requested. Instead she took some soil from the top of the grave and it remains at her home until today. Since that time her father has not visited any of them, and the family has been well.

It is not unusual for the dead to visit the living in their dreams. Described by the Khmer term *aoy yul sap*—which means literally "to give a dream"—these interactions are considered by many to be deliberate visits, determined by the dead. In these dreams the dead often make demands, which the living then fulfill. When my interlocutor's father visited her, before asking her to get his bones, he was crying, telling her he was with others and they were all suffering. Others told people it was really difficult where they were or that they were hungry. They asked for food or for particular actions to help alleviate their suffering. They cried because they were lonely, and some of them were lost.

Part of the Khmer Rouge's program was the reorganization of much of the population by repeated and forced movement around the country, dismantling families and communities in attempts to rupture connections to the old life and create linkages to the new one.[25] Many children were separated from parents and sent to work in youth brigades, while others were moved to different camps around the country. Huge numbers of people who were relocated subsequently died, and large numbers of people left the country as refugees. Families were split up and some were never reunited. This disconnection and movement meant that often people died far from their community, family, and friends. Like the living, the dead were scared and confused, but while the living could return to their homelands after the regime, the dead could not. This dislocation reportedly caused them a lot of distress. Several people I interviewed told me that in the immediate aftermath of the regime, the dead wandered the land looking for their family: "they were roaming around because they were worried about us" one elderly woman told me. "[T]hey were worried about their children, because we were very small." Some people think that some are still wandering.[26]

The haunting that I am describing was at its most prevalent in the immediate aftermath of the regime—in the late 1970s and early 1980s. My research participants attributed the haunting to the loss and confusion by the dead. Dislocated from their family and community, they became pitiful dead, wandering the land. The haunting did not only occur rurally—across urban and rural sites people reported stories of haunting and *kmoac* being widespread. Thus it related to social insecurity at every level of society: not only for the living, but also for the dead.[27]

Nowadays, there remains no haunting at the sites I visited. Most people told me that the ghosts had died or the dead had been reborn. Cambodia has a syncretic Buddhist-animist socio-religious system, and, as previously mentioned, the dead, ghosts, and other supernatural entities, not only belong to accepted realms of existence, but as with all other entities, can also die and be reborn within these realms.

The Khmer Rouge broke the bonds between the living and the dead. To rebuild these, the dead need re-incorporating into the social worlds of the living. While monks are usually the intermediaries between the living and the dead, in the aftermath of the regime people often fulfilled this role themselves, building reciprocal relations with the dead that helped both rebuild their lives. Uncovering their remains through grave-looting and excavation, for example, brought the dead back in to the social lives of the living, and taking valuables they found in the graves (while providing offerings in exchange), provided the living with material support in the aftermath of the regime. Annual rituals that provided care for the dead (such as the annual ritual for dead ancestors, *Pchum Benh*) were re-established in the 1990s, allowing those who had died to be cared for en masse.[28] As more people moved to different areas, they transformed the land from wild and insecure, to tamed and secure—the ghosts left the land or were reborn as a result of the karma they accumulated from the relations built with the living.[29] As the dead are reincarnated, the skeletal remains, displayed across the country in various memorial stupa, became "like wood."

If not taken seriously, these encounters could be dismissed as evidence of psychological trauma or approached solely as historical metaphor and a means of narrating the period.[30] But taking these interactions seriously gives us an opportunity to see beyond this to considering the role the dead played in re-ordering society, cosmology, and normal life; they are central to the reshaping of sociality[31] that is an essential aspect of dealing with mass violence.

Healing through Haunting

In its attempts to create a new society, the Khmer Rouge regime disrupted every aspect of Cambodian life, including politics, education, health care, religion, community, and family structures. As well as causing mass death, illness, and disease, the social order was disrupted. The re-establishment of control and order is central in any post-conflict society, and security is a vital aspect of this. Thus, when the regime was deposed in 1979, all of these aspects of life needed care. The dead, whose corpses covered large areas of the land, were one aspect of this.

Studies of healing after violence emphasize the role of communal rituals in rendering memories of violence into tolerable representations, building collectivity, and imagining the community.[32] These rituals offer ways to re-order sociality, bringing it back into regular order, and creating a temporal bridge between times of stability and times of disorder. Death in Cambodia is usually followed by specific rituals that control the dead and help them move on to their next life, while also providing mechanisms for re-ordering the social life of those surviving.[33] During Democratic Kampuchea, formal rituals were impossible.[34] This continued after the fall of the regime, with Buddhism still strictly controlled until the late 1980s.[35] With movement and rituals controlled, people could not conduct the usual rites for the mass dead that lay across the land. This related to the political and social environment, but also to the physical dislocation of the dead from their homes and family, and their commingling in mass graves where it became difficult to discern one from another. As one elderly participant told me: "Normally when we cremate the bones there has to be a family member to represent each family and take the ash to put in an urn to pay respects to. . . . However, in this case we don't know which bones belong to who."

Although no national rituals were conducted, some people made their own rites by piling the dead under sacred trees, or by burning their remains and offering some words of prayer.[36] They did this as they cleared the dead from the land to provide living space as they returned home, or moved to establish new villages and homes. Some continue to care for the dead in all their forms, giving offerings[37] to guardian spirits for protection, and other dead to help alleviate their suffering. For the most part, however, the dead have been incorporated into the annual ritual cycle, which allows offerings to be sent to the nameless dead at specific events throughout the year. Most significant in this is *Pchum Benh*—an annual ritual of fifteen days in September or October, when *preta* can return to the human realm and receive offerings from the living. During this time, the living gain merit (a positive force accumulated through life and related to karma, which aids in rebirth) by doing good deeds (*tvea bon*) for themselves and the dead—primarily by giving offerings at the pagoda, where the monks provide the pathway for communication with the dead. Pioneering anthropologist Anne Yvonne Guillou, who has conducted ethnographic research in Cambodia since the 1990s, notes how the re-establishment of this ritual in the 1990s provided much relief to people in her field site in Pursat, providing, as it did, a means of caring for the dead, both known and unknown.[38] Other rituals include the annual New Year's celebrations and the Chinese grave-sweeping ceremony of *Cheng*

Meng, all of which continue to be practiced today and incorporate those who died during the Khmer Rouge.

Despite this, ritual played only one part in the healing after the regime. I have written elsewhere about the key part the dead played in rebuilding security in post-Khmer Rouge Cambodia, and how through establishing reciprocal relations between the living and the dead throughout the 1980s and early 1990s, individuals acted as direct intermediaries with the dead—creating means for aiding them in their transition through *samsara* in the absence of Buddhist monks and ritual specialists such as *achaa* (lay priests), who would normally oversee this. Thus people were able to re-establish relations of support and rebuild stability and security after the regime.[39] Here I consider specifically the place haunting and the presence of ghosts has in relation to suffering and healing.

In *The Social Life of Spirits*, anthropologists Diana Espírito Santo and Ruy Blanes call for attention to be paid to the "work" spirits do in the societies and social worlds of the people we do research with.[40] As they note, spirits across many cultures have the ability to affect and alter people's fates and fortunes—to intervene in their lives at the everyday level, and effect social action. In Cambodia, there is an ongoing relationship between the living and the dead that is central to social identity, stability, and well-being. Both require care to move through the cycle of *samsara* and many incarnations of the dead share the human realm of existence and its related calm or discord. The presence of the dead and interactions with them in the immediate aftermath of the regime, therefore, was not necessarily, or not only, an articulation of suffering by the living, but also of suffering by the dead.

Spirits are integral to everyday life in Cambodia, and haunting and other interactions with supernatural others are common. Before major events people give offerings to local guardian spirits to ask for blessings and protection, and annual rituals, which are central to the calendar and functioning of the country, are aimed at directing care to the various types of dead in the Khmer cosmology. During his five-year rule of Cambodia (1970–1975), which followed a coup that overthrew the previous ruler (Prince Norodom Sihanouk), General Lon Nol relied heavily on relations with the supernatural realm for power and protection.[41] Although the Khmer Rouge attempted to dismantle Buddhism, in many areas they remained in relationship with local guardian spirits—offering sacrifices,[42] giving offerings, and engaging spirit mediums to provide protective amulets and tattoos. Before the Extraordinary Chambers in the Courts of Cambodia (ECCC)—the UN-backed trials of former Khmer Rouge—opened in 2006, a *neak ta* (guardian spirit) was invited to oversee the court; it was his presence as much as the legal framework that ensured truth telling in the court.[43] In contemporary Cambodia, some politicians consult spirit mediums before making major political decisions and appeal to the dead in public statements. The current

Prime Minister, Hun Sen, is acutely aware of the importance of connecting with the powerful spiritual world that orders Khmer society as a means of providing spiritual, and supernatural, legitimacy for his rule: for example, by proclaiming himself and his son to be reincarnations of powerful *neak ta* and other historic figures.[44] Thus the dead are involved in every major life event and every political and social engagement for many people in Cambodia.

As Carmen Goman and Douglas Kelley note, traumatic experiences have both psychological and sociological dimensions: "both the experience and the treatment of trauma need to be approached through a social perspective because human experience (e.g., trauma) cannot be abstracted from social context … That is, what individuals count or name as trauma emerges from their social context."[45]

Thus, an analysis of historical violence and its subsequent treatment should take both aspects into account, because in many cases it is as much the social, political, and structural upheaval that causes suffering as individual experience. The suffering of many Cambodians following the Khmer Rouge was not about psychology, or not only about psychology; it was also about ruptures in the social fabric, which required a redetermination of the world and the social relations within in. This extended to the dead as well as the living. This points to a disjuncture with the concept of trauma and healing as framed within the still dominant biomedical models, which do not allow an engagement with the idea that the dead themselves could be in pain, and therefore be the ones in need of consoling.

On Trauma in a Cambodian Context

In recent years work has begun to emerge that considers the cultural particularity of suffering in the aftermath of conflict and violence. Devon Hinton and Byron Good, for example, argue that there are locally specific "posttraumatic stress syndromes"—understandings of, and responses to, trauma that include local symptoms, meanings, and treatments, rather than the clinically defined posttraumatic stress disorder of the American Psychiatric Association's *Diagnostic and Statistical Manual*—the DSM-5.[46] Catherine Smith shows that the concept of trauma has been localized in Aceh, Indonesia, being deeply informed by Islam, local cultural values, and histories of violence that vary widely from clinical definitions and globalized discourse.[47]

Psychiatrists and clinical researchers meanwhile have established the multivariate symptoms and experiences of trauma, which have provided a nuanced understanding of its pathology and psychological effects. For example, Rachel Yehuda and Alexander McFarlane write that empirical research challenges the notion of PTSD as a normal stress response to traumatic events. They show that, rather than the homogenizing symptomology that was first presented in 1980, contemporary understandings of PTSD highlight its heterogeneity and may suggest "the manifestation of an underlying diathesis rather than a normative adaptation to environmental challenge."[48] This indicates that the idea of national trauma, or traumatized societies, is highly problematic. Andreas Maercker and Tobias Hecker, meanwhile, discuss how the broadening of assessment and therapy from the individual to the interpersonal and social aspects of life has the potential to improve understanding of the incidence and pathology of traumatic responses, as well as the success of treatment interventions.[49]

However, despite this, there persists an inclination to naturalize the incidence of trauma, and in particular the prevalence of Posttraumatic Stress Disorder, and its treatment, after mass violence. In an article published in 1997, Shelton Woods wrote: "if ever a whole society could be classified as suffering from Post-Traumatic Stress Disorder it would have to be Cambodia. Rarely can you find a person in Cambodia who was not directly affected by the loss of a family member as a result of the 1975–1979 Khmer Rouge reign of terror,"[50] while in their book, *Transforming Terror: Remembering the Soul of the World*, Susan Griffin and Karin Lofthus Corrington state that "trauma is the inevitable result of violence. Even the threat of violence produces measurable and enduring damage to both the body and the mind."[51]

The underlying assumption is that not only is traumatic stress a natural response, but that there is a universal response to suffering, which in turn determines a universal mode of dealing with it. This is usually framed within a Euro-American framework, and extends to justice mechanisms as well as psychological interventions, the two of which are often interlinked in post-conflict/post-genocide states. Both assume a nation in need of "healing," which is assumed to follow a particular pattern related to a linear temporal progression, and a transformation towards "justice" within liberal democratization.[52] Such approaches not only pathologize whole societies, but also leave little space for alternative understandings of both the past and the present or of pain and suffering. This gives no space for local means of dealing with historical violence, and, as Derek Summerfield argues, such approaches have the potential to become a form of bio-imperialism.[53]

In Cambodia there is no word that directly translates as "trauma," and the concept does not correlate with how most people understand or narrate pain and suffering. A number of different relations to suffering are recognized—for example, *bak sbat* (literally translated as broken courage) or *kut caraeun* (thinking a lot).[54] In addition, many survivors of Democratic Kampuchea understand the "traumatic" experience not in terms of personal disruption and anguish, but in socio-historical terms that are not necessarily related to them. The events of that era are largely understood as belonging to a particular time and place, and survivors and dead alike are not viewed as victims, or as witnesses to the genocide, but as beings who, while they may need special attention, have primarily become incorporated into the wider socio-cultural background of Cambodia.[55] Cambodians have been finding ways of managing their past, dealing with their suffering, and thereby "healing" for decades from within their own cosmological frameworks.[56]

Genocide, mass violence, disaster, and the like, are acts on entire worlds, not only the humans within them. Animals die, landscapes are scarred.[57] An elderly man who lived in one of the villages behind the Choeung Ek Genocidal Center, just outside Phnom Penh, described to me how on returning to his village in early 1979, he found rows and rows of rabbits, bred to feed the cadre who lived there during the regime, dead in their cages. A resident of another village I worked in told me that in the years after the regime the ground moved with the dead: rising and cracking as the bodies bloated with decomposition; sinking when the rains came and compressed the land. The dead suffered too. Dislocated from their families, alone and confused, they wandered around Cambodia, looking for their relatives and communities.[58]

Democratic Kampuchea not only destroyed individual and personal lives but also ruptured entire social worlds and networks of belonging and community. Suffering afterward cannot, therefore, be circumscribed to the individual level, but must also consider the communal and collective aspects of re-ordering society. Some of this is done at the national level, but much is done locally, through relations between people and their worlds. By reconstituting social worlds, meaning and order could be restored, and moves made toward re-establishing security. In all periods after the Khmer Rouge, relations with the dead have been significant in this. By re-establishing links with the dead, the living could also connect with the past, as well as the future. Reincarnation plays a part in this, providing a bridge between periods of (imagined) stability in the past and the present that the Khmer Rouge interrupted, but did not destroy.[59] Haunting allows the dead to manifest their suffering, and the living to console them.

The ghosts that haunted from the Khmer Rouge have largely left Cambodia now. Some died because they were not cared for, others have been reborn. However, while the ghosts have gone, those who died during the Khmer Rouge continue to be important members of society to be cared for and appealed to. Guillou writes that because of the emanation of *pārami*—a form of circulating spiritual power—the dead of the mass graves have come to resemble *neak ta* (tutelary spirits that demand respectful behavior but can also offer luck and protection).[60] Most notable of these is Pol Pot, whose grave has become a site of pilgrimage, and who, through his transformation into a powerful spirit, retains power and influence over politics and religion in Anlong Veng where his cremains are buried.[61] Throughout the trial of Duch (Kaing Guek Eav), former commandant of Tuol Sleng prison in Phnom Penh, at the UN-backed ECCC, the dead were vital participants in the trials, repeatedly brought in to the court by

Khmer participants, most noticeably to listen to the verdict of case 001, which was viewed as a form of *baŋ-skoul* (ceremony of offering to the dead).[62] They are called on for all sorts of other help in everyday life.[63]

Considering the presence of ghosts and haunting after historical violence to be either fragments of memory or evidence of psychological trauma dismisses their vital place in the constitution of social worlds in Cambodia. This negation of everyday reality could arguably increase suffering and pain, by not allowing people to engage in their own meaningful worlds—creating a cultural disconnect that could prevent healing rather than alleviate pain. Recovering from death is never an individual endeavor—it requires re-establishing social relations and identity as well as providing socially appropriate means of reconstituting the world without those who are lost. All of these are collective enterprises. This is even more the case when there has been massive national violence and death. People draw on local cosmologies and modes of making meaning to do this, drawing on everyday relations to the world to begin making sense of the violence and move beyond it. Paying serious attention to haunting and the presence of the dead in Cambodia provides a way for the living to re-establish social bonds broken by the genocide, and reconstitute the world fractured by the violence of the regime. In addition, the agency of the dead could be seen as a means of providing agency to the living: by tending to the needs of the dead they themselves can take an active role in healing and recovery, and thus assert control over their own lives.

Conclusion

In her influential essay "Taking People Seriously," Rita Astuti, a professor of anthropology at the London School of Economics, argues for an approach that rather than allowing simply for radical alterity (as advocated by those of the ontological turn[64]), takes people seriously by "paying resolute attention to the multiplicity of ways in which people create and deploy their knowledge in different contexts, at different ages, fueled by different kinds of experience."[65] This requires taking seriously that people whose ontological realities differ from our own—including those whose lives are entangled with ghosts and other supernatural beings—are complex, inquisitive, and critical, and that they "construct knowledge and ideas, not the other way around."[66]

Mass tragedy reconstitutes a society socially, politically, and physically. The violence of this must be negotiated and made sense of in the present. Part of this negotiation and sense-making requires finding ways by which people at every level of society can incorporate and make the past meaningful in the present. As Heonik Kwon notes: "it is in the process of eliciting the common origin [of war wounds] that we come to realize it necessary to contextualize the trauma of war in its proper historical context and, accordingly, to recognize the plurality of human culture to express traumatic memories of war."[67] Paying attention to the dead is one way of doing this.

In Cambodia, there is an ongoing relationship to the past, made visible through relations to the dead that must be negotiated in the present. This does not always fit in to the neat linear temporality that dominant discourses on trauma, healing, and transitional justice imply. Rather it is something that can be contained at some moments and break free at others. While theories of psychological trauma would see this as trauma or conflict surfacing, allowing for alternative conceptions of time and the past, including those who have died within it, offers an alternative mode of thinking about healing after historical violence. The reality of trauma is that it is neither uniform nor stable even within the same population. Its bounds are permeable, its form fluid, and in many locales across the world, the term itself does not correspond with how local people understand and relate to suffering.

Taking haunting and interactions with the dead seriously as something other than metaphor, memory, or psychological trauma, allows us to recognize the social and political ruptures that genocide engenders beyond individual psychological damage. If we engage with the dead as salient entities who need attention and care, we approach a world that recognizes the interrelation of all aspects of cosmology in creating meaning and belonging. By considering radically different ontological engagements, we also approach a mode of dealing with suffering that elevates it from the individual to the social, and as such, helps reconstitute collective, as well as individual, security and well-being.

Caroline Bennett is a social anthropologist with a background in forensic anthropology. She specializes in the study of politics and violence, with specific attention to genocide, human rights abuses, and the politics of death and the dead. Her current research examines mass graves in Cambodia, exploring the use of political violence and mass death in projects of nation and state building, as well as community relations to the genocide and its dead. Her research intersects the practical and theoretical approaches to mass grave investigation and the recovery and identification of human remains.

Notes

1. LaCapra, *Writing History, Writing Trauma*.
2. Astuti, "Taking People Seriously," 106.
3. To read more about the Khmer Rouge regime, see Becker, *When the War was Over*, and Kiernan, *Pol Pot Regime*.
4. See David Chandler, *Voices from S-21*.

5. The exact number who died during the Khmer Rouge remains unknown, with estimates varying from 741,000 to 3.3 million. See Sharp, "Counting Hell," for an analysis of the various different estimates. The most recent demographic analysis gives a range of 1.2 to 2.8 million, with a median of 1.9 million deaths. See Heuveline, "Boundaries of Genocide."
6. Although these deaths were a consequence of the Khmer Rouge regime, geopolitics also played a role. Related to Cold war politics, the Vietnamese invasion in 1978 to overthrow the Khmer Rouge and then governance of the PRK government until 1989 were viewed by many as an illegal invasion and occupation. As a consequence, the UN embargoed Cambodia, refusing trade, aid, and diplomatic relations (see Kiernan, "Cambodian Crisis"), and the Khmer Rouge received immense diplomatic support, including being supported to form a coalition government in exile, which retained the seat in the UN until the early 1990s. See Martini, *Invisible Enemies*.
7. Fein, "Genocide by Attrition."
8. Kiernan, *Blood and Soil*, 540–54.
9. "The killing fields": a term which has now become synonymous with mass violence across the globe was coined by Khmer journalist Dith Pran to describe his experience as he fled across Cambodia to Thailand during Democratic Kampuchea. See Schanberg, *Death and Life Dith Pran*.
10. Not its real name.
11. Parts of this section, and descriptions of the haunting are adapted from Bennett, "Living with the Dead."
12. See Kiernan, *Pol Pot Regime*, 444–65.
13. Laqueur, *Work of the Dead*, 81. Susan Lindee gives a wonderful analysis of the multiple meanings attributed to the same set of dead that shows their central part in meaning-making for all aspects of social and political life in her article on the repatriation of atomic bomb victim body parts to Japan. Lindee, "Repatriation Body Parts."
14. Despite popular belief, large numbers of dead bodies do not usually pose health risks. See Tidball-Binz, "Managing the Dead in Catastrophes."
15. Bennett, "Who Knows Who We Are?"
16. Bovensiepen, "Spiritual Landscapes," Perera, "Spirit Possession."
17. Chouléan, *Les êtres surnaturels*.
18. The state religion of Cambodia is Theravada Buddhism, and in the last census, more than 95 percent of the population self-identified as Buddhist. See National Institute of Statistics, *Cambodia Population Census 2008*.
19. This is not only the case in Cambodia of course; it is common across Southeast Asia and in many other parts of the world. Verdery, *Political Lives Dead Bodies*, 104, notes how twentieth century ethnography from Transylvania and Hungary detail the care needed for the dead, who were often buried under the house, and were considered to need nourishing with food and prayers, in return for which they would protect their ancestors, while Rojas-Perez, *Mourning Remains*, 74, discusses how those in the Quechua communities of Peru who suffered bad deaths wandered as dangerous spirits until the community took collective responsibility for their care, enabling their movement to the next plane.
20. Davis, *Deathpower*, 213–14.
21. Rechtman, "Survivor's Paradox."
22. Langford, *Consoling Ghosts*, Rechtman, "Survivor's Paradox."
23. For further discussion on this form of sleep paralysis, see Hinton et al., "'The Ghost Pushes You Down.'"
24. Houses in rural Cambodia are often one-roomed wooden, or wood and palm-leaf, stilted houses. They can be dismantled and moved when necessary.

25. Despite the way it is often reported as a homogenous rule, the implementation of the Khmer Rouge's rule varied by area and was heavily influenced by the local commander. Not all people, therefore, experienced the same regime—not everyone was moved from their homeland and in some communities, families and villages were allowed to remain together. Michael Vickery discusses the danger of a totalizing discourse on the Cambodian genocide in Vickery, *Cambodia 1975–1982*.
26. For this reason, many people I spoke to considered the collection and display of human remains at pagoda and memorial sites across the country to be good, because it brought the dead together into a community where they could be visited.
27. That said, I am not suggesting that everyone in Cambodia was haunted, or that Cambodia was a traumatized society—such totalizing rhetorics are damaging as well as false.
28. Guillou, "Alternative Memory Khmer Rouge."
29. See Bennett, "Living with the Dead."
30. Kwon, *Ghosts of War in Vietnam*.
31. Following Nicholas Long and Henrietta Moore, I use sociality to refer to the dynamic systems humans are engaged in, that create meaningful interactions and ways of being in, and understanding, the world. That is, the social relations between different agents (human and non), through which people "come to know the world they live in and find meaning and purpose in it." Long and Moore, "Sociality Revisited," 41.
32. Buyandelger, "Asocial Memories," 68.
33. For a comprehensive description of these rituals, see Davis, *Deathpower*.
34. Although as Levine, *Love and Dread in Cambodia*, shows, people found their own ways of honoring the dead, burying them under sacred trees, or uttering half-remembered words from Buddhist rituals attended before the regime.
35. Harris, *Cambodian Buddhism*.
36. See also LeVine, *Love and Dread in Cambodia*.
37. Offerings are usually food or other goods laid at gravesites, sites of death, or, more often, given to monks at the pagoda who are intermediaries with the dead. Sometimes, however, they take on more esoteric forms: for example, Bukong Tuon, writing about Chanrithy Him's poem, *Please Give Us Voice*, comments that writing "was Him's way of feeding those hungry spirits." Tuon, "The Ghostly Presence."
38. Guillou, "Alternative Memory Khmer Rouge."
39. Bennett, "Living with the Dead."
40. Espírito Santo and Blanes, "Introduction," 6.
41. Harris, *Cambodian Buddhism*, 168; Marston and Guthrie, *History, Buddhism*, 87–88.
42. Zucker, *Forest of Struggle*.
43. The "Lord of the Iron Staff"; see Hinton, *Justice Facade*, 180–83.
44. Norén-Nillson, "Performance as (Re)incarnation," Vannarin, "Hun Sen."
45. Goman and Kelley, "Conceptualizing Forgiveness," 83.
46. Hinton and Good, *Culture and PTSD*.
47. Smith, *Resilience Localisation of Trauma*.
48. Yehuda and McFarlane, "Conflict," 1,709.
49. Maercker and Hecker, "Broadening Perspectives on Trauma and Recovery."
50. Woods, "Myth Cambodia's Recovery," 420.
51. Lofthus Carrington and Griffin, "An Unbearable Heartache," 67.
52. See Bennett, "Karma after Democratic Kampuchea."
53. Summerfield, "Invention Post-traumatic Stress Disorder."
54. For an extensive discussion on trauma type symptoms among Cambodian people, see Hinton, and Good "Culturally Sensitive Assessment Trauma."
55. Guillou, "Alternative Memory Khmer Rouge."

56. See also Hinton, *The Justice Facade*.
57. At a conference on disaster victim identification in 2012, a relative of one of the victims of the Lockerbie bombing gave a talk about her experience after the disaster. The landscape was scorched, she told us, by burn marks from the bodies and debris from the plane, changing the landscape, perhaps forever. Mick North, the father of one of the children killed during the Dunblane massacre described the same: "For many years after the Lockerbie tragedy," he wrote, "the physical scars left by the crashed jumbo could be seen from the road . . ." North, *Dunblane*.
58. It is not only Cambodian spirits who have been noted as suffering: in his influential work on war trauma in Vietnam and Korea, Heonik Kwon notes that the wounds of war are those of the dead, not troubles continuing to haunt survivors. Kwon, "Can the Dead Suffer Trauma?" 208. Meanwhile, among Mongolian herders, Gregory Delaplace notes that ghosts are "imagined to be extremely lonely creatures, craving sociability and trying to lure the ones they loved during life into joining them in death." Delaplace, "What the Invisible Looks Like," 52.
59. Bennett, "To Live Amongst the Dead," 163–96.
60. Guillou, "Alternative Memory Khmer Rouge."
61. Guillou, "The 'Master of the Land'."
62. Hinton, *Justice Facade*.
63. A recent tweet from a collective of Khmer people outside Cambodia urging the dead of the Khmer Rouge to haunt Chinese investors and drive them from the country succinctly shows how the living appeal to the dead to help them in all aspects of life: "Ghosts (*khmauch*) of victims of KR/ex-KR genocide, please unite/occupy empty condos, and haunt/chase (*lorng*) living Chinese away, even after they burn tons & tons of fake money" KhmerPAC, "Ghosts (khmauch) of victims)."
64. The ontological turn is a theoretical shift in anthropology that suggests people live in vastly different realities—i.e., that there are multiple different worlds, and therefore differences between them is not so much a difference in culture, but in being. See Descola, *Beyond Nature and Culture*; Carrithers et al., "Ontology"; Viveiros de Castro, "Cosmological Deixis."
65. Astuti, "Taking People Seriously," 106.
66. Astuti, "Taking People Seriously," 120.
67. Kwon, "Can the Dead Suffer Trauma?" 219.

Bibliography

Astuti, Rita. "Taking People Seriously (the 2015 Robert H. Layton Lecture)." *HAU: Journal of Ethnographic Theory* 7, no.1 (Spring 2017): 105–22.

Becker, Elizabeth. *When the War Was Over: Cambodia and the Khmer Rouge Revolution*, Revised Edition. New York: Public Affairs, 1998.

Bennett, Caroline. "Karma after Democratic Kampuchea: Justice Outside the Khmer Rouge Tribunal." *Genocide Studies and Prevention: An International Journal* 12, no.3 (2018): 66–82.

———. "Living with the Dead in the Killing Fields of Cambodia." *Journal of Southeast Asian Studies* 49, no. 2 (2018): 184–203.

———. "To Live Amongst the Dead: An Ethnographic Exploration of Mass Graves in Cambodia." PhD dissertation. Kent: University of Kent, 2015.

———. "Who Knows Who We Are? Questioning DNA Analysis in Disaster Victim Identification." *New Genetics and Society* 33, no. 1 (2014): 239–56.

Bovensiepen, Judith. "Spiritual Landscapes of Life and Death in the Central Highlands of East Timor." *Anthropological Forum* 19, no. 3 (2009): 323–38.

Buyandelger, Manduhai. "Asocial Memories, 'Poisonous Knowledge,' and Haunting in Mongolia." *Journal of the Royal Anthropological Institute* 25 (2019): 66–82.

Carrithers, Michael, Matei Candea, Karen Sykes, Martin Holbraad, and Soumhya Venkatesan. "Ontology Is Just Another Word for Culture: Motion Tabled at the 2008 Meeting of the Group for Debates in Anthropological Theory, University of Manchester." *Critique of Anthropology* 30, no. 2 (2010): 152–200.

Chandler, David. *Voices from S-21: Terror and History in Pol Pot's Secret Prison*. Berkeley: University of California Press, 1999.

Chouléan, Ang. *Les êtres surnaturels dans la religion populaire Khmère* (Supernatural beings in Khmer folk religion). Paris: Cedorek, 1986.

Davis, Erik W. *Deathpower: Buddhism's Ritual Imagination in Cambodia*. New York: Columbia University Press, 2016.

Delaplace, Gregory. "What the Invisible Looks Like: Ghosts, Perceptual Faith, and Mongolian Regimes of Communication." In *The Social Life of Spirits*, edited by Ruy Blanes and Diana Espírito Santo, 52–68. Chicago: University of Chicago Press, 2014.

Descola, Philippe. *Beyond Nature and Culture*. Translated by Janet Lloyd. Chicago: University of Chicago Press, 2014.

Espírito Santo, Diana, and Ruy Blanes. "Introduction: On the Agency of Intangibles." In *The Social Life of Spirits*, edited by Ruy Blanes and Diana Espírito Santo, 1-32. Chicago: University of Chicago Press, 2014.

Fein, Helen. "Genocide by Attrition 1939–1993: The Warsaw Ghetto, Cambodia, and Sudan: Links Between Human Rights, Health, and Mass Death." *Health and Human Rights* 2, no. 2 (1997): 10–45.

Goman, Carmen, and Douglas Kelley. "Conceptualizing Forgiveness in the Face of Historical Trauma." In *Critical Trauma Studies: Understanding Violence, Conflict and Memory in Everyday Life*, edited by Monica J. Casper, and Eric Wertheimer, 78–98. New York: New York University Press, 2016.

Guillou, Anne Yvonne. "An Alternative Memory of the Khmer Rouge Genocide: The Dead of the Mass Graves and the Land Guardian Spirits (*Neak Ta*)." *South East Asia Research* 20 no. 2 (2012): 207–26.

———. "The 'Master of the Land': Cult Activities around Pol Pot's Tomb." *Journal of Genocide Research* 20, no. 2 (2018): 275–289.

Harris, Ian. *Cambodian Buddhism: History and Practice*. Honolulu: University of Hawai'i Press, 2005.

Heuveline, Patrick. "The Boundaries of Genocide: Quantifying the Uncertainty of the Death Toll During the Pol Pot Regime (1975–1979)." *Population Studies* 69, no. 2 (2015): 201–18.

Hinton, Alexander Laban. *The Justice Facade: Trials of Transition in Cambodia*. Oxford: Oxford University Press, 2018.

Hinton, Devon, and Byron J. Good. "The Culturally Sensitive Assessment of Trauma: Eleven Analytic Perspectives, a Typology of Errors, and the Multiplex Models of Distress Generation." In *Culture and PTSD: Trauma in Global and Historical Perspective*, edited by Devon E. Hinton and Byron J. Good, 50–114. Philadelphia, PA: University of Pennsylvania Press, 2016.

———, eds. *Culture and PTSD: Trauma in Global and Historical Perspective*. Philadelphia: University of Pennsylvania Press, 2015.

Hinton, Devon E., Vuth Pich, Dara Chhean, and Mark H. Pollack. "'The Ghost Pushes You Down': Sleep Paralysis-Type Panic Attacks in a Khmer Refugee Population." *Transcultural Psychiatry* 42, no.1 (2005): 46–77.
KhmerPAC (@KhmerPAC) "Ghosts (*khmauch*) of victims of KR/ex-KR genocide, please unite/occupy empty condos, and haunt/chase (*lorng*) living Chinese away, even after they burn tons & tons of fake money," Twitter, January 27, 2019, 7.14 p.m, https://twitter.com/PacKhmer/status/1089602442495512577.
Kiernan, Ben. *Blood and Soil: A World History of Genocide and Extermination from Sparta to Darfur*. New Haven, CT: Yale University Press, 2007.
———. "The Cambodian Crisis, 1990–1992: The UN Plan, the Khmer Rouge, and the State of Cambodia." *Bulletin of Concerned Asian Scholars* 24, no. 2 (1992): 3–23.
———. *The Pol Pot Regime: Race, Power, and Genocide in Cambodia Under the Khmer Rouge 1975–1979*, Third Edition. New Haven, CT: Yale University Press, 2008.
Kwon, Heonik. "Can the Dead Suffer Trauma? Religion and Science after the Vietnam War." In *Religion and Science as Forms of Life: Anthropological Insights into Reason and Unreason*, edited by Carles Salazar and Joan Bestard, 207–20. New York: Berghahn Books, 2015.
———. *Ghosts of War in Vietnam*. Cambridge: Cambridge University Press, 2008.
LaCapra, Dominic. *Writing History, Writing Trauma*. Baltimore, MD: John Hopkins University Press, 2001.
Langford, Jean. *Consoling Ghosts: Stories of Medicine and Mourning from Southeast Asians in Exile*. Minneapolis: University of Minnesota Press, 2013.
Laqueur, Thomas. *The Work of the Dead: A Cultural History of Mortal Remains*. Princeton, NJ: Princeton University Press, 2015.
Levine, Peg. *Love and Dread in Cambodia: Weddings, Births, and Ritual Harm under the Khmer Rouge*. Singapore: National University of Singapore Press, 2010.
Lindee, M. Susan. "The Repatriation of Atomic Bomb Victim Body Parts to Japan: Natural Objects and Diplomacy." *Osiris* 13, Beyond Joseph Needham: Science, Technology and Medicine in East and Southeast Asia (1998): 376–409.
Lofthus Carrington, Karin, and Susan Griffin. "An Unbearable Heartache: Trauma, Violence, and Memory." In *Transforming Terror: Remembering the Soul of the World*, edited by Karin Lofthus Carrington and Susan Griffin, 67–101. Berkley, CA: University of California Press, 2011.
Long, Nicholas, and Henrietta Moore. "Sociality Revisited: Setting a New Agenda." *Cambridge Anthropology* 30, no. 4 (2012): 40–47.
Maercker, Andreas, and Tobias Hecker. "Broadening Perspectives on Trauma and Recovery: A Socio-interpersonal View of PTSD." *European Journal of Psychotraumatology* 7, no.1 (2016): 1–9.
Marston, John, and Elizabeth Guthrie. *History, Buddhism, and New Religious Movements in Cambodia*. Honolulu: University of Hawai'i Press, 2004.
Martini, Edwin A. *Invisible Enemies: The American War on Vietnam, 1975–2000*. Amherst: University of Massachusetts Press, 2007.
National Institute of Statistics. *Cambodia General Population Census 2008*. Phnom Penh: Royal Government of Cambodia, 2017. Retrieved 1 December 2019 from https://www.nis.gov.kh/index.php/km/15-gpc/14-population-census-2008-final-result.
Norén-Nilsson, Astrid. "Performance as (Re)incarnation: The Sdech Kân Narrative." *Journal of Southeast Asian Studies* 44, no. 1 (February 2013): 4–23.
North, Mick. *Dunblane: Never Forget*. Edinburgh: Mainstream Publishing, 2000.
Perera, Sasanka. "Spirit Possession and Avenging Ghosts: Stories of Supernatural Activities as Narratives of Terror and Mechanisms of Coping and Remembering." In *Remaking a World: Violence, Social Suffering and Recovery*, edited by Veena Das, Arthur Kleinman, Margaret

Lock, Mamphela Ramphele, and Pamela Reynolds, 157–200. Berkeley: University of California Press, 2001.

Rechtman, Richard. "The Survivor's Paradox: Psychological Consequences of the Khmer Rouge Rhetoric of Extermination." *Anthropology and Medicine* 13, no. 1 (April 2006): 1–11.

Rojas-Perez, Isaias. *Mourning Remains: State Atrocity, Exhumations, and Governing the Disappeared in Peru's Postwar Andes.* Stanford, CA: Stanford University Press, 2017.

Schanberg, Sydney H. *The Death and Life of Dith Pran.* New York: Penguin Books, 1985.

Sharp, Bruce. "Counting Hell: The Death Toll of the Khmer Rouge Regime in Cambodia." *Mekong.net*, 2008. Retrieved 1 December 2019 from https://www.mekong.net/cambodia/deaths.htm.

Smith, Catherine. *Resilience and the Localisation of Trauma in Aceh, Indonesia.* Singapore: Asian Studies Association of Australia in association with the National University of Singapore Press, 2018.

Summerfield, Derek. "The Invention of Post-traumatic Stress Disorder and the Social Usefulness of a Psychiatric Category." *British Medical Journal* 322, no. 7278 (2001): 95–98.

Tidball-Binz, Morris. "Managing the Dead in Catastrophes: Guiding Principles and Practical Recommendations for First Responders." *International Review of the Red Cross* 89, no. 866 (2007): 421–42.

Tuon, Bukong. "The Ghostly Presence in Chanrithy Him's 'Please Give Us Voice.'" *Mosaic: An Interdisciplinary Critical Journal* 47, no. 1 (2014): 145–60.

Vannarin, Neou. "Hun Sen Tells of Eldest Son's Supernatural Arrival." *Cambodia Daily*, 3 May 2013. Retrieved 1 December 2019 from https://english.cambodiadaily.com/news/hun-sen-tells-of-eldest-sons-supernatural-arrival-21752/.

Verdery, Katherine. *The Political Lives of Dead Bodies: Reburial and Postsocialist Change.* New York: Columbia University Press, 1999.

Vickery, Michael. *Cambodia 1975–1982.* Bangkok: Silkworm Books, 2000.

Woods, L. Shelton. "The Myth of Cambodia's Recovery." *Contemporary Southeast Asia* 18, no. 4 (1997): 417–29.

Viveiros de Castro, Eduardo. "Cosmological Deixis and Amerindian Perspectivism." *Journal of the Royal Anthropological Institute* 4, no. 3 (1998): 469–88.

Yehuda, Rachel, and Alexander McFarlane. "Conflict between Current Knowledge about Post-traumatic Stress Disorder and Its Original Conceptual Basis." *American Journal of Psychiatry* 152, no. 12 (1995): 1,705–13.

Zucker, Eve Monique. *Forest of Struggle: Moralities of Remembrance in Upland Cambodia.* Honolulu: University of Hawai'i Press, 2013.

Chapter 8

A Field of Happiness

Space, Trauma, and Existential Precarity
among China's Sent-Down Youth

Hua Wu

Our Generation
We are of the same age as the People's Republic
We went up to the mountains and trained our backs
We went down to the country and strengthened our legs
Our Generation
We learned what endurance truly meant
We know how regret really tasted
Oh! The bitter-sweet wine of life
We drained so many cups of that.

—Wang Yougui, "Our Generation" A song written
by and for the Sent-Down Youth in China (2017)[1]

China's Sent-Down Youth and
Their Unique Generational Experience

China's Cultural Revolution (1966–1976) was a sociopolitical movement with significant and long-lasting impact on the country's social structure as well as the everyday lives of people across generations. The leaders of this social program intended to purge the remaining capitalist and traditionalist elements from within the Chinese Communist Party and society in general. Spreading from movements instigated by university students motivated by the ideology of class struggle, it became violent, damaged the economy, and led to massacres and widespread persecution. Several large-scale programs were launched during the Cultural Revolution, led by the Chairman of China's Communist Party Mao Zedong. One of them was the great rustication program. From 1968 to 1978, Mao led the "Up to the Mountains and Down to the Countryside" (*Shangshan Xiaxiang*) program, which aimed to place urban youth with peasants and was a socialist reeducation program. It resulted in one of the greatest rustication movements of youth in modern Chinese history. Scholars have debated its main motivations. Some have emphasized economic reasons by pointing out that it addressed the lack of employment in urban areas. Others have attributed it to Mao's personal biases against urbanization and the bourgeois ideologies he thought were related to urban life. Although the reasons for the rustication program were complicated, and despite the general unwelcome attitude from both parents and peasants, the administration of this program was efficient.[2]

During the rustication movement, seventeen million urban adolescents were relocated to rural communes, military farms, state cadre schools, and the frontier at the Inner Mongolia grasslands. In the midst of the Cultural Revolution, its administration was carried out with astonishing efficiency. The Sent-Down Youth spent, on average, seven years in rural communes, where most of them were subjected to hard labor and harsh living conditions, resulting in malnutrition, injuries, and trauma from structural violence administered by local cadres and peasants. Rapes and deaths were not uncommon. The education, careers, family formation, and intellectual development of this generation were consequently severely disrupted. Because of this, the Sent-Down Youth are usually referred to as China's Lost Generation.[3]

The life experiences of these Sent-Down Youth (or *Zhiqing*, a short form of *Zhishi Qingnian*, Educated Youth) has attracted much scholarly attention, especially in studies on historical transitions, economic change, and the social-structural transformation from the Maoist to the Post-Socialist era.[4] *Zhiqing* narratives, biographies, surveys, and interviews have focused on themes such as nostalgia, identity construction, recovery from political and historical trauma, and how the life course of affected individuals was affected by tremendous social changes.[5] This chapter traces connections between theories of trauma and memory, existential precarity,[6] and phenomenological understandings of embodiment and space. I employ a combination of life story narrations and participant observation to investigate the manifestation of non-verbal expressions as individuals go through traumatic emotional experiences in order to shed light on the immediate sensations triggered by memories.[7] This approach offers new perspectives in understanding trauma as it allows me to observe how traumatic memories surface as individuals navigate through specific spaces. The ethnographic data I have collected document historical and collective experiences by focusing on interpersonal interactions, communications, and the co-experience of life events by members from particular groups.[8] Both co-remembering a shared past and the immediate sensations people had as they went through the reunion trip that is central in this chapter constitute extraordinary experiences. I focus on a specific group as its members were undergoing this co-embodiment of time and space by bearing witness to each other's past and present, and then construct a common future as they renew their social relationships and provide emotional support to each other.

Embodiment and Emotion through Personal and Historical Transitions

This ethnography is part of a larger project that aims at documenting and presenting the ways people use their bodies to interact with changing social contexts and process their emotions across different life stages. The temporal, spatial, relational, and cross-cultural aspects of experience across the life course constitute my major focus in understanding the impact of social transition on human physical and psychological conditions. Among all members of these generational cohorts, the Sent-Down Youth group experienced one of the most shocking social, spatial, and cultural transitions, which not only affected their life choices and quality of life in the post-revolutionary era, but also influenced how they established social relations and understood their social roles, creating multi-generational impacts. Traumatic experiences including domestic, historical, and organized violence significantly affected the survivors as well as following generations.[9] During my ethnographic research, I conducted interviews and asked individuals to identify the most significant events they experienced and to elaborate on how they felt, both somatically and emotionally, before, during, and after such events. All of the participants, individuals who were born in the 1950s, identified the most dramatic changes across their life spans. At their early retirement stage when this research was conducted, many expressed concerns as they now face a future filled with uncertainty in a time that is vastly different from the era in which they grew up.

It is crucial to introduce the group I focus on and the cultural significance of their experiences. The Sent-Down Youth view themselves as "just some ordinary people in an extraordinary time." Their extraordinary experience provides scholars with a case study of massive social movements and their impact on people's embodiment and emotion. Their dislocation and the political changes that followed the Revolutionary period (1950s–1970s) up to the Market era (1980s to 2000s) altered the life course of the Sent-Down Youths.[10] As urban youths who joined the *Shangshan Xiaxiang* (The Up to the Mountains and Down to

Countryside) Movement, the forced separation from their original communities, the physically demanding agricultural labor, and the deprivation of material and social support were the major sources of their suffering.

I want to point out that, even though being a *Zhiqing* can constitute a collective identity, memories, interpretations, reflections, and feelings toward their Sent-Down time vary significantly between individuals during and after their *Zhiqing* years. Coming from different family backgrounds, a large number of the Sent-Down Youth experienced famine, hardship, and violence back home. The living conditions in the countryside varied depending on how they were assigned to production teams. Some of them went to frontier provinces and started on labor farms designed for prisoners. Others were put into peasant families or lived in isolated conditions in hostile villages. The primary determinant of their Sent-Down experience was their family background, which in turn determined their political status among their peers and in the labor teams, their expectations of the Cultural Revolution, and their choice of life and anticipated life course afterward.[11] Overall, children who came from "good" family origins (i.e., the proletariat class) that carried no political burdens generally evaluated their Sent-Down experience as positive or at least neutral. At times, the material conditions in Sent-Down farms were an improvement in comparison to their home situation. They became the privileged social group occupying a relatively safe political status and did not have to fear persecution or marginalization. Meanwhile, children from stigmatized groups and families, especially those who had higher expectations of their future before the Cultural Revolution, experienced not only economic and material deprivation as compared to their pre-Revolutionary childhood life, but also deprivation of dignity. They were more likely to perceive their Sent-Down experience as a process of forced separation from their families, and experienced despair due to displacement and lack of kinship support.[12]

The other important variable that influenced the *Zhiqing* experience depended on whether and how much violence they experienced during their Sent-Down years. In a number of counties, conflicts between peasants and *Zhiqing* escalated as violent class struggle ensued in addition to fights over natural resources.[13] Many *Zhiqing* and other people who went to the countryside for political reasons or as criminals ended up dead or severely injured.[14] Many survivors of extremely violent conflict and massacres were traumatized and reported a much worse overall emotional status throughout their lifetime.[15] Compared to these traumatized survivors, Sent-Down Youth who were middle-school graduates and worked in *Zhiqing*-only Production Teams had a much easier time because of internal group cohesion and comradeship. Regardless of the overall interpretation of their *Zhiqing* experience, the 1950s age cohort I studied all identified these years as the beginning of a series of turning points in their lives.[16] Being a *Zhiqing* became a unique experience of their generational cohort, a memorable life event that was often misunderstood, underrepresented, and under-discussed according to their narration and impression. "If you give me a million dollars I would never go back to that time in my life," one member indicated, quoting a popular saying from their cohort, "but I would never regret it or trade it with anything else in the world."

Team 3 Class 6: A Production Team at Happiness Field

I came to know the *Zhiqing* Reunion Group through a participant I met when I was conducting my dissertation research in Shanghai in the summer of 2018 and was invited to a *Zhiqing* reunion to commemorate the fortieth anniversary of their removal to Rural Hunan. Initially, my research aimed to conduct life story narrations by documenting everyday routines and important events to understand embodiment and emotion across transitional life stages. The Sent-Down experience stood out as a significant event for this 1950s cohort. One of my participants was a *Zhiqing* who currently lives in Shanghai and was a Sent-Down Youth in the Hunan district. According to her, time in this district was an unforgettable period in her life, and she explicitly said that she had many memories of hardship and trauma. Though she constantly talked about it, she never visited the Sent-Down farm as some other team members had done. When I asked her if she had contact with her former *Zhiqing* friends, she indicated that she had just re-established contact with her former *Zhiqing* Team members and was thinking of going to a reunion to revisit the site.

I accompanied twelve men and women who were on their reunion trip, which they named an act of "re-tracing the Sent-Down Route." For a few team members, this was the first time in forty years that they met the fellow members of their former *Zhiqing* group. After a majority of the *Zhiqing* returned to urban areas in the mid- to late 1970s, their life paths diverged. Some of them had grown up in the same community and had gone to the same school. Others had been transferred to labor farms with their whole families. Despite their diverse backgrounds and life course afterwards, their common experience formed a solid foundation for renewing their relationships. The main motive for these anniversaries and reunions, according to the organizers, were memorial in nature. Several team members had organized various trips to revisit the labor farm. The ones I attended were relatively intimate and only had a dozen or so participants. "We wanted to reinforce our friendship, recall our youth years, and maybe remind ourselves about the path we traveled. In today's world, nobody understood our experience. Sent-Down Youth Movement was unprecedented and won't happen again. We have no one to share it with but ourselves," suggested one of the team members. "Now we are in our old age, and we only have a few more years of freedom when we are not taking care of grandchildren or our own elderly parents. So, we get together to remember the past."

FIGURE 8.1. Farmer's Hut at the Happiness Field Cadre School. Image taken on August 21, 2017. © Hua Wu.

Most of the twelve people I interviewed during my field trips had mixed feelings when they looked back at their youth spent in the countryside. All of them considered their perseverance, their ability to endure hardship and suffering, and their broad set of skills and practical knowledge as positive qualities resulting from their Sent-Down experience. Eight of them came from former middle-class families; they expressed the strongest regret about having missed opportunities to receive an education, which was common to their generational cohort.[17] Four explicitly stated that the Sent-Down experience was one of the most traumatic experiences in their lifetime. Based on my observations, the origins of their lingering ill feelings were related to them having witnessed or being subjected to violence that had led to the deaths of peers, family members, and friends during conflicts between *Zhiqing* and local peasants. Violence and sexual assault were most pronounced on military farms.[18] Those who remained in the Happiness Farm Cadre School after it was converted into a military farm and labor camp suffered from violence and administrative abuse.

When I followed up with the larger group in 2018, a number of team members reported their experience as mainly positive because they had been able to gain economic and social independence from a young age. In sum, how people recollect and reflect on their Sent-Down experience is determined by a number of factors both before and after their time spent in the countryside. Despite the hardship they all had endured, such as the lack of material and intellectual resources, it is incorrect to conclude that the Sent-Down experience was a significant trauma for all *Zhiqing*. For this chapter, I will present ethnographic data, document the activities of the team members who played a significant role in organizing the event, and provide life story narrations before, during, and after the reunion trip. I have selected the accounts of three people from diverse backgrounds because they illustrate the varied experiences of *Zhiqing* people. Even though they shared a common space and their life paths intersected, their personal and psychological experiences were vastly different. What had been a place of trauma for one woman was, for another one, a site for natural transitions, which included a positive, nostalgic home base where a team spirit was nurtured. I show how their time in the countryside altered their life paths afterwards, and how the re-experience of embodying this space played a central role in strengthening their intersubjectivity by re-establishing meaning that allowed them to orient themselves toward a common future.

A Field of Happiness:
Re-visiting the Cadre School in Eternal County

August 2017 was unusually hot, even by the standard of Middle Southern China. Facing the middle reaches of the Yangtze River Plain, the Eternal County lays at the bottom of an area enclosed by mountains. The center of the county is 200 miles from the capital city of the province, the route crossing more than fifty tunnels through the mountains. Before high-speed trains made the whole area much more accessible in the late 2000s, the Eternal County was located far away from prosperous agricultural towns and fast-paced, industrial cities. For more than a thousand years, this place was inhabited by several ethnic minorities and served as a destination for exile. What makes the county famous in today's world—tourist attractions near mountain retreats; forests rich in animal and plant species, containing abundant resources; and unique metals and rare minerals— were once the reasons for its undesirable location and poverty. It is a place known for its poor soil, lack of water, scattered and uncultivatable land,

and steep hills; and therefore only fit for growing tea and experiencing extreme weather events throughout the year.

The Happiness Field Cadre School was located in the heart of this mountainous region. For Yumei, a 64-year-old woman who worked various jobs before retiring from the publishing industry in the Province's capital city, this was the first time that she visited the area since she left it in 1976. Yumei came from a family politically and socially marginalized during the Cultural Revolution; both her parents were imprisoned in 1957 as anti-revolutionist scholars and members of rightist political associations while she was branded as coming from a "bad" family. Yumei became a Sent-Down Youth after graduating from high school in a rural area. Suffering from extreme poverty and severe domestic violence as a teenage girl, Yumei's life before she arrived at Eternal County was, in her own words, "spiritually crushing." Freed from her uncle's abusive family, the initial stage of her Sent-Down experience was relatively easy. She imagined that she could become a team member and leave her past behind. She later suffered hardship because of the hard labor and the abuses inflicted by cruel and vindictive team leaders. She did not connect to any other team member, despite the usual tight bonding and friendship among teams, which created a considerable gap both socially and timewise until this reunion.

We arrived at Happiness Field during the early afternoon. The temperature was over 100°F (37°C) when our van parked near the only cement-paved road. One team member, who had participated in reunion trips several times, served as our guide. He pointed to a decaying, plain building near the end of the road, saying: "Here it is." He then led the way and gestured to the one-floor house with a locked yard: "That was our kitchen and dining hall! That was the place you worked, remember?" Laughing, chatting, and exchanging anecdotes all the way, Yumei froze on the spot, took a few slow steps, and burst into tears. Sobbing uncontrollably, she could not even hold herself up straight. Facing the site of her trauma, she experienced an emotional breakdown; her whole body appeared to give up. Other team members rushed to help her by holding her up, giving her tissues and repeating comforting words: "It is okay, it is okay. It happened to all of us. We all cried the first time we visited here." "Just let it all out," said another one: "let it all out. You've been holding these tears for so many years, let it all out so that *you can turn this page*."

While sobbing, Yumei pointed to the corner of the roof. I followed her gesture but saw nothing in particular, while she continued crying violently. She nodded and said: "That was the place." "What was the place?" I asked. Another teammate told me that on that part of a tin plate used to hang on a corner of the roof. Three times a day, kitchen workers, at times Yumei herself, would bang on the tin plate to signal mealtime. "That was the corner where she worked from 3 a.m. to start the fire and help with preparing food for three hundred people." We could only gaze at the roof through a locked yard, seeing an empty and abandoned room which was covered by an overgrown maple tree, which provided shade from the burning sun.

As we turned from the dining hall and continued on the country road, she pointed to a windowless hut in a state of disrepair with mud walls and a tiled roof, and she said while still in tears: "I was living in a place like that one. I repeated to myself every day: 'I shall not kill myself, I shall not lose my mind or go crazy, I will witness those who did me harm die before me, I shall live. I shall live no matter what!'" Then she cast another gaze at the hut and said: "I was terrified. See? Do you see it? There's nobody around. See how dark it is even in daylight? I *am* terrified. Do you know how dark it was at night? It's endless." I responded: "The night felt endless?" Yumei answered: "Everything . . . all of them. . . . The day is long, but I dreaded the night as well. . . . I don't know. *I'm terrified. I'm afraid of the dark* . . . and all alone . . . (it's) terrifying."

Because Chinese is a language indicating time with prepositions rather than with tenses, one can drop a time indicator at the beginning of a sentence and continue a narration without changing tenses. Given this characteristic, life story narrations in Chinese, especially in moments such as these, transforms expressions more like re-living the past than retrieving memories. Throughout Yumei's emotionally laden narration, it was hard to tell when she narrated the past, when traumatic emotions were emerging, and when she described how the suffering in the past influenced her life today.

Yumei's emotional breakdown lasted well into the night. During moments I was alone with her, I attempted to calm her down by initiating discussion or by encouraging narration. In between sobs, she said: "When I saw that dining place, it all came back to me. All the days and nights I spent here. I don't know . . . I don't know. . . . I'm not sure what to say. I cannot put it into words. I don't even know how to feel. I find it hard to get by (*nan guo*). Those (things) felt very real." I squeezed her hand, wanting to use this bodily contact to indicate that the moments with the team and with me were real as well. However, she did not respond to my gesture. Her hand laid soft and motionless in my palm, and she said: "I don't know what's real anymore."

A Place of Trauma

Yumei's intense emotions and her disorientation were clearly visible. Rooted in a bodily sensation of feeling dislocated in a site of ruin, what Yumei experienced was not only a re-living of traumatic emotions but also a fear of being trapped in time.[19] Entering the actual environment where one of the most traumatic experiences occurred during her early years, embodied emotions flooded Yumei in a serious episode of PTSD.[20] In addition to the buildings that served as a reminder of the past, her awareness of what was now missing from that particular site became a reminder of the years that had passed. What functioned as a trigger was not only the familiarity of a material space, but also the site which now appeared in ruins, which exacerbated the uncanny memory of ever-present suffering and the timelessness of hurtful feelings.[21] As the Sent-Down Team navigated through the half-abandoned village, their taking-in of the ruins produced another version of the same space, a space that reminded them not only of what had happened in the past, but also of what had been historically unclaimed.[22] The co-embodiment of a reproduced social space during their fortieth anniversary reunion allowed Yumei's unclaimed, individually embodied past trauma to be witnessed by her team members for the first time. This invested the space with an additional dose of meaning, this time the ruins, rather than the institution that had been located there in the past.

This unclaimed, under-discussed, and underrepresented experience created a traumatic experience as Yumei, as social actor, was trapped between the immediate sensations of seeing the ruins and dealing with the present. The most salient feature of a post-traumatic outburst is a strong sense of disorientation when Yumei re-traced the tracks she once covered on a daily basis but which she refused to look back to, discuss, or embody for a period of forty years. For Yumei, the forty years between her early adulthood and her later life as a successful entrepreneur in a changed world had created a void. Her intense disorientation and the bodily sensation of feeling dislocated from the here and now is typical when encountering sites of trauma, as she met the material environment that she had defined as a site of despair and torture. Trauma studies scholars have pointed out that both the presence of familiar sights (e.g., the kitchen and the pig pen) and the absence of significant elements (e.g., the office of the production team, the field that was now uncultivated) can create a profound disruption of our orientation toward the past and the future. Because of the profound difference between her life at Happiness Field and her life during the Reform Era, the experiential disconnect between Yumei's embodiment of her farm life and her later urban life created an emotional and cognitive gap that interrupted her ability to form a coherent sense of self.

The emotional processes described above all shared the same material space, yet the ruins and the site of trauma caused a constant mismatch between the site as mentally comprehended and the sit as emotionally perceived. On top of that, their intercorporeality of the time while they were Sent-Down Youth and their co-embodiment at the moment of witnessing Yumei's emotional breakdown reconstructed the site of ruin as well, as the repressed memories came to the surface. This experience caused a clash between the past and an immediate, on-going experience of being-in-the-world, occupying this space at a moment-to-moment pace.[23] However, I realize that beyond the sensations of disorientation and trauma, these complex processes of co-embodiments were also processes of claiming previously unclaimed trauma.

Jianguo

Jianguo was deeply concerned about Yumei's emotional breakdown. Not used to explicitly expressing or articulating his emotions, he followed Yumei around throughout the trip, busied himself with getting her water, offering her food, and, most of the time, mumbling comforting and encouraging words that were genuine but incoherent. Jianguo served as the driver, guide, and organizer of the trip. It was interesting to see that he occupied the leader's role, which mirrored the one he had played back when he was only sixteen years old and when he was the "captain" of Team Three immediately after graduating from middle school. Interestingly, although he was worried by Yumei's emotional state and offered to accompany her back to the city, it was Yumei who insisted that they continue the visit to see the entire village and the surrounding fields. Occasionally, he voiced regrets about taking Yumei and other team members on this trip. He stated: "If I ever knew you would be so heartbroken, I would not have taken you here. We were here before, all of us shed tears during our twentieth anniversary, but I didn't anticipate this trip to be so traumatic."

For Jianguo, the journey across the countryside was mostly nostalgic. He was very considerate about Yumei's emotional breakdown and was shocked, because it was the first time that he learned about Yumei's mistreatment. "I always knew that she was from the 'bad family' back then. But I never put any thought to that. I grew up in a community where there were a lot of engineers, scientists, and scholars who became targets of class struggle during the Cultural Revolution. However, they were and always had been just my uncles and aunties who worked with my parents." Class struggle and targeted families from other social classes influenced every family in Changsha city, where he was from. There had been violence and persecution on a daily basis. However, Jianguo's family maintained a traditional perspective by treating others as if they were semi-kinship members. He was educated by his parents to respect those who were knowledgeable. On a personal level, he was shielded from direct exposure to violent class struggle because he was a child from a nurturing, humanistic family. On a social level, his own family was of the proletarian class, so he was spared institutional violence and did not experience any discrimination. This resulted in a very different experience as compared to Yumei, even though they lived in the same physical space for at least ten years. Though Yumei and Jianguo had not met after Jianguo got a promotion when he was nineteen and left for a middle school teacher training college in a nearby county, their reunion brought back mutual bonding and friendship. The then fifteen-year-old was hand-picked to be a student leader by the teachers of his middle school based on his family background (all his family members were workers in suburban Changsha) and his outstanding performance in school, which, he pointed out to me, had nothing to do with academic prowess but only to his dedication to the "collective course." During their conversations on co-remembering their Sent-Down experience, prior to our arrival at the site and Yumei's emotional breakdown, I noticed differences between the way Jianguo and Yumei's described their experience and suffering. Jianguo maintained a positive attitude toward his Sent-Down experience as well as toward almost all of his team members, saying that their bonds were "pure" because of their young age. He also accepted the fact that he had not been able to choose a career when he had the chance to enter a college as a recommended Sent-Down member, something Yumei could not have dreamt of. "It definitely was not ideal that they sent me to a county school, but I had a good time and did receive some solid education. I never thought people or cadres were against me. I just accepted things and put an effort in whenever I could," Jianguo stated. "Even back then, I considered Yumei to be a very positive and aspiring young woman. She was three years older than me, so I sort of looked up to her. As the leader of the team, I learned about her family background. I knew that her parents were imprisoned during the anti-right campaign in 1956 and that she lived with her uncle's family as an adopted daughter. I never learned about how unfairly she was treated." He then said that he doubted his decision and enthusiasm to take Yumei on this trip. "I thought that it would be healthy for her to re-connect and, you know, . . . *turn this page*. I knew the Sent-Down experience was hard for her, but I did not know about the trauma she experienced after I was gone. I feel bad to drag her through all this."

When Jianguo and I were walking through the hilly village, his expression toward the changing landscape was very different than Yumei's emotional meltdown. He is currently a traditional Chinese garden designer and architect; not surprisingly, his visual-spatial sense and the accuracy of his memories were outstanding. He remembered clearly which field had which function back in the 1970s, even though most fields were now abandoned. We passed by houses and semi-ruined huts like the kitchen and the shed near a watermelon field. For Jianguo, these ruins served more as reminders of the passing of a youth that he could never return to. He recognized that urbanization constituted progress but could not help but think about the hard labor they had undertaken to make the farm a better place. "When you see all this, it must be very different from what I am seeing," he said as he pointed to the half-ruined little hut in the middle of the half-abandoned watermelon field. Urbanization had been so fast-paced that only seniors and children were left behind in the countryside. Most parts of the mountainous area of the Eternal County now derived their income from summer retreats instead of agriculture. "What are you seeing besides what I'm looking at?" I asked. "You must see a boring, backward ruin of a countryside," he said as both of us looked at the horizon. He was pointing to the place where the mountains seemed to cut the outside world off. "I am contemplating the youth we can never go back to, and this land stripped of any testimony of our labor and younger years. After we die, nobody will ever know what happened here." At that moment, the temporal aspects of our experiences—Jianguo's past and his identification of the spatial difference between now and then, Yumei's trauma and the clashing cognitive dissonance between what she recalled and what she was seeing, and my first-time exposure to this place while also bearing witness to their co-remembrance—overlapped with each other in the same physical space. For an instant that seemed to last forever, all of us were gazing to the horizon from the same point in time and space while seeing the same scene of ruin through very different filters, which determined our varied experience, knowledge, and purpose. In the quiet, hot afternoon everything seemed to be a framed picture. As Jianguo indicated, we were all history, and we were living in a moment that was transcendental and a space filled with memory.

One important purpose of this anniversary was to go on a trip as a sort of testimony to what had happened. Testimony therapy is a form of psychological intervention during which victims of trauma or torture narrate and address their experiences in front of others to attain proof, affirmation, and healing from their survival.[24] Even though they shared a perceived space, their lived space was vastly different because of their different family backgrounds and their varied experience during and after their Sent-Down years.[25] Individuals who were from "better" families, like Jianguo, expressed that, even during their Sent-Down years, they always knew that they would return to an urban area sooner or later. They had family support and were never in marginalized or isolated social positions. For Yumei, the ruins reminded her of the despair she experienced when she was trapped in a place that was like an ever-lasting exile, while for Jianguo it was a place of transition, which he interpreted as one of many life events he could not prevent but would nonetheless not regret. This reunion and co-experience of trauma, therefore, was as meaningful for Jianguo as it was for Yumei, for it not only re-established their mutual trust and friendship, but also enabled them to fully grasp what that period of history meant to all different participants. In a way, they were bearing witness to each other's unclaimed past.

Once this testimony was completed, a new present in time and space was established by their co-experience and emotional processing as they walked through the shared, physical space. Their presence at the site reshaped and redefined their lived space and the memory that went with that space. Although their trip was voluntary, its psychological effect was close to what testimony therapy can bring to trauma victims. The politically privileged faced the trauma of history and witnessed its occurrence. The marginalized and persecuted were able to reshape their memories of mutual trust and the absence of hostility, even back in the heated revolutionary years. As Yumei later commented in her narration: "It was comforting to know that they never looked down upon me, and it was even more reassuring to know that they never will."

Meiling

Meiling was the only person who had kept in close contact with Yumei. Although they had lost contact after Yumei moved to Shanghai in the early 2000s, they had frequently visited each other after all members of their *Zhiqing* cadre school came back to urban Changsha. After the reunion trip, they swiftly resumed their tight bond and remained in a relationship that was as close as those of family members. Meiling indicated that she had always saw Yumei as her big sister when they shared a dorm room during their Sent-Down years, and even took Yumei to her home for Chinese New Year when she was not welcome in her uncle's household. Among all the team members, Meiling maintained a very neutral attitude toward her Sent-Down experience: "Our generation has seen a lot, but it was not as horrible as going through the civil war as my parents' generation did, nor was it as competitive and ruthless as what my daughter's generation is going through." When I asked her about how she maintained a calm, spontaneous, and oftentimes humorous attitude as she was going through all these transitions, she said: "You see, there is the difference between people like Yumei and me. Yumei was smart and aspiring, but very insecure due to her childhood experience. Meanwhile, I grew up in a steady household and was content with being simple and ordinary."

Meiling's claim sounded true among the *Zhiqing* who were younger when they started the Sent-Down journey. Middle-school graduates joined Sent-Down groups when they were sixteen, while high-school graduates had spent many years wanting to go college only to have their dreams crushed when the Revolution descended into chaos and all universities were closed. For people like Meiling, who grew up in a civil servant's household, being a Sent-Down Youth was the first time that she had had a full stomach: "I had five siblings and only my father had a salary. My mother worked long hours to do handcraft jobs when she had the chance. Our family had always struggled to put a decent meal on the table." Although she also visited the farm for the first time, Meiling stayed close and comforted Yumei as much as she could, which reversed their adolescent roles of care-taking big sister and younger sibling. She stated: "I never had any interest in coming back and visiting here. I am only here because of Yumei. I knew this would be hard for her." When she learned about the unjust treatment Yumei had received, Meiling concluded that for Yumei, the Sent-Down experience was a series of unfortunate events at a personal, familial and social level. While we were visiting the village, she recalled both happy scenarios and horrifying moments. When I asked which Sent-Down experience had influenced her most in later life, we were passing the river that was the only waterway leading from the mountain regions. "My life is just like a small river," she said, "without any major raising or drops. Everything that happened in my life is like nature. People have entered and left my life, I had happy times and sorrowful moments. I felt content or in pain, or I echo other

FIGURE 8.2. Sent-Down Youth's Dorm at the Happiness Field Cadre School. Image taken on August 21, 2017. © Hua Wu.

people's joy or pain. All this is how it was meant to be. My younger brother and I were the only two children who were Sent Down, because half of our family's offspring had to go. It turned out that we were able to secure better jobs then my youngest siblings who stayed in Changsha. So, you never know."

We walked alongside the river, hearing Yumei's broken sobs. Meiling had tears in her eyes and said: "This is *Ming* (fate).[26] You realize that some major changes had to happen in your life and that there is no use resisting them." When I asked her to elaborate, she pinched me in the arm and teased: "I have not read enough books to explain such things! That is the job of scholars like you. I only know that the only boundary one has the right to maintain is that of your own body. Go with the flow!" She pointed to the river that vanished into the horizon: "the more relaxed you are, the less chance you're going to drown."

FIGURE 8.3. Visiting Old Town Center at the Happiness Field Cadre School. Image taken on August 21, 2017. © Hua Wu.

It is interesting to see that team members like Jianguo and Meiling tended to attribute the root of Yumei's trauma to her own personal misfortune, especially the domestic violence and mistreatment she suffered by her adopted families, while members of non-proletarian families were more likely to attribute her suffering to structural violence such as political persecution and unclaimed historical disaster. Aside from the different political positions all of these marginalized people occupied, we also see a significant difference in their mode of body-world interaction based on the surfacing of memory and emotion as they revisited the site. Instead of viewing part of her body as trapped in the traumatic site where time and space had frozen into a solid, dark moment as Yumei did, Meiling was able to maintain a constant, stable sense of self and body-boundaries as she saw her own self navigating from one environment to another. We should not see Meiling's orientation toward the world as passive, because she was able to utilize her agency and actively construct meaningful social relationships across different situations. As compared to Yumei, the former Happiness Field Cadre

School was a site of significant personal history, which definitely contained suffering but was not traumatic. Meiling also avoided looking back for forty years. However, her personal history did not become a cognitive void but rather existed on the periphery of her awareness, heavily weighing on her conscious yet not dragging her down.

Conclusion

From a phenomenological point of view, we can view space as having a dialectic triad feature: (1) the material aspects constructed by perception; (2) conceptually comprehended geometrical space, which in the case of the visiting Sent-Down Youth exists in their narration and life stories; and (3) the lived space in the unconsciousness and dreams, where looping time trapped the past self in unclaimed trauma. For Sent-Down Youth such as Yumei, the ruins of the farm were a space filled with unclaimed trauma. However, as supportive teammates pointed out, her encounter with the farm, her tears and emotional breakdown, and the fact that she reconnected with her friends created a co-embodiment and thus transformed these friends into witnesses to her suffering. Through their reunion and renewed social bonding, she not only was able to free herself from past trauma but also expanded the possibilities of herself as she entered the aging period in her life course. Bearing witness as a meaningful social group forty years after their traumatic experience ended broke the spell of the looping pain and freed the body from a lived yet inexpressible space, allowing her body to enter a new rhythm during which new social connections could be established. Time, in a way, started to flow again after her visit in that quiet afternoon. One year after the trip, I followed up with Yumei and some of her teammates. She had taken another trip to the farm, and this time she experienced no negative emotions at all. As her team member said: "the page was turned."

This ethnographic encounter was an attempt to understand historical transitions and trauma by focusing not only on the temporal aspect of experiences but also on the space where these experiences took place. In the case of the group of the former Sent-Down Youth visiting the farm in the summer of 2008, a space marking massive dislocation, functioned not only as an objective, physical site occupied by these Sent-Down Youth for a period of time, but also as a site of significant memories. Energized by the virtually supernatural strength that these social actors had mustered in living through their experience and then facing them again in the present, space was transformed first from a foreign site into a living habitat and political struggle, and, later, into an uncanny and haunting site of ruin that silently constituted a form of physical testimony for their historical trauma and struggle.[27] Then, finally, with a joint effort, co-embodiment and mutual witnessing, this space was once again transformed into a witness of unclaimed history.[28]

As I was writing up my project and contacted most of the team members two years later, they all maintained close contact with each other, and commented that this shared bond had been a great source of comfort in their lives. Yumei indicated that after her traumatic emotional breakdown in the Eternal County, she was no longer haunted by the nightmare of being stuck in the pig pen in the dark. She quoted what Meiling used to comfort her: "It was curious but I think I really turned the page. Now my friendship with Jianguo, Meiling, and many others were like the family I never had. We had such thorough understanding and helped each other out through some very difficult turns and we still will." Jianguo was accomplishing quite a few projects as an architect. Throughout the precarious and difficult times of the COVID pandemic, he often called on Yumei and other team members for emotional support. Meiling invited Yumei to her household whenever Yumei visited Hunan Province and added her to their family WeChat group. The Sent-Down experience was no longer an often brought-up topic since they now shared many new aspects in their lives.

Another interesting point that may stimulate future discussions on the understanding of body, space, and the history of trauma is the significant social gesture of my participants' constant effort to bring me into their co-embodiment throughout our trip. Growing up during the Reform Era, my urban upbringing and Western education highlighted my role as an outsider. However, my indirect, "bookish" knowledge of history and my interest in their stories allowed them to treat me as some sort of protégé. My presence, in some way, also bore witness to their history. The sense of timelessness was extremely salient as we visited a small museum dedicated to a Tang dynasty poet who wrote influential articles and poetry when he was exiled to the same county. The participants' empathy toward him during his exile that occurred a thousand years ago allowed them to articulate poetic expressions of their own existential tension.[29] In Asian culture, a continual relationship between the people and the land renews at every turning point of history, empowering one with an enlarged perspective on one's own life experience. The space of trauma provided the social actors with a powerful gaze onto both the past and the future and in the process turned the same space into a site of human resilience. The museum, the story of the Tang poet, and the reminder of the deep historical past were rich, culturally resonant symbols that allowed the spatial schemas to transcend personal experience and to serve as resources for psychological healing and new meanings of life.[30]

Hua Wu (Miranda) is a Ph.D. candidate in Psychological and Medical Anthropology at the University of California at San Diego. Her research interest includes mental health and the intergenerational experience of life transitions in Mainland China, the phenomenology of life experience, life course studies, the anthropology of the body, emotional experience and expression in East Asian context, and global mental health. Her dissertation, "Where Do I Place My Body and Heart:

Embodiment and Emotional Experience across Personal and Historical Transitions in Modern China," investigates emotional experience, health management, and the understanding of somatic and mental health across several generations in China. Miranda is also interested in the temporal-spatial aspects of everyday experiences, especially as people go through personal and social changes. She also collaborates with the Fudan-University of California Center at UCSD and Fudan University's anthropological team to explore the culturally shaped experience of mental health and subjective well-being in Shanghai.

Notes

1. Wang Yougui, "Wo Men Zhe Yi Bei" (Our Generation), 9 June 2017. Chinese Pop QQ Music.
2. Rene, *China's Sent-Down Generation*.
3. Zhou and Hou, "Children of the Cultural Revolution."
4. Deng and Treiman, "Impact Cultural Revolution."
5. Hung and Chiu, "Lost Generation."
6. Jørgensen and Schierup, *Politics of Precarity*.
7. Trigg, "Place Trauma."
8. Csordas, *Body, Meaning, Healing*.
9. See Kidron, "Toward an Ethnography of Silence" and Kidron, "Embodied Legacies of Genocide" on survivors of the Holocaust and their descendants' everyday life under the influence of transgenerational historical trauma. On the cross-generational experience and resilience of Australian Aboriginals see Herring et al., "Intersection Trauma, Racism, Cultural Competence."
10. Kleinman and Kleinman, "Suffering and its Professional Transformation."
11. Rene, *Public Administration*; and Zhou and Hou, "Children of the Cultural Revolution."
12. Hung and Chiu, "Lost Generation."
13. One of the most violent cases was the 1967 Daoxian Massacre in Hunan province. In his study of one specific massacre site, Hecheng Tan counts up to 4,509 deaths due to conflicts between local peasants, Red Guard groups, and Army forces. See Tan, *Killing Wind* 21–2.
14. Rene, *China's Sent-Down Generation*.
15. Tan, *Killing Wind*.
16. Lin, "Lost in Transformation?"
17. Deng and Treiman, "Impact Cultural Revolution."
18. See Chapter 5 of Rene, *China's Sent-Down Generation*.
19. Trigg, "Place Trauma."
20. Eleftheriou, "Bodies like Rivers."
21. Trigg, *Memory Place*.
22. Caruth, *Unclaimed Experience*.
23. Csordas, *Body, Meaning, Healing*.
24. Bichescu et al., "Narrative Exposure Therapy."

25. See Hess, "'Facilitating States,'" for an ethnographic assessment of the effects of Testimony Therapy for refugees and asylum seekers in the United States. On psychotherapeutic interventions with individuals who have had traumatic experiences and on using testimony therapy with victims of violence, see Van Dijk, Schoutrop, and Spinhoven, "Testimony Therapy."
26. The idea of *ming*, loosely translate into fate, fortune, and chance as in the interaction between personal choice, individual's life span, and the historical transitions one goes through. See Lupke, *Magnitude Ming*.
27. Grosz, *Space, Time and Perversion*.
28. Ng, "Toni Morrison's Beloved."
29. Bachelard, *The Poetics of Space*.
30. Garcia, *Pastoral Clinic*.

Bibliography

Bachelard, Gaston. *The Poetics of Space*. Translated by Maria Jolas. London: Penguin, 1958.

Bichescu, Dana, Frank Neuner, Maggie Schauer, and Thomas Elbert. "Narrative Exposure Therapy for Political Imprisonment-Related Chronic Posttraumatic Stress Disorder and Depression." *Behaviour Research and Therapy* 45, no. 9 (2007): 2212–20.

Caruth, Cathy. *Unclaimed Experience: Trauma, Narrative, and History*. Baltimore, MD: Johns Hopkins University Press, 1996.

Csordas, Thomas J. *Body, Meaning, Healing*. New York: Palgrave Macmillan, 2002.

Deng, Zhong, and Donald J. Treiman. "The Impact of the Cultural Revolution on Trends in Educational Attainment in the People's Republic of China." *American Journal of Sociology* 103, no. 2 (1997): 391–428.

Eleftheriou, Lyda. "Bodies like Rivers: Seeking for a Space for Body Memory in the Discourse of Trauma." *European Journal of English Studies* 19, no. 3 (2015): 315–30.

Garcia, Angela. *The Pastoral Clinic: Addiction and Dispossession along the Rio Grande*. Berkeley: University of California Press, 2010.

Grosz, Elizabeth. *Space, Time and Perversion: Essays on the Politics of the Bodies*. New York: Routledge, 1995.

Herring, Sigrid, Jo Spangaro, Marlene Lauw, and Lorna McNamara. "The Intersection of Trauma, Racism, and Cultural Competence in Effective Work with Aboriginal People: Waiting for Trust." *Australian Social Work* 66, no. 1 (2013): 104–17.

Hess, Sabine. "'We Are Facilitating States!': An Ethnographic Analysis of the ICMPD." In *The Politics of International Migration Management*, edited by Martin Geiger and Antoine Pécoud, 96–118. London: Palgrave Macmillan, 2010.

Hung, Eva P. W., and Stephen W. K. Chiu. "The Lost Generation: Life Course Dynamics and Xiagang in China." *Modern China* 29, no. 2 (2003): 204–336.

Jørgensen, Martin Bak, and Carl-Ulrik Schierup. *Politics of Precarity: Migrant Conditions, Struggles and Experiences*. Leiden: Brill, 2016.

Kidron, Carol A. "Embodied Legacies of Genocide." In *A Companion to the Anthropology of the Body and Embodiment*, edited by Frances E. Mascia-Lees, 451–66. Chichester: Wiley-Blackwell, 2011.

———. "Toward an Ethnography of Silence: The Lived Presence of the Past in the Everyday Life of Holocaust Trauma Survivors and Their Descendants in Israel." *Current Anthropology* 50, no. 1 (2009): 5–27.

Kleinman, Arthur, and Joan Kleinman. "Suffering and its professional transformation: Toward an ethnography of interpersonal experience." *Culture, Medicine and Psychiatry* 15, no. 3 (1991): 275–301.

Lin, Qianhan. "Lost in Transformation? The Employment Trajectories of China's Cultural Revolution Cohort." *The Annals of the American Academy of Political and Social Science* 646, no. 1 (2013): 173–93.

Lupke, Christopher. *The Magnitude of Ming: Command, Allotment, and Fate in Chinese Culture.* Honolulu: University of Hawai'i Press, 2005.

Ng, Andrew Hock Soon. "Toni Morrison's Beloved: Space, Architecture, Trauma." *Symplokē* 19, no. 1/2 (2011): 231–45.

Rene, Helena K. *China's Sent-Down Generation: Public Administration and the Legacies of Mao's Rustication Program.* Washington, DC: Georgetown University Press, 2013.

———. *Public Administration and the Legacies of Mao's Rustication Program.* Washington, DC: Georgetown University Press, 2013.

Tan, Hecheng. *The Killing Wind: A Chinese County's Descent into Madness during the Cultural Revolution.* Translated from the Chinese by Stacy Mosher and Guo Jian. Oxford: Oxford University Press, 2016.

Trigg, Dylan. *The Memory of Place: A Phenomenology of the Uncanny.* Athens, OH: Ohio University Press., 2012.

———. "The Place of Trauma: Memory, Hauntings, and the Temporality of Ruins." *Memory Studies* 2, no. 1 (2009): 87–101.

Van Dijk, Janie A., Mirjam J. A. Schoutrop, and Philip Spinhoven. "Testimony Therapy: Treatment Method for Traumatized Victims of Organized Violence." *American Journal of Psychotherapy* 57, no. 3 (2003): 361–73.

Zhou, Xueguang, and Liren Hou. "Children of the Cultural Revolution: The State and the Life Course in the People's Republic of China." *American Sociological Review* 64, no. 1 (1999): 12–36.

Chapter 9

PERFORMING SONGS AS HEALING THE TRAUMA OF THE 1965 ANTI-COMMUNIST KILLINGS IN INDONESIA

Dyah Pitaloka and Mohan J. Dutta

> The stigma attached to the PKI [Partai Komunis Indonesia; Indonesian Communist Party] has ripped away our social, political and cultural rights as human beings. Children grow up in fear and live with pain, carrying the stigma of the PKI for the rest of their lives. The families of the survivors have never received any trauma recovery treatment. This choir became a "safe space" for survivors and the families of the victims to share their pain. Singing and telling stories give us hope and strength to reach for the future, our future.
>
> —Uchi, speech on receiving the 2019 Gwangju Prize for Human Rights[1]

On Saturday, 18 May 2019, the Dialita choir—a group of survivors of the 1965 tragedy in Indonesia—was awarded the 2019 Gwangju Prize for Human Rights for "showing the path to reconciliation and healing through music." In her speech notes, which were shared on Dialita's Facebook page, Uchi recognized the suffering that community members have endured throughout the years and their struggle to regain their dignity as humans. Theirs was not a case of instant fame. For Uchi and the members of Dialita choir, everything started with the small hope that a community of survivors would be able to listen to and support each other. Today, Dialita is a more than just a choir. It has become a movement.

We started this study with many doubts and one big question: "How would the survivors of the 1965 communist purge ever be able to alter and replace mainstream discourse on the events of 1965?" In the years following the 1965 revolt, state discourse has framed this event as an instance of military heroism and triumph over the PKI. The emphasis of this dominant discourse, which has been upheld by the state-military apparatus, was on the murder of seven generals that were attributed to the PKI. Much less attention has been paid to the concurrent organized military operations that killed between 500,000 and 2 million Indonesians, tortured and raped many more, and incarcerated a large number of Indonesians without trial.[2] Younger generations, born long after 1965, have grown up reading history textbooks that portray Communists as "accustomed" to violence, evil, murder, and treachery. Indeed, many of these youths have grown up watching the (state-sponsored) film *The Treachery of the September 30 PKI Movement* (*Pengkhianatan G30S/PKI*), which glorifies Suharto's military power, his defense of the Indonesian nation, and the eradication of the PKI and its followers "down to its roots" (*sampai ke akar-akarnya*). The documentary film has been broadcast by the state-owned network (TVRI) for more than two decades since its release in 1984. For more than fifty years, Suharto's New Order regime has successfully detached the mass killings of 1965 from the social and political history of Indonesia and has employed the notion of "1965" as a latent threat (*bahaya laten*) of betrayal and anti-nationalism.

The Dialita Choir: Voices of the Silenced

Formally established in 2011, the Dialita choir is a group of elderly women bound together by their history and collective suffering. Currently, the choir has twenty members, comprised of former political prisoners, as well as those whose parents, relatives, and friends have been captured, tortured and exiled during the 1965/1966 communist purge in Indonesia. These women—wives, mothers, daughters, sisters—share a traumatic story of loss in which children were separated from their parents, parents lost their children, husbands lost wives, wives lost husbands, brothers lost sisters, and sisters lost brothers.

Dialita was not a choir from its outset. These women survivors first formed an organization called Mother and Child Care Community, or Komunitas Peduli Ibu dan Anak (KPIA), and focused on raising funds for fellow survivors—especially the elderly survivors—who suffered from illness or were in otherwise difficult conditions. Some of these KPIA members had, in the 1950s and early 1960s, been active in the Happy (*Gembira*) Singing and Dancing Ensemble, which collected funds by selling used clothing and goods.[3] Unable to earn much from this activity, women in the KPIA had the idea to form a vocal group for the purpose of securing additional funds. As many of the founding members were more than fifty years old, these women named their vocal group Dialita, which stands for *Di Atas Lima Puluh Tahun* (Over Fifty Years Old). Their founding

FIGURE 9.1. Dialita Concert *Songs of Survivors*. Taman Ismail Marzuki, Jakarta, 13 December 2017. © Dyah Pitaloka.

was announced on 4 December 2011, during a scheduled KPIA event at a small *kampong* in Bogor, West Java.

Uchi, currently the head of Dialita, has explained that in the first few years after their formation, the main focus of the choir was on providing support to fellow victims of the 1965 purges because they were facing tremendous struggles, challenges, suffering, and trauma. In those early years, some women activists who heard about Dialita (which at this time only had around eight to ten members) helped promote the choir to organizations or NGOs, after which Dialita began to receive invitations to sing at various events such as discussions, book launches, or seminars. The money collected in this manner was delivered directly to those in need.

In their early days, the Dialita choir did not perform prison songs, instead turning to pop songs or national songs that their audience would be familiar with. The process of collecting, memorizing, and re-arranging prison songs, for which the choir is well-known today, did not take place until recently. In 2000, Tati, a former political prisoner who is also a member of the Dialita choir, began writing down her memories and rewriting the songs that she and other fellow prisoners had composed while incarcerated. To date, Tati has collected about thirty songs, and some of them are regularly performed and included in Dialita's CDs. These silenced songs had long been forgotten; they were buried alongside unspoken stories of struggle for survival.

In 2015, the Dialita choir had an opportunity to reach out to young audiences at the Biennale Jogja XIII. Uchi described how the members of the choir felt anxious about performing for younger generations of Indonesians as they would be unfamiliar with their songs. "These prison songs are old, outdated, and, honestly, do not really fit young people's taste," Uchi said. She added: "We feel a bit anxious, a group of old women wearing *kebaya* singing songs about struggle and determination, will they listen to us?" The Biennale Jogja became a turning point for the Dialita choir because the event provided it with the opportunity to make their existence known to a wider public.

Dialita's first album, *The World is Ours* (*Dunia Milik Kita*), tells stories of solidarity. Their performance at Biennale Jogja had a profound impact on the young people in the audience, who came to collaborate with choir members in re-arranging these prison songs, in producing and recording the *Dunia Milik Kita* album, and in assisting its launch in 2016. Dialita's music penetrates the everyday discursive space, interrupts the dominant narrative of the events in 1965, and compiles a tangible record of a long-forgotten history.

Transforming Public and Private Experiences

It was 3:30 p.m. and I was at Tati's house with Uchi and Puji, both Dialita members. I had never heard about the choir and their songs, but I came with the assumption that these would be sad songs about the suffering and pain experienced by the community of survivors. I had not imagined that observing Tati and Puji singing their song would be an act of seeing an image of bodies that exist in the margin, nor that Tati and Puji would use their bodies to negotiate their public identity, reclaiming their dignity, and making sense of their well-being.

Tati winks her left eye at Puji, who in turn laughs aloud, before singing their song. Tati tells me: "You will love this song *Mbak Dyah*. It's about a man who adores Puji."

> I picked this beautiful red rose for you, my dear
> I give it to you with all my heart, a symbol of love
> Night fall and the cool breeze brought together the fragrance of the red rose.
> You must become a rose, a witness to my loyal vow, my love to her.
> The day after tomorrow, you and I will be apart. Don't worry.
> The night will go away, morning will come, and our future will surely be bright.
>
> —Field notes, 22 March 2017

The song, *Mawar Merah* (red rose), is about two young people, Puji and a handsome electrician who worked at the Bukit Duri women's prison in Jakarta. The song was composed by Sri Katon, Puji's fellow prisoner. Sri and other fellow prisoners used to tease Puji because this romantic young man always left a red rose with a prison guard before he went home, asking that the guard give the rose to Puji. During a Dialita concert in December 2017, this song was re-interpreted by a young musician by the name of Junior Soemantri. He provided a new musical arrangement, incorporating a happy and melodious bossa nova twist popular among young people, which inspired many to dance. The stage, the dim light, Soemantri's voice, and his romantic gestures amazed audiences. Afterward, he made Puji blush by inviting her on stage and handing her a red rose.

Mawar Merah would have never been heard by the public had Tati not tried to recall the lyrics and melody. Puji would have never wanted to share this life episode with anyone had Tati not teased her incessantly about it. Remembering this wonderful short episode made both Tati and Puji laugh. "It was one of the funniest moments that we had in prison. He would steal a look at her, and her face turned red, haha," Tati said. "It was just *cinta monyet* (monkey love)," Puji defended herself, blushing, "we never actually dated each other . . . both of us were imprisoned, so [there was] no chance." This song, according to Tati, was meant to lift up Puji's spirit. "The 1965 tragedy took away her life," Tati said. "She was only seventeen, one of the youngest, and she had no idea why she was inside [prison]," Tati continued. The last line, "the night will go away, morning will come, and our future will surely be bright," offers hope, not only to Puji, but also to many others who lost their loved ones, missed out on first dates, and were separated from parents, spouses, and families. A few days after the concert, Puji said:

> It was a great performance, right?! That song demonstrates a sense of love and support from my fellow prisoners. There is hope at the end of the tunnel, and I believe that God never leaves me. Soemantri made it more romantic and I'm happy that young people love it. Can't you see, they're dancing?! This is not a sad story, it was story of love . . . that someone recognize me, that I exist.

Prison walls across the nation have cut many people (600,000 to 750,000, according to Greg Fealy)—including teenagers like the then seventeen-year-old Puji—off from their families.[4] Not knowing her crime and without a trial, Puji was forced to spend fourteen years of her young life in prison: six years in Bukit Duri women's prison in Jakarta, and eight years in Plantungan prison in Kendal, Central Java. From Erving Goffman's perspective, performances such as Soemantri's create spaces of interpretation that forge connections between survivors and their audience.[5] In the instance described here, the song's performance provides Puji with the space to share her story. *Mawar merah* became a resource for Puji, a means to creating a self as well as a collective identity. Through this song, the community of survivors are able to share stories about shattered relationships and wrecked families that were never included in the dominant state discourse of 1965. According to our interpretation, the actions taken by the audience at the end of the performance—hugging Puji and the members of the Dialita choir—serve to celebrate the choir's bravery and spirit, and reflect a moment of cultural integration, of belonging and unity.

Bodies at the Margin: Reclaiming Identity and Dignity

> All traumatic experiences are painful. But not all painful experiences are traumatic. I want to share my strengths and hopes with the younger generation so that they can live a better life. By having young generations understand the history, or for the descendants especially, their parents and grandparents' history, I hope that they will take the opportunity to educate others about the effects of the mass killings and torture to humanity.
>
> —Mukti, survivor

Stigma, prejudice, and marginalization damaged the survivors' lives and identities by denying their trauma, silencing their voices, and reducing the potential to create communicative spaces. In their seminal works, the sociologist Erving Goffman and social psychologist Gordon Allport each made the claim that that stigma and prejudice are complex phenomena that encompass individual experience, the interaction between non-marginalized and marginalized groups, and broader structural and social phenomena such as power relations, historical contingencies, community practices, and program/policy design.[6] Goffman defined stigma as "an attribute that links a person to an undesirable stereotype, leading other people to reduce the bearer from a whole and usual person to a tainted, discounted one."[7] "Lower beyond the lowest, poorer beyond the poorest," is how one of the survivors described the life that she and her family endured after her father was killed and her mother was imprisoned.

During Suharto's New Order, telling stories about the violence perpetrated by his authoritarian regime remained a secretive business. The ending of Suharto's New Order in 1998 gave the community of survivors an opportunity to speak out about the discrimination and injustices they had experienced. Mary Zurbuchen explained that various elements in society and the state have driven these changes, including the rise of human rights NGOs and international human rights campaigners, the interest of prominent figures in the stories of survivors, and an international acknowledgement of some ex-political prisoners (*eks-tapol*).[8] Memoirs and other literary texts on and by *eks-tapol*, such as Pramoedya Ananta

Toer's, flourished, and national media coverage increased. The launching of *Prison Songs, Nyanyian Yang Dibungkam* (songs that were silenced), which was initiated by the Taman 65 community members in July 2015, attracted support and attention, not only from human rights advocates and grassroots organizations, but also from young musicians who interpreted, re-arranged, recorded and sang them to the public. Since then, Indonesian prison songs from the 1960s and 1970s started to emerge on YouTube. Young musicians embraced the songs, singing them on TV, and talking about the 1965 mass killings.

In exploring the role of songs as trauma healing, we made use of the Culture-Centered Approach (CCA) as a theoretical framework for listening to stories and remembering pain. This approach offers a lens through which one can understand the kinds of erasure performed by the state, the military, and transnational capital structures, and for making audible the voices of subaltern communities.[9] Against the backdrop of the mass killings and the erasure of the voices of victims of the 1965–66 purges, the CCA suggests co-constructive strategies for listening that invert the dominant narrative circulated by those in positions of power.[10] In this chapter we argue that songs and performance offer community members a sense of agency through which they are able to transform their traumatic past into courses of action that are meaningful to them. Agency, in this context, is expressed as "everyday participation of community members in negotiating structures of silencing, and in actively working collectively to transform the unequal structures of voicing and participation."[11]

Memory, according to George Lipsitz, is both the unexpected and the desired revisiting of the past.[12] It is both voluntary and involuntary. Music, as Lipsitz further argues, helps people learn about place and displacement.

> Laments for lost places and narratives of exile and return often inform, inspire, and incite the production of popular music. Songs build engagement among audiences at least in part through references that tap memories and hopes about particular places. Intentionally and unintentionally, musicians use lyrics, musical forms, and specific styles of performance that evoke attachment to or alienation from particular places.[13]

Researchers have identified the fact that that music, singing, and other cultural techniques play an important role in helping communities recover from trauma. Sports, games, creative writing, and other forms of art-based therapies have proven to be effective means of dealing with the aftermath of traumatic events.[14] It is generally accepted that music may be a tool for peace. Events such as drumming workshops in Burundi encouraging reconciliation between young Hutu and Tutsi people,[15] the "Songs of Divine Love" spiritual concert in Beirut that bridged Islamic and Christian audiences,[16] and the Colombian musician Cesar López who has turned shotguns into guitars are examples of music being employed as an instrument for peace around the globe.[17] Music has also been used as a healing agent in contexts that do not involve trained music therapists, for example in the case of the survivors of post-election violence in Kenya in 2007. In this context, a community musician used music to recall and experience trauma, and incorporated humor into their work with survivors to help them deal with the distress associated with both the initial violence and the resulting displacement.

Tati describes Dialita songs as "an invitation" for others to learn about their stories and history and participate in a dialogue.

> It's like reading a book. You'll find happiness, love, sadness, and hope in the lyrics. Through songs, we honor our memories. The joy is to have people listening to our songs and learn about us, our stories, and what we are capable of doing. They can write their own conclusion . . . yah.

For Puji, the choir provides collective support and energy for its members.

> There's always time when we feel down, that life is unfair, and we are questioning "why did it happen to me?" "What did I do wrong?" But as soon as I see my friends and we practice [singing], I forget about my sadness. This is life, you have ups and down. Here [in the choir], I can be me. I love singing, and I love laughing with them . . . doing silly things. Hahaha!

The Culture-Centered Approach seeks out entry points for listening to the voices of survivors that have otherwise been erased and explores the creation of co-constructive spaces that may give a voice to subaltern rationalities and imaginations. In this chapter, we invite readers to experience not only Dialita's songs, but how audiences—especially those comprised of young people—interact with the various elements of Dialita performances and how these audiences co-construct alternative narratives about 1965. To date, the erasure of the voices of the survivors of the 1965 community (and their descendants) as well as the stigma associated with the PKI and those deemed communists have helped reproduce the conditions of subalternity and debilitate the members of this community.[18]

The discursive process by which the community of 1965 was labeled as "polluted," which fostered the creation of "otherness" (othering) in a society where the dominant in-group ("Us," the Self) constructed one or many dominated out-groups ("Them," the Other) was one which, by emphasizing difference—real or imagined—identities could be undermined and stigmatized, providing a motive for potential discrimination.[19] Dialita women give their audiences opportunities to make sense of such experiences and moments captured in their songs and "to translate" these encounters into alternative narratives of survival, inclusion, strength, and humanity. Narratives presented by Dialita help audiences understand the tragedy of 1965, which has been named the "bloodiest anti-communist purges of the twentieth century."[20] The banning of movie screenings, discussions, book launches, and cultural activities that challenge official narratives by the authorities serve as enduring forms of collective punishment that restrict the possibility of mobilization for the community of survivors. Jasbir Puar, in her groundbreaking book *The Right to Maim: Debility, Capacity, Disability*, disrupts the category of disability and uses the concept of "debility" to describe the bodily injury and social exclusion brought on by economic and political factors. Interrogating Israel's policies toward Palestine, she outlines how the State of Israel relies on liberal frameworks of disability to obscure and enable the mass debilitation of Palestinian bodies.[21] Here, we are borrowing her argument to understand the injustice and the debilitating structure of collective punishment that the community of 1965 survivors experienced through the denial of their trauma, the obstruction of access to trauma healing, the limitation of communicative spaces, and inequal access to public space and place. We take this analysis as a starting point to explore how Dialita negotiates this system of punishment through song performance.

We have explored the agentic capacity of the Dialita choir and their songs through a study of their performances and through in-depth conversations with its members. This research included learning about the song repertoire, and participating in Dialita's monthly practices and rehearsals. Engaging in this way has helped us gain an understanding of the contexts and meanings that the composer(s) and choir members wished to convey. Five Dialita performances were experienced and the interaction between the Dialita choir and their audiences was closely observed. It was possible to observe the creation of communicative spaces as well as the negotiations and interactions that occurred within these spaces. In January 2019, the opportunity arose to observe and engage in "Dialita and Youth": a dialogue session between the choir and young people. Multiple sensory elements, from tones, vocals, lyrics, stage decoration, movement, and colorful dresses worn by the performers, contribute to the strategy adopted by Dialita, and offer audiences the tools with which to co-construct the collective re-interpretation of official narratives.

Songs as Dialogical Spaces

Bright, colorful *kebayas* (traditional Indonesian women's dress) and sarongs have become a characteristic of the Dialita choir. The choir not only invites audiences to "listen" to their stories, but also engages them in dialogic encounters with its members and other gestures that force their gaze inward. Below is a short dialogue from a Dialita choir rehearsal.

> The group was trying to decide which color they should use for their performance at one of the arts and humanitarian events:

DIALITA MEMBER. "Shall we use red or purple, uuhm . . . which one is better?"

AUTHOR. "I would go with red, bright, full of spirit, but . . . I don't know. The song is *Mawar Merah* right? So, it'll match the song."

DIALITA MEMBER. "What about purple? I love red, but you know . . . people may say: "Communist choir group, no wonder they choose red, right, hahaha!"

DIALITA MEMBER. "Hahaha . . . nothing is wrong with red. It makes us younger . . ."

AUTHOR. "And pretty!!"

DIALITA MEMBER. "OK, let's go with red. It matches the sarong, see . . . it has red-golden details in it."

This extraordinary conversation demonstrates the negotiation of identities that the community of survivors, including Dialita members, continuously conduct in their everyday lives. In our opinion, this conversation illustrates the ways existing forms of cultural knowledge can be adapted to communicate otherwise hidden narratives of structural violence as experienced by the 1965 survivors. This group has been labeled as "other." The mere presence of these survivors, and the presence of symbols, such as the number sixty-five (65), associated with the PKI in public spaces, threaten and endanger what is considered the status quo by the political establishment. When Uchi was asked how community members responded to this persistent stigma around the PKI and the events of 1965, she explained:

> If you rely on conventional reconciliation, nothing will happen. The only way would be through cultural reconciliation. Through songs, we can reach out to the younger generation. We're racing with time, many of us have "gone" and we're already old. We don't want to scare young people with stories about blood and killings. People can learn about history, our struggle, our hope, our strength, and our quality and capability as humans from Dialita songs.

Written in Bukit Duri prison, the two songs "Tetap Senyum Menjelang Fajar" (Keep smiling before dawn) and "Salam Harapan" (Greetings of hope) were each composed as gifts for fellow women political prisoners to celebrate their birthdays. These songs represent faith, strength, and support, and indicate that there is always hope even in moments of greatest darkness. Tati, Puji, and Nona explain that life inside the prison was so painful and bitter that the joyous celebration of birthdays was considered by many to be inappropriate. Tati still remembers that, on one particular birthday morning, fellow female prisoners lined up in front of her cell with bunches of wildflowers freshly picked from the prison garden, and sang the following two songs:

> It's not a beautiful scented flower
> Or fragrant incense
> Only greeting comes with love
> That I give to you
> My wish for you my friend
> That you will stay strong
> Although hit by sunshine or rain
> Keep smiling before dawn.
>   ("Tetap Senyum Menjelang Fajar," free translation)

> As the morning sun rising
> Jasmine starts blooming
> Greetings of hope to you my dear friend
> I wish you well and happiness
> Like a rock in the middle of the ocean
> You must stand tall against the waves
> Keep rowing, we'll soon arrive in our beach of dreams.
>   ("Salam Harapan," free translation)

Imprisonment took away many important aspects of everyday life, including birthday celebrations. Without the presence of their loved ones—parents, siblings, friends—these women had to turn to each other for support to ensure that these important episodes in life would not go unnoticed. Although imprisonment had taken away their freedom, the songs suggest that imprisonment was unable to crush these women's spirit, courage, and hope. The first author received these two songs as a birthday gift—songs that allowed her to interrogate her knowledge and the hegemonic meanings of 1965-related discourse.[22] Black propaganda campaigns disseminated false memories about PKI women through state-documentary films (as noted above) and public monuments, such as the Crocodile Hole Monument (*Monumen Lubang Buaya*).[23] The state narrative labeled communist women as brutal, sadistic, and evil. Growing up with these state narratives, people were taught to think of Gerwani (an Indonesian women's organization) as responsible for the mutilation of the generals killed in the G30S coup attempt. It was only later that it became known that Gerwani was, in reality, a women's organization consisting of educated, politically conscious middle-class women who had been active before the start of the war.[24] Prior to realizing this, the word "Gerwani" used to engender feelings of fear and frightful images of communist women. From our field notes:

The most memorable moment for me was when the Dialita women or in Indonesian, "*Ibu-Ibu* Dialita," introduced me to their songs.[25] Uchi put it succinctly: "This is our birthday gift to you, my dear child. When you're in doubt or in the lowest level of your life, please remember these songs. Never give up hope, keep smiling and stay strong."

Uchi's voice represents the voice of strong women—women who deserve to be called *Ibu* (mother), women who had gone through hardship but who refused to surrender. Uchi's message inspires the direction of this chapter to co-construct inclusive narratives of the individuals encountered in the field. Through the lens of the Culture-Centered Approach, this dialogue with Uchi provides an access point to building relationships of solidarity with the community of survivors, engaging them in the co-creation of knowledge.[26]

The word *Ibu* echoes the structural violence that impacted the lives of the hundreds of thousands of people accused of having affiliations with the communists. Some of these were only children and teenagers who were parted from their mothers and families, displaced and forced to adopt new identities, forced to deny their parents and family names, and, finally, exiled. During conversations with Uchi, she discussed the pride she held in her parents, a topic she had not discussed before. During these conversations, she struggled to express this pride, as both her parents were imprisoned because of accusations of communist affiliation, and, as such, she struggled to reclaim some aspect of her dignity. The tragedy had scattered her family across the country, and Uchi had to live with her grandmother. She grew up without the presence of her parents whom she missed. Tati was taken away from her parents and family, and imprisoned without her parents' knowledge. The song *'Ibu'* (Mother) was composed in Bukit Duri prison a year after she arrived there. Her concern over the state of her mother grew during that time, and she frequently wondered whether her mother had been informed of her situation: that her daughter was a political prisoner. In the face of this uncertainty and with these feelings of longing for her mother, Tati decided to compose a song in her mind and memorize it.[27] She would not see her mother for another eleven years.

In December of 2017, Endah Widiastuti, a talented Indonesian ballad musician, sang the song at the Humanitarian Concert in Jakarta, emotionally engaging the audience with the story of the injustices that these young women had experienced.

> I always remember your true love
> Your eternal, sincere, and pure love
> I always remember your care and gentle touch, mother
> Your words and advice kept ringing in my ears
> I imagine your face, mother
> My wish for you, that you will stay healthy.
>   ("Ibu," free translation)

The song reverberates not only with notions of fortitude and resilience, but with sincere acceptance (*keihlasan*). Imagining and remembering their mother's love helped to fortify these political prisoners' hearts and inner feeling (*batin*), especially the younger prisoners, against the experience of their incarceration. Songs, according to Tati, helped women prisoners to control the unbearable emotions they held inside: "There were times when we really wanted to scream out loud, but we couldn't. Songs helped us control these emotions and brought relief to the heart." Songs became a source of support and a way to entertain each other in times of hardship and uncertainty.

Reclaiming Identity and Enacting Agency: A Source of Health

Tears, exclamations of joy, and other emotional responses shown by audiences during the performances of the Dialita choir reflect the way dialogue and listening comprise moments of being-in-conversation. William Rawlins describes that as "[s]peaking constituted by your listening matters only if you actually do hear, only if you allow the other person's voice and stories to reach you, to change you."[28] Voicing through their songs and narratives of love and hope, the Dialita choir interrogates structural and communicative absences, inequalities and injustices such as discrimination, criminalization, and stigmatization perpetuated by hegemonic authorities. For the survivors, performance sites are transformative spaces where victims can become survivors, and where individuals who have lived through hardship find both the language and the audience with which to fearlessly talk about trauma. For audience members, these transformative sites "mark a structural transformation that allows them to expose, to experience, to appreciate and to engage bodily with different voices about 1965."[29]

In May 2019, the Dialita choir was invited to appear on the popular Indonesian talk show "Kick Andy." In their interview, one young artist who had collaborated with the choir explained that the social stigma tied to the PKI and its members had not stopped her from learning their stories and collaborating with the choir: "It's no longer about politics, or ideology, it's about humanity." Songs have the potential to give a community of previously silenced survivors a voice, something that in itself suggests both an internal and external transformation, both the development of a voice within a person, and a "social echo and resonance that emerges from collective spaces that build meaningful conversation."[30]

For Dialita, performing songs involves the embodiment of a sense of agency or "the intrinsic ability of cultural members and their families, and communities to make sense of structures and contexts and tone chart out courses of action that are meaningful to them."[31] Agency is expressed in the everyday participation of community members in meaning-making, in negotiating their bodily experiences of pain, in negotiating structures of silencing, and in actively working as a collective to transform these unequal structures. For Dialita members, performing songs is understood as a way of creating dialogic spaces in which shared meanings can be co-created. The collaboration of the choir with young and talented Indonesian musicians provides evidence of how these dialogic spaces are co-created and how alternative narratives are co-constructed.

Participants also experienced songs to be a source of strength. Songs confer an ability to battle fear—as expressed by one of the choir members—and, as such, songs act as an entry point for the achievement of health and resilience. By performing songs that had been all but erased from the nation's memory for so long, the members of the choir embark on their trauma-healing journey not as victims, but as survivors. Asti, one of the members of the choir describes it as follows:

> If you still look at yourself as a victim, it means you allow the past to control your life. You will live in constant fear, feel isolated, and miss a chance to have your stories heard. Being a victim means you are haunted by the past, always feeling scared and depressed. My life changed, singing makes me feel healthier. I make friends and I stop crying.

Performing songs help Dialita members to reclaim their dignity and to reconstruct their identities. Encounters and collaborations with young Indonesian musicians instill confidence. The boundaries between performers and their audience dissolves as audience members become "performers" of stories during their encounter with the survivors and the engagement with their hopes, dreams, aspirations, and imaginations. From the perspective of the theater of the oppressed, these engagements "rehearse action towards real social change."[32] Themes such as love, friendship, romance, and children, and imagery such as that of gardens, draw the audience's attention to sites of oppression, discrimination and injustice, assisting audiences in making sense of what happened to these 1965 survivors. Singing, as Uchi said, provides a safe and comfortable space for the choir members. It allows them to experience, identify, and express emotions and feelings in safe and manageable ways.[33]

Keeping Hope in a Marginalized World: Community Strategies for Trauma Healing

From the perspective of the Culture-Centered Approach, culture refers to shared values and practices that connect people within spaces and offers "recipes" for action. It is (re-)constituted through everyday interactions between community members—in this case, a community of 1965 survivors—and provides a framework for understanding suffering and trauma as well as strategies to heal. The survivors of the Acehnese conflict, as described by Catherine Smith, transformed their suffering into a strength by building a "new politics of care" in a post-conflict society.[34] In responding to trauma, both Acehnese women and Dialita women agree that crying, complaining, and emphasizing suffering will not solve their problems. Dialita women recount sensibilities such as strength, positive energy, solidarity, bravery, and the importance of fortitude in dealing with past traumatic events, and reframe their experiences as positive by fueling their everyday performance. "Today," Uchi said, "the Dialita choir members sing to support fellow survivors as well as for self-healing. Our songs convey a message of peace and solidarity, in the hope that it will educate the country about its forgotten past, in particular the younger generation."

Uchi and the other women survivors are no longer focused on the past, or on past suffering. Instead, their focus is on the future and how their songs can alter public perceptions of 1965 and those who survived the purge and its aftermath. Their source of strength, based on our observations and interviews, is their memories. "We want people to be able to connect our stories with their everyday life experiences—not with something that they cannot relate to," Tati explains. "We have trauma, but . . . we could never claim that, and we don't want to continue to linger on those pains." She adds that "we want people to see our ability and capability, our energy, to make change . . . to create a better future for our children." Here, Puji adds: "yeah, that we are also precious." The sensitive nature of these issues, and the deep-rooted stigma surrounding those accused of being affiliated with communism, has created boundaries that distanced the public from the community of survivors. Dialita choir members share a collective trauma born of mass killings and other state- and military-initiated atrocities. However, by their own description, they choose to articulate positive memories and, in doing so, liberate themselves.

For these survivors, the practice of singing becomes a strategy to express verbally the embodied emotions. However, in this study we have also argued that songs can play a powerful role in promoting social connections and a sense of solidarity. Performing songs challenges the broader structural, social, and cultural conditions in which individual survivors find themselves constructed as "other." Audiences, moved by Dialita songs, communicate Dialita's activities to people in their networks (such as friends, families, colleagues) and invite them to choir performances or to otherwise engage with its recordings. The new fans in turn share the music with their networks, and the circle grows. Indonesian musicians who collaborate with Dialita have invited their colleagues to join the project. University students who attended choir performances on campuses spread the word of the group's existence to their peers. Connected to their audiences through Facebook and Instagram, the Dialita choir is able to form networks of Dialita friends (*sahabat Dialita*) that reflect the same sense of support, togetherness, and solidarity that has become the survivors' source of health.

> Singing and dancing makes us excited. Looking great in *kebaya* and this make-up during our performance makes us believe that we are precious and all of sudden, you have your self-confidence and dignity back. It's a great feeling.
>
> —Ninik, Dialita choir member

Dyah Pitaloka is Senior Lecturer in Communications and Media Studies at the School of Arts and Social Sciences at Monash University Malaysia. Her research examines topics related to socio-cultural aspects of health, health inequalities, marginalization in contemporary healthcare, and activism and social change, with an emphasis on how various social, educational, economic, religious, racial, ethnic, gender, sexuality and policy contexts contribute to structural disparities in society. She has worked on these topics in relation to Indonesia, Singapore, and Australia. Together with Professor Mohan Dutta, Dr. Pitaloka conducted a study on meanings of health that explores the narrative of marginalization, injustice and health among the survivors of the 1965 Indonesia mass killings. An article on this study, titled "Embodied Memories and Spaces of Healing: Culturally-Centering Voices of the Survivors of 1965 Indonesian Mass Killings" was published by Palgrave Macmillan in 2018. Her opinions on the use of arts-based approach in trauma healing have appeared in the *Jakarta Post*, Indonesia's largest English language newspaper.

Mohan J. Dutta is the Dean's Chair Professor of Communication at the School of Communication, Journalism and Marketing at Massey University in New Zealand. He is also the Director of the Center for Culture-Centered Approach to Research and Evaluation (CARE), which develops culture-centered, community-based projects of social change, advocacy, and activism that articulate health as a human right. Professor Dutta's research examines the role of advocacy and activism in challenging marginalizing structures, the relationship between poverty and health, political economy of global health policies, the mobilization of cultural tropes for the justification of neo-colonial health development projects, and the ways participatory culture-centered processes and strategies of radical democracy serve as axes of global social change. He has published five books, including *Communicating Social Change: Structure, Culture, Agency* (Taylor & Francis), and, more recently *Voices of Resistance* (Purdue University Press).

Notes

All participants have given their consent to the authors to share their stories. In this chapter, we will only use participants' first names or nicknames, thus no full name will be disclosed. For other characters identified as non-participants or not a member of the Dialita choir, full names will be used together with descriptions of their titles, roles and/or profession.

1. Dialita, "Speech on Receiving the 2019 Gwangju Prize for Human Rights," Facebook, 18 May 2019, https://www.facebook.com/1314920403/videos/10219479975292764/.
2. Wardaya, *Keadilan bagi yang Berbeda Paham*.
3. The Gembira Ensemble was not institutionally part of LEKRA (The Institute of People's Culture), but several of its members were members of LEKRA—a very prolific literary

and social movement associated with the Indonesian Communist Party. During the late 1950s and early 1960s, Gembira was the ensemble the government most frequently invited to perform for state functions such as the welcoming foreign dignitaries. For more on this topic, see Lindsay and Liem, *Heirs to World Culture.*
4. Fealy, *Release Indonesia's Political Prisoners.*
5. Goffman, *Asylums.*
6. Goffman, *Stigma*; Allport, *Nature Prejudice.*
7. Goffman, *Stigma,* 11.
8. Zurbuchen, "History, Memory."
9. Dutta, *Communicating Health*; Dutta-Bergman, "Poverty, Structural Barriers and Health"; Dutta-Bergman, "Unheard Voices."
10. Dutta, *Communicating Health,* 45.
11. Pitaloka and Dutta, "Embodied Memories," 337.
12. Lipsitz, *Dangerous Crossroads.*
13. Lipsitz, *Dangerous Crossroads,* 4.
14. Akombo, "Music and Healing," Lawrence, De Silva, and Henley, "Sports and Games," McFerran and Teggelove, "Music Therapy."
15. Cohen, "Creative Approaches Reconciliation," 14.
16. King and Tan, *(Un)Common Sounds.*
17. Garcia, "Music and Reconciliation."
18. Dutta, *Communicating Health.*
19. Staszak, "Other/Otherness."
20. Gerlach, *Extremely Violent Societies,* 87.
21. Puar, *Right to Maim.*
22. Basu and Dutta, "Sex Workers and HIV/AIDS."
23. Crocodile Hole or Lubang Buaya is actually one of the districts located in East Jakarta where the bodies of the generals believed to be killed by Indonesian Communist Party (PKI) were dumped. Currently, the place is known as the location of the "Monument of the Seven Heroes" (*Monumen Tujuh Pahlawan*)—a site to commemorate the seven killed generals. See also Christie and Cribb, *Historical Injustice.*
24. Wieringa, "Two Indonesian Women's Organizations."
25. The word "woman" in Indonesian can be translated as *perempuan, wanita* or *Ibu*. Ibu in English means mother, but in Indonesian this word can be used interchangeably with other words to indicate a respected woman.
26. Dutta, "A Culture-Centered Approach to Listening."
27. Political prisoners could not keep any writing tools in prison. The only way for Tati to compose a song was by memorising the lyrics and the notes, and then to sing the song again and again and to share it with her fellow prisoners.
28. Rawlins, "Hearing Voices/Learning Questions," 122.
29. Pitaloka and Dutta, "From Victims to Survivors."
30. Lederach and Lederach, *When Blood and Bones Cry Out,* 7.
31. Pitaloka and Dutta, "Embodied Memories and Spaces of Healing," 349.
32. Prendergast and Saxton, "Theatre of the Oppressed." 69.
33. Crowe, *Music and Soulmaking.*
34. Smith, *Resilience Localisation Trauma.*

Bibliography

Akombo, David Otieno. "Music and Healing During Post-election Violence in Kenya." *Voices: A World Forum for Music Therapy* 9, no. 2 (2009). https://doi.org/10.15845/voices.v9i2.349.

Allport, Gordon W. *The Nature of Prejudice*, abridged version. Garden City, NY: Doubleday, 1958.

Basu, Ambar, and Mohan J. Dutta. "Sex Workers and HIV/AIDS: Analyzing Participatory Culture-Centered Health Communication Strategies." *Human Communication Research* 35, no. 1 (2009): 86–114.

Christie, Kenneth, and Robert Cribb, eds. *Historical Injustice and Democratic Transition in Eastern Asia and Northern Europe: Ghosts at the Table of Democracy*. London: Routledge Curzon, 2002.

Cohen, Cynthia. "Creative Approaches to Reconciliation." In *The Psychology of Resolving Global Conflicts: From War to Peace*, edited by Mari Fitzduff and Chris E. Stout, 1–62. Westport, CT: Greenwood, 2005.

Crowe, Barbara J. *Music and Soulmaking: Toward a New Theory of Music Therapy*. Lanham, MD: Scarecrow Press, 2004.

Dutta, Mohan J. *Communicating Health: A Culture-Centered Approach*. London: Polity, 2008.

———. "A Culture-Centered Approach to Listening: Voices of Social Change." *International Journal of Listening* 28, no. 2 (2014): 67–81.

Dutta-Bergman, Mohan J. "Poverty, Structural Barriers and Health: A Santali Narrative of Health Communication." *Qualitative Health Research* 14, no. 8 (2004): 1,107–22.

———. "The Unheard Voices of Santalis: Communicating about Health from the Margins of India." *Communication Theory* 14, no. 3 (2004): 237–63.

Fealy, Greg. *The Release of Indonesia's Political Prisoners: Domestic versus Foreign Policy, 1975–1979*. Melbourne: Monash Asia Institute, 1995.

Garcia, Maria Elisa Pinto. "Music and Reconciliation in Colombia: Opportunities and Limitations of Songs Composed by Victims." *Music & Arts in Action* 4, no. 2 (2014): 24–51.

Gerlach, Christian. *Extremely Violent Societies: Mass Violence in the Twentieth Century*. New York: Cambridge University Press, 2010.

Goffman, Erving. *Asylums: Essays on the Social Situation of Mental Patients and Other Inmates*. Harmondsworth: Penguin, 1968.

Goffman, Erving. *Stigma: Notes on the Management of Spoiled Identity*. London: Penguin, 1963.

King, Roberta R., and Sooi Ling Tan, eds. *(Un)Common Sounds: Songs of Peace and Reconciliation among Muslims and Christians*. Eugene, OR: Cascade Books, 2014.

Lawrence, Sue, Mary De Silva, and Robert Henley. "Sports and Games for Posttraumatic Stress Disorder (PTSD)." *Cochrane Database Systematic Review* (2010) 20, no. 1: CD007171. https://doi.org/10.1002/14651858.CD007171.pub2.

Lederach, John Paul, and Angela Jill Lederach. *When Blood and Bones Cry Out: Journeys through the Soundscape of Healing and Reconciliation*. Brisbane: University of Queensland Press, 2010.

Lindsay, Jennifer, and Maya H. T. Liem. *Heirs to World Culture: Being Indonesian, 1950–1965*. Leiden: KITLV Press, 2012.

Lipsitz, George. *Dangerous Crossroads: Popular Music, Postmodernism and the Poetics of Place*. London: Verso, 1994.

McFerran, Katrina, and Kate Teggelove. "Music Therapy with Young People in Schools: After the Black Saturday Fires." *Voices: A World Forum for Music Therapy* 11, no. 1 (2011). https://doi.org/10.15845/voices.v11i1.285.

Pitaloka, Dyah, and Mohan J. Dutta. "Embodied Memories and Spaces of Healing: Culturally-Centering Voices of the Survivors of 1965 Indonesian Mass Killings. In *Communicating for Social Change: Meaning, Power, and Resistance*, edited by Mohan Jyoti Dutta and Dazzelyn Baltazar Zapata, 333–57. Singapore: Palgrave Macmillan, 2019.

———. "From Victims to Survivors: The Healing Journey of the Dialita Choir." *Jakarta Post*, 27 September 2016. Retrieved 10 January 2020 from https://www.thejakartapost.com/life/2016/09/27/from-victims-to-survivors-the-healing-journey-of-the-dialita-choir.html.

Prendergast, Monica, and Juliana Saxton. "Theatre of the Oppressed." In *Applied Theatre: International Case Studies and Challenges for Practice*, edited by Monica Prendergast and Juliana Saxton, 69–83. Bristol: Intellect, 2009.

Puar, Jasbir K. *The Right to Maim: Debility, Capacity, Disability*. Durham, NC: Duke University Press, 2017.

Rawlins, William K. "Hearing Voices/Learning Questions." In *Expressions of Ethnography: Novel Approaches to Qualitative Methods*, edited by Robin Patric Clair, 119–25. Albany: State University of New York Press, 2003.

Smith, Catherine. *Resilience and the Localisation of Trauma in Aceh, Indonesia*. Singapore: National University of Singapore Press, 2018.

Staszak, Jean-François. "Other/Otherness." *International Encyclopedia of Human Geography*, (2008): 43–47.

Wardaya, Manunggal Kusuma. *Keadilan bagi yang Berbeda Paham: Rekonsiliasi dan Keadilan bagi Korban Tragedi 1965* [Justice for those who are standing on different sides: Reconciliation and justice for the victims of the 1965 tragedy]. *Mimbar Hukum* 22, no. 1 (2010): 1–200.

Wieringa, Saskia E. "Two Indonesian Women's Organizations: Gerwani and the PKK." *Bulletin of Concerned Asian Scholars* 25, no. 2 (1993): 17–30.

Zurbuchen, Mary S. "History, Memory, and the '1965 Incident' in Indonesia." *Asian Survey* 42, no. 4 (2002): 564–81

Chapter 10

HEALING OUR SACRIFICE

Trauma and Translation in the Burmese Democracy Movement

Seinenu M. Thein-Lemelson

On 8 August 2017, I headed toward downtown Yangon (also known as Rangoon) to join a group of peaceful demonstrators who gathered in Mahabandoola Park to advocate for a reparation law for former political prisoners. It was the anniversary of the 1988 pro-democracy demonstrations, and a local women's organization called Moksha[1] Volunteer Group was commemorating the protests by organizing an early morning rally. As the taxi approached the center of the park, I noticed about thirty protesters huddled together, wearing light blue and white shirts with the words "Reparation Law" on the back. On the front of the shirts were the initials "TJ," which stood for "transitional justice." After I stepped out of the car and onto the pavement, I was immediately greeted by one of the rally organizers who smiled and handed me a T-shirt. A few of the other women approached me and took my hand in theirs, squeezing it with affection. Like many of the events I attended that were organized by the former political prisoner community in Yangon, there was very little outrage, anger, or sadness on display. The women I stood with seemed to draw strength from gathering, laughing, and joking with one another as we waited for the main ceremony to begin.

A few weeks prior to the rally, I had attended a conference on "women and trauma" organized by Moksha, where several women sat side-by-side on stage as they took part in a panel discussion. After the moderator's introduction, each woman took the microphone in her hands and gave testimony about her journey as a *nainganyei akyinthu*[2] (former political prisoner). The conference was almost entirely in Burmese, but the participants and audience often injected English phrases such as "rehabilitation," "reparation," "trauma-healing," "transitional justice," "national reconciliation," and "truth-telling."

After Moksha's rally in Mahabandoola Park concluded, I rushed to a Buddhist monastery in Thingangyun Township for yet another gathering to commemorate the anniversary of the 1988 pro-democracy demonstrations. This event was organized by the 88 Generation Peace and Open Society, a group founded by some of the student leaders of the 1988 pro-democracy demonstrations—individuals who had since risen to prominence as some of the main heavyweights in Burmese politics. As the ceremonial aspect of the 88 Generation event began, a very different set of concepts was evoked—words that did not readily find a place in the transnational discourse on victimhood, survivorship, and reparations. Before introducing the first speaker, the master of ceremonies called out to the audience:

> MC: I would like to respectfully ask monks and people (laymen) who have arrived, all the people, to stand up. Pay tribute . . . to martyred leaders who fought for Burma's independence and fell in battle along with General Aung San! Pay respects! To honor monks, people, (and) students, who fell during the many battles for democracy, stay silent for eight seconds! At ease!

I bowed my head in respect and stood with hundreds of others in silence. This moment of silence and the ritual of assuming a somber stance with bowed heads (known in Burmese as the *aleipyu*) occurred at all commemorations and festivals that I attended during my six years of fieldwork in the community of former political prisoners in Yangon. The *aleipyu* appears to date back to 1988, when the democracy movement was founded. Before beginning her speech at the Shwedagon Pagoda in 1988, Aung San Suu Kyi, the main leader of Burma's democracy movement, asked the audience to lower their heads and observe a minute of silence, stating:

> (This) occasion has been made possible because the recent demonstrations have been spearheaded by the students and even more because they have shown their willingness to sacrifice their lives. I therefore request you all to observe a minute's silence in order to show our deepest respect for those students who have lost their lives and, even more, in order to share the merit of their deeds among us.[3]

By linking the sacrifice of student activists with the acquisition of Theravada Buddhist "merit" by those present, Aung San Suu Kyi rendered the nature of the moral relationship between those who lost their lives and those who survived. According to my informants, this was the first time in the democracy movement that civilians performed the *aleipyu* on a large scale. Prior to the rally at the Shwedagon, civilians performed the *aleipyu* only on Martyr's Day to pay

FIGURE 10.1. Naingkyin community and their supporters perform the traditional *aleipyu* ceremony during an anniversary memorialization of the 8888 pro-democracy demonstrations and massacres. © Seinenu M. Thein-Lemelson.

tribute to fallen leaders and on Independence Day in order to commemorate Burma's overthrow of British rule, which lasted from 1824 to 1948. Aung San Suu Kyi's use of the *aleipyu* drew an embodied connection between the struggle for independence against the British and what was then a fledgling movement for democracy. Her use of what was traditionally a "military salute" with lowered heads, downcast eyes, the arms hung by one's side, and a moment of silence, rather than the traditional erect posture with the hand brought to the forehead, constituted a symbolic "reversal."[4] It cast those who had been massacred by the military as national heroes rather than enemies of the state. The silence and lowered posture, however, signaled tragedy and loss in lieu of pride. Those who had perished in the great protests of 1988 were not merely victims of a massacre; they were martyrs who had selflessly sacrificed their own lives to help the struggle for nationhood and democracy.

At the commemoration in Thingangyun, after the *aleipyu* concluded, the first speaker approached the podium. Unlike the speakers at the women's trauma conference who conveyed their narratives of suffering in minute detail, referencing English terms such as "reparations" and "trauma-healing," the speakers at the 88 Generation festival gave testimony of their suffering through fiery political oratory, using the language of *anitnah* (sacrifice) and heroic struggle for a nation-state.

The Transnational Trauma Model and Its Historical Relationship to "Sacrifice"

Over the last three decades, the transnational public health model of trauma has become central to how societies make sense of suffering. Trauma is often represented as a psychic "wound" that typically requires intervention on the part of humanitarian psychiatrists or other trained professionals to facilitate processes of "healing."[5] The concept of trauma emerged as fundamental to how societies engage in meaning-making in the aftermath of violence, war, and displacement. Trauma and its associated meanings have also come to constitute a form of public testimony. Trauma survivors are viewed not only as preeminent witnesses to historical atrocities but also as silent victims. The silent victimhood of survivors and what has been described as the inexpressibility of traumatic pain compel those in the fields of human rights and humanitarian psychiatry to bear witness on their behalf.[6] Indeed, one of the main missions of humanitarian psychiatrists is not only to diagnose and treat those thought to exhibit symptoms of Posttraumatic Stress Disorder (PTSD), but also to serve as witnesses to mass violence and engage in forms of documentation that legitimize the rights of victims.[7] Proof of victimhood, validated by the work of those in the humanitarian aid industry, is offered as evidence of the need for reparations.

As much as the diagnostic category of PTSD and the transnational public health trauma model have been embraced, there have also been vocal critiques about their universality and cross-cultural relevance. While not questioning the veracity of PTSD, the Canadian medical anthropologist Allan Young illuminated the many ways the concept of trauma was inextricably linked to the "social, cognitive, and technological conditions through which researchers and clinicians come to know their facts and the meaning of facticity."[8] The penetration of the transnational trauma model into people's moral and social worlds has been so pervasive that it is perhaps easy to forget a historical period when the terminology of trauma was not referenced immediately in relation to human suffering. Prior to the discourse of trauma becoming prevalent, academics who observed the struggles for independence in other societies demonstrated a keen interest in the lives of "resistance fighters rather than the resilience of patients." For these scholars, the "focus was on understanding not the experience of people suffering, but the nature of social movements." Consequently, "those who were being defended were always oppressed, often heroes, never victims."[9] The emphasis upon the valor inherent in personal and bodily self-sacrifice was overturned in the profound social change that occurred whereby many societies came to accept the transnational public health discourse on trauma as the main epistemology through which to understand human suffering.

Scope of Chapter

This chapter examines what happens when the transnational public health trauma model began penetrating a local context that valorizes an indigenous moral concept known as *anitnah*, which shares a resemblance to the English concept of "sacrifice." Over the last six years, as part of a long-term ethnographic project on the Burmese democracy movement, I have been documenting how activists and former political prisoners in this community perform rituals; conceptualize moral personhood; construct their identities; sustain social relationships; provide one another with social support; and participate in material and monetary exchange. Each one of these elements of their complex cultural system is shaped to a large degree by the concept of *anitnah*. In previous writings and presentations, I have argued that both on a community and individual level, there is a great deal of resiliency in the Burmese democracy movement.[10] By "resiliency," I mean that even after repeated exposure to extreme forms of violence, dehumanization, and persecution, many of the former political prisoners appear to adapt and even thrive in ways that are locally meaningful.[11] The main participants in my ethnography demonstrated competence, agency, and generativity in their daily lives; displayed joy, awe, and happiness; expressed hope and excitement for the future; enjoyed high standing in their communities; expressed having a sense of purpose in their lives; and both offered and received a tremendous amount of day-to-day social support. Based on my fieldwork, I believe that many of these "resilient" qualities are due in large part to the beliefs and practices the activists maintain about the nature of sacrifice—*anitnah* in Burmese. These beliefs are instantiated on a daily basis as part of formal ceremonies and habitus. The suffering that resulted from their sacrifices are sublimated through art, literature, music, and political activism.

The elaborate cultural system of the Burmese democracy movement, centered on the concept of *anitnah*, is undergoing unprecedented change as part of a broader process of liberalization that Burma embarked upon starting around 2011. As a result of this liberalization process, the social movement community of the democracy movement, which was formerly an isolated group in a geopolitically isolated nation-state, came into more sustained contact with the transnational trauma model and its extensive network of humanitarian aid and public health organizations. Some of these aid organizations, sometimes in collaboration with Western universities and researchers, began setting up mental health programs to "treat" former political prisoners in Burma for their "trauma."

While much has been written about how "cultural idioms of distress" are co-opted to fit the epistemology and goals of humanitarian psychiatry and the international public health industry,[12] much less has been written about how local populations, with indigenous practices for giving testimony to their own suffering, bearing witness to the suffering of others, and ways of memorializing historically-situated suffering through ritual, art, literature, and habitus, both translate and transform the terminology of trauma. Indeed, communities often adopt the trauma model in a syncretic[13] fashion, combining it with local meaning-systems, practices, and habitus. Rather than simply importing globalized and medicalized terms, there is a dialogical[14] interplay between disparate epistemological and ideological systems.

Clinicians and other mental health professionals who disseminate the discourse of trauma through primary, secondary, and tertiary international public health programs are encouraged to incorporate indigenous concepts and frameworks into their repertoire as part of a push toward cultural sensitivity. Metaphors and terms that conjure cultural idioms of distress are referenced during the trainings, conferences, and clinical interventions that are carried out in local communities. While the purported goal of this approach is to diversify mental health symptomology and broaden the Western diagnostic system, it is also in large part to encourage local populations to dispel the stigma of mental illness so that they are more likely to utilize the services made available to them through aid programs.[15]

Two extensively researched topics—cultural idioms of distress and traditional healing—are both compatible with the medicalized public health model that conceptualizes trauma as a "psychological wound" that requires "healing." Practitioners and clinicians in local settings can easily overlook aspects of traditional life that do not readily fit this wound-healing model. This has been particularly true of "cultural idioms of resilience," a concept that anthropologists are only now beginning to name and unpack.[16] I define "cultural idioms of resilience" as the means by which members of sociocultural groups experience, understand, and express violence and suffering in ways that are non-pathologizing, affirmative of personal and group identity, and adaptive. Idioms of resilience increase the likelihood that individuals and communities will overcome their suffering in ways that are generative and sublimating, and that offer them meaning, solace, and hope. *Anitnah*, in addition to being a moral concept, is a cultural idiom of resilience for the social movement community of the democracy movement.

While clinicians and other mental health personnel are encouraged to incorporate local concepts and frameworks into their treatment paradigms, little is known about whether the syncretism of local and transnational epistemologies truly leads to increased wellness in the communities they seek to serve, or whether these communities become dispossessed of their own local idioms of resilience. In the case of a concept such as *anitnah*, there may be essential tensions between its localized meanings and the basic assumptions of the transnational public health trauma model. It is unclear whether the discourses associated with the transnational trauma model, rather than melding with local meaning-systems to produce hybrid discourses that are uplifting and empowering, strip concepts such as *anitnah* of their moral and relational meaning.

Brief Overview of the Burmese Democracy Movement

From 1962 to 2011, Burma was ruled by a military-led government that brutally suppressed its population through both violent and nonviolent measures. It was not until 1988 that a formidable opposition movement arose in reaction to the Burma Socialist Programme Party (BSPP) government. That movement for political change was instigated largely by university and high school students in Yangon. Large-scale protests organized by student activists in conjunction with local neighborhood and community leaders culminated in the 8888 pro-democracy demonstrations that at their peak on 8 August 1988 drew tens of millions of protesters from around the country. The military responded by engaging in large-scale massacres of protesters. During this period, the democracy movement in its nascent form caused the collapse of the BSPP and an end to the one-party system. Ne Win, Burma's dictator, had officially stepped down in July of 1988 after an earlier cycle of protest. As the BSPP was the main bureaucratic structure through which the military-led government ruled over civilian life, its collapse led to a brief period during August and September 1988 when the military seemed to withdraw from public life. This was short-lived, however, as on 18 September 1988 a new faction of the military staged a wave of massacres across Burma, recapturing control of the state.

After recapturing power, the military, first under a governing body known as the State Law and Order Restoration Council (SLORC) and later under the State Peace and Development Council (SPDC), continued and intensified the brutal suppression of its population. This military-state apparatus targeted individuals and families who participated in and supported the democracy movement. Many of these individuals were captured, tortured, illegally detained, and imprisoned by state authorities. Although there are no exact figures, the Assistance Association for Political Prisoners (AAPP) estimates that between 1988 and 2015, there were more than ten thousand democracy activists and their supporters who moved through Burma's prison systems.[17]

In the prisons, political prisoners were subjected to multiple forms of inhumane treatment, including being starved, beaten, psychologically and physically tortured, raped, and used as forced labor. Outside of the prisons, Military Intelligence constantly monitored democracy activists and their families. The goal of the military-state was to isolate and persecute democracy activists. The social movement community of the democracy movement and its cultural system based largely on the concept of *anitnah* took root under these extreme conditions.[18]

In March 2011, the ruling council of the military regime dissolved. Current and former members of the military and its main political party, the Union Solidarity and Development Party (USDP), continued to monopolize Burma's key industries. These industries had begun a slow process of privatization following the 1988 protests, which caused the collapse of the socialist system.

While a wealthy elite of military, ex-military, USDP, and ex-USDP members as well as their families and supporters continued to hold on to power through a variety of mechanisms, including a national constitution that they had ratified in 2008, a process of information liberalization began, and a nascent civil society emerged. During this same period, around three hundred former political prisoners were released; many were key leaders and intellectual figures in the movement. This led to a flourishing of the culture of the democracy movement as activists, forced for decades to carry out their rituals and commemorations surreptitiously, began holding festivals, rallies, gallery shows, poetry readings, and artistic performances in what constituted a small renaissance. Many of the renderings, performances, and public speeches concerned their experiences in prison, bearing testimony to their suffering and demonstrating, in the words of San Zaw Htway, a well-known artist and former political prisoner, that "torture and oppression can break a man's body but cannot take away the spirit within."[19] It was in this context that many international nongovernmental organizations (NGOs), humanitarian aid organizations, and representatives from schools of public health in Western universities entered the formerly isolated country, bringing with them the discourses, frameworks, and underlying assumptions associated with the transnational public health model of trauma.

Research Methods

I began working with the community of former political prisoners and democracy activists in Burma during the early part of 2013. Between 2013 and 2019, I visited the "field" on sixteen different occasions, with visits ranging from two weeks to five months. I carried out the ethnography and fieldwork primarily in Yangon, but because the social movement community of the democracy movement is not bounded territorially, I also traveled and conducted interviews and ethnography in other localities in Burma and around the world, including in Mandalay, Naypyidaw, Bangkok, Singapore, Rockville (Maryland), New York City, Buffalo (New York), San Francisco, Los Angeles, Jakarta, and Sydney.

My research methods consisted of deep immersion in the community. I observed participants and spent time with political prisoners and their families in their home environments; sat in on their organizational meetings; attended festivals, commemorations, ceremonies, rallies, and other public and private events organized by the community; toured with them as they engaged in their activist work; collaborated with them on creative projects; accompanied them on their medical appointments; and sustained long-term friendships with individuals in the community.

The Cultural System of the Democracy Movement

A Moral Concept and "Cultural Idiom of Resilience": Anitnah (Sacrifice)

Anitnah (or in its longer verb form, *anitnah-khan*) is most succinctly translated as the English term "sacrifice," but a more complete definition is the following: intentionally engaging in an act of self-sacrifice or willingly enduring a loss that is meaningful to the self in order to help or benefit (one) other(s). *Anitnah* is a concept that is evoked often and comprehended almost immediately by all Burmese-speakers whom I interviewed, across a range of ethnicities and religions, including in the political prisoner community and outside of it, inside of Burma and in the diaspora. Thus, while the concept of *anitnah* is linked to Theravada Buddhist notions of selflessness and the merit that is acquired while engaging in selfless acts of giving, the usage of the term transcends any particular religious tradition. As a moral and socio-relational concept, *anitnah* is salient to Burmese-speakers because it describes the moral obligations that exist between parents and children and between older and younger siblings. Parents are expected to *anitnah* (sacrifice) for their children; older siblings are expected to *anitnah* (sacrifice) for younger siblings.

Anitnah engenders a complex repertoire of emotions and motivations, which sets into motion cyclical patterns of mutual moral obligations. An individual's act of selfless sacrifice elicits feelings of warmth, love, admiration, respect, and gratitude. Those whom I interviewed reported feeling a deep sense of compassion for those who have sacrificed on their behalf. The sense of guilt and gratitude elicited by *anitnah* does not dissipate with time, and repaying someone who has *anitnah-khan* on one's behalf is not accomplished through a single act of reciprocation. The obligations associated with an act of *anitnah* extend across one's lifetime and, often, across generations.

Rites of Initiation: Anitnah and the Naingkyin's Body

The formal Burmese words for "political prisoner" are *nainganyei akyintha* for male prisoners and *nainganyei akyinthu* for females, but the majority of former political prisoners simply use the shortened and non-gendered term *naingkyin* to describe themselves and others. *Anitnah* is the foundational concept upon which the community of *naingkyin* and their supporters base their personal and collective identities. While the social movement community of the democracy movement values all forms of *anitnah*, it is the bodily form of sacrifice, personified by the figure of the *naingkyin,* that is idealized.

Naingkyin regard their experiences inside the interrogation centers and prisons as a necessary rite of passage.[20] Psychological preparations for these rites of passage began for future *naingkyin* well before they were arrested. One *naingkyin* reported that he slept on cold cement without a mattress or mat in order to prepare himself for the discomfort of prison. Another reported having her father, who was also *naingkyin*, describe in minute detail the brutalities that he endured inside the interrogation room during their evening meals together. Indeed, it was common for *naingkyin*, who had already been through the prisons, to tutor younger initiates on how they should cope.

Inside the interrogation rooms, the bodies of activists became objects of ritual sadism. During the interrogation, *naingkyin* were suspended in the air and beaten with sticks; males were sodomized with snakes or cobs of corn. *Naingkyin* were kicked, stabbed, choked, and raped. They were forced to hold stress position for hours at a time or made to crawl upon sharp rocks. Whatever mode of torture was utilized, it hurled them toward death, forcing them to pass through a "liminality" where everything they previously knew, including their former bodies, was destroyed.[21] It was only in destroying their former bodies that *naingkyin* could then be reborn into the larger body of the movement where they attained a symbolic immortality.

Rituals and Annual Cycle of Commemorations

The narratives of heroic self-sacrifice encapsulated by the notion of *anitnah* are the organizing themes for a variety of rites and rituals in the *naingkyin* community. The community of former political prisoners and democracy activists has its own annual calendar of ritual events that are commemorated year-round. These events, which are typically organized as a *pwe* (festival), involve memorialization of important protests, such as the annual *pwe* to memorialize the anniversary of the 8888 demonstrations. As the anniversary of important protests are also the dates when the community experienced significant forms of violence at the hands of the military-state, they also signify collective trauma suffered by the community.

Each *pwe* opens with the *aleipyu* described in the beginning of the chapter whereby there is a ritual silence and a bowing of the heads to pay tribute to fallen martyrs. The *pwes* often feature singing, commensal eating, drinking, political oratory, and the display of material artifacts pertinent to the movement. Between 1988 and 2010, Burma had repressive laws that forbade congregation of more than five individuals. Yet these commemorative events continued to be held surreptitiously in private homes and monasteries. Wherever democracy activists found themselves—whether it was Yangon, Mandalay, the Irrawaddy Delta, the Thai-Burmese border, or Rockville, Maryland—they attempted in whatever makeshift manner they could to continue to physically gather. These *pwes* affirmed their identity as a community, valorized their shared suffering, and reminded them of their continued struggle.

FIGURE 10.2. Photos and names of fallen martyrs from the democracy movement were put on display at a political *pwe* (festival) organized by the naingkyin community. © Seinenu Thein-Lemelson.

In current-day Yangon, an estimated one thousand members of this community regularly attend the *nainganyei pwes* (political festivals) held around the city on a weekly basis.[22] During a funeral, especially when the passing of more beloved and well-known community members is announced, the numbers of attendees swell to include a few thousand. During a single week, the community hosts up to five *pwes*, as well as numerous other meetings and informal gatherings. When I conduct fieldwork, I find myself shuttling from one event organized by the community to another, and I am still unable to attend all the events.

The Introduction of the Transnational Trauma Model into the *Naingkyin* Community

It was not until the period after 2010 when Burma ostensibly began a process of liberalization that transnational discourses of trauma were introduced to the *naingkyin* community inside the country in significant ways. In 2010, Aung San

Suu Kyi was released from house arrest. After her release, the National League for Democracy (NLD), the main political party of the democracy movement that was co-founded by Aung San Suu Kyi, submitted the names of more than six hundred political prisoners it wanted the transitional, quasi-civilian government to release. In January of 2012, a general amnesty was granted to more than three hundred former political prisoners on that original list.

Released political prisoners began regrouping and advocating for broader and deeper reforms. One of the most impactful of these organizations during this period was the 88 Generation Peace and Open Society, a group that I describe in the introduction to this chapter. The 88 Generation began holding large-scale rallies for constitutional reform, labor rights, land rights, and educational reform.[23] Many of the more prominent members of the 88 Generation who were newly released and recognized as international human rights figures traveled abroad during this period, interfacing with humanitarian organizations, including those explicitly concerned with offering their community rehabilitation and mental health services. Delegates from the 88 Generation, for example, traveled to Scandinavia on three separate occasions from 2013 to 2014. On one such trip in 2013, they attended a seminar on torture held by the Danish Institute against Torture (Dignity).

During this same period, there was an influx of NGOs, aid organizations, and other international actors into the formerly isolated country. These organizations began holding a range of workshops and conferences centered on themes such as "women's empowerment," "women's leadership," "federalism," "peacekeeping," "rule of law," and "national reconciliation." As described by locals who attended some of these workshops, few of the staff of these organizations had a direct archive of experience inside the country, but they brought with them new terminologies and discourses that had not yet penetrated Burma. One of these discourses was that of the transnational public health model of trauma. Schools of public health from universities in the West, including Harvard University, George Washington University, and Johns Hopkins University visited Burma during this time in order to assess mental health needs in the former political prisoner community.

It was also during this period that the Assistance Association for Political Prisoners (AAPP), an organization *naingkyin* founded on the Thai-Burma border in 2000, began implementing a peer-to-peer counseling program in Yangon and Mandalay. The program had initially been implemented in Mae Sot Thailand where the AAPP was headquartered as a collaboration between the AAPP, local clinics, and the Johns Hopkins Applied Mental Health Research Group, whose team utilized a method of mental health service delivery through peer-to-peer counseling. In October 2012, this program of peer-to-peer counseling was implemented in Burma with newly released political prisoners as their counseling staff. New counselors went through a six-month training program and then began delivering services around April and May of 2013.

The six-month training program typically consists of ten days of "life training," ten days of "in-house training," two months of practice, and roughly six weeks of delivering therapy to a "pilot client." Initially the program employed one supervisor and five counselors in Yangon, as well as one supervisor and three counselors in Mandalay. Counselors were trained in methods of assessment and cognitive behavioral therapy (CBT). Some of the counselors, supervisors, and trainers described the CBT as consisting of ten "components." A partial list of these components, based on ethnographic interviews, include "how to positively change hurtful thoughts," "how to engage in problem solving," "trust-building," "relaxation," "active participation," and an entire module on safety, which encompassed issues related to suicide, homicide, and domestic violence prevention. Counselors who worked inside Burma had little contact with psychiatrists and medication was not prescribed to clients.

Transnational Discourses of Trauma and the *Naingkyin's* Cultural System

The transnational discourses of trauma that penetrated the community differed significantly from *naingkyin's* beliefs about their own suffering at the hands of the military-dominated state. Perhaps one of the starkest points of departure was the extent to which the increasingly globalized discourse on trauma blurred the boundaries between those who directly experienced the traumatizing event and those who were impacted because they belonged to the same family, network, or nation-state. As written by Fassin and Rechtman: "Even though one had not lived through the war, endured the persecution, or experienced the sexual violence, it was now possible to be traumatized by virtue of the fact that one identified oneself as part of the same human community, the community affected by the event."[24]

The tendency on the part of practitioners and other interlocutors familiar with the language and literature of trauma to equate bodily suffering and psychic distress ran counter to core beliefs that *naingkyin* held about the nature of sacrificial giving. All members of the social movement community were expected to endure a loss on behalf of the movement by donating their time, resources, and labor. While each of these forms of *anitnah* were valued, those who had gone through the interrogation centers and prisons were viewed as having given the most profound sacrifice—that of their bodies. There could be no equivalency drawn between those who had endured the many small "deaths" of the prison and those who otherwise had a psychic wound. As is often the case with those who subjected to rites of terror, "[t]he memories for such experiences are unique and unrepeatable, specifying who else was present." Therefore, "[t]hose who were not present cannot be inserted into one's memories after the fact, nor can anybody who has been through the ordeals be excluded subsequently."[25] For the social movement community, boundaries between *naingkyin* and non-*naingkyin* were considered sacred and unchanging.

Even prior to Burma's liberalization process, which began in 2011, the *naingkyin* community possessed structures and mechanisms for creating intellectual content about their own suffering, including documenting atrocities, exposing human rights violations, and creating literary and artistic works. Since its founding in 2000, the Assistance Association for Political Prisoners released at least two dozen thematic reports. Between 1988 and 2019, *naingkyin* published dozens of memoirs and other literary works about their lives in prison. Some of these works were subsequently translated into English and published by international presses. *Naingkyin* who had migrated out of Burma, many of whom took up journalism, produced books, films, articles, and news programs that narrated the history of the movement and highlighted the struggle for democracy inside the country.

The existence of local rites, rituals, and structures for giving both oral and written testimony to political atrocities can render meaningless one of the main aims of humanitarian psychiatry: to bear witness. Victimhood is typically associated with powerlessness and passivity, but in activist communities where individuals devote their entire lives to a cause, the defining trait of community members is often their high sense of agency, even amid intimidation and violence. Under these circumstances, humanitarian psychiatrists are forced to contemplate what additional contributions they can make to alleviate suffering and what it means to "give voice" to individuals who already have feisty traditions of oratory in addition to well-developed mechanisms for producing intellectual and artistic content about the nature of their own suffering.

Perhaps it was some of these qualities of the *naingkyin* community—those that defied the usual logic and stereotypes of the voiceless "traumatized" victim—that contributed to a landscape in which by 2019 the Johns Hopkins Applied Mental Health Research Group peer counseling program on trauma had not expanded within the political prisoner community. Instead, counselors began treating other traumatized patient groups, such as "war victims, drug users, and [those who are] HIV positive." The program had grown somewhat between 2013 and 2019 in Yangon, with the number of counselors increasing from five to sixteen, but the program in Mandalay had shrunk from employing three counselors to one. Institutional development was slow and could even be said to have been stalled.

By the beginning of 2019, the main work of spreading the trauma model in the *naingkyin* community had fallen to a small, local women's organization known as Moksha Volunteer Group. In the following, I use Moksha as an ethnographic case study to unpack the ways the transnational public health model of trauma with its concepts, frames, arguments, and underlying ontological assumptions have been "translated" and "transformed" by the *naingkyin* community.

Case Study: A Support Group for "Those Who Have Sacrificed"

Ethnographic Background

Moksha Volunteer Group is a small, community-based organization founded in 2009 with a broad agenda of helping in the sphere of "women's affairs" and "rights." Its initial programs focused upon "community development," "community building," and "(community) awareness." Beginning in 2014, Moksha began focusing specifically on the empowerment as well as the economic and psychosocial needs of "female former political prisoners" and "female family members of former political prisoners."[26]

Moksha's programs for women political prisoners have been funded primarily by Southeast Asian Justice and Rights,[27] a non-profit organization based in Jakarta, Indonesia. Southeast Asian Justice and Rights was co-founded by an Indonesian national and focuses upon ending the cycle of impunity that exists in Asian countries in relation to mass atrocities and human rights violations. Moksha's programs for the political prisoner community were shaped by global discourses of trauma, human rights, and transitional justice, largely because its programs were formulated in conjunction with Southeast Asian Justice and Rights. The programs implemented in Burma utilize interventions that are modeled upon the premises of Participatory Action Research (PAR). The specific instruments and activities used in Burma were originally developed by the co-founder of Southeast Asian Justice and Rights for similar interventions carried out in Timor-Leste.

I first learned of Moksha's women's trauma support group through Yadanar,[28] a former political prisoner in her early fifties. As a young woman during the 1988 protests, Yadanar carried messages back and forth between different dissident groups. For her activities, Yadanar was imprisoned for more than ten years. I met Yadanar through a mutual friend, and as I was interviewing her, she told me about a support group for "women and trauma." She pulled out a small booklet that contained color photographs and brief biographical sketches of the women who participated in the group. She told me they would be meeting the following day and asked if I would join them.

Early the next morning, I drove to where the trauma group was to meet. Moksha's main office is located in an area of greater Yangon that feels more rural than urban. Livestock, including cows and chickens, run loose, and the roads are largely unpaved. The office consisted of a small brick house. Yadanar greeted me at the door. She smiled brightly as I got out of the car. Like many of the other *naing-kyin* with whom I interacted, she possessed a warm, positive, and irrepressible energy. Inside the house, I was introduced to Daw San,[29] who currently serves as one of the administrators of Moksha.

I chatted with Daw San for a bit, and she told me about being a participant in the first workshop that Southeast Asian Justice and Rights held in Burma in 2013.

It was there that she first encountered the Participatory Action Research model. She conveyed to me that she felt greatly "healed" after the workshop, which was led by a young staff member from Indonesia. When I met the staff member in Jakarta, she recalled how quiet and seemingly withdrawn Daw San had been during that first workshop. When she reencountered Daw San a couple of years later, the young staff member was surprised to find that Daw San was outspoken and confident, and had already begun disseminating the PAR method as the main administrator of Moksha.

After my conversation with Daw San ended, I followed her and Yadanar into the area where the trauma support group was held. There were six other women taking part in the support group that day, and each gave "testimony," conveying to me the narrative of their journey as a political prisoner from beginning to end. Subsequent to this initial contact with the support group, I attended three other events organized by Moksha, including a public conference on women and trauma; a conference and group gallery exhibition on women, trauma, and torture; and the public rally advocating for a reparation law, described earlier. Because the community of political prisoners in Yangon gathers regularly, I began seeing the familiar faces of many women in the support group at other public and private events that were not sponsored by Moksha. During these events, I was able to socialize with them during communal gatherings that were not organized explicitly around the themes of gender and trauma. During a visit to Jakarta, I was also able to visit the headquarters of Southeast Asian Justice and Rights, the organization that supports Moksha's activities and learn more about their mission and programs.

Healing Our Sacrifice: Anitnah as a Psychological Wound

At Moksha's conference on women and trauma I realized the support group that I had visited with the previous week was named the *peihsathu zagawine*. *Peihsa* is a word synonymous with *anitnah*; those who *peihsa* can be thought of as having endured a sacrificial loss. What Yadanar initially described to me as a "women's trauma support group" went by a very different name, which translated literally to a "discussion circle for those who have sacrificed." Rather than seeing one discourse displace the other, syncretic forms of understanding emerged as the community attempted to situate the concept of "psychological trauma" in the landscape of the moral and semantic universe with which they were already familiar.

Members of the Moksha community, particularly many of its leaders and administrators, often used *anitnah* to connote a "psychological injury" that needed to be "heal(ed)" and "treated." Daw San described to me during our conversation how accepting the reality of this psychic wound is one of the first steps in being cured:

> DS: In "trauma healing," number one, (it is important) for them to accept that they have a psychological injury.

DS: That is why we need to reduce psychological injury . . . this is not something that can be done after one lesson. There are people who are in a situation where they need treatment from medical doctors. We cannot do anything for these people . . . To the people who have psychological injuries, we . . . (need to teach them) how to (engage in) "management" of the psychological injury, how to "control" it.

As someone who attended and facilitated multiple workshops organized by Southeast Asian Justice and Rights both in Burma and abroad, Daw San occupied a unique position—that of a teacher and guide, who brought new forms of learning to the community of *naingkyin* and their supporters. As she conversed with me in Burmese, she continued to perform this aspect of her identity and positionality—as someone who brings privileged knowledge to a knowledge-seeker. Daw San described those carrying out the "trauma healing" as giving many "lesson(s)" that can "reduce psychological injury." She clarified, however, that if the injury is too great, those in the local community cannot help and medical doctors, who possess specialized forms of expertise, need to administer the treatment. While the transnational discourse of trauma creates equivalencies between those who are involved in a sacrificial relationship and outside parties, it often sets up power differentials between experts and nonexperts. Whereas *naingkyin* were accustomed to deriving meaning from their suffering by identifying with a group of fictive kin who offered them emotional, social, and material support, they were now told that those outside of that sacred group could, in most instances, be the best people to heal their wound.

Moving Past Our Sacrifice: Anitnah as a Negative Feeling-State

The transcultural model of trauma with its emphasis on pathogenic memories and symptoms, which are construed as diagnosable and treatable on an individual level through talk therapy and other forms of catharsis, placed an unprecedented emphasis upon *naingkyin's* interiority. This was evident in the keynote address delivered by a female leader at the conference on women and trauma:

KS: But for our future generations not to experience again what we have felt, faced, and sacrificed. We have a duty to take lessons from our stories and document them as a historical lesson so that in the future, the next generation would not experience it again. That is why, we, individually, these sacrifices . . . We cannot move past the sacrifices of the people who have sacrificed.

Whereas the customary meaning of *anitnah* as it is understood and utilized by Burmese-speakers references how acts of sacrifice by one generation engender similar acts by succeeding generations, the keynote speaker at Moksha's conference calls for the *anitnah* to be ended in this generation. *Anitnah* is transformed in this context from a morally meaningful cyclical action pattern that is recapitulated across generations to a negative feeling-state that needs to be "move(d) past."

The speaker's emphasis upon interiority and "experience," including what community members have "felt" and "faced," was in keeping with other aspects of the *peihsathu zagawine*. During political oratory, *naingkyin* often referenced their past suffering, but primarily through metaphor, imagery, and humor. Anecdotes about life in prison or under the military dictatorship were often infused into everyday conversation in a manner that was creative, spontaneous, and more likely to elicit laughter and nods of recognition than of grief, sadness, or anger. Recollections of this kind typically take place in the presence of fellow *naingkyin* and other members of the community with whom lifelong relationships based upon mutual feelings of warmth and trust are sustained. The women of the *peihsathu zagawine*, however, performed the act of "bearing testimony" by recounting their suffering in minute detail from beginning to end in front of large and small audiences consisting, sometimes, of individuals who were relative strangers.

The loss of relational and moral meaning is apparent when we compare the opening address given at the women's trauma conference to a speech delivered at the twenty-fifth anniversary of the 1988 demonstrations by one of the democracy movement's best-known orators and leaders, Min Ko Naing:

> MKN: (We) acknowledge how much we value our cause and how much we have sacrificed for it. We, mainly, thank . . . our parents and the people. Although this cause was started by students, if parents and the people were not involved, it would never have become such an important pivotal moment in history . . .
>
> MKN: We are continuing to walk on the path that they had created with their sacrifices because we cannot create such a pivotal moment by ourselves . . .

Min Ko Naing and the keynote speaker at Moksha's conference occupy a similar positionality; they are both engaging in public oratory as leaders of the social movement community using the authority conferred to them, as well as the particular context in which they were asked to speak, to share their assessment of the past, and offer a vision for the future. In Min Ko Naing's speech, *anitnah* is the very ground on which that future is laid, such that the present generation can "continu(e) to walk on the path that (past generations) . . . created with their sacrifices." Rather than being seen as an obstacle that needs to be surmounted or a "historical lesson" that signals a need to break with the past, memories of suffering are integrated into personal and collective identities, which become foundational to individual and community well-being.

The above examples highlight the limitations of the wound-healing metaphor that is often evoked in transnational discourses of trauma. The moral impetus in *anitnah* is not to "heal" from a "psychic wound" nor to "recover" from "violence."

The motivation in *anitnah* is to move through the liminality of violence, suffering, and loss in order to give to others. In moving through this liminality, the sacrificer experiences a sacred transformation of the self. Healing is neither necessary nor desirable because the new self that is symbolically reborn is not considered to be afflicted but made purer through the sacrificial act. The forms of translation that were occurring in the Moksha community often overturned these fundamental aspects of *anitnah*.

Conclusion

This chapter underscores the need to examine the hybrid discourses that emerge when local communities begin translating and transforming the transnational discourse of trauma. My research indicates that the increasingly globalized model of trauma, with its many associated meanings and ontological assumptions, is not necessarily contributing to a thoughtful syncretism that serves to bolster the status of the political prisoner community in Burma and help them overcome their suffering. Instead, it appears to be leading to a morass of epistemological stances and sentiments, which sometimes lends itself to social and moral confusion rather than to a clearer path toward empowerment and well-being. The findings of the current ethnography highlight the need to ask what role international public health programs and the field of humanitarian psychiatry have in societies that not only already possess meaningful, evocative, energizing, and non-pathologizing ways of making sense of violence and suffering but also have well-developed rituals and social structures through which to give testimony, document historical atrocities, and produce intellectual and artistic content devoted to memorializing and unpacking that suffering. It is unclear whether the shifts in meaning and the syncretic discourses that emerge from their contact with the transnational model of trauma are opening up new political opportunities for *naingkyin*. The women of Moksha did not seem any worse off for participating in exhibitions and workshops organized around the Participatory Action Research model, but they also did not strike me as any more empowered or agentic than others in the community, who continued to commemorate political atrocities using indigenous concepts and rituals that predated the prominence of the transnational trauma model. Moreover, practically all the women of Moksha appeared to participate in these many other forms of traditional commemoration and communal gathering. Moksha also continued many of the indigenous practices in their own events, including beginning each of the speaking events and discussion circles with the traditional *aleipyu*.

As this manuscript is being written, Moksha's advocacy has not led to a reparation law for political prisoners. During one of Moksha's events in 2018, I asked a female parliamentary member and *naingkyin*, who often joined the women of

Moksha for their events, whether a reparation law or health care benefits would be forthcoming to former political prisoners.

She explained that, given the scarcity of resources across the entire society, it was difficult to justify additional benefits only for "our people." She paused at the end of this statement and added, "*Naingkyin* will disappear after this generation, so the issue of benefits and reparations will no longer matter." Reparations can certainly be conceptualized as having an intergenerational component, so in some ways this statement reflects an incomplete knowledge of the transnational discourse of reparations. Yet it also signals the beginning of a significant change in the social movement community of the democracy movement.

The community's previous understandings of what constituted a *naingkyin* tied multiple generations of actual and fictive kin to one another in a seemingly unending cycle of sacrifice. This intergenerational connection infused *naingkyin* with a sense of meaning and symbolic immortality, as they continued the work of previous generations and prepared future generations to engage in similar forms of sacrifice. This aspect of *naingkyin* identity has now begun to erode. The term *naingkyin* is beginning to be regarded by some members of the community as a category of victimhood based upon particular forms of suffering that now seem to them to be historically bounded. The *naingkyin* community has moved from a sense of immortality to the prospect of extinction.

Seinenu M. Thein-Lemelson has been conducting long-term ethnographic and psycho-cultural research in Burma (Myanmar) since 2008. She received her PhD in Developmental Psychology, with a specialty in Culture, Brain, and Development, from the University of California, Los Angeles. From 2015 to 2016, she was a postdoctoral researcher at the Institute of Personality and Social Research (IPSR) at the University of California, Berkeley, and from 2016 to 2019, was a Visiting Scholar in the Department of Anthropology at the University of California, Berkeley. Dr. Thein-Lemelson has worked with former political prisoners and democracy activists in Burma since 2013 and is currently finishing a book-length ethnographic study on the Burmese Democracy Movement. She is also currently a lecturer in the Department of Anthropology, University of California, Los Angeles and a Research Scientist at the Foundation for Psycho-Cultural Research based in Los Angeles.

Notes

1. A pseudonym is used in order to protect the organization.
2. There is "no widely accepted standard system for the systematic romanization of Burmese" and as the transliteration system preferred by the publishers, provided by the American

Library Association–Library of Congress (ALA–LC), is incomplete for the purposes of this chapter, I am utilizing conventional romanization. Okell, *Burmese (Myanmar)*, 254.
3. Kyi, *Freedom from Fear*, 192.
4. Turner, *Ritual Process*, 172.
5. Fassin and Rechtman, *Empire of Trauma*, 22.
6. Scarry, *Body in Pain*; Malkki, "Speechless Emissaries."
7. Fassin and Rechtman, *Empire of Trauma*.
8. Young, *Harmony Illusions*, 10.
9. Fassin and Rechtman, *Empire of Trauma*, 160.
10. Thein-Lemelson, "A Cartography of Resilience"; Lemelson and Thein-Lemelson, "Fear and Silence."
11. See Kirmayer et al., "Rethinking Resilience" for an overview of the term "resilience."
12. Hinton and Lewis-Fernández, "Idioms of Distress"; Kaiser and Weaver, "Culture-Bound Syndromes"; and Saiba Varma's chapter in this volume.
13. See Stewart, "Syncretism and Its Synonyms" for a historical overview of the term "syncretism."
14. See Skinner, Valsiner, and Holland, "Discerning Dialogical Self" for a discussion of "dialogism."
15. Im, Ferguson, and Hunter, "Cultural Translation Refugee Trauma."
16. Cassaniti, "Keeping It Together,"; Kim et al., "Idioms of Resilience."
17. Tate Naing, personal communication to author, email, 2 October 2013.
18. See Hassan and Staggenborg, "Movements as Communities" for a review of the term "social movement community."
19. Thein-Lemelson, "Myanmar's Van Gogh Taken Too Soon."
20. Van Gennep, *The Rites of Passage*.
21. Turner, *Ritual Process*, 95.
22. This manuscript was written prior to the February 1, 2021 Myanmar coup. Presumably, these *pwes* have ceased since then.
23. Mon, "Burma's NLD and 88 Generation."
24. Fassin and Rechtman, *Empire of Trauma*, 105–6.
25. Whitehouse, "Dying for the Group," 31.
26. Moksha's executive director, interviewed by the author in Yangon, 8 July 2017.
27. A pseudonym is used in order to protect the organization.
28. A pseudonym is used and other minor details have been altered in order to protect the identity of the participant.
29. A pseudonym is used and other minor details have been altered in order to protect the identity of the participant.

Bibliography

Cassaniti, Julia. "Keeping It Together: Idioms of Resilience and Distress in Thai Buddhist Mindlessness." *Transcultural Psychiatry* 56, no. 4 (2019): 697–719.
Fassin, Didier, and Richard Rechtman. *The Empire of Trauma: An Inquiry into the Condition of Victimhood*. Translated by Rachel Gomme. Princeton, NJ: Princeton University Press 2009.

Hassan, Hatem M., and Suzanne Staggenborg. "Movements as Communities." In *Oxford Handbook of Social Movements*, edited by Donatella Della Porta and Mario Dian, 340–54. Oxford: Oxford University Press, 2015.
Hinton, Devon E., and Roberto Lewis-Fernández. "Idioms of Distress among Trauma Survivors: Subtypes and Clinical Utility." *Culture, Medicine, and Psychiatry* 34, no. 2 (2010): 209–18.
Im, Hyojin, Aidan Ferguson, and Margaret Hunter. "Cultural Translation of Refugee Trauma: Cultural Idioms of Distress among Somali Refugees in Displacement." *Transcultural Psychiatry* 54, 5/6 (2017): 626–52.
Kaiser, Bonnie N., and Lesley Jo Weaver. "Culture-Bound Syndromes, Idioms of Distress, and Cultural Concepts of Distress: New Directions for an Old Concept in Psychological Anthropology." *Transcultural Psychiatry* 56, no. 4 (2019): 589–98.
Kim, Andrew Wooyoung, Bonnie Kaiser, Edna Bosire, Katelyn Shahbazian, and Emily Mendenhall. "Idioms of Resilience among Cancer Patients in Urban South Africa: An Anthropological Heuristic for the Study of Culture and Resilience." *Transcultural Psychiatry* 5, no. 4 (2019): 720–47.
Kirmayer, Laurence J., Stéphane Dandeneau, Elizabeth Marshall, Morgan Kahentonni Phillips, and Karla Jessen Williamson. "Rethinking Resilience from Indigenous Perspectives." *Canadian Journal of Psychiatry* 56, no. 2 (2011): 84–91.
Kyi, Aung San Suu. *Freedom from Fear and Other Writings*. London: Viking, 1991.
Lemelson, Robert, and Seinenu M. Thein-Lemelson. "Fear and Silence in Burma and Indonesia: Comparing Two National Tragedies and Two Individual Outcomes of Trauma." In *Interdisciplinary Handbook of Trauma and Culture*, edited by Yochai Ataria, David Gurevitz, Haviva Pedaya and Yuval Neria, 377–91. Cham, Switzerland: Springer, 2013.
Malkki, Liisa H. "Speechless Emissaries: Refugees, Humanitarianism, and Dehistoricization." *Cultural Anthropology* 11, no. 3 (1996): 377–404.
Mon, Kyaw Hsu. "Burma's NLD and 88 Generation Team up to Push for Charter Reform." *The Irrawaddy*, 10 February 2014. Retrieved 1 December 2019 from https://www.irrawaddy.com/news/burma/burmas-nld-88-generation-team-push-charter-reform.html.
Okell, John. *Burmese (Myanmar): An Introduction to the Spoken Language Book 1*. DeKalb: Northern Illinois University Press, 2010.
Scarry, Elaine. *The Body in Pain: The Making and Unmaking of the World*. New York: Oxford University Press, 1985.
Skinner, Debra, Jaan Valsiner, and Dorothy Holland. "Discerning the Dialogical Self: A Theoretical and Methodological Examination of a Nepali Adolescent's Narrative." *Forum Qualitative Social Research (FQS)* 2, no. 3 (2001): Art. 18. https://www.qualitative-research.net/index.php/fqs/article/view/913/1995.
Stewart, Charles. "Syncretism and Its Synonyms: Reflections on Cultural Mixture." *Diacritics* 29, no. 2 (1999): 40–62.
Thein-Lemelson, Seinenu M. "A Cartography of Resilience: Mapping the Emotional, Cultural, and Social Landscape of the Burmese Democracy Movement." In 116th Annual Meeting of the American Anthropological Association (AAA), Washington, DC, 29 November–3 December 2017, 251. Arlington, VA: American Anthropological Association.
———. "Myanmar's Van Gogh Taken Too Soon: Leaves Legacy of Indomitable Beauty." *The Irrawaddy*, 16 January 2018. Retrieved 1 December 2019 from https://www.irrawaddy.com/opinion/guest-column/myanmars-van-gogh-taken-soon-leaves-legacy-indomitable-beauty.html.
Turner, Victor W. *The Ritual Process: Structure and Anti-Structure*. New Brunswick, NJ: Aldine Transaction, 1969.
Van Gennep, Arnold. *The Rites of Passage*. Chicago, IL: University of Chicago Press, 1960.

Whitehouse, Harvey. "Dying for the Group: Towards a General Theory of Extreme Self-Sacrifice." *Behavioral and Brain Sciences* 41, no. e192 (7 February 2018): 1–64. https://doi.org/10.1017/S0140525X1800024.

Young, Allan. *The Harmony of Illusions: Inventing Post-Traumatic Stress Disorder.* Princeton, NJ: Princeton University Press, 1995.

Chapter 11

BEYOND PTSD

The Politics of Visibility in a Kashmiri Clinic

Saiba Varma

> Except in urgent cases—an intestinal occlusion, wounds, accidents—the North African arrives enveloped in vagueness.
>
> —Frantz Fanon, "The 'North African Syndrome'" (1951)[1]

While psychological trauma in general, and Posttraumatic Stress Disorder (PTSD) in particular, have become issues of urgent public health concern in Indian-controlled Kashmir in the last decade, this chapter questions the prioritization of PTSD over other expressions of psychological distress in the region. In particular, it calls on public health, global mental health, and humanitarian experts to shift their gaze from PTSD to a form of distress called *kamzori*—a word often translated as chronic fatigue or pain, but which also connotes debility produced by colonial oppression. Turning our attention from PTSD to *kamzori* is not merely a question of shifting scale, from the "global" to the "local," but rather indicates the presence of a radically different bodily ontology in the Kashmiri clinic, one which must be taken seriously if well-being is to be achieved.

Kashmir: The "Vale of Tears"

For centuries, the region of Kashmir has been the site of intense territorial disputes[2]—Mughal and indigenous Kashmiri rulers vied for control in the sixteenth and seventeenth centuries, Afghan, Sikh, and British colonizers in the eighteenth and nineteenth centuries, the Russian and British empires during "the great game" in the nineteenth century, and India, Pakistan, and China in the twentieth and twenty-first centuries. In 1949, after India and Pakistan fought their first war over Kashmir, the region was partitioned into Indian (Jammu and Kashmir) and Pakistan ("Azad" Kashmir and Gilgit-Baltistan) controlled territories. Over the next few decades, India and Pakistan fought two additional wars over Kashmir. India lost the easternmost part of the state, called Aksai Chin, to China after the 1962 border war. In response to this long history of imperialism, since at least the 1930s, Kashmiris have demanded the right to self-determination and there has also been significant popular support for independence from both countries. In 1988, a militant group called the Jammu and Kashmir Liberation Front (JKLF), based in Indian-controlled Kashmir, launched an armed struggle for independence from India. Pakistan intervened in the conflict, sponsoring armed groups who supported Kashmir's incorporation into Pakistan. Pakistan's involvement allowed the Indian state to gloss the armed struggle as a case of "cross border terrorism" and a "proxy war," rather than an indigenous struggle for self-determination, fought primarily by Kashmiris themselves.[3]

In response, the Indian state massively scaled up its military presence and used extralegal tools—many of which were used by the British against India's own independence struggle—to quell the uprising. Since 1992, approximately 600,000 Indian security forces have been deployed to a region with 8 million people, a ratio of one soldier for every thirteen civilians, making Indian-controlled Kashmir the most militarized place on earth.[4] For the last thirty years, Indian-controlled Kashmir has been under a legal state of emergency, enabling Indian security forces to operate with exceptional powers, including preventive detention, the use of mercenary forces, torture, enforced disappearances and shoot on sight.[5] By the mid-2000s, Indian security forces' extrajudicial actions and sweeping counterinsurgency and counter-terror operations had led to massive human rights violations. While these tactics were successful in weakening the armed movement, desires for self-determination grew stronger.[6] While just a few hundred armed guerilla fighters remain active today, Kashmiris regularly protest Indian military occupation through nonviolent civil disobedience, including mass strikes, shutdowns, throwing stones at police, paramilitary and military infrastructures and personnel, and protests. More than 70,000 Kashmiris have lost their lives in the conflict, more than 8,000 have disappeared, and approximately one in six Kashmiri men has experienced state-sanctioned torture.[7] Thirty years since the armed struggle began, no political resolution is on the horizon, let alone one that addresses Kashmiri demands for self-determination.

Scholars, observers, and public health experts blame political instability for producing a psychologically distressed population. In 2018, the prevalence of adult mental distress in Indian-controlled Kashmir was 45 percent, with about 19 percent of Kashmiris suffering from PTSD.[8] Other epidemiological reports describe an "epidemic of trauma" plaguing the region.[9] In addition to war trauma, a devastating earthquake that struck Indian- and Pakistan-controlled Kashmir in 2005 and killed more than 85,000 people, further aggravated trauma and PTSD among civilians. These events have led to experts decrying a mental health crisis in the region.

Epidemiological mental health reports by Kashmiri psychiatrists and international humanitarian organizations have helped raise awareness around psychological suffering in Kashmir. However, this chapter argues that they have had the unintentional effect of foregrounding one specific form of psychological distress—Posttraumatic Stress Disorder (PTSD)—over others. In conversation with Seinenu Thein-Lemelson's piece in this volume, this chapter asks what happens when a transnational public health and humanitarian model of trauma reaches into settings with rich and expansive vocabularies of distress. Drawing on more than twenty-four months of ethnographic fieldwork in sites of psychiatric and humanitarian care in Indian-controlled Kashmir between 2009 and 2016, this chapter argues that knowledge of Kashmir's mental health crisis is structured by a "politics of visibility."

This concept is inspired by Didier Fassin's argument that a "politics of life" animates humanitarian aid work—in other words, despite the ethical commitments of humanitarian actors to a universal, egalitarian humanity, forms of inequality and the differential valuation of life persist.[10] Similarly, "politics of visibility" attends to how acts of revelation—such as making PTSD an "objective reality in the world" through epidemiological reports—are simultaneously acts of concealment.[11] In other words, I ask what is lost in the humanitarian and public health focus on PTSD? What diagnoses, experiences, and modes of distress are rendered unimportant, illegible or insignificant when PTSD is prioritized? In asking these questions, I consider how producing facts about mental health—which diagnoses are made visible, recognized, and legitimate—in clinical and humanitarian settings are not neutral or objective processes; rather, they may elide important political and ethical considerations.

Specifically, the presence of PTSD in Kashmir and elsewhere reveals a "hierarchy of suffering."[12] While Kashmir's "epidemic of trauma," particularly the high rates of PTSD, have gained global attention, focusing on PTSD comes at the expense of understanding more locally resonant complaints, including an ailment that Kashmiris refer to as *kamzōrī* (in Kashmiri) or *kamzorī* (in Urdu). *Kamzorī* is a polysemic word that signifies debility, tiredness, fatigue, or weakness, what, in some contexts, psychiatrists have described as somatized depression.[13] In Kashmir as elsewhere in South Asia, *kamzorī* can mean bodily weakness, a loss or lack of strength and vitality, a depletion of substances, such as blood or semen, as well as physical, social, or economic debility caused by caste or racialized oppression.[14] In Kashmir, people also use the adjective *kamzor* to describe the social, political, and psychological effects of living through colonial pasts and presents;

in other words, *kamzorī* is a means to highlight the psychic and bodily trauma of colonialism, the presence of a colonial wound.[15] Although trauma/PTSD and *kamzorī* share some symptomology, they occupied very different statuses inside and outside the clinic and prompted very different reactions from clinicians. While patients with PTSD symptoms were recognized as worthy recipients of psychiatric and humanitarian aid, patients experiencing *kamzorī*—particularly when *kamzorī* was the primary or only complaint—were treated with indifference or dismissed entirely. What might this trade off—focusing on PTSD and invisibilizing *kamzorī*—tell us about the operation of humanitarian and psychiatric knowledge?

The "politics of visibility" between trauma/PTSD and *kamzorī* is not only one of scale, of "global" versus "local" knowledge. *Kamzorī* has been documented as a pan-South Asian phenomenon, a diagnostic category relevant to at least one-sixth of the world's population.[16] It also resonates with other fatigue-related disorders, such as neurasthenia and chronic fatigue syndrome, which exist in other cultural settings. Thus, what is at stake in the comparison between PTSD and *kamzorī* is something more, or something other, than how a "local" idiom of distress (*kamzorī*) is being co-opted to fit international public health criteria (see also Thein-Lemelson, this volume). Relatedly, I am not arguing that *kamzorī* is more culturally resonant than PTSD; as we will see in the following section, PTSD has been localized and used to many different political ends in Kashmir. Rather, my argument is that, as clinical complaints, PTSD and *kamzorī* have fundamentally different moral and political stakes and each reveals a different ontology of violence, trauma and personhood. To elucidate this argument, this chapter begins with the distress most visible to clinical and humanitarian practices (trauma/PTSD) and progresses to the less visible/attended (*kamzorī*) to show what lies beneath PTSD.

Localizing PTSD

Kashmiri psychiatrists first noticed elevated levels of stress and anxiety in patients seeking mental healthcare in the early 1990s, at the peak of violence. In 2000, Kashmiri psychiatrists and members of the international medical humanitarian organization Doctors without Borders (Médecins sans Frontières) met for the first time to discuss the troubling signs of a burgeoning mental health crisis. In that meeting, they estimated that approximately 30 to 40 percent of the population was suffering from psychiatric problems. The following year, Médecins sans Frontières set up a pilot project to provide mental health services in Ganderbal district, an area severely affected by the Indian state's aggressive counter-terror operations. The pilot, which established the presence of a population desperately in need of mental health services, led to Médecins sans

Frontières establishing eleven psychosocial (non-pharmaceutical) counseling cells across the state, most of which were attached to existing public hospital structures. In addition, the organization committed itself to producing "psycho-educative" and "awareness raising" programs around mental healthcare, as well as conducting regular epidemiological surveys to establish mental health baselines. For example, one epidemiological report by Médecins sans Frontières from 2006 found that approximately 25 percent of Kashmir's population was suffering from mental distress in Kashmir, and of those, 93 percent had experienced conflict-related trauma.[17] These efforts were crucial in making Kashmir a global PTSD hotspot and justifying Médecins sans Frontières' presence in the region.[18]

Today, while therapeutic responses to PTSD are still hotly debated in the field of medical humanitarianism, scholars argue that "the disorder has become a taken-for-granted dimension of humanitarian assistance on a global scale."[19] In other words, signs of psychological trauma in local populations are widely accepted and recognized by international mental health experts. As British psychiatrist Derek Summerfield puts it, the central assumption in these narratives is that "a disease has an objective existence in the world, whether discovered or not, and exists independently of the gaze of psychiatrists or anyone else."[20] In other words, these studies helped cement a commonsensical truth: the psychological impact of war is consistent regardless of cultural or historical context or the subjective meaning brought to the experience by survivors.[21]

In addition to producing PTSD as a taken-for-granted category, media and humanitarian reports also established it as the most pressing mental health concern affecting Kashmiris.[22] These reports confirmed the existence of a damaged, civilian population in need of aid. As one article put it:

> With both Islamic militants and Indian security forces being held responsible for the turmoil, the . . . violence has caused a chronic trauma that affects *nearly all* of Kashmir's four million Muslims, countless numbers of Hindu and Sikh residents and those displaced . . . Public and private hospitals and mental health clinics are overwhelmed with the numbers of patients. Pain, depression and anxiety are the norm.[23]

Unlike earlier studies of PTSD, which were limited to specific population groups, such as Vietnam War veterans, refugees from Southeast Asia, or victims of political violence in the former Yugoslavia, now, an entire civilian population was diagnosed as traumatized. Kashmir's trauma studies thus broke new ground. Not only did they affirm the prevalence of PTSD among civilians, but unlike war veterans or refugees, who were removed from the site of war or trauma, they offered an understanding of what happens when people continue to live in traumatic environments.

However, while international humanitarian organizations helped spotlight PTSD, the growing popularity of PTSD as a discourse was because the term had resonance for Kashmiris themselves. As scholars have argued, unlike other diagnoses of psychological disorder, sufferers of PTSD are unique in that they "are seen as innocent victims and treated with patience and respect—a huge and valuable digression from the sense of suspicion and distrust that formerly pervaded the clinical phenomena associated with trauma."[24] In Kashmir, epidemiological mental health reports that established the prevalence of PTSD helped pro-independence and human rights activists argue that Indian militarization had caused widespread harm and suffering.[25] Because PTSD confers innocence on sufferers, the moral underpinnings of these studies were extremely useful for Kashmiris trying to counter Indian state discourse about Kashmiri Muslims as "terrorists." These studies thus served as contra-evidence to claims about the legitimacy of Indian rule. Local and international human rights groups used PTSD studies to argue that Indian militarism is inherently pathogenic, leading to culturally specific forms of distress such as "midnight knock syndrome"—people getting panic attacks at night as they imagine security forces or militants searching for them.[26] Kashmiri psychiatrists also described to me how long-term trauma had eroded people's capacities for coping and resilience.

Beyond being clinical diagnoses, trauma and PTSD have emerged as critical ethical and political languages through which Kashmiris can point to their victimization by state violence and occupation. At the same time, however, the Indian state and military has itself seized on Kashmir's mental health crisis and has offered a range of mental health and humanitarian interventions intended to demonstrate that it is a force of care and healing in the region, rather than a perpetrator of violence.[27] Mental health interventions around trauma and PTSD have been tightly woven with counterinsurgency goals, such as offering counseling to young stone throwers and the police providing free substance abuse treatment in mental health clinics as part of its "winning hearts and minds" strategy.

The multiple, contradictory uses of trauma and PTSD are not surprising. Scholars have noted how international humanitarian discourses of trauma/PTSD can turn survivors into victims, depoliticizing or medicalizing the experiences of political activists and actors.[28] For example, Erica James argues that the global attention and valuation of PTSD has led to the notion of victimhood having more utility for claims-making than notions of survivorhood.[29] James describes the harmful effects of a "political economy of trauma" in Haiti, an international humanitarian and development aid apparatus that commodified suffering and led to "false stories of injury as institutions and individuals authenticated and circulated portfolios of suffering."[30] Others worry that the popularization of PTSD is symptomatic of an increasingly "individualistic, rights conscious culture" in which restitution for "personal injury and grievances" are seen as increasingly morally necessary and urgent, leading to an increasing medicalization, and more specifically, "traumatization" of everyday life.[31] The imposition of these values is seen as particularly problematic in non-Western settings, where notions of community rights might be more highly valued than individual rights and where other forms of redressing violence (such as through ritual healing) might be more valued than narrating trauma.[32]

Thus, while the focus on PTSD in Kashmir and elsewhere comes with significant rhetorical advantages—such as disenfranchised communities receiving recognition for their experiences through an internationally valid category that constitutes evidence of suffering and confers moral innocence on suffers—it is far from liberatory. While trauma and PTSD may legitimize the suffering of Kashmiris, it may also reduce their agency, placing the capacity for healing in the hands of outside humanitarian and mental health experts.[33] By turning political actors into patients and victims, trauma and PTSD also offer perpetrators of violence—such as the Indian state—opportunities to cleanse themselves of harm and wrongdoing. Yet, despite these limitations, trauma and PTSD became hypervisible in Kashmir, in clinical settings and popular discourse.

In Search of an Epidemic

I arrived in Kashmir in the fall of 2009 to study this unfolding "epidemic of trauma." Like all diligent ethnographers, during my fieldwork preparation, I had tried to absorb as much research, human rights reportage, and journalism as I could on Kashmir's mental health crisis. Together, the overlay of war and natural disaster—what humanitarians describe as a "complex humanitarian emergency"—had produced a substantial literature on the subject, which I struggled to grasp before beginning fieldwork at Kashmir's only public psychiatric hospital, the Institute of Mental Health and Neuro Sciences (IMHANS) in Srinagar. However, like other ethnographers, I found that my research preparation and assumptions had misled—rather than led—me.[34] Yet, this misstep turned out to be a crucial part of my journey.

Together with hospital psychiatrists, I devised a protocol for my research. When patients suffering from PTSD symptoms came to the out-patient department, clinicians would refer them to me, if they were willing to be interviewed. Over the next few weeks, I spent long hours nervously waiting for patients to appear before me so I could begin my interviews. I wondered when the flow of patients would begin, when I could feel that my fieldwork had finally started. Psychiatrists reassured me that they would send patients to me, but I sensed something was wrong. Although the out-patient department (OPD) was crowded every day—with between fifty and a hundred patients with complaints ranging from headaches, body aches, anxiety, and obsessive-compulsive disorder

(OCD) arriving for care—only one or two patients had the classic PTSD symptoms of flashbacks, reenactments, and nightmares. Since psychiatrists assumed that I—like other foreigners who visited the hospital—was primarily interested in PTSD, rather than other forms of distress, they did not refer non-PTSD patients to me. After a few frustrating weeks of sitting empty-handed, I finally mustered up the courage to ask one psychiatrist with whom I had become friendly, Dr. Rather (a pseudonym), to see what I was missing. Where had all the PTSD patients gone? Why was there a discrepancy between clinical realities and the plethora of published work on PTSD, written by mental health experts, both Kashmiri and non-Kashmiri?[35]

To my surprise—and against what was written about mental health in Kashmir—Dr. Rather admitted that cases of PTSD had become rare. The decline in PTSD had to do with a number of factors, he said. First, overall levels of violence had declined significantly since the peak of the armed insurgency in the 1990s, when there were about 6,000 violent incidents in the state annually. At that time, psychiatrists saw between twenty-five and forty new cases of PTSD every day, Dr. Rather explained. But by 2009, there were only about 400 violent incidents a year, and psychiatrists were seeing only one new case of PTSD per day on average.[36] Put simply, Dr. Rather argued that the decline in PTSD corresponded directly with the decline in numbers of violent incidents. While the situation in Kashmir continued to be fraught, it was no longer dominated by live, active conflict between militants and Indian security forces, but rather, by counterinsurgency and collective acts of nonviolent civil disobedience, such as mass protests. Instead of being exposed to specific "traumatic episodes," as the definition of PTSD reads, Kashmiris described living in a generalized traumatic environment, which they call "turmoil" or "oppression" (*zulm*).

The problem, according to Dr. Rather, was that, despite changing levels of PTSD in the population, caused by changes in the nature of violence and insecurity, PTSD as a diagnosis had become fused with moral and political arguments about the harms caused by Indian militarization. He worried that revealing the truth about declining rates of PTSD might feed into arguments that Kashmir was "returning to normalcy" after two decades of insurgency, which the Indian state was actively pushing to demonstrate the success of its military and counterinsurgency programs to root out "terrorism." According to Dr. Rather, negating the prevalence of PTSD could be read as negating the need for demilitarization and for Kashmiri self-determination.

The second reason for the discrepancy between the clinic and published work did not have to do with the external realities of violence, but with the status of trauma and PTSD in biomedical and humanitarian psychiatry. Referring to Kashmiri psychiatry, Dr. Rather joked, "PTSD has become our bread and butter." While he applauded humanitarian organizations for helping to de-stigmatize mental illnesses in Kashmir, he also felt that the humanitarian and media focus on PTSD had led to the "traumatization of mental healthcare in Kashmir"—that is, a prioritization of trauma/PTSD over other forms of distress. Similar to James's account of a "political economy of trauma," Dr. Rather described how some Kashmiri psychiatrists had benefited greatly, both materially and professionally, from the international attention on Kashmir's PTSD crisis. His fellow psychiatrists—though he did not name names—had published extensively on PTSD in Kashmir in prestigious psychiatry journals, had been invited to international conferences, and had gotten lucrative consulting gigs with humanitarian organizations. His sardonic comment about PTSD becoming "our bread and butter" pointed to how some mental health experts had built their careers off PTSD, regardless of its relevance to Kashmiris themselves. These were the reasons for the overabundant discursive production of PTSD. The cache, legibility, and rhetorical power of PTSD had led psychiatrists and humanitarian experts to prioritize it in their clinical and research practices.

The Politics of Visibility

My conversation with Dr. Rather caused me to shift my research focus away from PTSD. Although I remained interested in how PTSD was being created as a matter of concern, I stopped waiting for PTSD patients to appear in the clinic. Instead, I expanded my inquiry to attend to other complaints patients were bringing into the clinic. Rather than wait for referrals, I began observing patient-clinician interactions directly. Gradually, a new object of study came into view.

In the wake of PTSD, I began noticing the ubiquitous presence of *kamzorī*. Patients in the OPD frequently complained of body aches, pain, restlessness, and a loss of strength (*kamzorī*). Not only was *kamzorī* omnipresent, it was a recurring complaint. Patients described it as resilient, as outlasting other psychiatric symptoms for which they were receiving treatment.[37] While psychiatrists often diagnosed *kamzorī* as part of a constellation of symptoms that marked major depressive disorder (MDD) or traumatic stress, *kamzorī* outlasted other symptoms of depression. For example, a patient might say, "my feelings of sadness have gone away, but now, because of the medication, I feel weaker (*zyādā kamzor*) than I did before." Patients often demanded specific treatments for bodily weakness, such as injections or Unani medicine (an indigenous, Islamic-Greek system of medicine), which are thought to restore bodily vitality.

Yet, because of the overcrowded and under-resourced setting in which they worked (there were just twenty-six psychiatrists in the public psychiatric hospital serving 4 million people), clinicians wanted to treat patients quickly and move them toward a trajectory of recovery. Patient-generated complaints of *kamzorī* were seen as holding back this progress. Particularly when *kamzorī* was the sole complaint with which patients came, it was dismissed as something patients had made up. Some psychiatrists felt complaints of *kamzorī*—particularly when they were "leftovers" of depression or trauma—distracted from more important mental health concerns and were ways for patients to receive "secondary gains," such as time off work, reproductive labor, or extra attention from kin. Jocelyn Chua has astutely argued that the clinical language of "complaint" refers to much more than just the symptoms or ailments that patients self-report.[38] Rather, she shows how, in South Indian clinics, complaints refer to distress patients might be experiencing and also include "processes of accusation, arbitration, and reportage" used by kin or clinicians against patients. In the Kashmiri context, clinicians used *kamzorī* to critique or undermine the suffering of female patients, in particular. Meanwhile, patients grew frustrated because they felt that doctors were not giving them adequate care and attention. Some felt that doctors were only interested in treating ailments that required expensive tests or surgeries; *kamzorī* was neither prestigious nor lucrative.

Kashmiri psychiatrists' dismissals of *kamzorī* were at least partly a product of their biomedical training, and thus would probably be replicated in other biomedical settings globally. In biomedical psychiatry, disease categories provide a universal language to understand and treat what is happening in people's minds, regardless of cultural background or history. Meanwhile, symptoms like *kamzorī* are examined as pathophysiological or neuropathological phenomena. As Angel Martínez-Hernáez argues, "in the same way that doctors deduce chicken pox from a rash on the skin, psychiatrists deduce diseases such as depression, brief psychotic disorder, or schizophrenia from auditory hallucinations."[39] Psychiatrists, like other biomedically trained medical professionals, are learned to distrust patient complaints that lack specific etiology and organic bases.[40] As the French physician and philosopher of science Georges Canguilhem noted, disease prestige is conferred based on the extent to which symptoms can—or cannot—be readily localized in the body.[41] *Kamzorī*, to borrow Frantz Fanon's phrasing, was "enveloped in vagueness"—it was non-localizable and invisible. For psychiatrists trained in Western biomedicine, *kamzorī* and other modes of "unspecified" fatigue thus lacked clinical integrity. Furthermore, while specific incidents or experiences of violence, such as a bomb blast or shooting were seen as underpinning PTSD, *kamzorī* often came without reference to any specific causes or external events.

Although unexplained fatigue is the most common "unspecified complaint" in Euro-American clinical settings—appearing in up to a third of all doctors' visits,[42] it is often explained as psychogenic: real but subjective. In cases when Kashmiri psychiatrists recognized *kamzorī* as psychogenic, they argued it was a form of somatization, particularly somatized depression.[43] Psychiatrists argued that complaints of chronic fatigue and bodily distress were pervasive because Kashmiris lacked knowledge of the psyche and thus expressed their mental or psychological distress through physical symptoms.[44]

Somatization has been a key theme in both the cultural psychiatry and medical anthropology of South Asia. In his now canonical work on "idioms of distress" in India, Mark Nichter found that somatization was an important way for Havik Brahman women to express distress.[45] He argued that somatization was an "adaptive response" to circumstances in which non-somatic expressions of distress were considered unacceptable. In this analysis, which was shared by some Kashmiri psychiatrists, psychiatric distress is translated into physical or bodily weakness; physical or bodily weakness is not a problem unto itself. When complaints of *kamzorī* lingered, and when they impeded the clinic's fast-paced function, psychiatrists reluctantly prescribed iron or calcium supplements or Unani tonics. These were seen as placebos to pacify patients.

Rather than receive the beneficial treatment and care assumed by the category of "secondary gain," patients who complained of *kamzorī* were treated more poorly—or often fell through the cracks—than those diagnosed with PTSD. For example, several medical humanitarian organizations in Kashmir, including Médecins sans Frontières, had a limited mandate to treat those deemed "most vulnerable" within a population; PTSD was a relatively easy and clear way to establish vulnerability, whereas *kamzorī* lacked validity. Although the political economy of PTSD in Kashmir was relatively limited, those diagnosed with PTSD received extra time, resources, counseling, and livelihood support from humanitarian NGOs. Meanwhile, patients who were *kamzor* were dismissed with minimal attention. These divergent responses to PTSD versus *kamzorī* clearly revealed the "politics of visibility" in the clinic, wherein PTSD mapped onto moral notions of worth and deservingness, while *kamzorī* did not.

Reading Kamzorī

Given the dismissive way patients with *kamzorī* were treated, I was curious why people might hold onto this complaint, even insist upon it, when there were so few tangible benefits from doing so. I began wondering what it meant to take *kamzorī*, not just PTSD, seriously, what it could tell us about how Kashmiris themselves understood and experienced the nature of political violence and trauma?

Medical anthropologists argue that symptoms like pain or fatigue should be seen as meaningful bodily experiences and read as "highly suggestive metaphors."[46] For example, Byron Good's analysis of heart distress (*narahatiye qalb*) in Iran showed how idioms of distress operate at literal and metaphorical levels.[47] At the literal level, heart distress connotes palpitations and heart flutters, and requires the intervention of a cardiologist. But heart distress also conveys difficult personal and social circumstances, feelings of loss or grief, or worries about health and financial affairs. Medical anthropological work shows how symptoms are not only physical or biological signs, but may be signs of social relations—such as a person's labor conditions, their familial ties, or their sense of economic and political precarity. Similarly, in war-torn contexts where it might not be safe or possible to speak about suffering directly, "idioms of distress" can be ways of speaking indirectly about intimate, social, and political difficulties, of maintaining what the New Zealand anthropologist Michael Jackson called a "practice of silence" in the face of suffering.[48] Yet, as I pointed out earlier, these approaches to "idioms of distress" are limited because they often imply that chronic fatigue or pain must be translated into something else in order to be meaningful. Such a perspective does not fully consider how ontologies of the body—that is, its presence, not just its meaning—may vary cross-culturally and how they may be disrupted by exposure to violence.[49]

The sense that Kashmiris' bodies had been both physiologically, psychologically and morally worn down by long-term violence became particularly palpable to me in August 2019, when Jammu and Kashmir's autonomy was unilaterally removed by the ruling Hindu nationalist BJP government. Eight million residents of the state were put under the longest internet blackout in history, which eventually lasted seven months, as well as months of communications restrictions, undeclared curfew, and the imposition of Section 144 of the Indian Criminal Code (which effectively bans protests and public gatherings). I was in Kashmir during the first month of the blackout and interviewed people about the effects of sieges and curfews on health systems, as well as on their sense of health and well-being. In Kashmir's largest public hospital, Srinagar city's Sri Maharaja Hari Singh (SMHS) hospital, I met a woman named Rubia, a woman in her early thirties who was being treated for severe anemia. Like other patients I met at SMHS during this time, Rubia and her husband had arrived at the hospital with great difficulty because of the ongoing curfew. They had been stopped several times by security forces and asked to show their identity cards. Despite security forces' ostensible promise that patients and their kin would be given unencumbered passage through the city, this is not how most patients experienced the city during heightened curfew. Rubia described the toll that Kashmir's conflict had taken on her health. "We've all become so weak (*kamzor*) and have so much stress (*tenshan*)," she said. "I feel tense all the time." I was struck by the way Rubia articulated her suffering as part of a collective suffering, a "we" who had been afflicted, rather than an "I." When I asked if Rubia had had any personal experiences with state violence—such as seeing someone be killed, wounded, or arrested in front of her, or if any of her family members had been victims of state violence—many of the same questions I had heard humanitarian aid workers ask in PTSD surveys, she said she had not. "No," she said, "I haven't seen anything personally. But it's the general atmosphere (*mahaul*) here. We're all affected."

Through this statement, Rubia located the etiology of *kamzorī* not in specific incidents of violence, but in a general milieu of militarism. She argued that this general atmosphere of violence had led to a weakening of her bodily capacities, which clinicians had diagnosed as anemia. Yet rather than describe her anemia as having just a biological cause—the lack of healthy red blood cells carrying oxygen in her body—she identified it as having social and political causes. Furthermore, rather than locate suffering only within her individual body, Rubia spoke in the collective pronoun "we," thus illustrating how suffering was lived and experienced as a social and relational process. Her body was a symptom of the sickness afflicting all Kashmiris.

I heard Rubia's perspective echoed in many other patients' narratives. People in Kashmir routinely told me: "no one is healthy in Kashmir." When I visited people's homes for interviews, along with a generous spread of tea, biscuits, and flaky bread fresh from neighborhood bakeries, they also invariably displayed their medical records, prescriptions, and strips of pharmaceuticals or tonics they were consuming. I saw this performative social display repeated over and over again, across class lines, in fieldwork trips over a decade.

I read these scenes as efforts to insist on the ongoing and expansive nature of injury and debility in Indian-controlled Kashmir. These enactments of *kamzorī* affirm that it is not merely an effect of specific incidents of violence, but is a product of living in a zone of militarization and occupation.[50] In contrast to PTSD, which translates experiences of political violence into a medical diagnosis, *kamzorī* retains a "political etiology."[51] In her work on dialysis patients in Egypt, Sherine Hamdy shows how Egyptian patients reliant on the public healthcare system understood renal failure in terms of Egypt's larger social, political, and economic failures, including corrupt institutions, polluted water, and environmental toxicity.[52] Similarly, Kashmiris describe *kamzorī* as caused by living in a generalized milieu of fear and anxiety. In contrast to PTSD, which reduces the cumulative effects of violence and trauma to specific, identifiable traumatic episodes, *kamzorī* appears in relation to Kashmir's unsettled status. Its nonspecificity corresponds to the enfolding and capacious nature of colonial violence itself. Thus rather than see its vagueness as a limitation, we can think of *kamzorī* as a more encompassing category than PTSD. While PTSD requires that a person has been directly involved in a singular event, Kashmiris locate *kamzorī* in the social and political realm. Because "no one is healthy in Kashmir," being *kamzor* means being in relation with fellow Kashmiris who have shared experiences of structural and physical harm.[53] Here bodily impairment is reconfigured away from being something that needs to be "fixed" to being a political claim. *Kamzorī* is a way to convey the commonsensical truth that relational lives have been profoundly disturbed because of histories of colonization and political violence.

Beyond "Global" PTSD and "Local" Kamzorī

In this final section, I address how shifting our gaze from hyper-visible PTSD to invisible *kamzorī* is not merely a shift from the global to the local. Relatedly, this piece is not a critique of humanitarian organizations and biomedical psychiatrists as insufficiently culturally sensitive. For more than a decade now, psychiatric and psychosocial humanitarian interventions have been translating and integrating "local" idioms of distress within "universal" categories such as PTSD. As Abramowitz notes: "Culturally sensitive, community-based mental health care" is now a widely idealized model for "post-conflict mental health and psychosocial intervention" around the world.[54] However, ethnographic work shows that even culturally sensitive public health and humanitarian models of trauma still maintain a "politics of visibility" that sustain hierarchies between what they deem "global" and "local" knowledges, and reduce and simplify local forms to those English-language, clinical terms that are more recognizable and legitimate.

For example, in her study of psychosocial humanitarian interventions in post-conflict Liberia, anthropologist Sharon Abramowitz found that organizations were keen to integrate local idioms of distress into their diagnostic manuals. One form of distress called "Open Mole"—which occurs in adults and involves symptoms of pain, dizziness, headaches, confusion, and social withdrawal, among others—appeared frequently as a clinical complaint. However, as humanitarian organizations incorporated "Open Mole" into their diagnostic practices, its meanings were reduced to fit PTSD symptomology and the specificity of war. Although Open Mole's meanings for Liberians include childhood illness, an aggravated response to bereavement, catastrophic life events, a consequence of African sorcery, through the work of humanitarian organizations, Open Mole became understood primarily as a "symbol of long-term suffering that is the consequence of war-related hardships, deaths, losses and post-conflict worries, vulnerabilities and fears."[55] In other words, nearly all narratives of Open Mole became "histories of trauma," and Open Mole was reduced to "an idiom of complaint" rather than an actual complaint with an ontologically valid status.[56]

Drawing on the experience of Open Mole, what would it mean to take *kamzori* seriously as an "actual complaint" rather than "an idiom of complaint," as Abramowitz puts it? Making this shift, I argue, is not as simple as creating a checklist of cultural competence, as many culturally sensitive providers and humanitarian organizations have done. Instead, it means a more fundamental shift, one that embraces a different ontology of the body and illness, as well as a different practice of listening.

As Susan Sontag famously described, patients and providers have very different orientations and goals in the treatment encounter; they occupy "two different kingdoms."[57] These ontological and epistemological divides are even more heightened in contexts of colonialism and violence. In his essay, "The North African Syndrome," written in 1952, Frantz Fanon argued that biomedicine, particularly when intertwined with colonialism, renders colonized patients and their bodies illegible. From the perspective of medical providers, the North African body arrives "enveloped in vagueness," Fanon writes, not due to a "lack of comprehension" on the part of doctors, but because of a profound ontological gap between the physician and patient. Because of the histories of colonization and mistrust that shape the clinical encounter, patients are unable to be understood on their own terms.[58] The patient does not feel at home in the clinic, it is not a space that belongs to them. Rather, the clinic is an extension of the colonial apparatus. These conditions produce a recalcitrant, vague—or, in many cases—a silent patient. It is only by accounting for the close connections between biomedicine, colonialism, and history, writes Fanon, that we have any hope of penetrating the patient's silence. It is only then that we can understand silence not as inarticulate, but as "a body beside itself with terror," a body that "bears the dead weight of all his compatriots."[59] The question, then, is not that patients are inarticulate or unable to express themselves, but whether doctors can truly "hear" what they have to say.[60]

Undoing the "politics of visibility" that structures biological psychiatry and psychiatric humanitarianism thus requires a radical transformation on the part of global mental health and humanitarian experts. Even when clinicians take seriously local "idioms of distress"—as in the case of Open Mole—they still translate them into more "real" and legitimate psychiatric or psychological complaints. They are not trained to take complaints of bodily vitality seriously as health concerns, despite the fact that, as Arthur Kleinman has argued, biomedicine is the only medical system in the world to banish vitality from considerations of health and well-being.[61] This gets to the heart of the gap between doctors and patients around *kamzorī*. *Kamzorī* not only indexes specific war-related experiences, but also reveals how war-time trauma is interwoven with other forms of everyday distress, including forms of gendered vulnerability. Like PTSD, *kamzorī* carries moral and political significance; it "preserves the moral integrity of the weakened against the weakener."[62] Yet, unlike PTSD, *kamzorī* reflects how distress is dispersed across social relations; it is not purely individual.

While psychiatrists and humanitarian aid workers are concerned with alleviating psychiatric symptoms, through *kamzorī*, patients express their concern with restoring the spiritual, moral, and political dimensions of the body, health, and well-being, in other words, its "biomorality."[63] Through *kamzorī*, patients signaled that regimes of violence disrupt more than just their psychic well-being—they also sap their collective moral and political well-being. Thus, rather than think of the difference between *kamzorī* and PTSD as culturally bounded versus universal disorders, by using the analytic of a "politics of visibility," I show how both diagnoses have distinct moral stakes. While PTSD individualizes and localizes distress, *kamzorī* locates the individual within a social fabric that is itself distressed. Rather than define "cure" as the erasure of past wounds, as psychological or psychiatric discourses of trauma might, an approach of decolonial healing emphasizes the "ethical dimension of the necessarily ongoing practice of healing."[64] Through *kamzorī*, people in Kashmir expressed their ongoing commitment to not just freedom from physiological or psychic pain, but a more complete liberation.

For providers committed to a decolonized future of healing, accommodating multiple epistemologies and ontologies of the body and illness in clinical practice is necessary to stop the endless cycle of patients returning to the clinic, day after day, year after year. *Kamzorī* is not merely or only a rhetorical strategy or an expression of need, dependency, or anger. To the contrary, it tells us about the very structure of lived experience in militarized Kashmir. It reminds us that wounds, whatever shape they may take, are inflicted not only on individual bodies but rather they reveal the interconnectedness between physical and moral well-being, and between individual and social bodies.

Saiba Varma is Assistant Professor of Anthropology at the University of California, San Diego, and an affiliate faculty in Ethnic Studies, Science Studies and Critical Gender Studies. She is a medical and cultural anthropologist working on questions of violence, medicine, psychiatry, and politics as they pertain to Indian-controlled Kashmir and South Asia more generally. Her book, *The Occupied Clinic: Militarism and Care in Kashmir* (Duke University Press, 2020), examines how militarism affects clinical and humanitarian practices and everyday life in the Kashmir Valley. Her research and teaching are driven by a commitment to feminist, anti-racist, and decolonial methodologies and approaches.

Notes

1. Fanon, *Toward the African Revolution*, 4.
2. Several newspaper articles and documentaries made about the conflict in Kashmir use this trope of suffering. See, for example, Journeyman Productions, *Kashmir: Valley of Tears, 28 min.* (SBS Australia, 2002); Barry Bearak, "Vale of Tears: A Special Report," *New York Times*, 12 August 1999. Retrieved 12 December 2020 from https://www.nytimes.com/1999/08/12/world/vale-tears-special-report-kashmir-crushed-jewel-caught-vise-hatred.html; and "Vale of Tears: Kashmir," *The Economist* 420, no. 9004 (25 August 2016). Retrieved 12 December 2020 from https://www.economist.com/asia/2016/08/25/vale-of-tears.
3. Kazi, *Kashmir*.
4. Kak, *Until My Freedom Has Come*.
5. See Duschinski and Ghosh, "Constituting the Occupation." According to Amnesty International, victims of enforced disappearance are people who have literally been disappeared from their loved ones and their community by state, military officials, or nonstate actors. Enforced disappearance is frequently used as a strategy to spread terror within society. The feeling of insecurity and fear it generates is not limited to the close relatives of the disappeared, but also affects communities and society as a whole. Enforced disappearances are a crime under international human rights law.
6. Varma, *Occupied Clinic*.

7. International Federation of Human Rights, *Report on Kashmir*.
8. Médecins sans Frontières, "MSF Scientific Survey"; Housen, Lenglet, and Pintaldi, "Prevalence." According to the *Diagnostic and Statistical Manual* (DSM), PTSD is defined by two major criteria: an exposure to a traumatic event and a set of psychiatric symptoms that occur (or recur) after the event. Originally framed as applying only to extreme experiences, PTSD has come to be associated with a growing list of relatively commonplace events, from accidents to muggings to sexual harassment to the shock of receiving bad news (see Summerfield, "Invention of Post-Traumatic Stress Disorder.") Tambri Housen, Annick Lenglet and Giovanni Pintaldi randomly sampled 5519 participants 18 years of age in the Kashmir valley between October and December 2015. They used the Hopkins Symptom Checklist and the Harvard Trauma Questionnaire; both instruments have been culturally adapted and translated.
9. Médecins sans Frontières, *Kashmir: Violence and Health*; Médecins Sans Frontières and University of Kashmir, *Muntazar*.
10. Fassin, "Humanitarianism as a Politics of Life."
11. Strathern, *Property, Substance, Effect*, 11.
12. Stone, "Disease Prestige."
13. Pereira et al., "Explanatory Models."
14. Cohen, *No Aging in India*, 230.
15. Varma, *Occupied Clinic*; Ureña, "Decolonial Embodiment."
16. Cohen, *No Aging in India*; Pereira et al., "Explanatory Models"; Ruddock, "Special Medicine"; Varma, *Occupied Clinic*.
17. De Jong et al., "Conflict Indian Kashmir Valley, I"; De Jong et al., "Conflict Indian Kashmir, II"; Tamim, "Kashmir's Mental Health Crisis."
18. Redfield, *Life in Crisis*; Varma, "From 'Terrorist' to 'Terrorized'."
19. Breslau, "Cultures of Trauma," 114. Scholars have written extensively about the expansion and globalization of trauma and PTSD in recent decades. By the turn of the century, psychological interventions focused on PTSD were playing an increasingly prominent role in the aftermath of disasters, including the Kobe earthquake of 1995 in Japan and Hurricane Mitch in Central America in 1998. See Breslau, "Cultures of Trauma"; Fassin and Rechtman, *Empire of Trauma*; Summerfield, "A Critique of Seven Assumptions"; Young, *Harmony Illusions*.
20. Summerfield, "Invention of Post-Traumatic Stress Disorder," 95.
21. Summerfield, "Invention of Post-Traumatic Stress Disorder," 95–96.
22. See, for example, Khan, "Violence in Kashmir Cast a Long Shadow"; Magray, "The Depth of a Scar"; Matloff and Nickelsberg, "Beyond the Breaking Point"; Mohan et al., *Blood, Censored*; Nickelsberg, "PTSD in Kashmir."
23. Nickelsberg, "PTSD in Kashmir," emphasis mine.
24. Bistoen, *Trauma, Ethics and the Political*, 44.
25. Varma, "From 'Terrorist' to 'Terrorized.'"
26. Mohan et al., *Blood, Censored*; Human Rights Watch, *Everyone Lives in Fear*.
27. Bhan, *Counterinsurgency*; Varma, "Love in the Time of Occupation"; Varma, "From 'Terrorist' to 'Terrorized'."
28. James, "Ruptures, Rights and Repair"; Malkki, *Purity and Exile*; Mahmood, "Perburbations."
29. As Derek Summerfield similarly puts it: "Once it becomes advantageous to frame distress as a psychiatric condition people will choose to present themselves as medicalized victims rather than as feisty survivors." See Summerfield, "Invention of Post-Traumatic Stress Disorder," 96.

30. James, "Ruptures, Rights and Repair," 112.
31. Fassin and Rechtman, *Empire of Trauma*; Summerfield, "Invention of Post-Traumatic Stress Disorder."
32. See also Derges, "Eloquent Bodies"; Jackson, "Prose of Suffering."
33. Mahmood, "Perburbations."
34. Cohen, *No Aging in India*.
35. The discrepancy could not be adequately explained by the time lag between what is described and the later date of academic publication. Many of the news reports and studies that I was reading were current.
36. Hussain, "Kashmir Coming out of Conflict Trauma."
37. Varma, *Occupied Clinic*.
38. Chua, "Register Complaint."
39. Martínez-Hernáez, *What's Behind the Symptom?*, 109.
40. Fanon, *Toward the African Revolution*; Stone, "Disease Prestige."
41. Canguilhem, *Normal Pathological*.
42. Shorter, *Bedside Manners*.
43. Weaver, "Tension Women North India."
44. See also Kleinman, "Depression, Somatization." See also Kirmayer, Dao, and Smith, "Somatization and Psychologization"; Nichter, "Idioms of Distress"; Nichter, "Idioms of Distress Revisited"; Weaver, "Tension Women North India."
45. Nichter, "Idioms of Distress."
46. Good, "Heart of What's the Matter"; Martínez-Hernáez, *What's Behind the Symptom?*, 109.
47. Good, "Heart of What's the Matter."
48. Jackson, "The Prose of Suffering."
49. See, for example, Alter, "Heaps of Health." My thanks to Sarah Pinto for this important point.
50. Somasundaram, "Collective Trauma in the Vanni."
51. Hamdy, "State and Your Kidneys."
52. Hamdy, "State and Your Kidneys."
53. The foundational criteria for PTSD require that an individual be involved with a traumatic event, defined as "actual or threatened death or serious injury, or a threat to the physical integrity of self and others" with a response of "intense fear, helplessness or horror." American Psychiatric Association, *DSM-III*, 467.
54. Abramowitz, "Trauma Humanitarian Translation," 354.
55. Abramowitz, "Trauma Humanitarian Translation," 368.
56. Abramowitz, "Trauma Humanitarian Translation," 364–65.
57. Sontag, *Illness as Metaphor*, 3.
58. Fanon, *Toward the African Revolution*, 7.
59. Fanon, *Toward the African Revolution*, 8.
60. Spivak, "Can the Subaltern Speak."
61. Kleinman, "'Everything That Really Matters'."
62. For example, writing about the presence of *kamzorī* among low-caste leather workers in north India, Lawrence Cohen notes: "weakening challenged the moral order of caste by substituting for it a different moral order, one equally rooted in the inevitability of organic difference. *Difference was embodied as weakness, not pollution: caste was a medical condition.*" See Cohen, *No Aging in India*, 232–33. Emphasis in original.
63. Alter, *Moral Materialism*.
64. Ureña, "Decolonial Embodiment."

Bibliography

Abramowitz, Sharon Alane. "Trauma and Humanitarian Translation in Liberia: The Tale of Open Mole." *Culture, Medicine & Psychiatry* 34 (2010): 353–79.
Hussain, Altaf. "Kashmir Coming out of Conflict Trauma," BBC News 6 December 2009. Retrieved 28 April 2021 from http://news.bbc.co.uk/2/hi/south_asia/8320178.stm.
Alter, Joseph S. "Heaps of Health, Metaphysical Fitness." *Current Anthropology* 40 (1999): S43–S66.
———. *Moral Materialism: Sex and Masculinity in Modern India*. New Delhi: Penguin, 2012.
American Psychiatric Association. *Diagnostic and Statistical Manual of Mental Disorders*. 3rd ed. Washington, DC: American Psychiatric Association, 1980.
Bhan, Mona. *Counterinsurgency, Democracy and the Politics of Identity in India: From Warfare to Welfare?* London: Routledge, 2014.
Bistoen, Gregory. *Trauma, Ethics and the Political Beyond PTSD: The Dislocations of the Real*. London: Palgrave Macmillan, 2016.
Breslau, Joshua. "Cultures of Trauma: Anthropological Views of Posttraumatic Stress Disorder in International Health." *Culture, Medicine, and Psychiatry* 28 (2004): 113–26.
Canguilhem, Georges. *On the Normal and the Pathological*. Translated by Carolyn R. Fawcett. New York: Zone Books, 1991.
Chua, Jocelyn. "The Register of 'Complaint': Psychiatric Diagnosis and the Discourse of Grievance in the South Indian Mental Health Encounter." *Medical Anthropology Quarterly* 26, no. 2 (2012): 221–40.
Cohen, Lawrence. *No Aging in India: Alzheimer's, the Bad Family and Other Modern Things*. Berkeley: University of California Press, 1998.
de Jong, Kaz, Nathan Ford, Saskia van de Kam, Kamalini Lokuge, Silke Fromm, Renate van Galen, Brigg Reilly, and Rolf Kleber. "Conflict in the Indian Kashmir Valley I: Exposure to Violence." *Conflict and Health* 2(1) (2008): 10–17.
———. "Conflict in the Indian Kashmir Valley II: Psychosocial Impact." *Conflict and Health* 2 (11) (2008): 8–16.
Derges, Jane. "Eloquent Bodies: Conflict and Ritual in Northern Sri Lanka." *Anthropology and Medicine* 16, no. 1 (2009): 27–36.
Duschinski, Haley, and Shrimoyee Nandini Ghosh. "Constituting the Occupation: Preventive Detention and Permanent Emergency in Kashmir." *Journal of Legal Pluralism and Unofficial Law* 49, no. 3 (2017): 314–37.
Fanon, Frantz. *Toward the African Revolution: Political Essays*. New York: Grove Press, 1964.
Fassin, Didier. "Humanitarianism as a Politics of Life." *Public Culture* 19, no. 3 (2007): 499–520.
Fassin, Didier, and Richard Rechtman. *The Empire of Trauma: An Inquiry into the Condition of Victimhood*. Translated by Rachel Gomme. Princeton, NJ: Princeton University Press 2009.
Good, Byron J. "The Heart of What's the Matter: The Semantics of Illness in Iran." *Culture, Medicine & Psychiatry* 1, no. 1 (1977): 25–58.
Hamdy, Sherine F. "'When the State and Your Kidneys Fail': Political Etiologies in an Egyptian Dialysis Ward." *American Ethnologist* 35, no. 4 (2008): 553–69.
Housen, Tambri, Annick Lenglet, and Giovanni Pintaldi. "Prevalence of Anxiety, Depression and Post-Traumatic Stress Disorder in the Kashmir Valley." *British Medical Journal of Global Health* 2, no. 4 (2017): e000419.
Human Rights Watch. *Everyone Lives in Fear: Patterns of Impunity in Jammu and Kashmir*. New York: Human Rights Watch, 2006. Retrieved 20 January 2020 from https://www.hrw.org/reports/2006/india0906/.

International Federation of Human Rights (FIDH). *Key Human Rights Issues of Concern in Indian-Administered Jammu and Kashmir,* 2019. Retrieved 11 December 2020 from http://jkccs.net/wp-content/uploads/2019/03/Briefing-Note_FIDH.pdf.

Jackson, Michael. "The Prose of Suffering and the Practice of Silence." *Spiritus* 4 (2004): 44–59.

James, Erica C. "Ruptures, Rights and Repair: The Political Economy of Trauma in Haiti." *Social Science & Medicine* 70 (2010): 106–13.

Kak, Sanjay. *Until My Freedom Has Come: The New Intifada in Kashmir.* New Delhi: Penguin, 2011.

Kazi, Seema. *Kashmir: Gender, Militarization and the Modern Nation State.* London: South End Press, 2009.

Khan, Suneem. "How Violence in Kashmir Has Cast a Long Shadow on Mental Health." *Daily O.* 25 January 2019. Retrieved 11 December 2020 from https://www.dailyo.in/variety/kashmir-crisis-stress-mental-health-violence-in-kashmir-militants/story/1/29091.html.

Kirmayer, Laurence, Thi Hong Trang Dao, and André Smith. "Somatization and Psychologization: Understanding Cultural Idioms of Distress." In *Clinical Methods in Transcultural Psychiatry,* edited by Samuel O. Okpaku, 223–65. Washington, DC: American Psychiatric Press, 1998.

Kleinman, Arthur M. "Depression, Somatization and the 'New Cross-Cultural Psychiatry.'" *Social Science and Medicine* 11, no. 1 (1967): 3–9.

———. "'Everything That Really Matters': Social Suffering, Subjectivity and the Remaking of Human Experience in a Disordering World." *Harvard Theological Review* 90, no. 3 (1997): 315–35.

Magray, Faisal. "The Depth of a Scar." *New Internationalist,* 2019. Retrieved 28 May 2019 from https://newint.org/immersive/2019/04/05/kashmir-ptsd-crisis.

Mahmood, Cynthia. "Perturbations of Violence in Kashmir." In *Resisting Occupation in Kashmir,* edited by Haley Duschinski, Mona Bhan, Ather Zia, and Cynthia Mahmood, 278–90. Philadelphia: University of Pennsylvania Press, 2018.

Malkki, Liisa H. *Purity and Exile: Violence, Memory and National Cosmology among Hutu Refugees in Tanzania.* Chicago: University of Chicago Press, 1995.

Martínez-Hernáez, Angel. *What's Behind the Symptom? On Psychiatric Observation and Anthropological Understanding.* Translated by Susan M. DiGiacomo and John Bates. Amsterdam: Harwood Academic, 2000.

Matloff, Judith, and Robert Nickelsberg. "Beyond the Breaking Point." *Dart Center for Journalism and Trauma,* 9 April 2009. Retrieved 11 December 2020 from https://dartcenter.org/content/beyond-breaking-point.

Médecins sans Frontières. *Kashmir: Violence and Health.* Amsterdam: Médecins sans Frontières, 2006. Retrieved 11 December 2020 from https://www.msf.org/kashmir-violence-and-mental-health.

———. "MSF Scientific Survey: 45 Percent of Kashmiri Population Experiencing Mental Distress." 18 May 2016. Retrieved 11 December 2020. https://www.msfindia.in/msf-scientific-survey-45-kashmiri-population-experiencing-mental-distress/, accessed.

Médecins Sans Frontières and Institute of Mental Health and Neurosciences (IMHANS) University of Kashmir. *Muntazar: Kashmir Mental Health Survey Report 2015.* New Delhi: Médecins Sans Frontières, 2016.

Mohan, Dinesh, Harsh Mander, Navsharan Singh, Pamela Philipose, and Tapan Bose. *Blood, Censored: When Kashmiris Become the 'Enemy.'* New Delhi: Yoda Press, 2018.

Nichter, Mark. "Idioms of Distress Revisited." *Culture, Medicine, and Psychiatry* 34 (2010): 401–16.

———. "Idioms of Distress: Alternatives in the Expression of Psychosocial Distress: A Case Study from South India." *Culture, Medicine and Psychiatry* 5, no. 4 (1981): 379–408.
Nickelsberg, Robert. "PTSD in Kashmir." *Getty Images Reportage*. Retrieved 12 December 2020 from https://www.reportagebygettyimages.com/features/ptsd-in-kashmir.
Pereira, Bernadette, Gracy Andrew, Sulochana Pednekar, Reshma Pai, Pertti Pelto, and Vikram Patel. "The Explanatory Models of Depression in Low Income Countries: Listening to Women." *Journal of Affective Disorders* 102 (2007): 209–18.
Redfield, Peter. *Life in Crisis: The Ethical Journey of Doctors without Borders*. Berkeley: University of California Press, 2013.
Ruddock, Anna Louise. "Special Medicine: Producing Doctors at the All India Institute of Medical Sciences (AIIMS)." Ph.D. dissertation. London: King's College London, 2017.
Shorter, Edward. *Bedside Manners: The Troubled History of Doctors and Patients*. New York: Simon and Schuster, 1985.
Somasundaram, Daya. "Collective Trauma in the Vanni: A Qualitative Inquiry into the Mental Health of the Internally Displaced due to the Civil War in Sri Lanka." *International Journal of Mental Health Systems* 4 (2010): 22.
Sontag, Susan. *Illness as Metaphor*. New York: Farrar, Straus and Giroux, 1977.
Spivak, Gayatri Chakravorty. "Can the Subaltern Speak?" In *Marxism and the Interpretation of Culture*, ed. Cary Nelson and Lawrence Grossberg, 271–313. (Basingstoke: Macmillan Education, 1988).
Stone, Louise. "Disease Prestige and the Hierarchy of Suffering." *Medical Journal of Australia* 208, no. 2 (2018): 60–62.
Strathern, Marilyn. *Property, Substance and Effect: Anthropological Essays on Persons and Things*. London: Athlone Press, 1999.
Summerfield, Derek. "A Critique of Seven Assumptions behind Psychological Trauma Programmes in War-Affected Areas." *Social Science & Medicine* 48, no. 10 (1999): 1449–62.
———. "The Invention of Post-Traumatic Stress Disorder and the Social Usefulness of a Psychiatric Category." *British Medical Journal* 322 (13 Jan 2001): 95–99.
Tamim, Baba. "Kashmir's Mental Health Crisis." *Al Jazeera*, 3 September 2016. Retrieved 20 January 2020 from https://www.aljazeera.com/indepth/features/2016/06/kashmir-mental-health-crisis-160620085520339.html.
Ureña, Carolyn. "Decolonial Embodiment: Fanon, the Clinical Encounter, and the Colonial Wound." *Disability and the Global South* 6 (1): 1,640–58.
Varma, Saiba. "From 'Terrorist' to 'Terrorized': How Trauma Became the Language of Suffering in Kashmir." In *Resisting Occupation in Kashmir*, edited by Haley Duschinski, Mona Bhan, Ather Zia and Cynthia Mahmood, 129–52. Philadelphia: University of Pennsylvania Press, 2018.
———. "Love in the Time of Occupation: Reveries, Longing and Intoxication in Kashmir." *American Ethnologist* 43(1) (2016): 50–62.
———. *The Occupied Clinic: Militarism and Care in Kashmir*. Durham, NC: Duke University Press, 2020.
Weaver, Lesley Jo. "Tension among Women in North India: An Idiom of Distress and a Cultural Syndrome." *Culture, Medicine & Psychiatry* 41, no. 1 (2017): 35–55.
Young, Allan. *The Harmony of Illusions: Inventing Post-Traumatic Stress Disorder*. Princeton, NJ: Princeton University Press, 1995.

Chapter 12

WAR MEMORIALS

Materializing Traumatic Pasts and
Constructing Memories of the Asia-Pacific War

Maki Kimura

I have been sitting on a stone bench for some time in the Nepal Himalaya Pavilion Park, Wisent, in Bavaria, Germany, watching a *Statue of the Girl of Peace*, the first and only statue so far erected in Europe to commemorate "comfort women," observing people passing in front of the statue. The statue is a replica of the original that was installed in front of the Japanese Embassy in Seoul in 2011 and was at first planned to be presented to the city of Freiburg. However, after the Mayor of the city renounced the acceptance of the statue, the owner of this private park agreed to accommodate it there. Most people who stop to see the statue took pictures, and quite a few of them sit on the empty chair next to the girl to be photographed. Sitting next to the girl, many men hold her shoulder and pose for the camera. Some admire the statue and look around curiously, but no information about it can be found, as the inscription plaque that initially accompanied the statue has been removed at the request of the Japanese government.

Possibly as a result of being the only statue of an ordinary human among numerous statues of Buddha and Hindu gods and goddesses, as well as other mystical figures, and the empty chair being inviting to onlookers, the statue of the girl seems to attract the attention of visitors to the park, developing a sense of intimacy through their interaction with the statue. While the statue is indeed designed to affect the visitors and generate intimate feelings, is that enough? Does the statue fulfill its intended purpose (of remembering)? Without any information about it, visitors will not know what the statue is for. Do they wonder why the statue is there? Does anyone link the statue with peace? The statue is covered with rich symbolism expressed through its materiality, but are any of these symbols identified? Do any of the visitors even recognize the girl's East Asian origin? Have any of them figured out who she might be? While the specific materiality of the statue—a girl with an empty chair next to her—seems to appeal to and affect the visitors, in the absence of any contextual information and knowledge, the practice of commemoration (of the victims of the "comfort women" system) can be said to have failed in this specific site. What do memorials make us remember and in what contexts can they truly be the medium of remembrance?

— Maki Kimura, Field notes, 16 July 2017 [1]

Over the past few decades, multiple museums, memorials, and heritage sites across the world have been either refurbished or newly constructed in order to engage with various "traumatic pasts" and to recognize the suffering of past victims. These sites include: (1) the Memorial to the Murdered Jews of Europe in Berlin, completed in 2004; (2) the War and Women's Human Rights Museum in Seoul, South Korea, featuring statues of victims of Japan's military sexual slavery during the Asia-Pacific War, completed in 2012; (3) the monument of a Mau Mau fighter unveiled in 2015 at the Memorial to the Victims of Torture and Ill-Treatment in the Colonial Era, in Nairobi, Kenya; (4) the National Memorial for Peace and Justice (also known as the National Lynching Memorial), in Montgomery, Alabama, opened in 2018, in memory of the past victims of racial terrorism in the United States; (5) a new monument paying tribute to the service of Aboriginal and Torres Strait Islander men and women erected at the Australian War Memorial, in Canberra in 2019; and (6) the Mother and Child sculpture to commemorate victims of wartime sexual violence—in particular those from the Vietnam War—installed in central London in 2019. The dramatic increase in recent memorial construction as well as the controversy surrounding global "Rhodes Must Fall" protests have sparked a keen worldwide interest in the role and impact of memorials on history, public memory, and people's identity.[2] This phenomenon raises questions not only regarding what these memorials specifically represent and commemorate, but also about the ways such memorials are designed—both physically and emotionally—along with how they are designed to "affect" the public viewer through their spatial arrangements and materiality while also constructing particular, often contested, traumatic memories and histories.

Since Kim Hak-sun, a victim-survivor from South Korea, came forward in 1991 to testify publicly about her wartime ordeal, the issue of sexual slavery organized by the Japanese Imperial Military during the fifteen years of the Asia-Pacific War has become the center of socio-political disputes in Asia and beyond.[3] While matters of war compensation, justice, and women's rights have been and are being debated in Japan and elsewhere, the "comfort women" issue

FIGURE 12.1. *The Statue of a Girl of Peace* in Wiesent, Germany, replica of the memorial in front of the Japanese Embassy in Seoul, South Korea. © Maki Kimura

in particular has developed into a battleground for the intense and complex politics of history and memorialization. Drawing on the several examples of memorials to the women who were sexually violated by the Japanese military—which have now been erected in Japan, South Korea, China, the Philippines, Germany, Australia, Canada, and the United States—this chapter explores how the conception, construction, and experience of these structures is intended to generate a sense of community and to offer a process of healing of psychological trauma. At the same time, I reflect on how these recent public constructions have heightened tensions over which historical experiences should be officially remembered and among which groups of Asian people and how public discussions of the memorialization process are divided by gender, race/ethnicity, age, ideology, and geo-political national boundaries.

Until recently, the issue of Japan's military sexual slavery and the politics of memorialization of this systematic violence over seventy-five years ago have been discussed in isolation, without being linked to other similar examples of traumatic pasts. To contextualize my analysis of "comfort women" memorials around the world, I will also introduce instances of memorials built in Japan to commemorate two other contemporaneous victim groups of the Asia-Pacific

War: first, men, women, and children who were killed by the atomic bombs in Nagasaki and Hiroshima in August 1945, including forced laborers from Korea and China; and second, the victims of the Battle of Okinawa. For the latter event, I will focus on the Himeyuri student nurse corps in Okinawa, mobilized during the war to work as assistant nurses. Some of these young women ended up committing suicide in order to avoid the dishonor of captivity and the risk of rape by US soldiers who had landed on the island in the spring of 1945. The act of remembering traumatic mass death is not limited to physical memorials: we can comparatively study other forms of memorialization, including literary and textual representations, as has been demonstrated by Holocaust Studies. The practice of and discussion around textual representations, however, has largely excluded the impact of emotion, affect, and bodily engagement in the act and politics of memorialization. Given this omission, I plan to focus on memorials in their material dimensions, and their emotional and psychological impact on remembering. In doing so, I attempt to engage the emerging scholarship in the social and human sciences on affect, emotion, and the new materialism, which shifts the theoretical focus from a social constructionist framework of representation toward materialist ontologies.

Japanese Military Sexual Slavery and the Emerging Redress Movement

Women who became victims of Japanese military sexual slavery during the Asia-Pacific War (i.e., the "comfort women" system) came from many different places, such as the former Japanese colonies and occupied territories as well as Japan itself. These women were of diverse nationalities and ethnicities including Japanese, Korean, Taiwanese, indigenous Taiwanese, Chinese, Filipina, Indonesian, Timorese, Dutch, Malay, Vietnamese, Thai, Burmese, Indian, Chamorro, and Eurasian. The majority of them were non-Japanese.[4] The existence of women who provided "sexual services" to Japanese military personnel and civilian employees was known by the Allied military forces through interrogations of prisoners of war and by reading diaries and memoirs of soldiers published after the war. However, at the time, these women were all considered simply "unfortunate" victims of war and poverty who had been sold into prostitution. Thus, the physical and psychological injuries and injustices that these women suffered only gained delayed recognition in the 1990s when Kim Hak-sun, and many other women, began to testify about their horrific past experiences, some fifty years after the end of the war. In the long interim period, most victim-survivors of the "comfort women" system had kept quiet about their agonizing ordeal during the war years. But as testimonies of women like Song Shin-do, a postwar Korean resident in Japan, Hwang Kum-ju from South Korea, and Yuan Zhulin from China have revealed, some women did disclose their traumatic experiences in attempts to gain recognition for their hardship. In 1979, the story of another Korean woman living in Japan, Bae Bong-gi, was made into a film titled *Okinawan Halmoni: The Testimony of a Military Comfort Woman* (directed by Yamatani Tetsuo). However, until the 1990s their collective voices of grievance were not heard and certainly were not taken seriously.[5]

The exact number of victims of wartime sexual slavery is still disputed, and the true extent of suffering will probably never be known. It has often been argued that at least 200,000 women fell victim to the system. To date, research has revealed that the first identifiable "comfort station" where women were raped and abused was established in Shanghai as early as 1932. Following this precedent, "comfort stations" spread throughout Japan, its colonies, occupied territories, and conflict areas in East, South East, and Pacific Asia, corresponding to the areas of Japan's colonial and military expansion during the period 1931–1945.[6] "Comfort stations" were varied in terms of their organization and operation. Some places were more structured and were operated directly by the military; other establishments were run as private businesses, building on the licensed prostitution system that existed in Japan at the time. Other facilities were more makeshift places where women were held and subjected to continuous sexual abuse as well as other forms of violence.[7] Women succumbed to this system of sexual exploitation through sex trafficking, kidnapping, deception, and forcible enlistment and recruitment by the military as well as by other Japanese officials and local collaborators.

The regulation of sex, along with the sexual exploitation of women (but sometimes also against men) is inherent in the operation of modern military forces. The outcome of the entire system is to produce and maintain gender and sexual binarism, in addition to traditional class and racial order.[8] The systematic sexual violence committed by the military during both armed conflicts and peacetime, therefore, has not in fact been uncommon in human history. Regulated prostitution (which controls male bodies through the exploitation of female bodies) was introduced and developed in European countries and the United States (and, needless to say, in Japan) during the nineteenth century in accord with mine colonial and military expansion and still prevailed even during World War II. Indeed, some scholars have suggested that the level of control of regulated prostitution often intensified in colonial territories. Regulating sexual practices linked issues of the military, gender, race, and public health.[9] Contemporary examples of widespread sexual assault, abuse, and exploitation in the US armed forces and among the United Nations Peacekeeping forces provides further evidence of this problematic connection between the military and sexual violence. Militarized sexual exploitation has also been used against an enemy as a form of physical, social, and psychological assault, that is, as "a weapon of war."[10]

In this light, it is necessary to acknowledge the past and present structural correlations between militarism, war, colonialism, gender, and sexual regulation and exploitation. The "comfort women" system that developed in many parts of Asia during the Japanese military expansion of the 1930s and the first half of the 1940s can also be understood within this context. At the same time, the unique nature of the Japanese system must be highlighted, especially regarding its extent, aggression, and severity. Researchers have now explored and documented its geographical spread, the scale of the victimization of women, their ethnic diversity, the level and duration of violence inflicted, and the extent of involvement by the military and other Japanese authorities.[11] The system is said to have been instituted by the Japanese military in order to prevent wartime rape, on the premise that the male sexual drive is "natural" and cannot be controlled.[12] Such a view, however, has been used historically to justify the exploitation of women's bodies and sexuality. Rather than reducing the incidence of rape, the "comfort women" system resulted in an unquestioning legitimization of sexual violence and exploitation of women, which came to be viewed as a "necessary evil."[13] In addition, the concept of naturalized male sexual "need" masks the fact that rape and other sexual violence during war often happens not simply as an expression of the biological sexual drive of men, but also as a collective "ritualistic" practice and a political strategy to exploit the biological, social, and symbolic meanings of the female body in a male-dominated social world. That is to say, rape is carried out both to harm women's reproductivity and to undermine the men of the enemy community.

In recent years, this aspect of the "comfort women" system has aroused intense division in Japan, South Korea, other Asian countries and beyond. The debate has opposed those campaigning for redress by seeking justice for the victims—including victim-survivors, transnational feminists, and other scholars and activists—against right-wing (Japanese) politicians and revisionist critics who deny the responsibility of the Japanese government for such an atrocity in the past and the associated violation of fundamental human rights. There are sharp disagreements regarding the degree of responsibility of the Japanese government, how and whether the injuries and voices of these women should even be acknowledged, and how their dehumanizing wartime experiences should best be represented and remembered today.

Discussions on the criminality of this system of sexual exploitation originally revolved around the role the Japanese military played in managing "comfort stations" and the level of coercion in the initial enlisting of women. Right-wing politicians and historical revisionists have claimed that the government authorities had only minimal involvement in the operation, arguing that their responsibility was restricted to regulating local private brokers who actually ran "comfort stations" and for protecting those civilians who managed and "worked" in "comfort stations." They have further maintained that "comfort stations" were organized on a commercial basis and asserted that the women were not forcibly recruited by the Japanese military but rather were usually sold into prostitution by their parents or guardians. In response to these assertions, survivors and activists have charged that, while the level of involvement of the Japanese military and other authorities did vary from place to place, they were responsible for introducing "comfort stations" and thereby sanctioned the overall arrangement. They have also maintained that what matters most today is not whether women were or were not coercively drafted, but rather that these women were taken unaware of their eventual degrading fate and were held captive against their will in these establishments.

Supported by feminist activists, historians, and other scholars, survivor-activists in recent decades have actively sought justice from the Japanese government. Liaising in the 1990s with feminist movements outside Japan that address other examples of wartime sexual violence—such as in the former Yugoslavia and Rwanda—they have successfully attracted the attention of the international community to their particular traumatic past and have helped gain recognition for systemic sexual violence not only as a serious war crime but also, more generally, as a crime against humanity.

Between 1991 and 2001, ten cases were filed by surviving victims against the Japanese government. All except one case, however, was either rejected or not accepted by District Courts and Appeal Courts. The outcome of the litigation brought by three victim-survivors and seven women from South Korea drafted for forced labor at the Shimonoseki Branch of the Yamaguchi District Court, the nearest Japanese court to Busan, Korea, was a partial acceptance of the plaintiffs' claims. Then, in 1998, the court recognized the failure of the Japanese government to fulfill its statutory duty to draw up compensatory legislation for "comfort women" and ordered the government to pay each of the victim-survivors of sexual slavery 300,000 yen ($2,800). This judgment, too, however, was subsequently overturned by the Hiroshima High Court in March 2001.

Meanwhile, over the past twenty-five years the Japanese government has made some, albeit limited, acknowledgement of the direct involvement of the Japanese military in managing the "comfort women" system. It has also acknowledged a certain level of coercion in its operation, as expressed in the 1993 Kono Statement issued by then Chief Cabinet Secretary of Japan, Kono Yohei. The Japanese government, however, has assumed the default position that, since all issues of reparation, restitution, and compensation had already been settled long ago by the San Francisco Peace Treaty, bilateral treaties and other agreements, in particular by the 1965 Treaty on Basic Relations between Japan and the Republic of Korea, no individual compensation was necessary at a later date. Yet, in recognition of its continuing moral responsibility, the Japanese government in 1995 established the Asian Peace and Friendship Fund for Women (also known as the Asian Women's Fund) in partnership with civil society as an expression of regret. The Fund has three provisions. First, it offers "atonement money" of 2,000,000 yen ($18,500) to victim-survivors donated by the public. Second, it issues a letter to victim-survivors from the Prime Minister expressing sincere remorse and apologizing to them. And third, the Fund provides medical and welfare support for victim-survivors through continuing government funding. While the Asian Women's Fund has been implemented, many affected women refused to accept the atonement money, criticizing it as an "alternative measure" to formal compensation that effectively blurs the legal responsibility of the Japanese government.

The request of survivor-victims for justice was further jeopardized by the 2015 Japan-Korea Agreement, which asserted that the "comfort women" matter would be resolved "finally and irreversibly" by the deal. Initially, the Japan-Korea Agreement was publicized as a "landmark" and a "breakthrough," being generally considered to represent the final achievement of a belated settlement on this divisive issue between Japan and South Korea (and other Asian countries concerned). However, survivor-activists and their allied groups have accused the governments of the two negotiating countries of failing even to consult, much less to seriously engage with, the victim-survivors themselves in negotiating the agreement. They expressed anger and frustration that the 2015 deal, despite asserting "the issue is resolved finally and irreversibly," excluded the voices of the victim-survivors, thereby disregarding and devaluing women's efforts for justice over the past twenty-five years.[14] The Japan-Korea Agreement ended up being condemned as an act of diplomatic complicity hammered out under pressure from the government of the United States, which was more concerned with political stability in East Asia than in addressing a historical injustice.

As recommendations made to the Japanese government in the 12th Asian Solidarity Conference on Japan's Military Sexual Slavery, held in 2014, clearly demonstrate, in their more than twenty-five-year effort to achieve justice, survivor-activists and their supporters have urged the Japanese government to genuinely resolve this issue. Their demands include recognizing the crucial role that it played in organizing the "comfort women" system, acknowledging the continuing suffering of women who fell victim to it, and admitting that the system was a historical violation of human rights. They proposed further that various reparation measures be undertaken with an offer of compensation to individual victims, as tangible evidence of the sincerity of their apology, and that preventative measures be taken against future reoccurrence.[15]

Remedial measures such as these had already been recommended to the Japanese government in the final judgment of the Women's International War Crimes Tribunal for the Trial of Japanese Military Sexual Slavery (WIWCT) held in Tokyo in December 2000. That Tribunal was organized by the transnational network of women's and human rights NGOs.[16] To similar effect, the Committee on the Elimination of Racial Discrimination in 2018[17] and the Committee on the Elimination of Discrimination against Women in 2016,[18] together with previous other concluding observations and recommendations within the

United Nations system, urged the Japanese government to formulate a lasting, victim-centered solution.

The Politics of Remembering Victim-Survivors

The practice of publicly remembering and memorializing war and trauma has never been gender-neutral. Nevertheless, commemorations of traumatic historical events have long been tone-deaf to militarized gender-based violence and have tended to completely ignore gendered experience and memory.[19] Exploring the world of war art, Joanna Bourke has pointed out that depictions of war rape in art are relatively rare. Drawing on the American feminist artist Judy Chicago's work "Double Jeopardy" in her *Holocaust Project* (1990), Bourke shows how Chicago sought to expose the absence of "women's sexual suffering" in "official" Holocaust narratives that seek to remember the death and suffering of Jewish and other groups in the Nazi genocide.[20]

In the ongoing campaign for redress, survivors and activists are challenging this lack of gender sensibility in the memorialization process. They are, furthermore, addressing the themes of recognition of and recovery from traumatic experience both during and after the war. In her now canonical study, *Trauma and Recovery* (1992), Judith Herman adopted social and feminist perspectives on the clinical analysis of trauma. The pioneering Harvard psychiatrist argued that an early fundamental step in overcoming any past trauma is that the traumatogenic event be identified and acknowledged by others as well as by individual victims. The Japanese government's continuing denial of responsibility has thus added a kind of therapeutic urgency to the struggle for recognition of the "comfort women" system.[21]

Herman identified three stages of trauma recovery and considered remembrance and mourning to be the second stage.[22] In the case of systematic political violence suffered by and in communities, remembrance and mourning are required at both the individual and collective levels. In fact, erecting a memorial and building an archive are among the listed demands presented to the Japanese government by the Korean Council for Justice and Remembrance for the Issues of Military Sexual Slavery by Japan (hereafter the Korean Council)—a grassroots organization in South Korea that has supported victim-survivors' campaign for redress since the early 1990s.[23] The final 2001 judgment of the Women's International War Crimes Tribunal for Japan's Military Sexual Slavery also recommended that the Japanese government "[r]ecognize and honor the victims and survivors through the creation of *memorials*, museums, and libraries dedicated to their memory and the promise of 'never again' as one of the 'remedial measures' that the Japanese government should undertake in order to 'fulfill its responsibility'."[24]

Constructing physical memorials to survivors, as well as those who perished, and acknowledging their past traumatic lives has thus been fundamental to the efforts of the redress movement to achieve a degree of psychological recovery of individual women. Survivor-activists have indeed repeatedly expressed how much they are emotionally attached to the memorials, which provide solace and reassurance.[25] Edward Vickers has identified three overlapping stages of the movement for redress: the first phase revolved around securing recognition, in particular by the governmental authorities in Japan, of legal responsibility. Phase Two, which took place mainly between the mid-1990s and the mid-2000s, sought to make the Japanese government accountable for the crimes and to secure reparations. And the third stage of the process, since the early 2000s, has focused on public commemoration.[26] Recognizing and remembering these women—at the local, national, and international levels—is vital for the psychological health of survivors and has also become important societally, because many women, who were already in their sixties and seventies when they started to be known as victim-survivors, have since passed away.

A range of campaigns about this haunting historical issue have now been mounted. These efforts include applications for UNESCO "Memory of the World" status for "Voices of the 'Comfort Women'" and for "Documentation on 'Comfort Women' and Japanese Army Discipline." The request for this second initiative was filed by several Chinese groups in 2014 and then again, two years later, by a number of trans- and multinational networks. In addition to the establishment of museums dedicated to the "comfort women" system—and to its survivors living in cities such as Tokyo, Seoul, Taipei, and Nanjing—the first International Conference of Museums on Japan's Military "Comfort Women" was held in Tokyo in April 2017.[27] Beginning in 2009, campaigns for erecting memorials have appeared in South Korea, in other Asian countries, and in Australia, Canada, and the United States. As the World War I historian Jay Winter has observed with reference to war memorials, such structures are vital locations where people can mourn both individually and communally.[28] Unfortunately, as the continuing case of the "comfort women" controversy exemplifies, such "sites of memory and sites of mourning" can also provoke emotionally charged battles of the politics of remembrance.

The first memorial to victim-survivors of the Asia-Pacific War's "comfort women" system located on public land was erected, of all places, in Palisades Park, New Jersey, near New York City, in 2010.[29] A Korean-American civil organization called the Korean-American Civic Empowerment (KACE) initiated the memorial.[30] The politics surrounding such acts of remembrance became more noticeable with the installation of the best-known memorial to the victims of Japanese military sexual slavery, *The Statue of Peace*—sometimes called *The Statue of a Girl of Peace*—which was completed in December 2011. That statue is situated in Seoul, South Korea, directly in front of the Japanese Embassy near Sejongno Park in the center of the South Korean capital. This striking bronze sculpture assemblage of a young barefoot woman sitting on a chair with an empty chair next to her was designed by the sculptor couple Kim Seo-kyung and Kim Eun-sung. It was erected to mark the 1000th Wednesday Demonstration in front of the Japanese Embassy by victim-survivors and other activists, a practice that commenced in January 1992.

Kim Seo-kyung, the main artist involved in creating the statue, explained how she, as a woman with a young daughter, carefully thought through the details of the memorial design, which consequently became rich in symbols (see Figure 12.1).[31] The Seoul statue portrays a young woman, or rather a girl, wearing traditional Korean dress to represent the loss of innocence from sexual abuse by Japanese soldiers. The figure's hair is cropped to demonstrate that women were forcibly taken from their families. Her bare feet and raised heels imply the hardship she had to endure. The clenched fists of the female figure convey the determination of survivors today to obtain an apology from the Japanese government. The shadow cast behind the girl is an old woman who represents the countless women who have been demonstrating for years in front of the Japanese Embassy. In Kim Seo-kyung's sculpture ensemble, the girl sits on a chair, just as many demonstrating survivors bring chairs to sit on during the demonstrations. The empty chair symbolizes the spirits of those women who were lost a long time ago and could not participate in demonstrations. Perched on the girl's shoulder is a bird, a sign of peace and freedom that also connects living survivors with deceased victims. The inscription on "The Statue for Peace" is based on the calligraphy of one of the survivors, Kim Bok-dong. Kim Seo-kyung also stated that the two artists conceptualized a memorial that would invite people to interact and communicate with it, thus the life-size dimensions of the memorial. The empty chair is crucial in enhancing communication between the viewers and the memorial; it seems to invite viewers to sit on it and to gaze at the Japanese Embassy, while generating compassion toward the victim-survivors.[32]

Since the original plan to erect the *Statue of a Girl of Peace* in front of the Japanese Embassy, the Japanese government has expressed its deep discontent and uneasiness with the statue and even tried to prevent it from being created. Since its completion, Japanese officials have repeatedly requested the memorial's removal. These interventions by the Japanese state continued and then increased as plans for erecting other memorials took hold across South Korea and in other countries. The government of Japan has expressed support for Japanese expatriate communities that oppose such memorials, which it sees as materializations of anti-Japanese sentiment, rather than as possible symbols of and aspirations for universal peace, as survivors and other activists intend these memorials to be. The Japanese government voiced its hostility toward the memorial in the South Korean capital directly and diplomatically in the Japan Korea Agreement of 28 December 2015. As noted above, the Japan Korea Agreement was sharply criticized by survivor-activists and activist organizations in South Korea and Japan, including by the Korean Council. What infuriated these groups the most was that the demand by the Japanese for the removal of the *Statue of a Girl of Peace*, was integral to concluding the deal of the agreement. In response to this subterfuge, activists, and particularly South Korean students, began to organize all day sit-in protests that lasted for many months and were intended to protect the statue from removal.[33] Amid these protests, another *Statue of a Girl of Peace* was placed close to the Japanese consulate in the southern port city of Busan at the end of 2016, initially without seeking the permission of Busan City.[34] In a gesture of protest against this move, the Japanese government temporarily recalled its ambassadors to South Korea and suspended high-level economic talks. As these events indicate, the official recognition and memorialization of this past historical crime has in the last generation become a flashpoint in intra-Asian foreign relations.

The Practice of Commemorating Historical Trauma in Contemporary Japan

As a country and culture, Japan has a history memorializing traumatic episodes in the Asia-Pacific War. By far, the best-known example of this national practice is the Hiroshima Peace Memorial Park, which powerfully commemorates victims of the atomic bomb. Hiroshima Peace Memorial Park opened in 1956,[35] Nagasaki Peace Park, opened two years later,[36] and the Nagasaki National Peace Memorial Hall for the Atomic Bomb Victims, opened in 2002.[37] These famous commemorative sites have become popular destinations for both Japanese school trips and sight-seeing foreigners. Numerous memorials within these parks and the surrounding areas have been built to honor the victims of the atomic bombs from many different places, ages, and occupations. These commemorative sites deploy a variety of designs, forms, and spatial arrangements to create an emotionally moving space for contemplation and compassion. For instance, the Memorial Cenotaph for the Victims of the Atomic Bomb and The Peace Flame are both located in the center of Hiroshima Peace Memorial Park. The Cenotaph frames the nearby Peace Flame as well as the "A-Bomb Dome," located a few hundred meters away, where visitors can read the inscription "please rest in peace, as we will not repeat the mistake" (Figure 12.2).[38] Similarly, in entering the Remembrance Hall of the Peace Memorial Hall for the Atomic Bomb Victims in Nagasaki, visitors encounter a sign explaining that "This is the place to pray for everlasting peace and eternal rest for the souls of all those who perished in the atomic bombings." Walking outside, the visitor finds two large walls of glass and a sculpted basin (Figure 12.3) with the following signage:

> The two walls of glass that jut up out of the sculpted basin are the upper section of the glass pillars in the Remembrance Hall two floors below. The line they form points in the

FIGURE 12.2. The Memorial Cenotaph for the Victims of the Atomic Bomb with a stone inscription in the Hiroshima Peace Memorial Park framing the Peace Flame and the A-Bomb Dome. © Maki Kimura.

FIGURE 12.3. The Peace Memorial Hall for the Atomic Bomb Victims in Nagasaki. © Maki Kimura.

direction of the place where the atomic bomb exploded. . . . The sculpted basin, which is twenty-nine meters in diameter, was designed for the great number of people who craved water after experiencing the atomic bombing. Please walk all the way around it, proceeding counterclockwise in order to calm your mind before entering the Hall.

These are only a few of the many structures that demonstrate the affective power of memorials to wartime trauma in Japan through the effective use of design, form, and spatial arrangements. While such an act of remembering trauma is crucial in facilitating the recovery of victims and in fostering human empathy, it is also important to note that, as a general rule, the perpetrator of the original historical crime being remembered "does everything in his power to promote forgetting."[39] This fact most likely explains why officials in Japan have also been reluctant to support memorials for victims of other violent atrocities committed by Imperial Japanese troops during the Asia-Pacific War. Foremost among these other events is the Nanjing Massacre of 1937—also known as "the Rape of Nanjing"—in East China.

This does not mean, however, that all traces of past Japanese colonial and imperial mass violence have been expunged from official memory. Memorializing the catastrophic human effects of the atomic bombs in 1945 could also open up the possibility of acknowledging other historical traumas. In Hiroshima and Nagasaki, tens of thousands of Korean and Chinese people who had been drafted during the war for forced labor were also killed by the atomic blasts. In both Hiroshima and Nagasaki, memorials now stand to the Korean and Chinese victims of the bombs, thus admitting the complicity of Japan's colonial past in the deaths of these innocent non-Japanese Asians.[40] Now recognized around the world as sacred places for peace, Hiroshima and Nagasaki are unique spaces in which multiple traumatic pasts associated with war can be acknowledged and where a diversity of war narratives from the perspective of both victims and perpetrators are displayed simultaneously for all the world to see.

The role of place in the practice of remembrance is also embodied on the island of Okinawa, Japan, where the Peace Memorial Park was opened in 1972.[41] Despite being a semi-tropical archipelago of beautiful islands with a rich biodiversity situated in the East China Sea, Okinawa has suffered a history of oppression, war, and militarization. Invaded and colonized by Japan in the early seventeenth century, and then annexed in 1879, Okinawa and its people have experienced systematic discrimination, exploitation, and oppression for centuries. Worst of all, in 1945, toward the end of the Asia-Pacific War, Okinawa became an actual battlefield, in fact the only battlefield located on Japanese territory. The awful fate of the Okinawan people was to be attacked by both US and Japanese armed forces. Instead of protecting the native inhabitants, the Japanese army used the islanders as human shields, forcing them at times to commit suicide

FIGURE 12.4. Steps leading to the memorial for Korean victims in the Okinawa Peace Memorial Park with the Peace Memorial Hall behind. © Maki Kimura.

in order to avoid the "dishonor" of being captured by US soldiers. It is said that one in five Okinawans was killed during the ferocious Battle of Okinawa, which lasted from early April to late June 1945.[42]

Today, Okinawa continues to host over 70 percent of US military bases and facilities in Japan. With this everyday presence and violence of foreign militarization, combined with the knowledge of their complex history, the people of Okinawa have a strong awareness of the trauma of war and commemoration. A memorial to the Korean victims who were drafted and forced to become civilian employees of the Japanese military (Figure 12.4) is clearly visible next to the Okinawa Peace Memorial Hall.[43] Unveiled in 1995 and located in the town of Itoman on the southern tip of the main island, the Cornerstone of Peace is another key memorial in the Park. It features a central Flame of Peace surrounded by 118 screen-like walls spreading out in concentric semi-circles facing toward the sea (Figure 12.5). On the walls are inscribed the names of over 240,000

FIGURE 12.5. Monument walls of the Cornerstone of Peace in the Okinawa Memorial Park. © Maki Kimura.

people—civilians and soldiers of all the combatant nations—who died in the Battle of Okinawa.[44] Okinawa's history of successive invasions and occupations leaves room for memorializing the multifaceted victimization of war and oppression on the island.

Okinawa is one of the few places in Japan that present a gendered memory of war trauma. The tragic story and fate of over two hundred Himeyuri students from a teacher training college and another women's college who were mobilized on Okinawa to work as assistant nurses at army and field hospitals in 1945 has long been known. The Himeyuri Cenotaph was completed in 1946, and a dedicated museum, the Himeyuri Peace Memorial Museum, opened beside the Cenotaph in 1989. Himeyuri students faced the nearly impossible task of treating injured soldiers without adequate facilities or medical supplies while living under the constant threat of bombing and invasion. The casualty rate among the students escalated at the war's end after the military demobilization order of June 1945; at that time, students were ordered to leave hospital shelters and caves and had to protect themselves from bullets, gas attacks, and bombs. Many of these young women became victims of these attacks; others had been instructed by the Japanese military to take their own lives rather than suffer the dishonor of capture by the enemy. In particular, women were felt to be at risk of rape by

FIGURE 12.6. A memorial for the *Himeyuri* Students at Arakawa Shore, Okinawa. © Maki Kimura.

invading US soldiers who had landed on the islands. More than half of the students who had been mobilized were killed.⁴⁵

A couple of miles away from the Museum at Arasaki Shore lay memorial stones to the Himeyuri students who died there, ten of them by killing themselves with hand-grenades while under attack by US Marines armed with machine guns (Figure 12.6). By standing in front of these memorial stones on the remote rugged shoreline, with a list of names and emotive poems to mourn their death, the present-day visitor senses the pain and lost lives of these helpless young women. The narratives of Himeyuri students' experience against the background of Okinawa history illuminates an invaluable practice of gendered commemoration of war and trauma. At the same time, the memorialization of the student nurse corps reveals how dominant discourses continue to "reinforce, reproduce, or silence particular gendered trauma."⁴⁶ As the strategic importance of Okinawa increased in the 1940s, rape by Japanese soldiers and later by American soldiers became prevalent and by 1944 the Japanese government started to organize "comfort stations" in Okinawa; to date, 146 "comfort stations" have been identified on the island.⁴⁷ The firsthand stories of sexual violence experienced and witnessed by local Okinawa women and men and by the Himeyuri students, however, are not incorporated into the memorialization.⁴⁸

The Affective Politics of Memorialization

The examples that I have discussed above of the practice of the commemoration of trauma in Japan's twentieth-century history illustrate how specific designs, forms, and spatial fields, as well as existing narratives of time and place, powerfully affect visitors and create, reinforce, and exclude particular memories of trauma and war. As the collective perpetrator of these traumatic pasts, the Japanese government is inclined to disapprove of any form of recognition of the "comfort women" system, a criminal episode in their national history that they prefer to deny or forget. Thus, the memorial to the sexual slaves of the Asia-Pacific War has become a critical battleground in the contemporary politics of memorialization. To date, there seems to have been, however, insufficient awareness and discussion of the very divergent affective potentials of the memorial, or, to put it differently, of how particular styles, representations, and spatialities elicit different political responses.

As I noted above, the *Statue of a Girl of Peace* originally installed in front of the Japanese Embassy in Seoul in 2011 conveys many symbolic meanings. Compassion and determination may be generated in some visitors, especially when sitting on the empty chairs next to the girl or dressing her with hats, scarves, gloves, and shoes. Kim Seo-kyung's memorial also has a specific relation to its site. Not only does it commemorate victims and survivors of the "comfort women" system, it also pays homage to the twenty years of activism (up to 2011), including the weekly Wednesday Demonstrations in front of the Japanese Embassy.[49] The inscription on the memorial clearly expresses this intention in written form:

> December 14, 2011 marks the 1000th Wednesday demonstration for the solution of Japanese military sexual slavery issue after its first rally on January 8, 1992 in front of the Japanese Embassy. This peace monument stands to commemorate the spirit and the deep history of the Wednesday Demonstration.[50]

This text stands in stark contrast to the inscriptions on the memorials in Hiroshima, Nagasaki, and Okinawa, which are designed to mourn and commemorate the dead. In addition, while this is a statue specifically of a Korean girl, rather than remembering trauma within a nationalist framework or shaming the Japanese government (as it is often misinterpreted to do), the installation is ultimately a monument for "positive peace" situated in a specific geo-historical setting. Through the Wednesday Demonstrations, survivors have created a space for interaction, dialogue, and empathy with people from South Korea as well as the rest of the world. Recalling the painful memories of their experiences during and after the war, survivors initially could only focus on their individual ordeals. Through group demonstrations and public activism, they become peace activists at this very site, now called Peace Street by activists with a much wider context of history.[51]

Stylistically speaking, it is difficult to determine if realistic or abstract forms arouse greater affective responses in visitors to these commemorative sites. The Hiroshima, Nagasaki, and Okinawa memorials show how public structures in an abstract and minimalist style, often accompanied by emotive texts, can move people in body and mind. In his well-known discussion of World War I memorials, Jay Winter illuminates the potential power of abstract or non-representational memorials that provide space and time for collective remembrance and mourning.[52] At the same time, in the instance of the *Statue of a Girl of Peace*, it is a realistic representational style—a sitting girl with an empty chair next to her—that compels the visiting viewer; survivor-victims at the site regularly remark how they feel passionately connected to the memorial seeing it as their sister, while other visitors demonstrate the intimate act of placing scarves and hats on the figure of the girl. Whether realistic or abstract, the material aspects of the memorial are vital.

If this is the case, then, what do other "comfort women" memorials cast in the same style but located in different places with different local narratives of war memorialize? Kim Seo-kyung and Kim Eun-sung have also created other memorials. They based their other commemorative work on four different, loosely categorized design types, which they choose and finalize through consultation with the local people commissioning the memorial.[53] These memorials to "comfort women" have been erected in Busan, South Korea, and Glendale Central Park, east of Los Angeles, California, in 2013. Both of them are almost identical in form to the site-specific *Statue of a Girl of Peace* in central Seoul. So, what does the Glendale memorial commemorate, and whose trauma is being memorialized? The relative success of campaigns for constructing such memorials around the world can in part be attributed to transnational feminist networks as well as to coalition-building of diaspora politics and transnational commemoration.[54] Many memorials outside of South Korea have a similar design, although they stand today in places with their own local and national narratives of trauma and war, which could well generate different affective experiences of memorialization.

Between the years 2010 and 2017, an exhibition of photographic images of survivors of Japan's military sexual slavery in Indonesia, the former Dutch colony of the East Indies, toured different cities in the Netherlands, Indonesia, Japan, France, Germany, and the United States. The show was produced to convey the memories of women's suffering, by a Dutch photographer, Jan Banning, and a Dutch journalist and anthropologist, Hilde Janssen, who has lived many years in Jakarta.[55] Using the example of this exhibition, Katharine McGregor and Vera Mackie have observed how different audiences around the world interpreted the images in the traveling show differently, through "local mnemonic practice and knowledge system."[56] In a similar way, monument designers aspire to create a shared, affective experience and generate a process of transnational commemoration. Yet, when established in places away from the site it was originally created for, the statue of the Korean girl could, in ways that are unexpected and unintended, result in commemorating very exclusive national or ethnic/racial collective traumas.[57] Or alternatively, the sculpture can fail to be perceived as commemorating anything at all, due to a lack of relevant local knowledge or narrative traditions. This contextual possibility is exemplified in my own comment on the *Statue of a Girl of Peace* in Wiesent, Germany, which I cited at length at the beginning of this chapter.

The possibility of performing true transnational feminist commemorative acts can only emerge by addressing cosmopolitan concerns transcending a national heritage of injury that travels across the globe to arouse transnational nationalism. For the successful realization of a new cosmopolitan sense of community founded on equality, justice, and women's rights, therefore, memorials of the victims and survivors of Japan's military sexual slavery need to be planned carefully and thoughtfully. The individual affective experiences evoked through the materiality of the memorials should inspire us to develop "empathic connections for others" beyond regional, national, linguistic, or racial boundaries. Such emotional responses, however, can also be translated and interpreted within specific geographical locations with local knowledge and memory practices.[58] Many challenges need to be overcome in order to effectively achieve transcultural feminist commemorations, not least of all resistance to these acts by government authorities with powerful invested interests. Despite this counter-current of opposition, the process of feminist commemoration continues apace with two newly erected memorials outside of Japan and South Korea in the past few years: in Shanghai, China, on the campus of Shanghai Normal University, in 2016, and in downtown San Francisco, California, near Saint Mary's Square, in 2017. Interestingly, these recent memorials in Shanghai and San Francisco were both designed specifically for their respective sites. The Shanghai installation, which is the first memorial of its kind in China, portrays two girls—one Korean, the other Chinese—sitting next to one another beside an empty chair. Shanghai Normal University was chosen as the site because the campus also houses the Chinese "Comfort Women" Museum. The statue in San Francisco represents three young women—from China, Korea, and the Philippines—positioned in a circle on a plinth holding hands, with an additional figure of the sculptor Kim Hak-sun nearby looking at them. Located close to Chinatown in culturally diverse San Francisco, within the visible presence of different Asian diaspora communities, this memorial represents "a genuine pan-Asian American movement." It conveys a universalist message of women's rights as human rights and the determination never to let the past violation of these rights be forgotten.[59]

Maki Kimura is Lecturer in Gender and Politics at University College London, in the UK. Her research interests are in gender and race equality, feminist activism, and war and peace. She is the author of a book on Japan's military sexual slavery during World War II entitled *Unfolding the "Comfort Women" Debates: Modernity, Violence, Women's Voices* (Palgrave Macmillan, 2016). She continues her research into war, gender, and memorialization.

Notes

1. Field notes by the author, 16 July 2017.
2. Originally started in March 2015 at the University of Cape Town in South Africa, the protest movement campaigned to remove a statue of nineteenth-century British arch-colonialist Cecil John Rhodes. The campaign resulted in the removal of the statue, attracted worldwide attention, and has since sparked similar protests in South Africa, the UK, the United States, and elsewhere.
3. Victim-survivors have repeatedly expressed their discontent at being called "comfort women," since their experiences during the war were far from what the term "comfort" implies. They argue that "sexual slaves" is a more appropriate designation. In this chapter, I avoid referring to the victims of Japanese military sexual abuse as "comfort women." I do, however, use the term to refer to the system of Japan's military sexual slavery during the Asia-Pacific War (e.g., to the system of "comfort women") and to memorials in homage of these victims, but always with inverted commas in order to indicate the problematic nature of the term.
4. Fight for Justice, "Who Were the Japanese Military 'Comfort Women'?"
5. Kimura, *Unfolding "Comfort Women" Debates*, 194–95; 200–2.
6. Yoshimi, "Dai isho," 3.
7. Women's Active Museum on War and Peace (WAM), *Nihongun "Ianfu"*, 9–10.
8. Kimura, *Unfolding "Comfort Women" Debates*.
9. Enloe, *Maneuvers*, 64.
10. Nagahara, "Ianfu," 63–65.
11. Tanaka, *Japan's Comfort Women*, 95–96.
12. Yoshimi, "Dai isho," 9–10.
13. Hasegawa, "Girei to shite no seiboryoku," 287–88.
14. Kimura, "Japan's Military Sexual Slavery."
15. 12th Asian Solidary Conference on the Issue of Military Sexual Slavery by Japan, *Recommendations to the Government of Japan*.
16. Women's International War Crimes Tribunal for the Trial of Japanese Military Sexual Slavery (WIWCT), *Final Judgement*, paragraph 1086. Since this Tribunal is a people's tribunal, the judgment does not carry any formal authority, nor is the ruling legally binding. Nevertheless, prominent international lawyers were involved in the Tribunal so within the transnational feminist community the judgment is highly respected.
17. United Nations Committee on the Elimination of Racial Discrimination (CERD), *Concluding Observations*.
18. United Nations Committee on the Elimination of Discrimination against Women (CEDAW), *Concluding Observations*.
19. Duriesmith, "Memory, Trauma," 267, 269; Peto and Altinay, "Introduction."
20. Bourke, "Rape in the Art of War," 319–20.

21. Herman, *Trauma and Recovery*.
22. Getz, "Honour and Dignity," 64; Herman, *Trauma and Recovery*, 175–95.
23. The Korean Council, "Our Demand." The organization originally started as the Korean Council for the Women Drafted for Military Sexual Slavery by Japan, but was renamed after its merger with the Foundation for Justice and Remembrance in 2018.
24. Women's International War Crimes Tribunal for the Trial of Japanese Military Sexual Slavery (WIWCT), *Final Judgement*, paragraph 1086, no. 6. Emphasis mine.
25. Okamoto, "'Heiwa no shoujyozou'," 76–77.
26. Vickers, "Commemorating 'Comfort Women.'"
27. Mackie and Crozier-De Rosa, "Remembering the Grandmothers"; Vickers, "Commemorating 'Comfort Women'"; UNESCO, *International Memory of the World Register*.
28. Winter, *Sites of Memory, Sites of Mourning*, 79.
29. This was the first memorial in a public setting for the victims of the "comfort women" system. However, an earlier memorial was erected in Chiba near Tokyo in 1985 on the premises of the Kanita Women's Village, a rehabilitation and care institution for women, following the wishes of Shirota Suzuko, who was a survivor of the system and lived in the Village.
30. McCarthy and Hasunuma, "Coalition Building and Mobilization," 417.
31. Okamoto and Kim, "Hitobito to ishisotsu," 25–30.
32. Okamoto and Kim, "Hitobito to ishisotsu," 21–34.
33. The Japanese government had been planning to upgrade and modernize their Seoul Embassy, and in 2015 the Embassy and consulate service were moved to the nearby Twintree Tower Building. At that time, the former Embassy buildings were demolished. However, in the meantime, due to the discovery of archaeological artifacts on the new planned site and to various political complications, the development of the new buildings has been delayed. Sasaki, "Kankoku no nihontaishikan."
34. KH Digital2, "Seoul Faces Dilemma."
35. Hiroshima City, "Heiwa kinenkouen ni tsuite."
36. Nagasaki City, "Negai no zoon."
37. Nagasaki Peace Memorial Hall, "Kinenkan ni tsuite."
38. Hiroshima Convention and Visitors Bureau, "Cenotaph for the A-bomb Victims."
39. Herman, *Trauma and Recovery*, 8.
40. Hiroshima City, "Kankokujin genbakugiseisha ireihi," Nagasaki City, "Tsuitou Nagasaki genbaku."
41. Okinawa Peace Memorial Park Foundation, "Okinawa Memorial Park."
42. Kimura, "The Anti-US Military Base Struggle in Okinawa, Japan."
43. Okinawa City, "Okinawa kinen kouen."
44. Okinawa Peace Memorial Park Foundation, "The Cornerstone of Peace."
45. Himeyuri Peace Museum, *Himeyuri gaidobook*; Women's Active Museum on War and Peace (WAM), *Katarogu 10*.
46. Duriesmith, "Memory, Trauma," 265.
47. Women's Active Museum on War and Peace (WAM), *Katarogu 10*, 14.
48. It should be noted, however, that one of the few memorials located in Japan to Japan's wartime sexual ill-treatment of women stands on Ishigaki Island in Okinawa. It was erected, on private grounds, in 2008.
49. Okamoto and Kim, "Hitobito to ishisotsu"; Yang, "Heiwa no hi"; Mackie and Crozier-De Rosa, "Remembering the Grandmothers."
50. Okamoto and Kim, "Hitobito to ishisotsu," 26.
51. Yang, "'Heiwa no hi'," 16–18.
52. Winter, *Sites of Memory, Sites of Mourning*, 98–116.

53. Okamoto and Kim, "Hitobito to ishisotsu," 24.
54. Hasunuma and McCarthy, "Creating Collective Memory"; Kwon, "Sonyŏsang Phenomenon"; McCarthy and Hasunuma, "Coalition Building and Mobilization"; Yoon, "Erecting 'Comfort Women' Memorials."
55. McGregor and Mackie, "Transcultural Memory." Portraits of women from these exhibitions can be viewed at Jan Banning's website "Comfort Women (Troostmeisjes)."
56. McGregor and Mackie, "Transcultural Memory," 141.
57. Kwon, "Sonyŏsang Phenomenon"; Rooney, "Politics of Shame"; Shepherd, "Cosmopolitanism Nationalism."
58. Yoon, "Erecting 'Comfort Women' Memorials," 84.
59. McCarthy and Hasunuma, "Coalition Building and Mobilization," 421.

Bibliography

12th Asian Solidarity Conference on the Issue of Military Sexual Slavery by Japan. *Recommendations to the Government of Japan for Resolution of the Japanese Military "Comfort Women" Issue*. Tokyo: Women's Action Museum on War and Peace (WAM), 2014. Retrieved 1 December 2019 from https://wam-peace.org/main/wp-content/uploads/2014/07/20140602_EN.pdf.

Banning, Jan. "Comfort Women (Troostmeisjes)" Jan Banning Photographer. 2019. Retrieved 1 December 2019 from http://www.janbanning.com/gallery/comfort-women/.

Bourke, Joanna. "Rape in the Art of War." In *War and Art: A Visual History of Modern Conflict*, edited by Joanna Bourke, 316–23. London: Reaktion Books, 2017.

Duriesmith, David. "Memory, Trauma, and Gendered Insecurity." In *Routledge Handbook of Gender and Security*, edited by Caron E. Gentry, Laura J. Shepherd, and Laura Sjoberg, 262–72. New York: Routledge, 2018.

Enloe, Cynthia H. *Maneuvers: The International Politics of Militarizing Women's Lives*. Berkeley: University of California Press, 2000.

Fight for Justice. "Who Were the Japanese Military 'Comfort Women'?" Retrieved 1 December 2019 from http://fightforjustice.info/?page_id=2356.

Getz, Gudrun. "Honour and Dignity: Trauma Recovery and International Law in the Issue of the Comfort Women of South Korea." *Journal of International Women's Studies* 19, no. 1 (2018): 63–77.

Hasegawa, Hiroko. "Girei to shite no seiboryoku [Sexual Violence as a Ritual]." In *Nashonaru Hisutori wo Koete* [Transcending national history], edited by Yoichi Komori and Tetsuya Takahashi, 287–88 (Tokyo: Tokyo University Press, 1998).

Hasunuma, Linda, and Mary M. McCarthy. "Creating a Collective Memory of the Comfort Women in the USA." *International Journal of Politics, Culture, and Society* 32, no. 2 (2019): 145–62.

Herman, Judith Lewis. *Trauma and Recovery: The Aftermath of Violence, from Domestic Abuse to Political Terror*. New York: Basic Books, 1992.

Himeyuri Peace Museum. *Himeyuri Heiwakinen shiryokan koushiki gaidobook* [Himeyuri Peace Museum official guidebook]. Okinawa: Himeyuri Peace Museum. 2010.

Hiroshima City. "Heiwa kinenkouen ni tsuite [About Hiroshima Peace Memorial Park]." Hiroshima: Hiroshima City, 2019. Retrieved 1 December 2019 from http://www.city.hiroshima.lg.jp/www/contents/1483699383190/index.html.

Hiroshima City. "Kankokujin genbakugiseisha ireihi" [Cenotaph for Korean atomic bomb victims]. Hiroshima: Hiroshima City, 2019. Retrieved 1 December 2019 from http://www.pcf.city.hiroshima.jp/virtual/VirtualMuseum_j/tour/ireihi/tour_11.html.

Hiroshima Convention and Visitors Bureau. "Cenotaph for the A-bomb Victims (Memorial Monument for Hiroshima, City of Peace)." Hiroshima: Hiroshima Convention and Visitors Bureau, 2019. Retrieved 1 December 2019 from https://www.hiroshima-navi.or.jp/en/post/007122.html.

KH Digital2. "Seoul Faces Dilemma over 'Comfort Women' Statue in Busan." *Korean Herald* 3 January 2017. Retrieved 1 December 2019 from http://www.koreaherald.com/view.php?ud=20170103000764.

Kimura, Maki. "The Anti-US Military Base Struggle in Okinawa, Japan." *OpenDemocracy* 13 February 2016. Retrieved 1 December 2019 from https://www.opendemocracy.net/en/anti-us-military-base-struggle-in-okinawa-japan/.

———. "Japan's Military Sexual Slavery: Whose Agreement?" *OpenDemocracy* 20 January 2016. Retrieved 1 December 2019 from https://www.opendemocracy.net/en/5050/japans-military-sexual-slavery-whose-agreement/.

———. *Unfolding the "Comfort Women" Debates: Modernity, Violence, Women's Voices*. Basingstoke: Palgrave Macmillan, 2016.

The Korean Council. "Our Demand: The Korean Council Demands to the Government of Japan." Retrieved 1 December 2019 from http://womenandwar.net/kr/history-of-the-movement/.

Kwon, Vicki Sung-yeon. "The Sonyŏsang Phenomenon: Nationalism and Feminism Surrounding the 'Comfort Women' Statue." *Korean Studies* 43 (2019): 6–39.

Mackie, Vera, and Sharon Crozier-De Rosa. "Remembering the Grandmothers: The International Movement to Commemorate the Survivors of Militarized Sexual Abuse in the Asia-Pacific War." *Asia-Pacific Journal* 17, no. 4 (2019): Article ID 5248. Retrieved 1 December 2019 from https://apjjf.org/2019/04/MackieCrozierDeRosa.html.

McCarthy, Mary M., and Linda C. Hasunuma. "Coalition Building and Mobilization: Case Studies of the Comfort Women Memorials in the United States." *Politics, Groups, and Identities* 6, no. 3 (2018): 411–34.

McGregor, Katharine E., and Vera Mackie. "Transcultural Memory and the Troostmeisjes/Comfort Women Photographic Project." *History & Memory* 30, no. 1 (2018): 116–50.

Nagahara, Yoko. "'Ianfu' no hikakushi ni mukete [Developing comparative historical research on 'comfort women']." In *"Ianfu" mondai wo/kara kangaeru: Gunjiseibouryoku to nichijyoseikai* [Thinking about/from the "comfort women" issue: Militarized sexual violence and the everyday world], edited by Historical Study Association and Japanese History Study Association, 63–79. Tokyo: Iwanami Shoten, 2014.

Nagasaki City. "Negai no zoon kinenzou chiku [A zone for hope: Memorials area]." Nagasaki: Nagasaki City, 2019. Retrieved 1 December 2019 from http://www.city.nagasaki.lg.jp/heiwa/3030000/3030100/p005151.html.

Nagasaki City. "Tsuitou Nagasaki genbaku chosenjin giseisha" [Commemorating Korean victims of the Nagasaki atomic bomb]. Nagasaki: Nagasaki City, 2019. Retrieved 1 December 2019 from https://nagasakipeace.jp/japanese/map/zone_inori/tsuito_chosenjin_giseisha.html.

Nagasaki Peace Memorial Hall. "Kinenkan ni tsuite" [About the hall]. Nagasaki: Nagasaki Peace Memorial Hall, 2019. Retrieved 1 December 2019 from https://www.peace-nagasaki.go.jp/about.

Okamoto, Yuka. "'Heiwa no shoujyozou' wa 'hannichi' no shocho nanoka?" [Q3: Is *The Statue for a Girl of Peace* a symbol of 'anti-Japanese sentiment?']. In *Naze 'Heiwa no Shoujyozou' wa Suwaritsuzukeru noka* [Why does "The Statue for a Girl of Peace" remain seated?

Engaging with the memory of harming], edited by Yuko Okamoto and Pu-ja Kim, 76–77. Yokohama: Seori Shobo, 2016.

Okamoto, Yuka, and Pu-ja Kim. "Hitobito to ishisotsu ga dekiru monyumento wo" [Creating a monument that can communicate with people]. In *Naze 'Heiwa no Shoujyozou' wa Suwaritsuzukeru noka* [Why does "The Statue for a Girl of Peace" remain seated? Engaging with the memory of harming], edited Yuko Okamoto and Pu-ja Kim, 20–34. Yokohama: Seori Shobo, 2016.

Okinawa City. "Okinawa kinen kouen" [Okinawa Peace Memorial Park]. Okinawa: Okinawa City. 2019. Retrieved 1 December 2019 from http://www.city.itoman.lg.jp/kankou-navi/docs-kankou/2013022300322/.

Okinawa Peace Memorial Park Foundation. "Okinawa Memorial Park." Okinawa: Okinawa Peace Memorial Park Foundation, 2019. Retrieved 1 December 2019 from http://sp.heiwa-irei-okinawa.jp/index.html.

Okinawa Peace Memorial Park Foundation. "The Cornerstone of Peace." Okinawa: Okinawa Peace Memorial Park Foundation, 2019. Retrieved 1 December 2019 from http://sp.heiwa-irei-okinawa.jp/stone/stone.html.

Peto, Andrea, and Ayşe Gül Altinay. "Introduction: Uncomfortable Connections: Gender, Memory, War." In *Gendered Wars, Gendered Memories: Feminist Conversations on War, Genocide and Political Violence*, edited by Ayşe Gül Altinay and Andrea Peto, 1–22. New York: Routledge, 2016.

Rooney, Sierra. "The Politics of Shame: The *Glendale Comfort Women Memorial* and the Complications of Transnational Commemorations." *De Arte* 53, no. 2/3 (2018): 86–102.

Sasaki, Kazuyoshi. "Kankoku no nihontaishikan, tatekae ga susumazu akichininatamama yonen ga tatta riyuu" [Reasons why four years have passed without any progress in building a new Japanese Embassy in Seoul]. *Newsweek* 17 April 2019. Retrieved 1 December 2019 from https://www.newsweekjapan.jp/stories/world/2019/04/post-11992.php.

Shepherd, Robert. "Cosmopolitanism Nationalism and the Heritage of Shame: Comfort Women Memorials and the Legacy of Slavery in the United States." *International Journal of Cultural Policy* 25, no. 2 (2019): 125–39.

Tanaka, Yuki. *Japan's Comfort Women: Sexual Slavery and Prostitution During World War II and the US Occupation*. London: Routledge, 2002.

United Nations Committee on the Elimination of Discrimination against Women (CEDAW). *Concluding Observations on the Combined Seventh and Eighth Periodic Reports of Japan (CEDAW/C/JPN/CO/7–8)*. New York: United Nations Office of the High Commissioner for Human Rights (OHCHR), 2016. Retrieved 1 December 2019 from https://tbinternet.ohchr.org/_layouts/15/treatybodyexternal/Download.aspx?symbolno=CEDAW/C/JPN/CO/7-8&Lang=En.

United Nations Committee on the Elimination of Racial Discrimination (CERD). *Concluding Observations on the Combined Tenth and Eleventh Periodic Reports of Japan (CERD/C/JPN/CO/10–11)*. New York: United Nations Office of the High Commissioner for Human Rights (OHCHR), 2018. Retrieved 1 December 2019 from https://tbinternet.ohchr.org/_layouts/15/treatybodyexternal/Download.aspx?symbolno=CERD/C/JPN/CO/10-11&Lang=En.

United Nations Educational, Scientific and Cultural Organization (UNESCO). *International Memory of the World Register Recommended Nominations List 2016–2017*. New York: UNESCO, 2017. Retrieved 1 December 2019 from https://en.unesco.org/sites/default/files/mow_recommended_nominations_list_2016-2017.pdf.

Vickers, Edward. "Commemorating 'Comfort Women' Beyond Korea: The Chinese Case." In *Remembering Asia's World War Two*, edited by Mark R. Frost, Daniel Schumacher, and Edward Vickers, 174–207. London: Routledge, 2019.

Winter, Jay. *Sites of Memory, Sites of Mourning: The Great War in European Cultural History.* Cambridge: Cambridge University Press, 1995.

Women's Active Museum on War and Peace (WAM). *Katarogu 10: Guntai wa Jyosei wo Mamoranai—Okinawa no nihongun ianjyo to beigun no seiboryoku* [Catalogue 10: The military does not protect women: Japanese military comfort stations and sexual violence by the US military in Okinawa]. Tokyo: Women's Active Museum on War and Peace, 2012.

———. *Nihongun "Ianfu" mondai Subeteno Gimon ni Kotaemasu* [Answering all questions concerning Japan's military "comfort women" issue]. Tokyo: Godo Shuppan, 2013.

Women's International War Crimes Tribunal for the Trial of Japanese Military Sexual Slavery (WIWCT). *The Final Judgement.* Tokyo: Violence against Women in War Research Action Center (VAWWRAC), 2001. Retrieved 1 December 2019 from http://vawwrac.org/war_crimes_tribunal.

Yang, Ching-ja. "'Heiwa no hi' ga tatsubasho 'Heiwaji'" ['Peace Street,' where 'The Statue for Peace' stands]. In *Naze "Heiwa no Shoujyozou" wa Suwaritsuzukeru noka* [Why does "The Statue for a Girl of Peace" remain seated? Engaging with the memory of harming], edited by Okamoto Yuka and Kim Pu-ja, 14–19. Yokohama: Seorishobo, 2016.

Yoon, Rangsook. "Erecting the 'Comfort Women' Memorials: From Seoul to San Francisco." *De Arte* 53, no. 2/3 (2018): 70–85.

Yoshimi, Yoshiaki,. "Dai isho: Nihongun ianfu to wa nanika" [Chapter 1: What are Japanese military comfort women?]. In *Kyodo Kenkyu: Nihongun Ianfu* [Japanese military comfort women collaborative research], edited by Yoshiaki Yoshimi and Hirofumi Hayashi, 3–13. Tokyo: Otsuki Shoten, 1995.

Afterword

TRAUMATIC PASTS, HAUNTING FUTURES

Byron J. Good

Gathered together by the editors under the heading "traumatic pasts," this fascinating collection on Asian societies begins to carve out a critically important and original field of study. Linked to Mark Micale and Paul Lerner's collection on *Traumatic Pasts: History, Psychiatry, and Trauma in the Modern Age, 1870–1930*,[1] this collection takes on issues of Asian traumatic pasts, carries the project forward to the present, and joins historical and ethnographic studies. In the process, the vision of such a project is expanded and opens space for genuine comparative research.

The volume takes on big questions. What do we mean by "trauma," particularly when associated with the most profound historical forms of violence and warfare unleashed against whole populations? What is "historical trauma," and what are the tools for examining "traumatic pasts"? How do we carry such a project across societies, civilizations, and time? Is there something particular about responses to historical trauma in Asian societies? How has Asian psychiatry—psychiatric professions and institutions in particular Asian societies—been shaped by the demand to respond to soldiers incapacitated by some form of "shock" during major wars of the twentieth century? How have local forms of Asian psychiatry been changed by the demand to respond to populations who have lived through devastating wars, internal violence, or natural calamities? How have interactions with humanitarian organizations shaped local meanings of trauma and trauma treatments? What does it mean to talk about trauma as "past"? The fact that this remarkable collection is so nearly equally divided between historical and ethnographic accounts is a reminder that traumatic pasts are never truly past. What might it mean to suggest that traumatic pasts are at the same time present? How are traumatic pasts hidden from view, how do they haunt the present, and under what conditions do they reappear? How can traumatic pasts be studied in the present? How do we investigate traumatic memory at the communal level, as well as in lives of individuals, and how are traumatic memories contested and fought in the present? It is precisely questions such as these, relevant for all societies, that are central to the chapters in this collection.

This volume is important, however, not only for what it does do, for the large questions it addresses through empirical case studies, but also for what it does not do. Running throughout the chapters in this collection are a set of questions about the contemporary formulation of Posttraumatic Stress Disorder (PTSD). Essays either directly or indirectly challenge a set of assumptions common in psychiatry today that PTSD is a timeless entity, "discovered" more than "invented." These assumptions are usefully engaged by reading histories of psychiatry in Asian societies, particularly military psychiatry, alongside histories of US and European psychiatry, and by reading present understandings of trauma in light of the past. The ethnographic studies not only describe distinctive ways of experiencing the "remainders of violence,"[2] both societally and individually, but also the remarkable naiveté of global trauma specialists bringing their reductive conceptions of trauma and post trauma mental health problems, as well as technologies of treatment, into settings such as postwar Vietnam, as Narquis Barak's chapter brilliantly demonstrates. But while questions about the status of PTSD are present, the chapters in this volume are not caught up with reductionist questions about whether individuals in Asia really suffer PTSD or not. Neither the historical nor ethnographic analyses are obsessed with the question of whether PTSD is real or merely a "pseudocondition," in Derek Summerfield's terms,[3] imposed on settings by global trauma specialists. And they do not focus narrowly on the local cultural shaping of diagnostic criteria of what can indeed be assumed to be a universal condition with local manifestations. While referencing Summerfield's critique of an obsession with PTSD in global humanitarian responses to war or disaster, the authors in this volume do not get caught up by his claims that this is a uniquely Western condition. Implicitly, the book outlines a field that places the larger questions about traumatic pasts at the center rather than narrow questions about a specific diagnostic entity.

In this volume, the terms "trauma" and "traumatic pasts" stand in for some of the most horrifying periods of Asian—and global—history. "Trauma" here does not refer to individuals' experiences of acute accidents or domestic violence or abuse, however critical these may be for individuals, producing PTSD symptoms susceptible to psychological interventions. Instead, several chapters take up Japan's colonial violence in China, Taiwan, and Korea. In these chapters, "traumatic pasts" refer to the nuclear bombing of Hiroshima and Nagasaki, and its aftermath, to the devastation of the Korean War, in which 3 million out of a population of 30 million Koreans were killed. In other chapters, the term refers to the devastation of what the Vietnamese call the "American War," with forms of suffering incomprehensible to those assuming a similarity between experiences of US and Vietcong soldiers. Traumatic pasts refer to the killings of nearly one million persons labeled "Communists" by Suharto and the military in 1965 Indonesia and to the imprisonment of hundreds of thousands of other Indonesians. It refers to the genocidal killings of the Khmer Rouge in Cambodia, to the systematic imprisonment and torture of members of the democracy movement in Burma, and to the devastation of China's Cultural Revolution. And the term refers to massive natural disasters, such as the catastrophic earthquake in central Taiwan in 1935. The chapters of this book thus take on a weightiness, a reminder of the horrifying violence and destruction that are central to the histories of Asian societies, and raise questions about their role in the making of contemporary societies and their medical systems.

In this Afterword, I look back briefly over the chapters in this volume, adding my own reflections to the preview provided by the editors in the Introduction. As I do this, I read from the perspective of having worked in post-tsunami, post-conflict Aceh, collaborating with the International Organization for Migration in surveying mental health problems and assessing "needs" for "psychosocial" programs to respond to those problems. This work brought me face to face with the immediate aftereffects of both the devastating tsunami and a conflict that loosened horrifying violence on local communities, raised questions about the meaning of trauma in this context, and forced me to think again about the utility of psychiatric diagnostic categories and medical responses in settings such as these. I read this collection from this perspective, and will return at the end to the relevance of the work my colleagues and I carried out in Aceh for some of the issues raised by the chapters in this collection. In the conclusion, I suggest a critical role for a hauntology in the larger project framed by this book.

Historical Studies of Traumatic Pasts in Japan, Korea and Taiwan

I address the chapters of this volume in three clusters. I begin with the first four case studies written by historians of Japan, Korea, and Taiwan. In these chapters, one is immediately placed in the world of Japanese militarism and imperial expansion during the first half of the twentieth century and the Japanese colonial administration of Korea and Taiwan. The vast majority of historical analyses of colonialism, "postcolonial disorders," and the haunting history of colonial violence, as well as indigenous resistance, independence movements, and postcoloniality, focus on settings of European colonialism and colonies.[4] A more recent body of writing on "historical trauma" has developed in the context of indigenous peoples and the long-term effects of the violence of settler colonialism (especially in the Americas, Australia, and New Zealand).[5] While the case of Japanese colonialism is well known to scholars of East Asia, writings on postcolonialism seldom refer to Korea and Taiwan, for example, or to Manchuria or to later efforts by the Japanese to bring Malaya and the Dutch East Indies under colonial control. In this context, the focus of these chapters on trauma associated with the Japanese imperial armies and the long-term effects of Japanese colonialism is particularly interesting.

We are reminded by Eri Nakamura that "nervous breakdowns," often dubbed "hysteria," were rejected by Japanese propogandists and by psychiatrists associated with "the Emperor's Army." The Imperial Japanese Army defined national manhood in terms of strength, bravery, and the ability to be an effective fighting soldier, idealizing the "samurai spirit." They contrasted the response to combat of Japanese, racially, with the weakness displayed by members of the Allied forces in World War I, who were said to have high rates of breakdown due to shell shock, neurasthenia, and hysteria. "Hysteria" was also seen as feminine, and psychological breakdown among Japanese soldiers was both hidden and stigmatized. It would be interesting to ask how this resistance to recognizing trauma among the forces of the Imperial Army influenced Japanese psychiatry in the postwar years. One hint: Joshua Breslau suggests that Japanese psychiatry was slow to take up PTSD as a category, and that the massive earthquake in Kobe in 1995 was the first time that response to the suffering associated with such a disaster began to be responded to as "trauma" and as PTSD.[6] Interestingly, Breslau notes further that this response was understood locally as a new attention to *kokoro* as opposed to *seishin*, and that the field of intervention for supporting those affected by the disaster came to be known as *kokoro no kea* (care for the heart). He contrasts *kokoro* to *seishin* as female to male, noting that *seishin*, the Japanese "spirit," figured prominently in wartime propaganda during the military period. Does the resistance to taking up the term PTSD suggest a long continuity with psychiatry during the Imperial years, and that the response to the Kobe earthquake represents a turning point in Japanese psychiatry's recognition of and response to "trauma"?

Ran Zwigenberg's essay on the lack of formal attention to "trauma" of those who suffered the devastation of the nuclear bombing of Hiroshima and Nagasaki continues the theme of the resistance of Japanese psychiatry to attend formally to trauma, linking it further with ties to German medicine, which shared the idealization of the masculine represented by the soldier, and an important source of the use of the category neurasthenia, seen to be a more acceptable category than psychological categories such as hysteria. This apparent resistance to addressing the local traumatic experiences of the nuclear bombs was amplified by the US occupation and the United States' refusal to allow any studies of the traumatic effects of the bomb. Remarkably, this remained true until the publication of Robert Lifton's 1968 book, *Death in Life, Survivors of Hiroshima*.

The chapters by Harry Wu and Jennifer Yum-Park carry us into the Japanese colonial and immediate postcolonial worlds of Taiwan and Korea. Japanese claims of "tropical madness" suffered by colonial agents from Japan residing in Taiwan, and the near exclusive development of mental health services for colonial administrators rather than for the Taiwanese population is so common in the European colonies as to sound unexpectedly familiar. Few services were thus available for those who suffered from the massive earthquake in central Taiwan in 1935, and "tropical neurasthenia" was preferred to any conceptualization of "trauma" among responders to the disaster. Ironically, Wu demonstrates that studies by Japanese psychiatric researchers of symptoms associated with the earthquake, while following the model of statistics developed by colonial administrators, turned out to be one of the earliest examples of psychiatric epidemiological studies of the effects of disaster on populations.

Park's case study of the transformation of Korean psychiatry through the interactions of US and Korean psychiatrists dealing with the effects of military trauma on troops during the horrors of the Korean War carries this work into the immediate period of Korea as a post colony—indeed a post colony caught in the horrifying violence resulting from the Cold War between the Soviet Union and the US allies. While Japanese colonial psychiatry left a resistance to attending to mental breakdowns among soldiers among Korean psychiatrists, the US psychiatrists, deeply affected by having dealt psychologically with American soldiers who fought in World War II, transformed Korean psychiatrists' understandings of the effects of warfare on soldiers. Park's fascinating case study shows how neo-Freudian ideas had become central to US psychiatrists dealing with the effects of conflict on US soldiers, and how these in turn transformed Korean psychiatrists' understandings of the effects of trauma on Korean combatants, ultimately leading to the wholesale Americanization of Korean psychiatry.

While Park's essay focuses on Korean psychiatry, the profound violence of the Korean War and the partition between North and South continue to have enormous resonance into present-day writings, particularly by anthropologists. There has been a flurry of recent reflections on the afterlife of the Korean War by Korean American anthropologists.[7] It will be interesting to see how historical studies represented by Park's chapter become linked with current reflections on traumatic pasts by ethnographers.

Ethnographic Studies of Traumatic Pasts in the Present

The second set of papers that make up a cluster, in my mind, while not in the chronological order of the chapters of the book, are the remarkable ethnographic studies of the traumatic effects of the war in Vietnam, the violence in Kashmir, the devastation of the Khmer Rouge, and the Cultural Revolution in China. Narquis Barak's extraordinary study of the absence of PTSD in Vietnam resulting from the "American War" is based on her research in the early 1990s. It takes up most directly the question with which Vietnamese psychiatrists would respond to the visiting international psychiatrists, intent on finding a plethora of PTSD among those who had lived through the war: "why do we have no PTSD in Vietnam, whereas you have so much in your countries?" The answer of the psychiatrists with whom Barak worked tended to be that either the Vietnamese had developed particular coping mechanisms or that adverse events were so common that they had ceased to have the psychological effects on the Vietnamese people that outsiders expected to find. Barak makes a broader argument: Vietnamese psychiatry's understandings of the effects of the horrifying events of the war were grounded in a combination of indigenous understandings, linked to Chinese/Vietnamese medicine (including *ying/yang* models) and to Pavlovian psychiatry, both of which focused on psycho-physical balance and imbalance. She argues that this establishes an entirely different framing of the immediate and long-term effects of acute or traumatic events than did Western civilizational ideas focused on memory, on the view that certain forms of memory are pathogenic, that such memories may be latent and hidden from view, and that they may emerge causing symptoms and suffering requiring treatment. Linking research in the psychiatric hospital's archives, ethnographic work in clinical settings, and research in rural public health clinics and families, Barak makes a strong argument that PTSD did not and does not exist in Vietnam, although there is psychological distress associated with acute psychological experiences, both negative and positive, and that trauma is far more deeply social and less individual than understood by Western psychiatrists. This then raises the serious question of whether a syndrome of experience described in North America as PTSD is actually present in some societies, not others, and what conditions are necessary to produce not merely medicalized diagnoses but such syndromes of experience.

Saiba Varma, writing about the effects of the long and violent conflict in Kashmir, makes a related but somewhat different argument. Kashmiri psychiatrists received international attention and acclaim for their focus on PTSD in the early stages of the war. Varma, an anthropologist conducting research in Kashmir between 2009 and 2016, sought cases of PTSD but instead found *kamzori*. When she confronted local psychiatrists, they confessed that there were now relatively few cases of PTSD, but that international interest led them to maintain their focus on this syndrome. Varma, in turn, shifted her attention from PTSD to complaints she heard about both in clinics and in the community, described as *kamzori*, a set of symptoms including weakness, loss of energy, and physical distress classically described as neurasthenia, somatized depression, or mixed anxiety and depression. Here she picks up a different part of Summerfield's critique—not that PTSD is a "pseudocondition," but that global agencies often focus near exclusive attention on PTSD as a major public health problem, thus extending the clinical and research interests of Western psychiatry but ignoring the more common mental health sequelae of violence. Varma analyzes this in terms of the "politics of visibility," noting that the international visibility of PTSD, which resonated politically in establishing Kashmiris as "innocent victims," led to "acts of concealment," here to the neglect of the most important local forms of suffering.

Caroline Bennett's study of ghosts and haunting in the aftermath of the murderous years of the Khmer Rouge in Cambodia places us not in the local worlds of psychiatrists and patients, but in the world of the ghosts of the dead who died badly and the efforts of post-Khmer Rouge Cambodians who were reclaiming their villages and lands, turned "wild" by the violence, to give peace to the ghosts of those who died at the hands of the Khmer Rouge. Bennett, an anthropologist, argues that re-establishing relations among the living and the dead was central to reasserting control and security as Khmer villagers returned to their communities desecrated by the Khmer Rouge, providing rituals to release the ghosts of those who had died anonymously and out of place, and to allow them to move on to successful rebirths. She rejects recent "ontological" claims of anthropology—that one has to accept local ontologies in their own terms, absolutely—as well as reductions of the haunting ghosts to psychological forces. Instead, she argues for a more grounded, therapeutic dimension to responding to ghosts, as well as to haunting itself: "haunting allows the dead to manifest their suffering, and the living to console them." Interestingly, we are placed not in the ever-unfinished world of haunting by "traumatic pasts." Bennett argues that the ghosts that haunted Cambodians after the end of the Khmer Rouge "have largely left Cambodia now." Some expired because they were not cared for, others have been reborn. Nonetheless, she argues, those who died "remain important members of Cambodian society to be cared for and appealed to."

This set of ethnographic papers concludes with Hua Wu's fascinating study of the youth sent to China's countryside as part of the Cultural Revolution, a generation now in their sixties, many of whom are attempting to come to terms with this violent disruption that radically altered their life course. The study describes a Reunion Group of twelve persons from Shanghai who in 2018 returned to the site in rural Hunan where they had been together, a site of genuine trauma for many, in an effort to "turn the page" on their past. What is remarkable about this study is what we learn about the great diversity of memories about this period, in some measure depending on the social position of the families of those who were sent down, and about the diverse reactions of those who revisited this site of their past. While not explicitly taking up the issue of PTSD, the ethnographer provides a rich account of one woman who experienced a full-blown traumatic reaction upon returning to the setting that she associated with enormous suffering. The chapter describes how a seemingly shared period in their lives was experienced differently and shaped their lives quite differently, for some quite tragically, and how members of this generation are seeking ways as they age to come to terms with and repair their experience of China's traumatic past.

Testimony and the Remaking and Memorializing of Traumatic Pasts

The final four chapters that I would group together challenge medicalized notions of trauma in ways other than the ethnographic accounts discussed above, taking us out of the world of psychiatry, diagnoses, and trauma treatments. They take us instead to community-based efforts to give testimony while at the same time repairing, challenging, and memorializing traumatic pasts and projecting futures of common humanity. Two of these chapters deal with Indonesian political prisoners following the wave of killings in 1965 that brought Suharto to power. A third provides a case study of prisoners of the Democracy Movement in Myanmar, and a fourth of the ongoing memorialization of "comfort women" in Korea. Issues of local forms of testimony and bearing witness to "traumatic pasts," and the rejection of victimization of those who have engaged in struggle, are central to these four studies.

The events of 30 September 1965 in Indonesia, in which six Army generals and a lieutenant were killed, were blamed on members of the Indonesian Communist Party and initiated a campaign, led by Major General Suharto, to suppress the party and its followers. Between 500,000 and 1 million persons were killed, and another million were imprisoned and detained. Vannessa Hearman provides a fascinating account of an "epistolary friendship," a friendship between a British Quaker woman and an Indonesian woman incarcerated as a political prisoner, which developed through an exchange of nearly 300 letters between 1982 and 1992. Drawing on theorizing of the way testimony gives shape and meaning to traumatic experience, Hearman develops a powerful analysis of the way that letters, smuggled out of the prison, provided an increasingly safe space for the Indonesian woman to bear witness to her interminable imprisonment, her loss of contact with her children and her husband, and her physical hardships. Here, the exchange of letters provided one means of giving testimony, of "regaining the capacity to speak" and transforming "unassimilated scraps of overwhelming experience" into narrative form.

Pitaloka and Dutta provide an account of a second form of testimony: the formation of a choir of women who were former political prisoners of the 1965 events using song as a means of witness. The Dialita choir was formed in 2011 by a group of elderly women, bound together by their history of struggle and collective suffering, to create an intimate space through singing, and ultimately to give embodied testimony through singing. The group began performing popular Indonesian songs, but went on to relive the poetry and songs composed during their imprisonment. In this post-Suharto era, the Dialita choir has been able to perform publicly, to engage with audiences through music, to engage other performers in a creative recasting of their prison songs, and to begin to challenge and revise the state narrative of the events of 1965 and the state's claims about those who were imprisoned over many years. Here the women reject silencing and the stigma imposed on them as dangerous political outcasts, and also their alternative framing as victims, and instead link audiences and performers in acts of "trauma healing" and the constituting of new forms of subjectivity.

Seinenu Thein-Lemelson provides a critically important account of persons who were imprisoned for their role in the Burmese Democracy Movement—an account made all the more devastating by the actions of the Burmese Army, just unfolding as I sit, now in 2021, to write this Afterword, to quash the democracy movement and reimprison many of the persons who played a key role in the story Thein-Lemelson has to tell. Her research with this group of activists shows the extent the "transnational public health model" of trauma and trauma treatment stands in contradiction to the activists' framing of their experience in terms of sacrifice, sacrifice as a moral commitment on behalf of democracy and future generations of Burmese by those who endured interrogation camps as a rite of passage. Honored as resistance fighters, the majority of those with whom she worked "demonstrated competence, agency, and generativity in their daily lives; displayed joy, awe, and happiness; . . . sublimated [their sacrifice] through art, literature, music, and political activism."

Finally, this section and the book conclude with an analysis of the establishment of recent memorials in front of the Japanese Embassy in Korea on behalf of "comfort women" as a reminder that memorializing war and trauma has never been gender neutral. Memorials such as this, Maki Kimura argues, become sites of memory and sites of mourning, as well as sites for positive activism, and have emerged as global sites of feminist commemoration.

A Return to Aceh

As I have read and reflected on the case studies in this volume, I have at the same time been rethinking some aspects of our work in Aceh.[8] On 26 December 2004, the Great Indian Ocean Tsunami struck the coast of Aceh, the northernmost province of Sumatra in Indonesia, killing nearly 200,000 persons and destroying entire communities settled along the coast. As more than three hundred humanitarian organizations from around the world swept into Aceh, many began for the first time to take notice of the violent conflict between the forces of the Free Aceh Movement (Gerakan Aceh Merdeka, GAM) and the Indonesian army. The conflict had been ongoing since the late 1980s, hidden from international attention—as much as possible—by the Indonesian government. Knowing that we had already spent nearly a decade working on mental health issues in Indonesia, particularly in Java, the International Organization for Migration (IOM) invited my wife Prof. Mary-Jo DelVecchio Good and me to consult about IOM's role in providing mental health and trauma services in response to the tsunami. On 15 August 2005, representatives of GAM and the Government of Indonesia completed negotiations and signed a peace agreement in Helsinki, an Memorandum of Understanding (MOU) which turned out to be remarkably effective. Knowing that IOM would have a significant role in the implementation of the peace accords, we agreed with the director of IOM in Jakarta that we should focus our primary attention on mental health or psychosocial responses to the conflict rather than the tsunami.

By late in 2005, we had agreed to help IOM conduct a "psychosocial needs assessment" in three districts of Aceh. Along with Jesse Grayman, our then Ph.D. student who had begun working as staff for IOM as part of his thesis project, we led an intensive study of 596 adults in high conflict subdistricts of the three selected districts, and by April delivered an initial report of our findings to IOM Indonesia.[9] Finding extremely high levels of traumatic experiences, associated with high levels of symptoms, we urged IOM to undertake a pilot intervention program, consisting of sending IOM teams of trained physicians and nurses, along with nurses from the local public health centers, into twenty-five selected villages in one district, run clinics aimed at case-finding for mental health problems, then provide continuous care, including monthly visits lasting nearly a year, for persons who suffered diagnosable mental illnesses, finally referring those who needed ongoing care to their local primary health care centers after the program concluded. When this pilot project demonstrated the feasibility and overall effectiveness of this model of active outreach mental health care, we raised funds through IOM and the World Bank for an initial scaling up of the project to fifty new villages and undertake a rigorous pre- and post-intervention study to determine effectiveness. The IOM doctors and nurses were trained to make basic psychiatric diagnoses, with a focus on depression, anxiety disorders, and PTSD, and to provide medications and basic counseling. While patients were often visited in their homes and the clinicians developed close relationships with patients and families, listening to their stories, no classic PTSD interventions were conducted as either individual or group therapy.

The interventions proved extremely beneficial to the patients, both in reducing symptoms and enabling individuals to work. But reviewing this project from the perspective of questions raised in this book, why were the clinicians trained to make psychiatric diagnoses, including PTSD, given that trauma responses are shown here to be culturally and historically contingent? Did the IOM teams indeed find cases of PTSD? Was the condition recognized by members of the community, was medical treatment effective, and if so why? If there is "no PTSD in Vietnam," as Barak shows, why would we have expected to find PTSD in post-conflict Aceh? In an important article cited by some authors in this volume, Derek Summerfield has argued that

> for the vast majority of survivors posttraumatic stress is a pseudocondition, a reframing of the understandable suffering of war as a technical problem

to which short-term technical solutions like counseling are applicable. These concepts aggrandize the Western agencies and their "experts" who from afar define the condition and bring the cure. There is no evidence that war-affected populations are seeking these imported approaches, which appear to ignore their own traditions, meaning systems, and active priorities.[10]

Was the IOM project that we helped design and shape an example of precisely such "reframing of the understandable suffering of war as a technical problem"? Did the treatments provided by the IOM teams reframe a collective struggle and sacrifice or resilience as individual pathogenic or traumatic memories? If the treatments were indeed effective for individuals, what was the source of their efficacy? What effect did they have on their communities?

PTSD as a Clinical Phenomenon in Post-conflict Aceh

Our design of the post-conflict mental health intervention in Aceh was quite pragmatic.[11] IOM teams had spent weeks—in January and February of 2006, six months after the peace agreement—conducting a "psychosocial needs assessment" or PNA. Teams of experienced Acehnese researchers went into villages, sampling households and adults, and carrying out interviews, asking about whether people had experienced particular traumatic events, asking about symptoms they experienced using formal symptom checklists translated and adapted for this community, asking how they managed their symptoms or sought medical care, and asking about what kinds of services they would like. Team leaders conducted in-depth qualitative interviews with key informants in each community. The research team members heard terrifying stories, and as the data emerged from the analysis, it became clear just how widespread these horrifying experiences were. In the district in which we conducted the pilot study, for example, 85 percent of adults surveyed reported having experienced conflict, 49 percent had been beaten, 25 percent reported being tortured, 3 percent reported a spouse having been killed, 5 percent reported one of their children had been killed, 66 percent a family member or friend. Rates for certain traumatic experiences varied by gender and age—for example, 48 percent of young men aged seventeen to twenty-nine reported being beaten on the head. But rates were extremely high for all groups.[12] Not surprisingly, six months after the conflict formally ended, there were still remarkably high levels of symptoms of depression, anxiety, and PTSD reported by adults living in these rural communities—levels among the highest reported in similar research conducted around the world.

Having spent time in the villages listening to stories, we felt compelled to take mental health care directly to villagers; we knew that villagers would be unlikely to bring mental health problems associated with the violence to primary health care centers, which had been under surveillance by the military during the conflict as part of their search for combatants. Our basic design was to develop mobile mental health teams to go directly into the most highly affected villages. To initiate the project, IOM recruited a number of its best Acehnese physicians and nurses to serve as clinicians on the teams. One of the few psychiatrists in Aceh, who also worked part-time for IOM and was deeply committed to caring for persons affected by the conflict, trained the outreach teams to recognize basic psychiatric clinical syndromes and the appropriate medications to treat those. PTSD was simply one of the syndromes he taught them to recognize, using the Indonesian translation of the International Classification of Disease (ICD) manual. When the teams initiated clinics in the villages, the psychiatrist met with the team members and the patients they identified as suffering a significant mental health problem to review their diagnoses and recommend treatment. After several months, the mental health teams felt comfortable seeing patients on their own, with the psychiatrist as supervisor.

Several important observations grew out of our consultation and collaboration with these teams. First, they found a significant number of persons with conditions that looked phenomenologically like PTSD.[13] Individuals reported intrusive memories of having been tortured, of being forced to humiliate family members in public settings of interrogation, of having watched family members tortured or killed. Acute intrusive memories would come in the day, leading to a sense that the events were occurring again, in the present, and provoking feelings of panic or acute anxiety. And they would come at night, as vivid nightmares, disrupting sleep. Some reported not having slept through a night for years; others described traumatic events they had experienced as though in the very recent past, only to later tell clinicians that these events had happened many years before.

Second, the initial PNA survey, conducted just six months following the MOU, found extremely high levels of symptoms—with 65 percent, 69 percent, and 34 percent of persons reaching cutoff levels for "caseness" of depression, anxiety, and PTSD using international standards. However, when providing clinical services in the community, beginning one year after the PNA research, the IOM clinicians diagnosed only 11 percent of the adult population in the fifty villages in which outcome data were collected as suffering a diagnosable mental health problem. Of those, only 33 percent (40 percent of males, 29 percent of females) were diagnosed by the doctors and nurses as suffering PTSD. Thus, the treated prevalence of PTSD in the community was only about 4 percent of all adults. In no way were whole communities pathologized as suffering from PTSD.[14]

Third, while PTSD was not a known concept in Acehnese villages, the word "trauma," pronounced essentially as "trauma," was common parlance as villagers discussed what had been inflicted on them and the suffering that remained in the community. Indeed, as Leslie Dwyer and Degung Santikarma have described, the term trauma made its way into Indonesian popular discourse in very specific politicized settings—following the Bali bombing; in the aftermath of the violence against the Chinese community in Jakarta, which included significant sexual violence, immediately preceding the fall of Suharto; in settings of ethnic and religious violence; and in Aceh during the conflict.[15] Indeed, when the mental health outreach teams wanted to conduct general mental health clinics in the villages, a method for case-finding, simply saying that they were providing care for "trauma" was enough to bring an important part of the village to care.[16] And when we would visit villages, describe our interest in mental health care, using the term trauma, we would often be urged to visit some particular individual, often someone who had suffered a traumatic brain injury, who represented for the community the effects of the terror enacted against them. Indeed, rather than saying "no PTSD in Aceh," community members would be more likely to say that over the years of the conflict, a vast majority of the population suffered "trauma" at the hands of the Indonesian military forces. Depression, anxiety disorders, somatic symptoms, and PTSD were all described broadly as "trauma," and there was virtually no stigma in seeking care for such experiences. PTSD served as a useful category for clinicians providing mental health care in these communities. It is important to reiterate that our understandings of trauma and PTSD in Acehnese villages was not based on clinical work with persons identified as suffering diagnosable mental illnesses and not with groups within the community at large.

Human Rights, "Warrior Women," and Resilience

How did our work relate to Thein-Lemelson's observation that the majority of the Burmese activists with whom she worked described themselves as having made a "sacrifice," rather than as having suffered trauma? They had sacrificed for future generations, were recognized by other activists and the masses for their sacrifices, and did not wish to be considered victims, as implied by the use of the terms *trauma* and *PTSD*. Early in our IOM project, members of our team met with a group of former GAM combatants and leaders to enlist their support. We described our project, talked about US veterans having experienced trauma, suggesting—rather naively, I think in retrospect—that members of their group, "veterans" of the struggle, might also be suffering from something akin to PTSD. Their response was immediate: "Our language is human rights; it is not trauma!" They were clear that they considered themselves as having been freedom fighters, members of a struggle for Acehnese independence, and now advocates for human rights—claims not unlike those made by the Burmese Democracy fighters Thein-Lemelson came to know. However, as we went forward with our conversations, a number of members of the GAM group began to talk about how family members, persons who were living in villages and supporting them but were not combatants, had suffered even more than they had. Combatants had had the support of their comrades in the struggle, but family members in the villages suffered terrible violence because of them, because the Indonesian military knew that many villagers had family members who were combatants, and suffered violence and torture as the military interrogated individuals and whole villages as the military sought information about the GAM guerillas. Indeed, in our PNA study in the district where we conducted the pilot intervention, 55 percent of adults said they had been forced to help members of the military search for family members who were members of the GAM forces (listed among possible traumatic experiences). Thus, these GAM members recognized the need for care for family members who had suffered trauma because these GAM members had participated in the conflict as combatants.

The experience of the villagers was highly gendered. On the one hand, men were more likely to be suspected of being combatants, whatever their age, and were even more likely than women to have been tortured as part of interrogation. On the other hand, as Mary-Jo Good has dramatically demonstrated, women were often idealized—and idealized themselves—as "warriors," Women Warriors following in the historical tradition of women sultans and as members of brigades of women warriors.[17] Acehnese women are owners of their homes and were often powerful defenders of their men, going en masse to protest the imprisonment of men from the village, seeking their release. Public health discourse often describes "women and children" as being vulnerable, a group at special risk for health problems, particularly mental health problems. Mary-Jo's work shows clearly that women were powerful activists, and moreover that many women in the villages of Aceh rejected the notion that they were 'vulnerable,' a group vulnerable to being victims of violence. Instead, their narratives of the conflict made clear that they considered themselves protectors of the land, the homes, and the men.

This self-identification as powerful participant in the struggle did not prevent village women from seeking care from the mobile mental health teams. Indeed, as in other primary care settings, women sought care at approximately twice the rate of men. This should not be used, however, to argue that women should be grouped with children as constituting a particularly vulnerable populations.

Clinical Care as a Site of Testimony

A number of the chapters in this volume make clear the power of "testimony" in the process of recovering agency. Diverse forms of testimony were shown to be critical to claim legitimacy for their struggle and to receive public acknowledgement, a means of rejecting a society's stigma and images of being victims, which are often associated with the terms *trauma* and *PTSD*. The letters exchanged with those imprisoned by the Suharto regime enabled individual prisoners to constitute themselves narratively, and to have others bear witness to their conditions, as Hearman shows. The Dialita choir is explicitly engaged in "testimony," as Pitaloka and Dutta demonstrate, and thus in a reconstitution of their subjectivity. And Thein-Lemelson shows just how critical the testimony of those who were prisoners in Burmese interrogation camps was in establishing their identity as members of a group who had "sacrificed" on behalf of the future of Burmese democracy and freedom. We see this struggle emerging once again in the present struggle for democracy in Myanmar.

Our work in Aceh was not primarily with former GAM combatants. We explicitly did not keep data on who among those treated were former combatants and who were not, and we do not know how many members of the combatant groups, many of whom were imprisoned and tortured, suffered "trauma" as did the villagers with whom we worked. However, what is clear is that the clinical work done by the IOM mental health teams (*Tim Psikososial*, as they called themselves) was a site of witnessing.

One of the first experiences we had, which provided a model for the intervention we designed, was to participate in a special mental health clinic conducted in a village in Aceh that members of the PNA research teams had identified as having suffered terribly at the hands of the military.[18] We arrived in that village in IOM vehicles—a powerful symbol of international recognition and witnessing. The villagers were prepared to meet in the *meunasah,* the village center and prayer house, for a kind of proto trauma clinic. When we along with the psychiatrist and the IOM team went in procession to the *meunasah*, we were first met by a man who had clearly suffered anoxia and brain damage during his torture. He was immediately treated, given a sedative by the psychiatrist. The whole village gathered, then one after another came and told their stories to the psychiatrist in a public setting. They all knew each other's stories. They exchanged their stories for a few days' worth of pills.[19] But what became clear was that this was a site of testimony, a site in which members of the community could give witness to what they had experienced at the hands of the military. It mattered that the clinicians were Acehnese, who understood them and could respond with medications. But it mattered deeply that they came in IOM vehicles, accompanied by foreigners, who served as witness to their testimony. This one-time mental health outreach clinic, conducted during the PNA research, served as a model for the intervention we designed. In retrospect, as with the other forms of witnessing described in this volume, the medical services provided by the IOM mobile mental health outreach teams over several years were also sites of witnessing. Whether the clinical encounters were rather short and public, or whether they occurred in village homes alongside the families of identified patients, the clinical services were likely effective in significant measure because they served as sites of testimony.

Clinical Services and Efficacy

The outcome studies we conducted, along with the longitudinal case studies we conducted, clearly demonstrate that that persons treated by the IOM teams got better. At the end of the second phase of the intervention program, in which 1,063 individuals were treated and interviewed before and after treatment, 1 percent reported their symptoms got worse, 16 percent that their symptoms remained the same, and 83 percent that their symptoms had improved. Whereas the group reported being able to work an average of only 11 hours per week prior to their treatment, they reported working an average of 41 hours per week at the end of the IOM intervention. How do we understand this? What were the sources of efficacy of the medical services provided?[20]

It should be clear that the end of violence was the most critical public mental health intervention. The Helsinki Accord ended the violence, but they also defined distinctive forms of local autonomy and allowed GAM to launch local political parties and contest elections. These were also powerful interventions. The IOM clinical intervention for which we have outcome data was launched eighteen months after the signing the MOU. Clearly many persons had already recovered from the most acute symptoms of distress. The development of mental outreach teams was aimed at identifying a cohort of persons who had not recovered, who continued to suffer after the end of the conflict, and who constituted a group suffering significant mental health problems as longer-term remainders of the violence. How were the clinical interventions effective with this group?

The IOM mental health outreach teams focused on those with common but debilitating mental health problems, many of which were subsumed under the rubric of "trauma" by community members. This program differed from a large program developed by the national and provincial offices of the Ministry of Health.[21] The MOH project focused on giving specialized training to all general practitioners and to a select group of nurses in the subdistrict-level *puskesmas* or community health clinics as well as to a new group of village *kader* specialized in mental health care. However, following WHO advice, this program focused almost exclusively on persons suffering psychotic illnesses, viewed as the priority for building up public mental health care. In the IOM program, only 2 percent of persons treated suffered psychotic illnesses. Ironically, a mental health program launched by the Ministry of Health in response to the tsunami and the conflict focused attention on only a tiny minority of persons most affected by these conditions.

A number of international NGOs developed specialized trauma treatment programs, usually conducted as group therapy sessions, using classic evidence-based models of psychological interventions. While not requiring psychiatrists, doctors, or nurses, these groups did require therapists with intensive training, and often depended on persons from outside Aceh. Little outcome data from these interventions have been published. However, anecdotal evidence suggested that a very significant number of persons dropped out of these therapy groups after the first several meetings.

The IOM program was based on a medical outreach model. Doctors (largely female), supported by nurses (largely male), all Acehnese, identified villages that had been settings of high conflict and committed to providing outreach care over the period of a year. Open medical clinics were used to identify persons suffering "trauma" or diagnosable mental health problems—in particular, anxiety disorders, mixed depression-anxiety, serious depressions, or PTSD (and psychoses when relevant). General supportive counseling, along with antidepressants or anti-anxiety medicines, provided the basic mode of care. In some villages, community support groups were formed. In a 20 percent subsample of villages, mental health services were linked to a "livelihood" program. But no specialized PTSD interventions were used. We have argued elsewhere that the use of relatively sedating antidepressant medications as well as anxiolytics may have promoted sleep among persons whose sleep had been disrupted by trauma-related nightmares for years. They may have also had some effect in reducing the acuteness of panic experiences related to intrusive memories. These may in turn have allowed local forms of practice—individual and public prayers, socializing with friends and family, participation in local rituals, returning to work—to be effective in promoting "acceptance" (*ikhlas*) and recovery. And here we also return to the role of clinical care as sites of testimony and clinical listening to be a form of acknowledgement and witnessing. Our research thus suggested that explicit—but not exclusive—attention to PTSD using outreach services, linked to the larger integrated system of public health services, provided an important model for care in this post-conflict setting.

Final Thoughts: Traumatic Pasts, Haunted Futures

This collection has provided a rich set of case studies of traumatic pasts in East and Southeast Asia. As I suggested at the beginning of this Afterword, the volume opens a whole field of comparative studies. Quite importantly, and it should be noted that this is far from common practice in academic projects, the volume includes historical case studies, ethnographic studies of the recent past or present as they relate to traumatic pasts, and reports on community-based efforts at testimony, again focused on giving voice to the past. Clearly, traumatic pasts are never past. As with slavery and institutionalized racism in the United States, as with historical trauma of indigenous communities in settler colonial states, the past haunts the present and the future.

I would argue that a "hauntology," in Derrida's terms, is a necessary part of a project such as this.[22] If we take Derrida seriously, we are not talking only about the pasts. We are talking always about futures. For Derrida,[23] learning to live in the present is always about learning to live with ghosts.

> to learn to live *with* ghosts. . . . To live otherwise and better. No, not better, but more justly. But *with them*. . . . And this being-with specters would also be, not only but also, a *politics* of memory, of inheritance, and of generations. . . .
>
> It is necessary to speak *of the* ghost, indeed *to the* ghost and *with* it, from the moment that no ethics, whether revolutionary or not, seems possible and thinkable and *just* that does not recognize in its principle the respect for those others who are no longer or for those who are not yet *there*, presently living, whether they are already dead or not yet born.

I close this Afterword with a reminder, densely and poetically argued by Derrida, that in this volume we are not dealing with some small issues from the archives or from ethnographic observation. The real issue is not some internal debate about Post Traumatic Stress Disorder and passing psychiatric diagnostic systems. We are dealing in this book with some of the most astonishing events of world history—colonial violations and murderous wars, the nuclear destruction of whole populations, creative forms of torture of activists and civil populations, massive levels of confinement, imprisonment and abandonment, and though not part of this book, environmental degradation that threatens all futures. Is there any wonder I close with reminding us of ghosts? We are in this book, in the words of Derrida, standing before "the ghosts of those who are not yet born or who are already dead, be they victims of wars, political or other kinds of violence, nationalist, racist, colonialist, sexist, or other kinds of exterminations, victims of the oppression of capitalist imperialism or any of the forms of totalitarianism." At the heart of this book is what Derrida calls this "*non-contemporaneity with itself of the living present,* without that which secretly unhinges it." "Traumatic pasts" are critical to the "living present," as well as to those "not yet born." This volume is filled with ghosts, the "non-contemporaneity with itself of the living present." We can take on Asian "traumatic pasts" in ethically distant, academic ways. But this volume is a reminder that there are stakes here, that we are dealing with a "*politics* of memory, of inheritance, and of generations." Feminist memorials of comfort women matter not just about the past but about the future. The voices of those who sacrificed for the Burmese Democracy Movement, and who are sacrificing again today, and the voices of the Dialita choir, are always about a politics of memory. Our work in this field is filled with ghosts. Our work is not simply to learn to live with ghosts, but as Derrida says, to live with ghosts more justly. This is the challenge set forth in this volume.

Byron J. Good is Professor of Medical Anthropology and former Chair in the Department of Global Health and Social Medicine, Harvard Medical School, and the Department of Anthropology, Harvard University. He received the 2018 Lifetime Achievement Award from the Society for Psychological Anthropology. Dr. Good's present work focuses on research and mental health services development in Asian societies, particularly Indonesia. For more than a decade, he collaborated with Prof. Mary-Jo Good and the International Organization for Migration (IOM) in developing mental health services in post-tsunami and post-conflict Aceh, Indonesia. The Goods are currently leading a team of Indonesian psychiatrists and psychologists in Yogyakarta, developing, evaluating, and beginning to scale up a model of recovery-oriented mental health services centered in the public primary health care system – with funds from USAID, the Harvard-Dubai Center, and Indonesian government sources.

Notes

1. Micale and Lerner, *Traumatic Pasts*.
2. We first used this term in a conference we organized, *The Future of Aceh: The Remainders of Violence and the Peace Process in Nanggroe Aceh Darussalam*, which brought together representatives of both sides of the conflict and peace process, as well as key humanitarian and mental health actors, at the Harvard Asia Center, 24–27 October 2007.
3. Summerfield, "Critique Seven Assumptions."
4. I take the term "postcolonial disorders" here from DelVecchio Good et al., *Postcolonial Disorders*.
5. On settler colonialism, see, for example, Kauanui and Wolfe, "Settler Colonialism Then and Now"; Snelgrove, Dhamoon, and Corntassel, "Unsettling Settler Colonialism"; Wolfe, "Settler Colonialism Elimination Native." On historical trauma, see, for example, Brave Heart and DeBruyn, "American Indian Holocaust"; Hartmann et al., "American Indian Historical Trauma"; Kirmayer, Gone, and Moses, "Rethinking Historical Trauma"; Ball and O'Nell, "Square Pegs Round Holes."
6. Breslau, "Globalizing Disaster Trauma."
7. See, for example, Han, *Seeing Like a Child*; Kwon, *After the Korean War*; Kim, *Memory, Reconciliation, Reunions*.
8. For an overview of our work in Aceh, consult Good, Good, and Grayman, "Complex Engagements"; Good and Good, "Perspectives Politics Peace Aceh"; Good, "Haunted by Aceh"; Good, Grayman, and Good, "Humanitarianism and 'Mobile Sovereignty.'"
9. The report on this study was published by IOM as: Good et al., *Psychosocial Needs Assessment Aceh*.
10. Summerfield, "Critique Seven Assumptions," 1449.
11. We have taken up these issues more directly in Good and Good, "Toward Cultural Psychology Trauma." See also Good, Good, and Grayman, "PTSD 'Good Enough.'"
12. See Good et al., *Psychosocial Needs Assessment Aceh*, 14-16.
13. Good and Good, "Toward Cultural Psychology Trauma."
14. See Good et al., "Humanitarianism and 'Mobile Sovereignty'"; and Good and Good, "Toward Cultural Psychology Trauma," for more in-depth analysis of these issues.
15. Dwyer and Santikarma, "Posttraumatic Politics."
16. For a discussion of the differing meanings of "trauma" and "stress" in Indonesia, and Aceh in particular, see Grayman, Good, and Good, "Health Activists and Trauma Contagion."
17. Good, "Acehenese Women's Narratives"; Good, "Spectral Presences."

18. For more details of this initial village clinic, see Good et al., "PTSD 'Good Enough'."
19. Good, "Trauma and Psychopharmaceuticals."
20. For further discussions of the effectiveness of the IOM model, see Good et al., "PTSD 'Good Enough.'" See also Good and Good, "Toward Cultural Psychology Trauma."
21. For a detailed discussion of the history of national and international mental health interventions in Aceh, including the IOM program, see Good, Good, and Grayman, "Pelayanan Kesehatan Jiwa di Aceh."
22. See Good, "Hauntology." See also Good, "Haunted by Aceh."
23. All Derrida quotations here are from Derrida, *Specters of Marx*, xviii–xix.

Bibliography

Ball, Tom, and Theresa D. O'Nell. "Square Pegs in Round Holes: Understanding Historical Trauma in Two Native American Communities." In *Culture and PTSD: Trauma in Global and Historical Perspective*, edited by Devon E. Hinton and Byron J. Good, 334–58. Philadelphia: University of Pennsylvania Press, 2016.

Brave Heart, Maria Yellow Horse, and Lemyra M. DeBruyn. "The American Indian Holocaust: Healing Historical Unresolved Grief." *American Indian and Alaska Native Mental Health Research* 8 (1998): 60–82.

Breslau, Joshua. "Globalizing Disaster Trauma: Psychiatry, Science, and Culture after the Kobe Earthquake." *Ethos* 28, no. 2 (2000): 174–97.

DelVecchio-Good, Mary-Jo, Sandra Teresa Hyde, Sarah Pinto, and Byron J. Good. *Postcolonial Disorders*. Berkeley: University of California Press, 2008.

Derrida, Jacques. *Specters of Marx: The State of the Debt, the Work of Mourning, and the New International*. New York: Routledge, 1994.

Dwyer, Leslie, and Degung Santikarma. "Posttraumatic Politics: Violence, Memory, and Biomedical Discourse in Bali." In *Understanding Trauma: Integrating Biological, Clinical, and Cultural Perspectives*, edited by Laurence J. Kirmayer, Robert B. Lemelson, and Mark Barad. New York: Cambridge University Press, 2007.

Good, Byron J. "Haunted by Aceh: Specters of Violence in Post-Suharto Indonesia." In *Genocide and Mass Violence: Memory, Symptom, and Recovery*, edited by Devon Hinton and Alexander L. Hinton, 58–82. Cambridge: Cambridge Univeristy Press, 2015.

———. "Hauntology: Theorizing the Spectral in Psychological Anthropology." *Ethos: Journal of the Society for Psychological Anthropology* 47, no. 4 (2020): 411–26.

Good, Byron J., and Mary-Jo DelVecchio Good. "Toward a Cultural Psychology of Trauma and Trauma-Related Disorders." In *Universalism without Uniformity: Explorations in Mind and Culture*, edited by Julia L. Cassaniti and Usha Menon, 260–79. Chicago, IL: University of Chicago Press, 2017.

Good, Byron J., Mary-Jo DelVecchio Good, and Jesse H. Grayman. "Is PTSD a 'Good Enough' Concept for Postconflict Mental Health Care? Reflections on Work in Aceh, Indonesia." In *Culture and PTSD: Trauma in Global and Historical Perspective*, edited by Devon E. Hinton and Byron J. Good, 387–417. Philadelphia: University of Pennsylvania Press, 2016.

Good, Byron J., Mary-Jo DelVecchio Good, and Jesse Hession Grayman. "Mereka-Ulang Pelayanan Kesehatan Jiwa Pasca Tsunami dan Pascakonflik Aceh [Reimagining mental health care in post-tsunami post-conflict Aceh]." In *Jiwa Sehat, Negara Kuat: Masa Depan Layanan Kesehatan Jiwa di Indonesia*, edited by Hans Pols, G. Pandu Setiawan, Carla Marchira, Irmansyah, Eunike Sri Tyas Suci, Mary-Jo DelVecchio Good, and Byron J. Good, 7–40. Jakarta: Penerbit KOMPAS, 2019.

Good, Byron J., Mary-Jo DelVecchio Good, Jesse Grayman, and Matthew Lakoma. *Psychosocial Needs Assessment of Communities Affected by the Conflict in the Districts of Pidie, Bireuen, and Aceh Utara*. Jakarta: International Organization for Migration, 2006.

Good, Byron J., Jesse Grayman, and Mary-Jo DelVecchio Good. "Humanitarianism and 'Mobile Sovereignty' in Strong State Settings: Reflections on Medical Humanitarianism in Aceh, Indonesia." In *Medical Humanitarianism: Ethnographies of Practice*, edited by Sharon Abramowitz and Catherine Panter-Brick, 155–75. Philadelphia, PA: University of Pennsylvania Press, 2015.

Good, Mary-Jo DelVecchio. "Acehenese Women's Narratives of Traumatic Experience, Resilience and Recovery." In *Genocide and Mass Violence: Memory, Symptom, Recovery*, edited by Devon E. Hinton and Alexander L. Hinton, 280–300. Cambridge: Cambridge University Press, 2015.

———. "The Spectral Presences of *Si Pai*: Begoña Aretxaga's *Cipayo* and Uncanny Experiences of *Si Pai* in Aceh 2008." *Ethos: Journal of the Society for Psychological Anthropology* 47 (2020): 480–88.

———. "Trauma in Postconflict Aceh and Psychopharmaceuticals as a Medium of Exchange." In *Pharmaceutical Self: The Global Shaping of Experience in an Age of Psychopharmacology*, edited by Janis H. Jenkin, 41–66. Santa Fe, NM: SAR Press, 2010.

Good, Mary-Jo DelVecchio, and Byron J. Good. "Perspectives on the Politics of Peace in Aceh, Indonesia." In *Radical Egalitarianism: Local Realities, Global Relations*, edited by Felicity Aulino, Miriam Goheen, and Stanley J. Tambiah, 191–208. New York: Fordham University Press, 2013.

Good, Mary-Jo Delvecchio, Byron J. Good, and Jesse Grayman. "Complex Engagements: Responding to Violence in Postconflict Aceh." In *Contemporary States of Emergency: The Politics of Military and Humanitarian Interventions*, edited by Didier Fassin and Mariella Pandolfi, 241–66. New York: Zone Books, 2010.

Grayman, Jesse Hession, Mary-Jo DelVecchio Good, and Byron J. Good. "Social Configurations, Awareness and Contagion: Cultural Epidemics and Reconsiderations of Trauma in Post-conflict, Post-tsunami Aceh." In *Configuring Contagion: Ethnographies of Biosocial Epidemics*, edited by Lotte Meinert and Jens Seeberg. New York: Berghahn, 2021.

Han, Clara. *Seeing Like a Child: Inheriting the Korean War*. New York: Fordham University Press, 2021.

Hartmann, William E., Dennis C. Wendt, Rachel L. Burrage, Andrew Pomerville, and Joseph P. Gone. "American Indian Historical Trauma: Anticolonial Prescriptions for Healing, Resilience, and Survivance." *American Psychologist* 74, no. 1 (2019): 6–19.

Kauanui, J. Kēhaulani (Kanaka Maoli), and Patrick Wolfe. "Settler Colonialism Then and Now." *Politica & Società* 2 (2012): 235–258.

Kim, Nan. *Memory, Reconciliation, and Reunions in South Korea: Crossing the Divide*. Lanham, MD: Lexington Books, 2017.

Kirmayer, Laurence J., Joseph P. Gone, and Joshua Moses. "Rethinking Historical Trauma." *Transcultural Psychiatry* 51 (2014): 299–319.

Kwon, Heonik. *After the Korean War: An Intimate History*. Cambridge: Cambridge University Press, 2020.

Micale, Mark S., and Paul Lerner, eds. *Traumatic Pasts: History, Psychiatry, and Trauma in the Modern Age, 1870–1930*. New York: Cambridge University Press, 2001.

Snelgrove, Corey, Rita Dhamoon, and Jeff Corntassel (Cherokee). "Unsettling Settler Colonialism: The Discourse and Politics of Settlers, and Solidarity with Indigenous Nations." *Decolonization: Indigeneity, Education & Society* 3, no. 2 (2014): 1–32.

Summerfield, Derek. "A Critique of Seven Assumptions Behind Psychological Trauma Programmes in War-Affected Areas." *Social Science & Medicine* 48, no. 10 (1999): 1449–62.

Wolfe, Patrick. "Settler Colonialism and the Elimination of the Native." *Journal of Genocide Research* 8, no. 4 (2006): 387–409.

INDEX

Abramowitz, Sharon, 281
Adler, Adolf, 36
Advocacy. *See under* Trauma: Advocacy
Affect Studies, 291, 292, 306–308
Alexander, Franz, 107
Algoso, Theresa, 60
Allport, Gordon, 231
American Atomic Bomb Casualty Commission. *See under* Japan: atomic bombing of
American Psychiatric Association, 99
Amnesty International, 10, 165, 168, 174
    See also humanitarian actors and NGOs
Andreasen, Nancy, 3–4
Anh, Nguyen Quoc, 134–35
Anitnah. See under Rituals: sacrifice
Asian Peace and Friendship Fund for Women (Asian Women's fund), 295–296
Asylums, 36, 39, 44, 99
    Ninsaiin, 40, 41
    Yomeito, 40
    See also Prisons
Astuti, Rita, 186, 187
Atomic Energy Commission. *See under* Japan: atomic bombing of
Australia, x, xiii, 5, 129, 167, 174, 290, 291, 317

Bälz, Erwin, 36, 42, 46, 48–49
Banning, Jan, 307
Battle of Okinawa. *See under* Japan: Battle of Okinawa

bearing witness, 12, 117, 207, 217, 221, 250, 260, 262, 292–293, 297, 302, 322, 328
Blanes, Ruy, 193
Borden, William, 107
Bourke, Joanna, 297
Breslau, Joshua, 318
Briquet, Pierre, 64
Brooke General Hospital, 107
Brures, Austin, 89
Buddhism, 10, 15, 64, 129, 132, 134, 148, 156, 188, 191, 192, 193, 246, 253, 289
Burma
    88 Generation Peace and Open Society of, 246–247, 256
    8888 Demonstrations in, 247, 251, 254
    aleipyu salute, 246–247, 254, 263
    Assistance Association for Political Prisoners in, 251, 256, 258 (*see also* Prisons: political prisoners)
    Democracy movement in, 245–247, 249–256, 259, 262, 322, 327
    liberalization process of, 258
    Martyr's Day, 246
    military violence in, 251, 254
    Moksha Volunteer Group of, 245–246, 258, 259–263
    National League Democracy Party of, 256
    Socialist Programme Party of, 251
    State Law and Order Restoration Council of, 251

State Peace and Development Council of, 251
Tingangyun, 247
Union Solidarity and Development Party of, 251–252
Yangon, 245, 257, 258, 260
Burundi, 232
Busch, Noel F., 44

Cambodia
  Choeung Ek Genocidal Center, 189, 190, 196
  Democratic Kampuchea, 187, 188, 189, 192, 195, 196
  diaspora of, 189
  Khmer Rouge, 1, 12–13, 153, 171, 186–188, 190–196, 198, 316, 319, 321
  "killing fields," 12, 187–188, 189
  People's Republic of Kampuchea, 188
  Pursat, 192
Canada, 5, 167, 291, 298
Canguilhem, Gorges, 277
Cannon, Walter, 139
Carmichael, Hugh T., 106, 110
Caruth, Cathy, 278
censorship, 8, 17, 81, 82, 85
  and self-obfuscation, 85, 166
  See also silence
Chamorro peoples. *See under* Mariana Islands
Charcot, Jean-Martin, 63–64, 70
Chicago, Judy, 297
children
  and illness, 63, 64, 119, 328
  loss of, 168, 171, 174, 178, 227, 237, 292, 322, 325
  raising of, 61, 113, 148, 153, 165, 172, 208, 219, 226, 240
China
  Anti-Right Campaign in, 212, 216
  Changsha City, 215
  Chinese Communist Party of, 206
  Cultural Revolution in, 13, 14, 205–206, 208, 212, 215, 317, 321
  Eternal Country, 211, 216, 222
  Happiness Farm Cadre School of, 211, 212, 214

Hunan, 209, 321
Nanjing, 17, 117, 298, 302
reform era in, 214
revolutionary period of, 207
sent-down youth (*zhiqing*) in, 206–218
Shanghai, 209, 293, 308, 321
Shanghai Normal University, 308
Chisholm, G. Brock, 70
Chin, Sŏng-gi, 106, 107
Chua, Jocelyn, 277
chronic fatigue and chronic fatigue syndrome, 15, 38, 71, 83, 140, 268, 270–271, 277–278, 279
  See also kamzori
Cleveland-Peck, Patricia, 165–167, 170, 172–178, 180
colonization and colonialism, 7, 38, 39, 41–42, 89, 98, 268, 270–271, 280–282, 293, 302, 309, 319
  See also postcolonialism
"comfort stations." *See under* sexual violence: comfort women
"comfort women." *See under* sexual violence: comfort women
compensation, 80–82, 86–88, 295
  See also reparations
conscription, 60, 61, 62, 72, 102
Corrington, Karin Lofthus, 195
cretinism, 40
Crile, George, 139
Crouthamel, Jason, 19
culture-centered approach, 232, 233, 237, 239, 241

Darling, George, 89
Delay, Hean, 135
Deniker, Pierre, 135
Derrida, Jacques, 331–332
Dialita Choir, 10, 226–240, 322, 328, 332
diagnosis
  Diagnostic and Statistical Manual of Mental Disorders, 3, 50–51, 100, 101, 133, 194
  ethno-psychiatry as, 41, 96
  International Classification of Disease Manual, 326
  nomenclature in, 100, 115, 116

physical examination and, 109–110, 113, 131, 144–145, 147
psychiatric, 96–97, 112–113, 119
statistics and, 39–40, 41, 46
symptoms and, 45–46, 80–81, 83–84, 86, 99–100, 101, 133, 140, 151, 153
Doctors without Borders (*Médecins sans Frontières*), 271–272, 278
  See also: humanitarian actors and NGOs, World Health Organization
Dower, John, 73
Dutch East Indies, 5, 18, 21, 41, 46, 318

East Java. *See* Indonesia, East Java
Edwards, Robert, 115
embodiment, 175, 206–207, 209, 211, 213–214, 219–220, 221–222, 238, 240–241, 247, 253, 302, 322
emotional paralysis (*emotionslähmung*), 36, 42, 46, 48–49
eunuchoids, 108–113

Fanon, Franz, 36, 268, 277, 281–282
Fassin, Didier, 14, 257, 270
Fealy, Greg, 230
Freud, Sigmund, 16, 20, 98, 119, 133, 135, 137
  neo-Freudianism, 9, 100–101, 107, 110, 114, 117, 118, 319
  talking cure, 135–136, 179
France, 9, 10, 18, 59, 62–64, 88, 189, 307

genocide, 12, 35, 187–188, 195–196, 198, 297
Gatot, Lesario, 165, 167, 170, 171, 174, 177
Germany, 289, 291
ghosts, 165, 167, 170, 171, 174, 177
  offerings to (*pchum benh*), 289, 291
  See also hauntology
Goffman, Erving, 230, 231
Goltermann, Svenja, 81
Goman, Carmen, 194
Good, Byron, xii, 157, 194, 278, 315–336
Good, Mary-Jo DelVecchio, 157, 323, 328
Glass, Albert, 8, 104, 105–107, 115, 116
Griffin, Susan, 195

Guillou, Anne Yvonne, 192, 196

habitus, 249–250
Hak-sun, Kim, 280, 290, 292, 308
Harrington, Anne, 101
Hart, Onno van der, 176
hauntology, 186, 188, 189–191, 193, 196–198, 317, 321, 331
  and cadavers (*kmoac*), 188–189, 191
  and dreams (*aoy yul sap*), 190, 191, 192, 193
  see also ghosts
Harvard University, 256, 297, 333
Hayao, Torao, 65
Hecker, Tobias, 195
Herman, Judith, 170, 175, 179, 298
heroism, 58, 247
  heroic self-sacrifice and, 254, 257, 258, 260, 327
Hinduism, 1, 272, 289
Hinton, Devon, 170, 171, 194
Hitsuda, Heizaburō, 82
holocaust, xxi, 4, 16, 18–19, 86, 88–89, 292, 297
Hosokoshi, Masakazu, 64, 68
hospitals, 44, 58, 59, 62, 64–72, 96, 97, 105, 109, 115, 117, 118, 279
  See also Asylums; Brooke General Hospital; Kōnodai Military Hospital; Korea: Capital Army Hospital, Korea: Chosŏn Ch'ongdopku Ŭiwŏn; Korea: Kungnip Chŏngsin Pyŏngwŏn; Sri Maharaja Hari Singh Hospital; Taiwan: Keelung Hospital; Taiwan: Taichung Hospital
Htway, San Zaw, 252
humanitarian actors and NGOs, 2, 19, 44, 79, 129, 132–133, 232, 248, 249, 252, 256, 258, 259, 263, 268, 270–282, 297, 316, 330 *See also* Médecins sans Frontières (Doctors without Borders)
humiliation. *See under* memory
hysteria, 59, 62–63, 64, 73, 140, 144, 146, 151, 318
  See also masculinity: male hysteria and

Iijima, Shigeru, 63–64

India
  British colonial occupation of, 15
  militarization of, 269, 273, 275, 279, 280
  partition of, 1
Indonesia
  1965 Mass killings, 226–227, 232, 233, 236, 238, 322
  Aceh, 317, 323–324, 327, 329, 330
  Acehnese Conflict, 239
  Bukit Duri Women's Prison, 230, 237
  communist party (*Partai Komunis Indonesia*), 10, 167, 227, 235, 236, 238
  Crocodile Hole Monument (*Monumen Lubang Buaya*), 236
  East Java, 168, 175
  Free Aceh movement (*Gerakan Aceh Merdeka*), 323, 326–328, 330
  Java, 39, 323
  Mother and Child Care Community (*Komunitas Peduli Ibu dan Anak*), 117
  Plantungan prison, 230
  propaganda in, 169, 170
  war of independence, 175
  West Java, 228
  women's organizations in, 167, 236
infectious diseases, 135, 136, 141, 146, 187, 258
Israel, 88–89, 129, 130, 234
International Organization for Migration, 323–324, 325–326, 329, 331

Jackson, Michael, 279
James, Erica, 273
James, William, 36
Janssen, Hilde, 307
Japan
  2015 Japan-Korea agreement, 296, 299
  atomic bombing of, 8, 78–79, 81, 83–84, 86–87, 89, 292, 300, 303–304
  Battle of Okinawa, 292, 303–304
  collective morale in, 43, 46
  occupation of Korea. *See under* Korea (Japanese occupation of)
  Emperor's Army, 64–65, 73. *See also* Japan (Imperial Army of)
  German scholarship within, 39, 82, 98
  Government Statistical Office (*Kanbō Tōkeika*), 40
  Himeyuri Student Nurse Corps, 292, 304–305
  Hiroshima, 8, 78–79, 81–87, 89, 292, 295, 300–302, 306, 307, 318
  Imperial Army of, 59–61, 63–64, 66, 71–72, 290, 302, 317–318
  Imperial Government of, 36, 40–42
  Kōnodai Military Hospital, 58, 59, 62, 64–72
  Kobe, 37, 50
  Nagasaki, 8, 84, 86, 89, 292, 300–302, 306, 307, 318
  National Survey (*Kokusei Chōsa*), 39
  occupation of Korea. *See under* Korea (Japanese occupation of)
  Okinawa, 292–293, 302–307
  psychiatry in, 6–7
  perception of superiority in, 7, 38, 39, 43, 66–67, 80
  southern expansion policy (*nanshin ron*), 36, 38
  Tokyo, 36, 39, 42–44, 46, 48, 297, 298
  Tokyo Imperial University, 36, 39, 60–61
Johns Hopkins Applied Mental Health Research Group, 256, 258
Johnson, James, 38
Junior Soemantri, 230

kamzori, 15, 268, 270–271, 276–283, 320
  See also posttraumatic stress disorder: comparison to *kamzori*; fatigue and chronic fatigue
Kagan, Richard, 157
Kamata, Shirabe, 80
Kang, Chun-Sang, 106–107
Kashmir
  Aksai Chin, 269
  colonization and occupation of, 268–269, 273, 275, 279–280
  Institute of Mental Health and Neuro Sciences, 274–275
  Jammu and Kashmir Liberation Front, 269
  Pakistan and, 268–269

Sri Maharaja Hari Singh Hospital, 279
Kelley, Douglas, 194
Kim, Bok-dong, 299
Kim, Eun-sung, 299
Kim, Seo-kyung, 299, 306
Kim, Sŏng-jin, 106, 108
Kolk, Bessel van der, 176
Kondo, Toshiyuki, 83
Kono, Yohei, 295
Konuma, Mashiho, 79–82, 83–85, 87–88
Korea (North and South)
   2015 Japan-Korea Agreement, 296, 299
   Americanization of, 96–97, 99, 104, 117, 120
   Capital Army Hospital, 96, 105, 109, 115, 117
   Chosŏn Ch'ongdopku Ŭiwŏn (Governor General Hospital), 97
   Council for Justice and Remembrance for the Issues of Military Sexual Slavery by Japan, 297, 300, 310 See also Sexual Violence ("Comfort Women")
   Japanese Embassy in, 298–299, 306, 323
   Japanese occupation of, 97–98, 318
   Kyŏngsŏng Imperial University, 97, 102, 109
   Kyŏngsŏng Medical College, 97
   Military alliance with United States, 97, 102, 105, 118
   National Mental Hospital (Kungnip Chŏngsin Pyŏngwŏn), 118
   neuropsychiatry in, 108, 118
   Pusan, 101, 295, 300
   Republic of Korea Army, 102–103, 105, 106, 108, 113
   Seoul, 97, 105, 289, 290–1, 298–299, 206–207
   Seoul Child Guidance Clinic, 119
   Seoul National University, 102, 103, 108, 118
Kleinman, Arthur, 282
Kraepelin, Emil, 39, 98
Kubo, Yoshitoshi, 79, 83, 85–87
Kure, Bunso, 39
Kure, Shūzō, 39–40, 62–63
Kwon, Heonik, 197, 201
Kyi, Aung San Suu, 246–247, 255–256

LaCapra, Dominic, 186
Lestario, Gatot, 165
Laqueur, Thomas, 188
Laub, Dori, 178, 179
Leese, Peter, 19
Lerner, Paul, xi, 58, 315
letter writing, 164, 176, 179–180, 322
Liberia, 281
Lifton, Robert, 79, 89
Lindemann, Erich, 36
Lipsitz, George, 232
Lucas, Anton, 177

Maercker, Andreas, 195
Mackie, Vera, 307
major depressive disorder, 276
Mariana Islands, 292
Martínez-Hernandez, Angel, 277
Martyrdom, 246–247, 254–255
Maruyama, Chijun, 98
Masculinity, 12, 58–62, 101, 110–111
   effeminacy and, 61–64, 70–71, 113–114, 318
   male hysteria and, 59, 63–64, 67–71, 146
   national character and, 62–64
   self-mastery as a form of, 58, 61
mass graves, 12, 186, 187, 191–192, 196
materiality, 292, 297, 299, 300, 302–304, 306, 308
Matsumoto, Scott, 87
Maybin, Janet, 172, 179
McFarlane, Alexander, 194
McGregor, Katharine, 307
medical training, 7
memorials, 245–247, 250, 252, 254, 263, 289–290, 291, 297, 298, 300, 305, 307
   Australian War Memorial, 290
   Cenotaph for the Victims of the Atomic Bomb, 290
   Himeyuri Peace Memorial Museum and Cenotaph, 304
   Memorial to the Murdered Jews of Europe, 290
   Memorial to the Victims of Torture and Ill Treatment in the Colonial Era (Nairobi, Kenya), 290

museums, 13, 22, 108, 290, 297–298
National Lynching Memorial (Alabama, USA), 290
National Memorial for Peace and Justice, 290
Okinawa Peace Memorial, 303
Peace Flame of Hiroshima, 300–301
Peace Memorial Park, 302
Statue of a Girl of Peace, 289, 298–300, 306, 307, 308
War and Women's Human Rights Museum, 290
memory, 13, 144, 192, 206, 209, 217, 232, 257, 289
flashbacks and, 6, 133, 212–213, 326
humiliation and, 170 (*see also* trauma)
politics of, 36, 290, 297
storytelling and, 176, 207, 212, 258, 262, 325 (*see also* letter writing)
See also Memorials
Menninger, William, 99, 100, 107
Modi, Narendra, 16
  Bharatiya Janata Party (BJP), 16, 279
Mooij, Annet, 80
Mosse, George, 58–59
Micale, Mark M., 59, 315
militarization, 269, 273, 275, 279, 280, 293, 297, 302, 303
Miller Beard, George, 71–72
Min, Pyŏng-gun, 101, 103, 117
Myanmar. *See under* Burma

Naing, Min Ko, 262
Naka, Syuzo, 36, 39, 41, 44, 48–49
Nakai, Hisao, 38, 50
Nakamura, Yuzuru, 39–40
nationalism, 16, 20, 37–38, 50, 59, 306
natural disasters, 1, 2, 6–7, 10, 35–37, 42, 46–50, 79, 133, 274, 315, 317, 323
earthquakes, 1–2, 6, 7, 19, 35–37, 42–44, 46–51, 79, 90, 270, 317–318
health responses following, 7, 37–39
neurasthenia, 38, 63, 64–65, 67, 68, 71–73, 83, 140
"tropical neurasthenia," 38, 41, 48
New Zealand, 48, 317
Nichter, Mark, 278

Nikichi, Okumura, 82
"non-effective soldiers," 114–117
Non-Governmental Organizations. *See under* humanitarian actors and NGOs

O, Sŏk-hwan, 100, 104–105, 107, 108
Obersteiner, Henrich, 39
ontology, 197–198, 201, 268, 271, 281, 321
  See also: hauntology

Pak, In-ho, 102, 106, 107
Palestine, 234
Parrish, Matthew, 119
participatory action research, 259–260, 263
Pavlov, Ivan, 137–138, 139, 143–144, 320
Pepys, Samuel, 35
Peterson, Donald, 115
Philippines, 17, 38, 167, 291, 308
political etiology, 7, 280
postcolonialism, 36, 268–269, 317, 318
posttraumatic stress disorder (PTSD), 2, 35, 51, 79, 88, 96, 117, 128–134, 141, 152, 156–157, 194–195, 213, 248, 268, 270–273, 278, 280, 316, 319–320, 321, 324, 326–328, 331, 332
  comparison to *kamzori*, 271, 276–278
  cultural significance of, 35
  symptoms of, 14, 35, 275
  globalization of, 271, 274
Pot, Pol, 1, 12, 153, 196
  See also Cambodia; Khmer Rouge
Prisons, 1, 10–11, 15, 164, 167, 171, 173, 175, 212, 230, 321, 236–237, 317, 322, 328, 329, 332
  and prison camps, 6, 10, 12, 83, 88, 170, 204, 208, 323, 329
  confinement within, 15, 38, 40, 98–99, 174, 178, 332 (*see also* Asylums)
  political prisoners, 10-12, 15, 165–180, 208, 216, 227–228, 231, 235, 237–238, 245–247, 249, 251–254, 256, 258–260, 263–264, 322
  prisoners of war, 292
propaganda, 89, 142, 169–170, 236, 318
  See also Indonesia: propaganda
Puar, Jasbir, 234

Pudji, Aswati, 165–178, 180
  Pudji Fund, 167
Puji, 229–231, 232, 234, 236, 240

Quakers (Religious Society of Friends), 165–166

radiation (nuclear), 79, 82, 83
reaction psychosis, 144–145
Rechtman, Richard, 14, 189, 257
Red Cross. *See under* Humanitarian actors
Religious Society of Friends. *See under* Quakers (Religious Society of Friends)
reparations, 86, 102, 179, 245–247, 248, 260, 264, 295–296, 298
  See also compensation
rituals, 13, 192–193, 294
  and healing, 10, 98, 232, 247, 248, 250, 260–261
  and sacrifice, 15, 247, 249–250, 251, 253–254, 257, 260–263
Robbins, Arthur, 96, 109
Rondpierre, Jacques, 135
Rothberg, Michael, 19
Rwanda, 295

Sakel, Manfred, 135
Sakurai, Tonao, 68, 70
San Francisco Peace Treaty, 295
Santo, Diana Espírito, 193
schizophrenia, 72, 85, 100, 103, 114, 118, 130, 152–153, 277
Schneider, Kurt, 81
Schreiner, Olive, 167
Segal, Henry, 105
sexual violence, 170, 211, 251, 327
  "comfort women," 17, 289–298, 306–308, 309
  and sexual slavery, 1, 17, 290–300, 306–308
  as torture, 169 *See also* memory: humiliation; torture
  Wednesday Demonstrations on, 306
  Women's International War Crimes Tribunal for the Trial of Japanese Military Sexual slavery, 296
shame. *See under* stigma

Shen, Mingzong, 62
shell shock, 58, 64–66, 69, 73, 80–81, 130, 147, 153, 157, 159, 162
Shephard, Ben, 99
Shikiba, Ryūzaburō, 67
Shimizu, Hiroshi, 67
Shimoda, Mitsuzō, 69
Shimozawa, Zuisei, 61
Showalter, Elaine, 58–59
Siem, Nguyen Van, 128–129
Sin, Yu-hŭi, 110, 111, 112
silence, 7, 85, 177
  See also censorship
sleep cure, 143–144
Smith, Catherine, 194, 239
somatization, 270, 277–278, 320
Sontag, Susan, 281
Southeast Asian Justice and Rights, 259, 260, 261, 262
southern expansion doctrine. *See under* Japan: southern expansion doctrine (*nanshin-ron*)
Soviet Union, 1, 10, 18, 135–136, 138, 140, 165, 319
Spirituality, 10, 15, 133–134, 149, 165, 175, 188, 191
Stanley, Liz, 167, 169
statues. *See under* memorials: statues
stigma, 8, 66–67, 140, 170, 175, 231, 318, 323
storytelling, 35, 42, 47, 176, 230
  singing and, 226, 229, 230, 232, 234, 235–236, 238–239, 254
  See also letter writing; memory; testimony
Suharto, Major General, 168, 227, 317, 322, 328
  New Order Regime under, 227, 231
suicide, 84, 98, 257, 292, 302
Sugita, Naoki, 66, 69
Summerfield, Derek, 195, 272, 316, 320, 324
Suwa, Keizaburō, 67
syncretism, 250, 260, 263

Taiwan, 316–319
  earthquakes in, 1, 36, 37 (*see also*: earthquakes)

Hainan Island, 41–42
Indigenous peoples of, 292
Japanese occupation of, 318
Keelung Hospital, 40
National Taiwan University, 41
occupation of, 38–39, 41
Taichung, 44–46
Taichung Earthquake Rehabilitation Office, 46
Taichung Hospital, 44
Taihoku Imperial University, 36, 41, 44, 50
Taipei, 298
Tati, 228, 229, 230, 233, 240
testimony, 176, 178–179, 328–329
Tetsujirō, Inoue, 60–61
torture, 165, 169–170, 251–252, 254, 256, 260
  anti-torture campaigns, 165
  See also sexual violence: as torture
trauma
  advocacy, 11
  collective, 43, 174, 176, 186, 194–198, 200, 201, 248, 254, 316
  colonialism and, 7, 19, 234, 248
  complex trauma, 171
  cultural factors associated with, 4, 10, 82, 132, 175, 315
  disclosure of, 179, 261–263
  healing of, 192–194, 195–196, 197, 198
  idioms of distress, 278–279, 281–282, 249–250
  intergenerational, 4
  memorialization of. (*See under* memorials)
  men's experiences of. *See under* masculinity: male hysteria
  physical, 83, 84, 86, 257, 278
  place and, 6, 43–44, 103, 213–214, 220–221, 232, 234, 248, 315
  relating to social loss, 171, 195
  in survivors of war, 8, 48, 66, 106, 132, 140, 258
  treatment and counseling, 4, 14, 40, 48, 71, 135, 144, 192–197, 256, 257, 258, 272, 278, 324–325, 331

  universalization of, 4, 171, 248–249, 250, 252, 255
  veterans and, 7, 114–117
  women's experiences of, 12, 66–67, 146, 247, 260, 277
  See also posttraumatic stress disorder (PTSD)
Trident. *See under* Trisula operation
Trisula operation (Trident), 168, 170
Tse Tung, Mao, 1, 187, 206
  See also China: cultural revolution

Uchi, 226, 228, 229, 235, 237, 239–240
United States of America, 7, 8, 291, 293, 296, 298, 302–303, 305, 316, 317
Usa, Shizuo, 64

veterans of war and conflict, 6–7, 9, 16, 80–81, 82, 88, 118, 129, 131–134, 136, 141, 147–148, 151–153, 156–157, 272, 327
Vickers, Edward, 298
Vietnam
  American psychiatric perspectives in, 133, 138
  American war in, 6, 16, 130, 133, 142–143, 151, 154, 156–157, 272, 316, 319
  bombing of, 142–143, 151, 153, 154
  French occupation of, 134, 140
  post-war psychiatry in, 134
  Soviet influence in, 135–138, 148
  Thuong Tin, 129–130
  traditional medicine of, 139, 146, 320
visibility (politics of), 270, 271, 276, 282, 320
Voltaire, 35

war
  in Afghanistan 147, 157
  Asia-Pacific, 8, 17, 37, 59, 64, 66, 69, 74, 80, 289–308
  atomic bombs. *See under* Japan: atomic bombing of
  China-Japan, 17, 81
  Cold war, 9, 319
  in Iraq, 147, 157

in Korea, 96–97, 99, 101–104, 108
Nanjing Massacre (Nanking Massacre), 17, 302
neuroses relating to, 7, 9, 103, 104. (*see also*: trauma)
Russo-Japanese, 40, 81
Sino-Japanese, 59, 64, 69, 73
US Civil, 152
Vietnam. *See under*: Vietnam: American war in
World War I, 7, 58, 63–64, 66, 69, 71, 80, 130, 298, 307
World War II, 1, 4, 6, 36–38, 44, 46, 48, 104, 136, 147, (*see also*: holocaust)
Wang, Yougui, 205
Widastuti, Endah, 237
Win, Ne, 251
Winter, Jay, 298, 307
Withuis, Jolande, 80
witnessing. *See under* bearing witness

World Health Organization (WHO), 65, 330
    See also: humanitarian actors and NGOs

Yawata. Takeuchi, 41
Yehuda, Rachel, 194
Yei, Malis, 189
Yei, Mean, 190
Yei, Youch, 190
Yi, Chŏng-gyun, 103
Yi, Pong-gi, 101, 106, 109, 110–114, 119
Yi, Tong-u, 113
Yoshioka, Ichirō, 83
Young, Allan, 133, 248
Yu, Sŏk-chin, 100, 101–115, 119
Yugoslavia, 295
Yūshi, Uchimura, 82

Zhang, Zhongjing, 63
Zondek, Hermann, 109–110
Zurbuchen, Mary, 232

www.ingramcontent.com/pod-product-compliance
Lightning Source LLC
Chambersburg PA
CBHW071332080526
44587CB00017B/2804